'*Invisible Worlds* offers convincing proof of the central role played by con-
ceptions of the supernatural and the afterlife in the religious upheavals
of the early modern period. It also highlights the untidy complexity of
the shift from one set of beliefs to another, thus giving us a nuanced
understanding of the passage to modernity, the rise of scepticism and the
so-called disenchantment of the world brought about by the Protestant
Reformation. Peter Marshall's work is indispensable reading for anyone
who desires to understand the intellectual and spiritual shaping of early
modern England and of the Western imagination as well.'

Carlos Eire, Professor of History and Religious Studies, Yale University

'With characteristic elegance and subtlety, Peter Marshall investigates
the contested realms of heaven, purgatory and hell in early modern
England, and probes persisting assumptions about angels, ghosts and
fairies. Painting a rich and intricate picture of the transactions between
traditional religion and Reformed theology, his book shows how pastoral
imperative sometimes bowed to popular belief, and how, simultaneously,
Protestantism sowed the seeds of scepticism about the supernatural.
Full of intriguing insights, *Invisible Worlds* will be warmly welcomed by
scholars, students and general readers alike.'

Alexandra Walsham, Professor of Modern History
University of Cambridge

Peter Marshall is Professor of History at the University of Warwick and co-editor of *The English Historical Review*. He has published widely on many aspects of the religious culture of early modern Europe, particularly in the British Isles, and his books include *Mother Leakey and the Bishop: A Ghost Story* (2007), *The Reformation: A Very Short Introduction* (2009) and *Heretics and Believers: A History of the English Reformation* (2017).

INVISIBLE WORLDS

Death, religion and the supernatural in England, 1500–1700

PETER MARSHALL

First published in Great Britain in 2017

Society for Promoting Christian Knowledge
36 Causton Street
London SW1P 4ST
www.spck.org.uk

British Library Cataloguing-in-Publication Data
A catalogue record for this book is available from the British Library

ISBN 978–0–281–07522–5
eBook ISBN 978–0–281–07523–2

Typeset by Fakenham Prepress Solutions, Fakenham, Norfolk NR21 8NN
First printed in Great Britain by Ashford Colour Press
Subsequently digitally reprinted in Great Britain

eBook by Fakenham Prepress Solutions, Fakenham, Norfolk NR21 8NN

Produced on paper from sustainable forests

In memory of
John Bossy (1933–2015)
and Cliff Davies (1936–2016)

Contents

Contents

Introduction

The chapters in this volume – updated versions of essays first published between 2000 and 2015 – seek to make a significant contribution towards understanding the dramatic impact of the Protestant Reformation on the society and culture of sixteenth- and seventeenth-century England, and (particularly in Chapter 1) to place that impact in a larger international context. They do so by adopting a distinctive angle of vision. The focus is not so much upon concrete matters of church governance, ecclesiastical politics and the day-to-day organization of worship as upon the wanderings and fixations of the religious and cultural imagination. In particular, I seek in these essays to chart the shifting borders and boundaries between the known and the unknown, the natural and the supernatural; between worlds of daily travail and the 'invisible worlds' that contemporaries believed were there to be discovered after death, or that lay hidden within the folds and crevices of ordinary lived experience.

The book is in two parts. The first five chapters consider the intellectual and cultural consequences of the Reformation's assault on established doctrines about the afterlife, and the experience of human souls following death. The second part looks at deeply held beliefs around angels, ghosts and fairies, and the ways in which these were reappropriated and reimagined once they were cut loose from their traditional theological moorings.

The effect of the Reformation upon the imagination is not, I contend, a marginal or trivial subject; rather, it points us towards crucial aspects of human identity and experience. Nor, in making reference to a symbolic realm of the imagination – something which French cultural historians have usefully christened the *imaginaire*[1] – do I intend to pass negative or condescending judgement on the veracity of the beliefs of the historical actors written about in these pages. In the twenty-first century we are not really in any better position than our ancestors to know what, if anything, lies in wait for us beyond the grave or the incinerator, and our speculations on that subject are inevitably as influenced by the cultural presumptions of our own time as those of sixteenth-century people were by those of theirs.

Many, I expect most, readers of this book will share my own instinctive assumption that creatures such as ghosts and fairies are not 'real', and that people who reported having dealings with them are not in fact supplying us with reliable evidence for the objective existence of these supernatural entities in the past. But, in terms of historical understanding, such an observation does not take us very far. There is a difference between the duty to explain and the temptation to explain away: the latter can too easily lead to a 'reductionist' approach to the more challenging and uncomfortable aspects of pre-modern belief or action, one which seeks to translate them into terms that make sense to us. We should be suspicious of modern historians offering definitive explanations of what was 'really' going on, when those explanations are couched in terms which would have made no sense at all to the people actually involved.

The integrity, the autonomy, the strangeness of the past is always something to be respected, and, as far as possible, to be imaginatively recovered and reconstructed. The invisible worlds of sixteenth- and seventeenth-century England are places of the imagination that we should seek to explore sensitively and seriously, not to smile at knowingly as bizarre curiosities or monuments to obsolete credulity. E. P. Thompson's famous stricture about the imperative to rescue seemingly outlandish people and ideas from 'the enormous condescension of posterity' can simply never be cited too often.[2]

At the same time, it is a responsibility of historians – arguably their key responsibility – to explain patterns of change over time, and to help us understand how the societies of the past evolved into the societies of today. The Reformation was, without doubt, an engine of momentous change. It simultaneously transformed and divided English society, breaking institutional and doctrinal ties that had for centuries bound England to a wider European religious culture, while forging important new ones with networks of Protestants overseas.

Scholarly interpretations of the English Reformation have long been contested and controversial. They are themselves to a considerable extent cultural artefacts of the world the Reformation helped to create, rather than detached assessments formed in some sealed oxygen chamber of the intellect. The dominant scholarly narrative, well into my own lifetime, was one whose broad outlines Protestant reformers themselves might have recognized. The Reformation represented an inevitable challenge to a corrupt and oppressive ecclesiastical institution, saddled with a deeply flawed theology and some highly suspect rituals and practices. The initial trigger, in England, may have been the marital difficulties of Henry VIII, and changes were certainly enacted under the mantle of an all-embracing 'Act of State'. But anticlerical feelings on the part of the people, and a yearning for the Bible and more authentic forms of Christian expression, ensured that reforms were broadly welcomed and effectively

implemented. The Reformation was itself a relatively short period of transformation and transition, drawing for all important purposes to a close
with the Elizabethan 'Settlement' of 1559; it was more an 'event' than a
long-drawn-out 'process'.[3]

There had always been a Catholic counter-narrative to this triumphalist
refrain, stressing the tragedy of division and the cruelties that often
accompanied it, but only in the last couple of decades of the twentieth
century did a refined version of this 'minority report' achieve a significant
measure of academic respectability. 'Revisionist' historians of the English
Reformation were, and are, thoughtful individuals rather than a disci-
plined school, but certain themes characterized their overall approach:
convinced Protestants were for long a small minority of the population as
a whole; changes were enforced by authority but often deeply unwelcome,
and even resisted, at the local level; the nation as a whole was only ever
patchily and incompletely converted to the new ideas.[4]

Revisionism enjoyed something approaching total ascendancy around
the turn of the twenty-first century, yet as a self-conscious, forensic rebuttal
of an earlier historical paradigm it inevitably invited its own critiques and
correctives. Much, if not most, historical writing on the Reformation
since the 1990s has been avowedly 'post-revisionist' in its interests and
emphases, and even Christopher Haigh, whose influential collection of
essays, *The English Reformation Revised* (1987), coined the revisionist label
for this period of history, has made the concession that 'we are (almost)
all post-revisionists now'.[5] Post-revisionism usually accepts the revisionist
premises that the changes of the Reformation were in no sense inevitable,
that the late medieval Church was in various respects doing a good job
and that, initially at least, Protestant ideas exercised only a limited popular
appeal.

Many post-revisionists, however, reject what they see as a false
dichotomy between models of enthusiastic embrace of reform and of
determined resistance to it. They draw attention to patterns of continuity
within change, and they often advance the paradoxical claim that in the
end the Reformation was remarkably successful in transforming English
society precisely because it represented much less of a clear, clean and
complete break with pre-Reformation practices and habits of thought than
we were at one time accustomed to think.[6]

The essays in this volume are broadly in line with a post-revisionist
approach to the Reformation in England. But at the same time they dissent
from a tendency in some (by no means all) post-revisionist writing to
overstate the character and extent of cultural continuity, and to interpret

apparently dramatic changes in terms of the substitution of one socially utilitarian doctrine or practice for another. When, some years ago, an early version of Chapter 4 was given as a talk at a university faculty seminar, the chair introduced me by saying that, while other scholars argued for a 'fast' or 'slow' Reformation in England, my scholarship was infused with the notion of a 'messy' Reformation. I was momentarily nonplussed, but almost immediately recognized this to be both a reasonable and perceptive assessment of emphases in my work. The following surveys of the 'invisible worlds' sensed and imagined by sixteenth- and seventeenth-century English people certainly recognize the continuing presence of the old within the new. But, rather than straightforward 'continuity', recurrent themes here are the complexities, confusions, dissonances and disjunctures of post-Reformation religious culture. A principal concern is with the ways in which – intellectually, imaginatively and emotionally – people tried to come to terms with irrevocable change, and the extent to which their attempts to adapt took unusual, unexpected and sometimes unsatisfactory turns.

At the heart of most of the discussions in this book, and arguably at the heart of the English Reformation itself, there lies a gaping absence. We could describe it as a definitive deletion, though it was one that arguably raised as many questions and perplexities as it resolved. Shortly after the break with Rome, in the first official doctrinal formulation of a newly independent Church of England, the Ten Articles laid down that, while it was a deed of charity to pray for the dead, 'the place where they be, the name thereof, and kind of pains there . . . be to us uncertain by scripture'. It was therefore necessary 'that such abuses be put clearly away, which under the name of purgatory hath been advanced'. A few years later, in his King's Book of 1543, Henry VIII commanded that people 'abstain from the name of purgatory, and no more dispute or reason thereof'. Within a year of Henry's death, the Chantries Act of 1547 declared 'devising and phantasing vain opinions of purgatory' to be a matter of 'blindness and ignorance', and the Forty-Two Articles, issued in King Edward VI's name in 1553, roundly declared purgatory to be 'a fond thing, vainly feigned, and grounded upon no warrant of scripture'.[7]

Purgatory has been described as '*the* defining doctrine of late medieval Catholicism'.[8] Purgatory was a state of being, but it was also a location in the cosmos. It was a way of explaining (and of enabling) salvation, of regulating relations between the living and the dead, and of understanding the nature of time itself. As I elaborate in Chapter 1, purgatory was a spur to memory, of the recently dead, and of the denizens of the longer-term past, around which much of the material culture, the imaginative energy and the institutional structure of the medieval Catholic Church in the West was organized.

The emphatic repudiation of purgatory by Protestant reformers across Europe in the sixteenth century was intended to be a tidy clinical exercise in therapeutic doctrinal amputation. There was no 'third place' in the afterlife. There was only the heaven and hell spoken of in Scripture, to which the souls of the departed went straight away after death, according to God's intents for them. Nor was there any necessity for such a place to exist. Christian souls had no need to purge or expiate their sins post-mortem; that had been done for them, once for all, in Christ's self-sacrifice on the cross. Similarly, there was no justification for Christians to pray for the souls of the dead – the activity that teaching on purgatory had galvanized and institutionalized. The condition of the dead was subject to no degree of change or amelioration through the imprecations of the living. The beloved dead might be properly and appropriately commemorated by the survivors, but not in any fashion that implied there were still active connections between them and human society on earth.

In the event, matters were not nearly so simple. The wound left by the excision of purgatory from the social body of post-Reformation Christianity was from the outset a bleeding source of puzzling and challenging questions of faith. Was it really the case that souls went straight to enjoy eternal bliss in heaven? Some Protestants were not so sure, believing that such interim and provisional blessedness detracted from the full glory of the final resurrection, when souls would be reunited with bodies, and dwell with a triumphantly returning Christ in the new heavens and new earth promised by the book of Revelation (21.1). Perhaps the soul was simply without any consciousness at all while it waited, or 'slept', in anticipation of the resurrection – the view that in time became known as Christian mortalism. And if so, in what place did the soul rest during this interim time?

The Bible was by no means as informative or clear-cut on these questions as magisterial Protestant reformers might have liked it to be. And it raised other unanswered, and unanswerable, questions, such as where the soul of Lazarus of Bethany had resided (John 11.1–44) in the four days between his passing from this world and Jesus' raising him from the grave. For that matter, where was Jesus' own soul between his death on the cross on Good Friday and his rising again on Easter Sunday? Did he literally 'descend into hell', as the ancient Apostles' Creed confidently asserted?

Medieval Christianity had the answers to these questions, though they were answers that Protestant reformers found both fanciful and unscriptural, involving the posited existence of a 'limbo of the fathers' (*limbus patrum*) in addition to the fiery prison of purgatory itself. But assertions of *sola scriptura*, the sole authority of the Bible, were scarcely a guarantee of unanimity in scriptural interpretation, and Protestants, in England as elsewhere, debated these matters among themselves without consensus. The growing availability of vernacular Scripture also encouraged a wider range of literate people to speculate on these and other abstruse questions of belief. In Chapter 3, I re-examine the case of Ellis Hall, a divinely inspired layman from mid-Tudor Manchester, who employed a deep knowledge of the Bible in English to give shape to a personal account of spiritual experience which was deeply indebted to medieval traditions of vision literature and the recording of otherworldly journeys. To the Protestant clergy who examined him, this was a thoroughly alarming adaptation of the new to the old.

The erasure of purgatory from the list of post-mortem destinations was intended to have no deleterious effect on the status of heaven and hell; indeed it was assumed they would now be able to shine forth more vividly and effectively in their colours. A recurrent theme of Protestant polemics against purgatory was that its supposed existence undercut the deterrent power of hell.[9] Yet, as I attempt to show in the first part of this book (particularly Chapters 2 and 4), there were unanticipated yet profound knock-on effects from the Protestants' theological assault on purgatory. Perhaps not entirely unanticipated, for in 1536 the humanist writer Thomas Starkey had written to Henry VIII to warn him about what he saw as the unsettling effects of radical preaching on the people: 'with the despising of purgatory, they began little to regard hell'.[10]

Cultural and intellectual historians have long suspected that Starkey may have been on to something; that the abrogation of purgatory was indeed in some way connected with the emergence of rising levels of scepticism about the eternal punishments of hell through the later seventeenth century and beyond.[11] In the first part of this book, I make the attempt to fill in some of the crucial detail on this connection. These chapters aim to show how the demands of religious controversy and polemic, and the desire to denounce and denigrate Catholic pieties about the character of post-mortem experience in purgatory, produced a growing willingness to admit to uncertainty about the precise nature of the afterlife in general. We can start to discern what I have called a 'reverential agnosticism' about the lineaments of the world to come. This expressed itself principally in a preparedness in some (though not all) Protestant quarters to interpret teaching on Christ's descent into hell, or the nature of fire in hell, in a non-literalist sense. It also promoted a greater willingness to 'despatialize' the afterlife, and to deny that its constituent parts could readily, or with any certainty at all, be located in relation to the known physical world. The Reformation's assault on established beliefs about the afterlife had profound intellectual and cultural consequences: debates about the existence of purgatory acted as unwitting agents of modernization, and sowed the seeds of a later harvest of scepticism and secularization.

From the perspective adopted in this book, the Reformation was more a matter of unsettling existing patterns of thought and belief than of rapidly implanting universally agreed replacement models. Nor was it ever a process in which ideas simply filtered downwards from intellectual elites to reorientate the priorities of lay and popular religion. Ellis Hall was an extreme and unusual case, but it is an important cumulative argument of the essays in this collection that the disruptions of the Reformation provided scope for ordinary people to think through some fundamental matters of life, death and belief, and to practise a kind of vernacular theology. Here it is of undoubted relevance that, usually more so than before the Reformation, the theologians who composed works of argument or instruction were often also themselves parish-based pastoral clergymen, or at least preachers, who on a regular basis encountered the laity and their frequently searching questions.

This too may have contributed to longer-term reconfigurations of the afterlife in ways that the leaders of the Protestant Reformation would not necessarily have wanted or expected. Increasingly, after the middle of the sixteenth century, Calvin's doctrine of double predestination became the normative teaching on salvation among English Protestant clergy. God had picked out, before the world was even created, and without respect to any good works performed in their lifetime, those who would dwell with him eternally in heaven, and those who would suffer for ever with the devil in hell.[12] The logic of predestination was that only a minority of Christians were chosen, 'elected', by God, and there was always a fair number of clergymen prepared to assert in print that the number of the elect was likely to be very small indeed.[13]

But the clergymen dealing with bereaved parishioners in a pastoral capacity (and these were sometimes the very same clergymen) were often in their funeral sermons willing to declare without qualification that an individual deceased person was now a 'saint' in heaven. They were also usually prepared to answer in the affirmative an even more theologically

sensitive question emanating from members of their flock: whether ancestors dying in time of popery – and in the sixteenth century these may
often have been parents or grandparents – could actually be saved. Before
the Reformation, purgatory had been the default destination at point of
death for all except the exceptionally wicked and the unusually virtuous.
In a process of unacknowledged negotiation with the anxieties and hopes
of ordinary people, there are signs that, increasingly, heaven took over
that role: another milestone in the long-term decline of hell. And, as
I discuss in detail in Chapter 5, the expectation that deceased friends
and family members were now in heaven, combined with an inability to
perform works of intercession on their behalf in this world, had another
unanticipated effect. There was a lively interest in the prospects for post-
mortem 'reunion', something which was at odds with the preoccupations
of spiritual purists, and which gives the lie to any suggestion that commemoration of the dead in post-Reformation Protestant culture was
overwhelmingly 'retrospective' in nature and increasingly secular in tone
(see also Chapter 1).

Still, there is little doubt that, among wide swathes of the population,
the Reformation produced a fair amount of doubt and uncertainty about
the state and status of the departed. It is otherwise hard to account for the
persistence and prevalence in post-Reformation England of stories about
the revenant dead – the principal theme of Chapters 8 and 10 in this book.

Belief in ghosts, the unquiet spirits of the dead, undoubtedly predates
the advent of Christianity itself, and its deep-rootedness in folkloric
culture probably helps to explain its long-term (and even continuing)
survival in England after the Reformation. Nonetheless, ghost belief was
cheerfully appropriated by Christianity and had been rendered more or
less theologically respectable over the long course of the Middle Ages.
Once again, it was purgatory that supplied the rationale for some degree
of contact between denizens of the visible and invisible worlds. Medieval
ghost-apparitions were typically visitations of souls from purgatory, permitted by God to appear on earth, either to issue warnings about the
consequences of bad behaviour, or to request the masses and prayers that
would help alleviate their own pitiful situation. To Protestants, of course,
this was on every level impossible: purgatory did not exist, and the souls
of the departed were either blissfully safe in God's heaven, or secure
prisoners of the devil in the eternal incarceration of hell. There were no
'appearances of the dead' in this world.

Yet the ghosts stubbornly refused to go away, and their continued
presence had to be explained. Here, it is not quite enough to say that the

Reformation 'failed' to eradicate belief in ghosts, for 'popular belief', like belief of any kind, is never static, and perceptions and attitudes evolved and mutated in significant ways over the sixteenth and seventeenth centuries. As I argue in Chapter 8, this was an area of often unacknowledged but nonetheless extensive dialogue between orthodox Protestantism and local cultures of belief; a dialogue in the course of which Protestant orthodoxy moved some considerable way from its emphatic starting point that supposed appearances of the dead (assuming they were not simple human frauds) were nothing but deceptive tricks of the devil. The material in Chapter 10 explores further the idea that an ultimate effect of the Reformation was to 'de-theologize' the ghost story, opening it up to a creative range of moral and cultural purposes.

This pattern of mutation, adaptation and pluralization in thinking about the boundaries of the invisible world was an unintentional, even counter-intuitive effect of the Reformation in England. As Darren Oldridge has recently persuasively demonstrated, a recurrent concern of Protestant reformers was to regulate and reform the unruly world of spirits; their aim was 'to establish a biblical model of the supernatural world'.[14] As with the conceptual geography of the afterlife itself, this proved considerably easier said than done, for the Bible was a much less precisely prescriptive, or compendiously comprehensive, text than its proponents liked to believe.

For a start, there were some creatures of the imagination on which Scripture was to all intents and purposes silent: fairies, elves, hobgoblins, brownies and the like; supernatural beings which had never really fitted in an orthodox Christian cosmology, but whose presence in the English cultural landscape had for many centuries been attested to by writers of various kinds. The initial instinct of Protestant reformers was to bundle fairy belief into the broad category of outdated 'popish' superstitions which would inexorably fade under the light of the gospel. As with ghosts, however, the intractability of popular belief in this area was something which began as a problem and came over time to seem an opportunity – albeit an often ambiguous and double-edged one. In Chapter 11 I discuss how, in the later seventeenth century, growing concerns about religious scepticism and unbelief led a number of Protestant writers to seize on almost any manifestation of the presence of the invisible world as a means of refuting the 'atheists' of their day – a strategy which, particularly as it pertained to fairies, left its exponents open to the ridicule of fashionable 'Enlightenment' opinion.

We should note but not necessarily endorse the ridicule. The writers who chronicled visitations from the invisible world were typically men of 'science' as well as faith: one of their principal concerns was to place apparitions and other supernatural events on a firmly factual basis, using techniques of recording and verification which would have seemed quite appropriate to members of the nascent Royal Society (which many of them were). But the new empiricism sat uneasily with the older traditions of Protestant biblicism. If such manifestations had to be proved by the evidence of the senses, then they became negotiable, debatable, uncertain – and, to some at least, increasingly implausible.

Protestant biblicism was on seemingly solider ground when it came to the most heartening of supernatural visitors and messengers. Between them, the Old and New Testaments provided an impressive 250 or so references to angels, as they set about their business of instructing, admonishing, guiding or comforting God's people. Pure spirits, created but immortal, angels represented an authorized channel of communication between worlds, as well as a welcome source of spiritual support and succour for people in a theological system from which the other supernatural helpers of the medieval period – in the form of the saints – had largely been evicted, and one in which Satan and his legions of demons loomed increasingly large.

Angels were undoubtedly an important pastoral resource for Protestant preachers in their efforts to reform and refocus the religious preoccupations of the people. But they were always a decidedly ambivalent asset, and belief in angels can in many ways be seen to exemplify the cocktail of continuity, conflict, compromise and confusion which was the cultural legacy of the Reformation in England. Angels 'appear' in the Bible in both senses of the term. Yet many reformers – wedded to the notion that an apostolic 'age of miracles' was firmly over, allergic to any suggestion of 'new revelations' and alert to the danger of angels being venerated as they had been in the Catholic past – were wary of any suggestion of angels appearing visibly to mankind. They were, in the words of the mid-seventeenth-century Calvinist bishop Joseph Hall, 'invisible helpers', to whose ministrations on earth there were now no 'ocular witnesses'.[15] Protestant authors raised the possibility that some reported apparitions of ghosts might in fact be misinterpreted sightings of angels almost immediately to dismiss it (see Chapter 8).

Yet this too proved a line almost impossible to defend, and by the end of the seventeenth century some Protestant clergy had themselves given up trying to defend it. The possibility that angels might manifest themselves directly to the human senses was one which across the seventeenth century was conceded in learned treatises as well as in ballads and popular print.[16] An arena in which visions of angels were regularly reported was the deathbed, a place where faithful Christians were reported as crying out that they saw the spirits who had come to carry them to their place of eternal rest. I explore this theme in detail in Chapter 6, identifying it as a key point of cultural continuity across the Reformation divide, but also as a study in how, with some difficulty, familiar motifs might be reworked to address the needs of a new theological framework.

There was a similar admixture of the inherited and the reinvented in the case of another medieval concept with a vibrant post-Reformation afterlife: the idea that humans were assigned by God a 'guardian angel', for protection in this world and oversight of their spiritual progress towards the next (Chapter 7). Here, once again, the Bible proved an uncertain guide, with much debate among Protestants, stretching over a century and more, as to whether the doctrine of individual angelic guardianship could actually be discerned in, or inferred from, Scripture. The notion was an understandably appealing one, and also proved distinctly malleable. It lent itself to the purposes of a variety of devotional and theological positions, from crypto-Catholicism through to a doctrinally rigorous Calvinism (in the idea that the provision of guardian angels was a token of God's special care for his elect). The angel beliefs of early modern England were remarkably dynamic. Since angels (believed to constitute distinct orders in heaven) were a useful means of interpreting and commenting on hierarchy, there seems to have been a surge of interest in them in periods when hierarchies were being challenged and tested, particularly in the revolutionary decades of the mid-seventeenth century.[17] With respect to angels, and, I would argue, the supernatural world more broadly, the picture is not so much one of a managed and coherent reform as of far-reaching fragmentation, a process making constituent parts available for various forms of creative redeployment.

The longer-term implications of this pattern constitute almost too large a theme to do more than glance at here. Like others written in recent years on aspects of supernatural belief in early modern England, this book sits in the shadow of a monumental work of twentieth-century scholarship: Sir Keith Thomas's *Religion and the Decline of Magic* (1971). The story that book sought to tell was one of disaggregation as well as decline. The Reformation, which Thomas saw as an intrinsically rationalizing force, drove magical mentalities and a powerful sense of the immanence of the sacred out of the official purview of the Church. These, for a time, flourished in social settings largely separated from official religion, but their subsequent inevitable erosion helped to usher in the advent of the modern world.

While there is no doubt that, in comparison with the world of our late medieval ancestors, modern Western society has been desacralized and secularized to a remarkable degree, the routes that journey has taken, and the significance of the Reformation as a crucial fork in the road, remain very much open to discussion and debate. At the very least, the essays in this book add weight to a perception that the divorce between 'religion' and 'magic' was a considerably slower and messier business than a casual reader of Thomas might be able to infer. In the person of John Quick (the subject of Chapter 9), we encounter a nonconformist minister, and orthodox Calvinist, of the late seventeenth century, who was to a remarkable degree interested in ghosts, portents and forms of providentialism bordering on the miraculous. He was far from unique in this.[18]

Behind Keith Thomas's work lies an older and still influential paradigm: the German sociologist Max Weber's famous proposal that the Reformation, particularly in its Calvinist manifestations, promoted a 'disenchantment of the world' (*Entzauberung der Welt*): a rejection of magical, numinous and supernatural beliefs in favour of faith in a more distant and transcendent deity.[19] For some time now, religious and cultural historians have been sceptical about key aspects of this thesis, and some have even sought to turn it on its head by arguing that, in the medium term at least, the Reformation promoted an intensified preoccupation with intrusions of divine power into the created world. This pattern of 're-enchantment' is seen in Protestantism's magnified concern with the activity of Satan, and in its emphasis on an activist, interventionist God whose will was inscribed in the natural world through providential signs and occurrences. England was no exception to the pattern of post-Reformation societies elsewhere in Europe in exhibiting rich Protestant subcultures of folk belief and popular magic.[20]

The essays in this volume share a viewpoint adopted in much of the best recent work on these topics: that we need to shake off any inherited assumption that Reformation Protestantism was intrinsically more 'rational', more content with solely naturalistic explanations for strange phenomena, than the religious system it displaced: the age of the witchcraft trials was scarcely one of caution about the reality of supernatural forces. There was no progressive, straight and widening path from credulity to Enlightenment to modernity. But at the same time, seeds of scepticism and disbelief were surely planted in the fields from which so many of the great oaks of medieval theology had been torn down. Those seeds were nurtured and watered in post-Reformation England's jarring experiences of religious pluralism, of polemical argument, of rival and incompatible explanations of truth, and of various forms of DIY theology. Ultimately, the disenchantment of the world was a delayed consequence of the deregulation of the supernatural.

Part 1

HEAVEN, HELL AND PURGATORY: HUMANS IN THE SPIRIT WORLD

1

After purgatory: death and remembrance in the Reformation world

Wherever it took hold, the Reformation changed the meaning and experience of death. More specifically, it picked apart a rich and complex cultural grammar of commendation and commemoration for the dead. This grammar involved ritual, doctrine, liturgy and material objects, as well as deeply ingrained habits of thought, language and gesture. What bound it together was the conviction that the dead were in a dynamic condition of change and improvement in the next life, something which kept them connected in intimate ways with the motives and actions of those left behind in the world. The living had responsibilities towards the dead, to remember them in specific ways and in specific contexts. The aim was not to bind, but to release them, to help see them safely to journey's end and to their final heavenly home. To pray for the dead was to partake in the process of their redemption, and in so far as society was geared up and equipped for this task, it collectively volunteered itself to support the salvific work of Christ.

The great strength of the medieval scheme of commemoration was that it aligned an emotional impulse to do right by the dead with a cosmological explanation of their condition and location. Purgatory – that crowning achievement of the medieval social imaginary – was at once a place of confinement, a state of being and a clarion call for acknowledgement and response. Death, paradoxically, served to affirm the claims and character of common humanity, exemplified in the ubiquitous medieval legend of the three kings who encounter a trio of animated rotting corpses: 'What you are, so once were we; what we are, so you shall be.'[1] Such imagery, in addition to its *memento mori* function, pointed towards the powerful unwritten contract between generations past and present. Precisely because the living would come to share the fate of the dead and their condition of need, they must not forget them, but stir themselves to action to alleviate their plight. Do unto others as you would have them do unto you.

But right across Europe in the course of the sixteenth century, that contract was challenged, tested at law and found to be without validity. Purgatory – so the reformers taught their congregations – was a lie, a fiction and an invention. From an early date, Europe's disparate reform movements were remarkably unanimous in this conclusion. Unlike the Eucharist, baptism or predestination, the question of purgatory was hardly ever a cause of doctrinal dissension among Protestants. It may have taken Luther more than a decade from the time of his protest over indulgences in 1517 to finally and explicitly deny the possibility of any middle state for souls in his *Widerruf vom Fegefeuer* (Repeal of Purgatory) of 1530. But already in 1521 he was denouncing masses for the dead, and he soon came to regard all forms of post-mortem intercession as *Gaukelwerke*, works of trickery.[2] Other early reformers were less hesitant. In the preaching and polemic of English evangelicals like William Tyndale or Hugh Latimer, purgatory was simply 'purgatory pickpurse'. In a still more resonant phrase, the early Swiss reformers Pamphilius Gengenbach and Nicholas Manuel denounced traditional teaching about the afterlife by the Catholic clergy as *Totenfresserei*, feasting, or rather guzzling, upon the dead.[3]

The ferocity of such assaults has perhaps never been thoroughly accounted for. It is often pointed out that purgatory had uncertain scriptural foundations, but then so did other key doctrines largely uncontentious within mainstream Protestantism, such as infant baptism and the Trinity. The rage seems to come from a deeper place – a sense of anger and betrayal at being hoodwinked by the clergy, certainly. Or was the revulsion in any way fuelled by ambivalent feelings towards the dead themselves, that fear and resentment which can sometimes accompany the grief of bereavement? Whatever the psychological imperatives in play, wherever Protestantism came to power, it was agreed that the dead had no right to demand the prayers of the living, and the living had no obligation to supply them. In the space of a few years, the doctrinal rationale for a plethora of ritual observances and material constructions was entirely swept away, and the whole basis on which the dead were to be honoured and remembered was open for renegotiation.

For Catholic observers, this was frequently an occasion of bewilderment, shock and trauma. Johann Leyp, the last remaining Catholic pastor in Chemnitz in Lutheran Saxony, looked around him in 1534 and saw how 'the dead are buried without a cross or candles in silence, like senseless beasts, like dogs'. Similarly, in France in 1556, a Catholic writer caustically observed how Huguenots would 'throw the body into the grave without saying anything or making any more ceremony than for a dog or a horse'.

Another French Catholic considered the heretics' 'miserable treatment of the dead . . . tearful to see'.[4] The Elizabethan English Catholic William Allen looked across the channel from exile in 1565 and lamented that 'nowe there is no blessing of mannes memorie at all'. Towards the end of the century, the Dutch humanist Arnoldus Buchelius bewailed the fact that Protestants 'neglect the monuments of the ancients, and do not attend to the memorial masses of our ancestors, saying that their names have already been written in heaven, so that some of them seem more barbaric than the Goths themselves'.[5] Such statements are evidence of an immediate and instinctive reaction to sacrilegious transgression, in the setting aside of familiar and valued rituals, but they also point to a wider unease about a kind of social amnesia, an abandonment of the crucial symbolic connections between current and past tenants of the earth.

II

Modern scholarship does not in the main share the spiritual anxieties and regrets of sixteenth-century Catholics, but it has been inclined to echo the perception that in this area, even more than in others, the Reformation initiated dramatic and long-lasting patterns of change, with implications far beyond the world of ecclesiastical ritual and doctrine. It is commonly asserted, for example, that what the Protestant reformers effected was nothing less than a thoroughgoing redefinition of human community, severing all connections between the living and the dead, and casting out the latter from the position they had enjoyed as an honorary 'age group' in medieval society.[6] The dead were not just dead; they were dead and gone. This did not necessarily mean that they were forgotten, but rather that they were remembered in profoundly new ways, ones which brought about far-reaching changes in the meaning of memory itself. Medieval concepts of memory were profoundly structured by what, in a classic discussion, the German historian Otto Gerhard Oexle called 'Die Gegenwart der Toten' – the presence of the dead. Subsequent scholarship has done much to elaborate the concept of *memoria* as an organizing principle of medieval social and cultural life, noting how it was constituted through a multitude of gift exchanges, and a ritualized refiguring – literally re-membering – of the dead through the recital of their names in a variety of liturgical and quasi-liturgical contexts.[7] Medieval *memoria*, it is argued, served to collapse the gap between past and present which is central to modern ideas of memory. The Reformation, however, by ejecting the dead from a ritual and intercessionary 'present', demarcated the past more clearly and endowed it with a new ontological status. 'The rejection of *memoria*', suggests Craig Koslofsky, 'was essential to the modern order of memory based on linear, directional time and a past of dead individuals, absent, with whom the living could have only the most disturbing contact.'[8] Thus, it would seem, the origins of the modern discipline of history itself turn out to be surprisingly closely entwined with the eschatological concerns of the Reformation.

Such models of explanation are based in part upon developments in twentieth-century art-historical theory, particularly around the interpretation of tombs and monuments. A seminal study of *Tomb Sculpture* by the German art historian Erwin Panofsky argued that post-Reformation monuments were fundamentally 'retrospective', seeking to enumerate and commemorate the achievements of the dead person during a life now terminated; quite unlike the 'prospective' monuments of the Middle Ages, with their evident concern for the still mutable condition of the deceased in the afterlife.[9]

This, then, was a new idiom of commemoration with potentially far-reaching social and cultural consequences. One line of development scholars have spotted leads towards a greater emphasis on the lived identity of the dead person, and intersects with the rise of modern individualism.[10] Here, a greater biographical emphasis in tombs, monuments and epitaphs seems of a piece with the abandonment of collective rituals for the achievement of a good death, and successful navigation of the afterlife. For had not Luther preached in a sermon of 1522 that 'everyone must fight his own battle with death by himself, alone'?[11]

A second and related argument sees the retrospective and this-worldly character of Protestant memorial culture as a symptom of a larger process of conceptual reorientation, one of desacralization or secularization. Funerary monuments in churches came to be much more about celebrating honour and lineage, and about articulating the social and political order, than about providing symbols of Christian hope.[12]

It is not hard to find examples to support the thesis, whether in the apparently excessive concern with heraldic display that can be found on elite monuments across northern Europe, or in seemingly merely naturalistic and unspiritualized representations of the recumbent form. It was of such sepulchres that the English playwright John Webster was thinking when he has a character in *The Duchess of Malfi* exclaim:

> Princes images on their tombes
> Do not lie, as they were wont, seeming to pray
> Up to heaven: but with their hands under their cheekes,

(As if they died of the tooth-ache) . . . not carved
With their eies fix'd upon the starres; but as
Their mindes were wholly bent upon the world
The self-same way they seeme to turne their faces.[13]

It has seemed, moreover, to some modern commentators that in promoting a stronger sense of the finality of judgement at death, the Reformation sharpened a contrast between worldly achievements to be celebrated and conserved, and the dark oblivion that awaited beyond.[14] In his brilliant and provocative *Very Brief History of Eternity*, Carlos Eire suggests that the abrogation of purgatory and what followed from it was no less than 'a significant first step toward the elevation of this world as the ultimate reality and towards the extinction of the soul'.[15]

It is clear, then, that the Reformation's rethinking of the meaning of commemoration, shaped by the reformers' unmasking of 'fraudulent' purgatory, has been asked to do a lot of historical work. As an important foundational component, both of a modern sense of individual selfhood, and of a profoundly secularizing impulse, it would seem as if the abolition of purgatory is being made into one of the defining conditions of modernity itself. It is of course the task and responsibility of historians to construct ambitious explanatory models of historical development, to suggest connections between disparate synchronous phenomena, and to identify the processes and dynamics at work in effecting changes we might well want to regard as epochal. But, attractive though they are, grand theories about the relationship between the assault on purgatory and the emergence of the modern world pose some significant problems, as grand theories always do.

In the first place, there is the need to consider the existence of the very different patterns of funerary ritual and commemorative culture to be found in different parts of the Protestant world. Second, and still more pertinently, such theories have a convenient tendency to forget that most parts of western Europe did not abandon purgatory, because they did not ultimately adopt the Reformation. In much of Catholic Europe, as several studies have noted, interest in post-mortem intercession and the cult of the holy souls actually intensified in the post-Reformation era.[16] If radical reform of the afterlife is made the condition of modernity, then Catholicism is by definition excluded from a role in the making of modernity, which seems not so much discriminatory as deeply implausible. Third, now that historians have caught up with sociologists of religion in becoming sceptical about the secularization thesis itself, and as it has become increasingly evident that secularity is hardly the most prominent feature of the world we collectively inhabit, a need to identify so emphatically its putative historical roots is arguably a less pressing task.

III

The rest of this chapter seeks to probe some of these concepts a little further, asking what patterns of mortuary and commemorative practice in the post-Reformation world can tell us about the priorities of different reform movements, about the interplay of social and spiritual motives in the continuing response to the biological imperative of death, and about the sometimes remarkable plasticity and adaptability of reforming initiatives in particular cultural and geographical settings. The story, without doubt, is a much untidier and more perplexing one than any simple 'before' and 'after' binary might suggest.

Did the Reformation act to sever connections between the living and the dead? There are some senses in which that is obviously true. Reformed doctrine insisted that the dead had no awareness of what was transpiring in the world; that they were insensible of, as well as unable to respond to or benefit from, the prayers or devotions of the living.[17] The motive here was a desire to undercut the cult of the saints, as much as it was to prevent people making representations to or for the more ordinary dead, but it was a line Protestant orthodoxy was determined to hold. Yet in other ways and contexts the metaphor of the severed connection begs some significant questions.

Was, for example, this separation of the dead from the living purely metaphysical and conceptual, or did it have a physical, spatial component? For Germany, the case has been strongly made that it did, for example, by Koslofsky and Susan Karant-Nunn. They note that in many parts of Germany and Switzerland through the sixteenth century and into the seventeenth, the traditional graveyards encompassing the parish church were being closed down and relocated outside town and city walls.[18] Here, the removal of cemeteries is symbolic of a spiritual shift, a parallel distancing of the bodies and the souls of the dead from the habitats and habitus of the living.

But as these scholars are compelled to admit, the story is a little more complicated than that. Luther was in favour of extramural burial on the basis of both scriptural mandate and decent pious practice,[19] but the stated reasons for closing traditional graveyards always involved public health arguments rather than theological ones – graves were believed to exude foul and dangerous miasmas – and it was a process that had begun already

22

in the fifteenth century. Moreover, it was patchily implemented, and sometimes fiercely resisted.[20] Even in Germany, the relocation of burial sites was an exclusively urban phenomenon, and it was far from normative for the wider Protestant world: Carlos Eire exaggerates when he states that the removal of bodies to suburban churchyards was a composite 'spiritual apartheid and physical apartheid', which 'came into existence rapidly and thoroughly wherever Protestantism took root'.[21] Burial in traditional medieval churchyards continued, for example, in both Lutheran Sweden and Calvinist Scotland, though here individual grave markers were becoming more common in the seventeenth century than they had been before the Reformation.[22] In Protestant England too, even in towns, burial in the ancient churchyards remained the usual pattern throughout the sixteenth century. In London, as Vanessa Harding has shown, some new suburban parish cemeteries were established, but they were largely shunned by parishioners of status, and became repositories for the marginal dead: strangers, paupers and victims of the plague.[23]

Social status had always been a prime determinant of burial location, and across Europe the general pattern here seems to be one of broad continuity rather than of radical innovation. In medieval times, the most desirable location was inside the parish church itself, preferably in the chancel near to where the sacrifice of the mass was offered. Burial within the church continued to be the aspiration for local social elites in Protestant England, Lutheran Germany, the Reformed Netherlands, even some Swiss cities like Basel.[24] As Diarmaid MacCulloch has put it, 'far from tombs disappearing from church buildings, in most European settings the protestant dead made their presence felt ever more stridently and in greater numbers'.[25]

This was neither an inevitable nor an uncontentious development. The case of Scotland is instructive here. Leaders of the Kirk took the line that the dead had no place among the worshipping community of the living. Since kirk burial originated from a desire for proximity to saints' relics, and for benefiting from masses and prayers, its continuation was a dangerous invitation to popish relapse. Prohibitions of the practice were passed at General Assemblies in 1588, 1597, 1638 and 1643.[26]

Serial prohibitions are usually an indication that a policy isn't working, and so it proved in Scotland. There was an official and legitimate way of circumventing the ban: the construction of aisles or small transepts on the side of churches as the site of often very elaborate family mausolea. These were not technically part of the church, but allowed landowners to continue to reap the prestige associated with burial at the heart of the worshipping community. There was also much simple defiance of the ban. In response to popular demand, and in return for an appropriate fee, local kirk elders regularly allowed the placing of bodies and monuments within the building itself. Such monuments were not invariably modest and discreet, as can be seen, for example, from the imposing figural tomb for Sir George Bruce placed in the former monastic church turned parish kirk at Culross in Fife in 1642. Commenting on the burial ban, the American historian of Scottish Protestantism, Margo Todd, remarks that 'there is surely no louder testimony to continued lay reverence for sacred space . . . than the utter failure of this effort in the face of popular insistence on kirk burial, and its eventual transformation into yet another fundraising device'. More speculatively, she adds that the annual payments of so-called 'burial silver', required to keep bodies in their places, seem 'reminiscent of the expense of those pre-Reformation commemorative masses, the "months minds" and obits on the anniversary of a death'.[27]

All of this raises the key question of cultural meanings, both of those explicitly declared and of those implicitly assumed. The continuities in physical patterns of burial need not imply or require the persistence of pre-Reformation habits of religious thought. It is here indeed that advocates of a secularized concept of commemoration anchor their case, supposing that tombs and monuments assumed overwhelmingly social and political functions, entirely divorced from their original spiritual rationale. Yet to characterize Protestant memorial culture as fundamentally secular in intention and expression is a serious misreading.

Commemoration of the dead began, of course, with the funeral, just as it had before the Reformation. Here, diversity and disagreement within the Protestant camp about the permissible extent of religious ceremonial was at its most marked. German Lutheranism, predictably, was at one end of the spectrum, building on Luther's own understanding of the honourable burial of the dead as a required act of Christian piety. As it developed in the Empire, Lutheran funeral ritual retained numerous ceremonial elements of a traditional stamp, most evidently in the solemnity of a communal procession to the graveside led by the clergy.[28] The burial service of the Church of England similarly had discernible roots in the medieval services. In both England and Germany, patterns of ritualized almsgiving to the poor remained a notable feature of funerary practice.[29]

To Calvinist observers, much of this looked unacceptably popish. Within the English church, there were persistent tensions around the form of the burial service, with Puritans taking particular exception to the phrase appearing to offer all the recently deceased 'sure and certain hope of the resurrection'. English Puritanism enjoyed a short moment of political triumph during the mid-seventeenth-century civil wars, and the Directory of Public Worship which replaced the Anglican Book of Common Prayer in 1645 mandated that corpses were to be 'decently' attended to interment, but without any prayers, readings or singing.[30] This was the ideal of Reformed practice. When Calvin himself was laid to rest in Geneva in 1564 it was without pomp, and by his own request in an unmarked grave.[31] Reformed burial rites, suggests Philip Benedict, were performed with 'breathtaking restraint'. In France, ministers might take part, but only as private individuals. Both here and in Scotland, set readings and singing of hymns were prohibited because of the fear that, as the Scots First Book of Discipline put it, 'some superstitious think that singing and reading of the living may profit the dead'.[32]

Yet the ultimate logic of burial as an entirely civil and secular occasion was virtually nowhere observed in Europe, outside a few small separatist and sectarian groups. And there seems to have been an almost universal tendency for ritual elements to seep back through the cracks of Reformed doctrinal rectitude. Ringing was a case in point. Protestant orthodoxy was usually suspicious of bell-ringing because of its historical legacy as a Catholic 'sacramental', and as a traditional form of intercessory action for the dead. Ecclesiastical authorities thus sought to regulate its practice and extent, but without much effect. In England, parish performance stretched to breaking point, and several hours beyond, the episcopal directives that there should be only a 'short' peal of bells after the funeral. Reformed synods in France found themselves unable to prevent the ringing of church bells during the funeral procession, while in Scotland, and in defiance of ministerial opinion, local kirk sessions set about pragmatically establishing fee structures for different levels of tolling.[33]

The clergy were more directly implicated in another concession to lay expectations with links to the pre-reformed past: the preaching of funeral sermons. It was of course always unlikely that the Reformed ministers would willingly forgo any opportunity to expound the Word of God to a captive audience. In some churches formalized funeral sermons were discouraged for seeming in their timing and function uncomfortably close to Catholic invocations. This was the case in Zürich and Geneva, in France and Scotland, and in England under the regime of the Directory of Public Worship. But in all these places ministers were still permitted to make an 'exhortation' or 'remonstrance', putting people in mind of their Christian duties. Puritan anxieties about funeral sermons being 'put in the place of trentals' signally failed to dampen growing enthusiasm for them in later sixteenth-century England.[34] Even in Scotland, the distinction between an impromptu exhortation and the fully fledged funeral sermon was far from rigidly observed, and John Knox himself preached at the funeral of the earl of Moray in 1570, just as Luther had preached at the funerals of those earlier political patrons of Protestant reform, Frederick the Wise and John the Constant.[35]

It was above all in Lutheran Germany that the Protestant funeral sermon established its definitive form, and a secure place in the ritual management of death. Pastors were in fact generally required by the authorities to preach at the funerals of parishioners, and literally hundreds of thousands of sixteenth- and seventeenth-century funeral sermons have survived in printed form. This genre has attracted considerable scholarly attention, much of it occasioned by funeral sermons' utility as a source for social, cultural and gender history, with much close reading of the biographical and obituary elements of the texts. But these were not in intention eulogies, and a recounting of the life and character of the deceased was usually only one element of a larger scheme which sought to expound doctrinal messages about death and the hope of resurrection.[36] Virtually nowhere in the Protestant world around the turn of the seventeenth century can the experience of attending a funeral be usefully characterized as a 'secular' one.

IV

The same can surely be said of the experience of anyone contemplating a funeral monument or other type of commemorative epitaph in a post-Reformation parish church or cathedral. It seems scarcely contentious to assert this for those parts of Lutheran Germany and the Baltic world where textual or heraldic commemorative cues were regularly included on elaborate votive altarpieces.[37] In the Reformed churches there was much greater anxiety about all forms of imagery and representation, and about the possible dangers of idolatry. A consequence was that carved or painted likenesses of the human form on funerary monuments were sometimes the only form of directly representational imagery to be found in the church. This could in itself represent a source of anxiety, and invite the attention of overscrupulous iconoclasts. It was to head off this possibility that Elizabeth I of England issued a proclamation in 1560 asserting that monuments to dead persons in churches were a matter solely of civil honour and respect: they had been 'set up for the only memory of them to their posterity . . . and not for any religious honor'.[38] But the medieval tombs and brasses found in countless English parish churches, and protected from damage under the terms of the proclamation, often had inscriptions asking bystanders for prayers to ease their passage through purgatory. Nor was the survival of large numbers of medieval Catholic monuments in Protestant churches by any means an exclusively English phenomenon.[39]

New monuments placed in churches did not ask for prayers, or only very rarely. Neither – in Reformed settings – did they include representations of Christ or the saints, though there is some evidence of angels finding their way back on to memorials in Calvinist settings.[40] Post-Reformation monuments were, like their late medieval predecessors, often heavily freighted with statements about family and lineage. But this in itself hardly renders them deracinated of religious meaning. In the first place, we might well suspect that the messages about virtue and honour with which early modern tombs are imbued are really inexplicable without reference to the biblical and Christian humanist culture within which they were formed.[41] Moreover, it seems simply unlikely that any culturally complex artefact, situated within the measured spatial relationships of a church building, and endlessly washed over with the utterance of prayer and the mimetic codes of ritual performance, could remain entirely innocent of religious meaning. Here we might reflect on how new and emerging forms of com-memorative media – epitaph paintings, and half-length effigies in relief, for example – were being placed in churches in positions from which earlier religious imagery had been removed or obscured: frequently on the whitewashed walls of the nave.[42]

In any case, the textual and iconographic features to be found on post-Reformation funerary monuments do not generally require much deep or counter-intuitive interpretation to establish that these were in quite evident ways still sacral objects, with important religious messages to impart. Panofsky's influential notion that Protestant tombs were typically 'retrospective' constructions, overwhelmingly concerned with the record of an historical past rather than with the prospect of an eschatological future, is hard to reconcile with a trope which emerges with great clarity from a wide variety of commemorative media in various parts of northern Europe: an expression of faith in the resurrection and a concern with the ultimate destiny of the resurrected body.[43]

The resurrection was hardly a doctrinal discovery of the Reformation, of course. But it does seem that this was often a relatively subordinate theme in the material culture of commemoration in the late Middle Ages, when so much emphasis was placed on intercession for the intermediate period. However, it asserted itself with greater confidence in the post-Reformation decades. The resurrection, unsurprisingly, was also a central theme of Protestant funeral sermons.[44]

Closely linked to this was the growing tendency to employ the metaphor of sleep to characterize the condition of the body over the period between death and resurrection. Soul-sleeping, the idea that the dead had no consciousness of any kind before the Last Judgement, was widely regarded in later sixteenth-century Europe as an Anabaptist heresy, despite the fact that Luther himself had been drawn to the notion. But any anxieties that using the language of sleep might undermine the idea of an individual judgement on souls at the point of death seem to have dissipated fairly quickly, in the Reformed as well as Lutheran churches. It was certainly ubiquitous in English memorial culture, and by one recent calculation the comforting term 'avsomnat', fallen asleep, had replaced 'died' on a quarter of Swedish gravestones before the end of the seventeenth century.[45] As well as being pastorally reassuring for the dying and the survivors, the imagery of death-as-sleep had the advantage of being able to draw on strong scriptural precedents: both Old and New Testaments are full of references to the dead sleeping in the Lord.[46] It also constituted an ongoing argument against the existence of purgatory, for the dead could hardly be resting in the Lord if they were being tormented with purgatory fire.

The awakening which came after sleep, so the clergy taught, was to a rapt contemplation of the Godhead through all the senses of a resurrected and perfected body. But quite possibly this was not what all laypeople were looking forward to with keenest anticipation. A striking feature of Protestant memorial discourse is the interest which many monuments and funeral sermons display in the prospect of the reunion of spouses, parents and children in the next life. The poignant question 'Shall we know one another in heaven?' was generally answered in the affirmative by preachers and pastors in the early modern era.[47] This undoubtedly makes further nonsense of the idea that the post-mortem gaze of the post-Reformation was entirely retrospective, or that it contemplated the land beyond death solely as a vista of darkness and annihilation. It also argues against the notion of the key signature of Protestant commemoration being a heightened individualism, at least in its strictest sense. For family – in either lineage or nuclear forms – was almost everywhere a dominant motif of monumental sculpture and epitaph paintings.

The families in question, moreover, were not historically correct and chronologically ordered ones, but composite and reconstituted families, in which dead as well as living children have their place, and serial wives sit or kneel patiently alongside each other together with their common husband. Perhaps the aim was to draw attention to the fruitfulness of a successful patriarch.[48] But it is hard to think that we are not looking on scenes in which enduring human relationships are at once celebrated, idealized and projected forwards on to an imagined future. Just how the donors envisaged the domestic arrangements in heaven working out is a question on which, alas, our sources are generally silent.

All of this should, I think, remove any lingering suspicion that the commemorative culture of Protestant Europe was a simply residual one, its structure and logic determined solely by the fact of a purgatory-shaped hole. There were distinct, and distinctively Protestant, repertoires of mortuary and memorial practice, responding to a variety of social, psychological and religious needs. Perennial spiritual questions were addressed in new ways, and new patterns of iconography were pressed into service. Naturally, there was a complex blend of continuity and innovation in all of this, as there was in virtually all aspects of the Reformation's impact on society. The point which is often made – that post-Reformation commemoration of the dead was deeply concerned with status display, and with articulating the social and political order – seems likely to be rather one of the key continuities than otherwise. Questions of the location of the burial site, of the style and scale of funeral obsequies, and of the size of tomb or monument were all matters of more than purely spiritual significance, before the Reformation, as after it. The spiritual continuities are harder to discern, amidst the sound and fury of a doctrinal revolution. But they are surely there. It is hard to believe that the earlier associations of holiness attaching themselves to processional routes to churchyards, to patterns of commensality and charity, or to specific locations in the churchyard and places of interment within the church were simply obliterated from people's minds.

V

So far, this chapter has been discussing the development of Protestant commemorative culture without much reference to the ongoing confessional rivalries of sixteenth- and seventeenth-century Europe. In conclusion, we might then turn to consider, not just what the Reformation did for the memory of the dead, but what the memorializing of the dead did for the Reformation. It has already been noted that Catholic Europe responded to the attack on purgatory by flamboyantly reasserting the importance of prayer for the dead. Local studies of Spain and France show that real-term spending on intercessory masses rose dramatically in some places from the latter part of the sixteenth century. The condition of the holy souls became a more common motif for new altarpieces in the Counter-Reformation Church than it had been in the Middle Ages.[49] It is possible to track the progress of Counter-Reformation teaching in Ireland in the later sixteenth century through the inclusion of more emphatically Tridentine sentiments in memorial inscriptions.[50] Protestant memorial iconography meanwhile, even in the visually rich Lutheran tradition, was confessionally and assertively distinctive, demoting and historicizing saints and martyrs, and promoting the image of Christ the divine redeemer over Jesus the suffering man of sorrows. Danish Lutherans might even record on their tombs that they died in the 'true religion'.[51] As Catholics and Protestants attacked each other's funerary practices as superstitious or impious, death itself acquired an explicitly confessional face.

But as historians of the Reformation are very well aware, the process of demarcating religious divisions that we have come to call 'confessionaliza-tion' was seldom swift, complete, or unidirectional in origin and impetus. Because the dead belonged in one sense to the past, their role might be to complicate the delineation of confessional identities in the present, asking searching questions about the boundaries of community and the role of the Church in defining them. Protestant laypeople seem often to have pondered a poignant family-focused dilemma, though one heavy with theological implications: are all our ancestors damned? In the main, the Protestant clergy answered 'no' in response to this, thus implicitly conceding that the medieval Church contained within it some means of salvation.[52]

The importance of maintaining the connection to one's ancestors – with all the social, cultural and political capital that connection carried with it in deeply conservative societies – lay at the root of one of the most characteristic problems of co-existence to be found in bi- or multi-confessional areas of Europe: disputes over places of burial. The right to burial in consecrated ground, preferably in a place of honour, was a long-standing marker of full membership of the community. Those who were excluded under medieval canon law – Jews, heretics, suicides, the unbaptized and the excommunicated – constituted a roll call of marginals and deviants. Where separate minority confessional communities formed in the sixteenth century, their almost invariable instinct was not to seek separate places of burial, but to continue to assert a right to interment in the traditional cemetery or churchyard, irrespective of what Protestants were supposed to believe about there being nothing intrinsically special about so-called consecrated ground. Huguenots in France, Calvinists in the Lutheran territories of Saxony and Brandenburg, and Catholics in the Dutch Republic, England and Ireland all wished to be buried with their ancestors, and presumably hoped to rise in their company on the Last Day.[53]

Local practical arrangements often allowed this to take place. English ministers and churchwardens frequently turned a conveniently blind eye to the burial in their churchyards of officially excommunicate Catholic recusants. Catholics in Ireland not only managed to be buried within the now officially Protestant churches, but often included overtly Catholic inscriptions and iconography on their monuments, indicative of some degree of accommodation with their Protestant neighbours.[54] In the politically Catholic but confessionally mixed German diocese of Münster, Catholics, Lutherans and Calvinists were buried together in churchyards throughout the middle decades of the sixteenth century with little apparent difficulty or protest.[55] Even in France, where the issue was at its most fraught, local solutions could be found well into the seventeenth century, which, as Keith Luria has demonstrated, could involve the partitioning of the parish cemetery.[56] Burial practice, then, might seem to represent an area of potential cross-confessionalism or counter-confessionalization, where religious distinctions could become blurred in the interests of avoiding damaging conflict. Perhaps it went even beyond this, to become a forum for respecting the claims of common humanity, and for exercising what the Dutch historian Willem Frijhoff has termed 'the ecumenicity of everyday life'.[57] Benjamin Kaplan has argued that because, unlike weddings and baptisms, in no confession were funerals a sacrament, church authorities tended to police participation in them less strictly. There is evidence, particularly from the Dutch Republic, of neighbours joining in funeral processions without much regard for confessional allegiances.[58]

Yet these matters were far from immune to the wider pressures of the confessional era. In late sixteenth-century northern Germany, popular Lutheran hostility to perceived crypto-Calvinism led to mob attacks on funerals and dishonouring of corpses. In Münster, the election in 1585 of a counter-reforming bishop, in the person of Ernst of Bavaria, signalled a drive to reassert control over sacred space, and an era of intensified burial disputes with lay Catholic opinion slowly beginning to shift in clerically approved directions.[59] The Dutch and English Catholics who continued to request burial in Protestant cemeteries meanwhile were not necessarily allowing social considerations to trump spiritual ones, still less affirming some wider sense that neighbourhood and community should transcend confessional difference. Completely shunning the burial rites of the religious establishment, they wanted to be buried in or near its churches precisely because they considered them to be *their* churches, temporarily in the hands of the heretics. They wanted and expected to get them back. As the Dutch priest Petrus den Hollander exclaimed from his deathbed, 'My dry bones will shout out that the Church occupied by the uncatholic belongs to the Catholic.'[60]

Tensions around burial were at their most acute in France, fuelled by a growing sense on the part of many Catholics that their places of burial had been 'polluted' by the presence of heretics' corpses. The widespread disinterment and ritual humiliation of corpses that accompanied the progress of the Wars of Religion is well known, and was brought to a ragged end only by the establishment of separate Protestant burial sites under the terms of the edicts of pacification.[61] Violence against the dead was always a possibility when community and confessional tensions were sufficiently inflamed. During the Irish Rebellion of 1641, the bodies of Protestant victims were denied burial and disposed of shamefully – left 'lying in ditches', as Protestant atrocity propaganda took care to announce. Protestant remains, moreover, were exhumed from churchyards where the Catholic forces took control. At Waterford in 1642, the corpses of a Protestant minister, his wife and four others were dug up and boiled to make saltpetre for improvised gunpowder.[62] The ritual punishment of corpses, inverting all codes of civility due to the dead, was designed to make the loudest and most aggressive of statements, expelling the deceased from membership of the community of honour and respect, as well as from symbolic expectation of the resurrection. Even in more settled times, such metanarratives of dishonour were almost everywhere codified under the law: in the treatment of the bodies of traitors (ritually dismembered), suicides (buried shamefully at crossroads) and heretics (destroyed by fire).

In summary, then, the cultural responses to the dead that emerged out of the upheavals of the Reformation were complex and multilayered, too much so to lend themselves convincingly to any simple or programmatic thesis about individualism, secularization, confessionalization, or the historicization of memory. But at the same time, the fact that death and remembrance were, and are, universal and irreducible facets of human experience invests them with exceptional potential as tools of comparative historical analysis. If the Reformation caused considerable confusion about both the status and the treatment of the dead, it also invited a range of creative and imaginative responses about how best to remember them.

It is a fascinating paradox, though not necessarily an inexplicable or nonsensical one, that commemoration of the dead in post-Reformation Europe encompassed some of the extremes of continuity and discontinuity, of compassion and intolerance, of inclusion and exclusion.

2

'The map of God's word': geographies of the afterlife in Tudor and early Stuart England

The idea of the survival of the human personality after death has from the earliest days been a hallmark of Christian belief. Moreover, like most other religions, Christianity came to assign the souls of the dead to locations invisible to and (usually) unreachable by the living; not merely to one undifferentiated 'place of the dead', but to a variety of places with distinct orientations both in respect to the created world and to each other. In their reconstructions of the intellectual outlook and spatial imagination of the Middle Ages, historians have recognized that the formation of a 'geography of the afterlife' was a process not peripheral but central to contemporary religious and eschatological concerns.[1] In modern Christian thought, by contrast, life after death (in so far as it impinges at all) tends to be imagined in terms of some kind of radical transformation of consciousness, rather than an experience of spatial relocation to another place in the universe. One 'history of heaven' concludes that in the late twentieth century heaven became 'a state of vague identity'. As for hell, another modern survey puts it bluntly: 'hell has become something of an embarrassment'.[2]

As this chapter will demonstrate, however, unease with the affirmation of a precise spatial location for disembodied souls is not an exclusively modern phenomenon. In the course of the seventeenth century an increasing number of English religious radicals would be prepared to reject the very notion of a localized afterlife, to assert that heaven and hell were no more than spiritual states experienced in this life.[3] At the same time more respectable intellectual sceptics would begin that process of interrogation of traditional eschatologies which D. P. Walker styled *The Decline of Hell*, a recognizable milestone on the road to those happy hunting grounds of the historical profession, Modernity and Secularization.[4] In tracing the origins of seventeenth-century rejections of heaven and hell it has been usual to cite the rapid dissemination of sceptical ideas in the turmoil of civil war, or to point to a substratal tradition of sceptical and 'atheistical' speculation, a lineage of true unbelievers.[5] The emphasis here will be rather different, concerning itself in the main not with the opinions of deviants and dissidents, but with the discourses of generally 'respectable' theologians. It will be argued that over the period from the break with Rome up to roughly 1630, distinct cracks in the edifice of conventional belief about a localized afterlife can be detected spreading slowly, almost imperceptibly, from within the bastions of orthodox Christianity itself. This took place primarily because over the course of the English Reformation, reformers of all kinds were determined to dissociate themselves irrevocably from the typologies and language of pre-Reformation 'geographies of the afterlife', in particular from the notion of a 'third place', purgatory. In doing so they can be seen to prepare the ground and set the terms for a fundamental reappraisal of the relationship between the known physical world on the one hand, and what David Cressy has called the 'conceptual geography of salvation', on the other.[6]

I

The 'geographies' of the future life which reformers would discard with such vehemence in the sixteenth century were the product of a long collective process of imaginative construction. They drew eclectically on classical traditions, scriptural exegesis and visionary accounts of otherworldly journeys. The vision literature of the early Middle Ages popularized the idea that souls would pass to various locations in the next life, and it made the association between entrances to the other world and places on this earth, such as Mount Etna, or the so-called 'St Patrick's Purgatory' in Ireland.[7] Yet as Aaron Gurevich has observed, early medieval beliefs about the afterlife lacked 'spatial integrity': 'the Other World of visions is a conglomerate of uncoordinated points'.[8] The magisterial work of Jacques Le Goff has traced a process which he terms a growing 'spatial conception' of the afterlife, and the emergence by the twelfth century of 'a new geography of the other world, which was no longer made up of tiny receptacles . . . but consisted rather of vast territories'. The crucial development came towards the end of the twelfth century with the coining of the noun 'purgatorium' as the definitive identification of the place where the majority of souls would be confined for a lengthy period after death.[9] In fact, by the late Middle Ages, the clear consensus of theological opinion was that there were five distinct places occupying the 'space' of the next life: heaven, hell, purgatory, a *limbus infantium* for the souls of children who had died before receiving baptism, and a *limbus patrum* which had housed the souls of the patriarchs who died before the Incarnation, and which Christ had visited after his death on the cross in the so-called 'harrowing of hell'.

There were, however, latent in medieval teaching about the afterlife a number of disputed or unanswered questions. The existence and theological rationale of purgatory had been formally defined by the councils of Lyons in 1274 and Florence in 1439, but no such official sanction had been provided for the teaching on the limbos. Nor had any definitive answer ever been offered to the question posed by the Cistercian Caesarius of Heisterbach in the thirteenth century: 'ubi est purgatorium?' (Where is purgatory?)[10] Nonetheless, there seems to have been little objection to the idea that this was a question worth asking, and that it ought in principle to be possible to 'map' the afterlife, to establish schema for the geographical relations of the constituent parts. Most firmly established was the idea of the proximity of purgatory and hell, resulting in what Le Goff, following Arturo Graf, has called an 'infernalization' of purgatory.[11] Aquinas thought it likely that 'the place of purgatory is situated below and in proximity to hell, so that it is the same fire which torments the damned in hell and cleanses the just in purgatory; although the damned being lower in merit, are to be consigned to a lower place'.[12] Among pre-Reformation English sources, *The Ordynare of Crysten Men* of 1502 stated that paradise and hell were at the extremes of geographical distance, that 'this present worlde is bytwene Hell & paradyse' and that purgatory was 'one part of Hell'.[13] Still more categorical was the *Lytel Boke, that speketh of Purgatorye*, appearing on the very eve of Henry VIII's break with Rome. This laid down that hell, *limbus infantium*, purgatory and *limbus patrum* were situated under the earth, stacked one on top of the other in that ascending order.[14] By the early 1530s, however, pronouncements of this sort were already anathema to an undercurrent of reformist opinion, a current that was shortly to merge with the inexorable spate of official policy.

II

The story of the campaign against purgatory and prayer for the dead, culminating in the Edwardian dissolution of the chantries, is an increasingly familiar one in the historiography of the English Reformation.[15] Yet to date the scholarship has shown relatively little interest in continuing Protestant attacks on purgatory after the climacteric of 1547, and it has scarcely engaged at all with what will be the central concern of this chapter, debates about the 'geography' of the afterlife. As I hope to demonstrate, intense hostility to the Roman teaching on the next life remained a staple of anti-papal polemic throughout the Reformation period. While this polemic attacked purgatory on a number of fronts – its association with clerical abuses, its inculcation of unchristian fear, its alleged disparagement of Christ's Passion – a persistent theme was the absurdity of the Catholic geography of the afterlife, its tendency to particularize and localize imaginary realms, to map out the confines and borders of the hereafter.

Unsurprisingly, the vision literature of the Middle Ages, with its vivid material evocation of the topography of purgatory and hell, its paths, bridges, rivers, valleys and angelic guides, proved an irresistible target for Protestant satire. In the Elizabethan burlesques *Tarleton's News out of Purgatory* and *Greenes Newes both from Heaven and Hell*, bemused souls undertake taxing journeys in search of the 'third place that all our great-grandmothers have talked of'.[16] Arguably of greater literary merit, but of similarly polemical intent, was John Donne's *Ignatius his Conclave* (1611). Here the writer falls into an ecstasy and with the help of a pair of miraculous spectacles, 'the same by which Gregory the Great and Beda did discern so distinctly the soules of their friends', he was able to see 'all the roomes in Hell open to my sight'.[17]

In the same work, Donne epitomized limbo and purgatory as 'the Suburbs of Hel', an image employed by other anti-papist writers including Pierre Viret, Anthony Wooton, Sir Edward Hoby and Thomas Beard.[18] With their contemporary resonances of sprawl, disease and disorder, the suburbs well evoked the sense of squalid materiality these writers wished to associate with the Romish teaching on purgatory.[19] Another tack was to link the subdivisions of the afterlife with the theme of unlawful possession. In his 1567 *Defence of the Apology of the Church of England*, Bishop John Jewel made scornful reference to 'your lists and gainful territories of Purgatory'.[20] To the Jacobean bishop Thomas Morton, the papists' *limbo puerorum* (limbo of children) was 'like a new inclosure . . . lately taken out of the common of Hell . . . our Adversaries limite the borders of Hell according to their own fancies'.[21]

To some writers what was most staggering about the Church of Rome's imaginary landscape of the afterlife was the certainty with which its apologists claimed to be able to place its every feature. A character in Jean Veron's 1561 dialogue *The Huntyng of Purgatorye to Death* is made to remark that notaries are not as careful in their deeds to record the situation of lands and houses as popish doctors are 'to measure and limite Hell, the lymbe and purgatorie'.[22] According to William Fulke, perhaps the most energetic of all Elizabethan writers against purgatory, 'there is no man knoweth his owne house better the[n] we may know every corner of Purgatory'.[23]

Yet while on the one hand castigating the Catholics for their utter and absurd certainty about the geography and topography of the afterlife, an equally, if not more, fruitful line of attack was to draw attention to the extent to which Catholic teaching was hopelessly inconsistent and contradictory on this score. The charge that papists were unable to agree 'about the place where Purgatory should be' became a leitmotif of anti-popish polemic, William Barlow noting that authorities were unresolved whether it was 'extensive as a cover over Hell, in latitude; or collaterall with Hell, severed by a partition, in longitude, or circular about Hell, in severall celles, as the spottes of an apple about the quore'.[24] As to *limbus patrum*, James Ussher pointed out that as it was now redundant, papists disagreed about its distinction from the limbus of children.[25] The English translation of a work by the Huguenot Pierre Du Moulin helpfully suggested that since

> the Franciscans, according to their rule, do not goe into Purgatory single, but by two and two . . . this Limbo lying in the way to Purgatory, seemeth a very convenient place to lodge him who being departed hence alone, must attend his companion.[26]

At the beginning of the seventeenth century, no papist defence of purgatory was more carefully pored over than the *Liber de Purgatorio* of Rome's most renowned controversialist, the Italian cardinal Robert Bellarmine. This work had given cautious approval to a tradition, originating with Bede, that within purgatory there was a place free of punishment, for souls not yet ready to receive the beatific vision, a place described as a fresh and pleasant meadow.[27] This had Protestant polemicists falling over themselves to argue that Bellarmine had unilaterally invented a fifth place in hell.[28] James I himself joined in mocking Bellarmine on this score, and was able to combine his two great passions, theology and hunting, by asking Bellarmine to tell him 'if that faire greene Meadow that is in Purgatorie, have a brooke running thorow it; that in case I come there, I may have hawking upon it'.[29]

III

It should by now be clear that a central component of the Protestant strategy for demolishing purgatory, *limbus patrum* and *limbus infantium* was to epitomize them in terms of their spurious geographical locations, and spatial relationships to each other, to demonstrate the unreality of these places through an ironic evocation of their very concreteness. But the ramifications of this *modus operandi* could be felt beyond the specific doctrinal dispute with the Catholics over the existence of purgatory and limbo. The problem of the appropriateness of envisaging the condition of the soul after death in terms of its spatial location lay quite clearly near the heart of two internecine conflicts which beset English Protestantism. The first of these was the sixteenth-century debate over the destination of the soul immediately after death, the so-called 'sleep of the soul'.[30] The second was the long-running 'Descensus Controversy', the debate over how Protestants should understand the article in the Apostles' Creed that Christ 'descended into hell', a phrase which in its very construction clearly raised questions about the location of the devil's abode.[31]

The idea that the souls of the faithful did not proceed immediately to the beatific vision, but 'slept' until the end of the world, was associated in the early sixteenth century with the teaching of Martin Luther. It appealed to a number of early English reformers, William Tyndale and John Frith among them, because it seemed to restore soteriological meaning to a final judgement which could otherwise appear a kind of eschatological rubber-stamping.[32] By the mid-Tudor period, however, the idea was coming to be decisively rejected by the Protestant establishment, partly because it had acquired an association with Anabaptism, but also because it seemed to revive in Reformed theology the notion of a third place in the next life, distinct from heaven and hell. John Hooper spoke for an emerging English Protestant orthodoxy on this question when he repudiated 'the fond opinion of the sleepers, which affirm that the spirits of the saints are not yet in Heaven, but do sleep in a certain place unknown to us'.[33] In fact, early proponents of soul-sleeping ideas had shown a clear determination not to get caught up in questions about where exactly the souls of the dead would reside. According to Tyndale, this was 'a secret laid up in the treasury of God', and Frith remarked that 'God would that we should be ignorant where they be'.[34] The most eminent continental opponent of the soul-sleepers, John Calvin, expressed himself in almost identical terms by noting that 'many torment themselves greatly with discussing what place they occupy . . . It is foolish and rash to enquire into hidden things'.[35]

Rhetorical diffidence of this sort was characteristic of mature Protestant discussion of the destinations of the dead, but it found itself tested in the tilt-yards of polemical debate. Protestant taunts about the inability of the Catholics to pinpoint or agree about the location of purgatory invited an obvious riposte. A man 'may have both the example and the like doubt of Hell itself', observed the exiled William Allen in 1565.[36] The same conclusion was reached in the course of the Jacobean debate between Sir Edward Hoby and the Jesuit John Floyd. Noting the disparate locations in which medieval authorities had placed purgatory, Hoby observed, '*Quod ubique est, nullibi est*, it is in so many places, that indeed it is in no place.'[37] Floyd in turn accused Hoby of incipient atheism: 'Doe not learned christians likewise dissent about the situation of Hell? . . . Will any true Christian argue in your forme? Hell is in so many places, that it is indeed noe where?'[38] Hoby's response was to ground himself upon a founding principle of the Reformation: 'As for Hell, though Learned men exactly know not the site thereof, yet doth the word of God plainly teach that there is a Hell . . . so that we are tied to a necessitie of beleefe . . . But as for Purgatorie, it is neyther averred nor described in the Mappe of Gods word.'[39]

That the existence of hell could be established definitively from the 'map of God's word', the Scriptures, was a position accepted by all mainstream reformers, but further than this the cartographic analogy was hopelessly misleading. Dispersed through a series of more or less gnomic Old and New Testament texts, the scriptural teaching on hell was cryptic and encoded, and required for its deciphering the negotiation of a whole series of historical and philological problems.[40] As the Elizabethan and Jacobean controversies over the meaning of Christ's descent into hell were to show, appealing to Scripture to pin down the likely location of hell proved hugely divisive. Protagonists on what we might loosely call the 'Puritan' side of these debates, those who preferred a spiritual interpretation of the credal article, tended to stress the variety of figurative uses of 'hell' in Scripture, and usually argued that the Hebrew word *sheol* was better translated as 'the grave' or 'death' rather than hell, and was more properly applicable to bodies than to souls.[41] Some controversialists made much of the passage in Ephesians 2.2 which implied the devil's abode was in the air; thus to have visited hell in the literal sense, Christ would have had to have *ascended*.[42] Hugh Broughton (a learned if somewhat eccentric hebraist) went as far as to say 'they are much deceaved who thinke Hell to be in this world, lowe in the earth'.[43] None of the main participants in the Descensus Controversy ever sought explicitly to deny that there was a place, commonly called hell, which God had reserved for the souls of the damned. Yet clearly inscripted within the theological positions adopted by even 'moderate Puritans' like William Whitaker, William Perkins or Andrew Willet was a palpable unease with the conception of the afterlife as a series or even a pair of concatenated localities, allowing, however exceptionally, of travel between the constituent parts: 'Christ's locall descension was but to the grave'.[44]

On the other side of the debate, 'conformist' spokesmen like Thomas Bilson, Adam Hill, Richard Parkes and John Higgins vigorously upheld a more literalist interpretation of the descent, and at times were prepared to assert that hell was situated under the earth.[45] Yet common to virtually all the participants in these controversies was a growing coyness about where precisely hell might be, a pragmatic consensus that since Scripture did not pronounce definitively on the question, to enquire of it too closely was presumptuous and dangerous.[46] As Archbishop Ussher piously admonished, 'it is not to be inquired in what place it is situated, but by what means rather it may be avoided'.[47] Even conformists such as Adam Hill and John Higgins who were prepared to make the case against their Puritan opponents that hell was beneath us felt that no more precise enquiry was warranted.[48] Preaching in 1626 on the text 'in my Father's house are many mansions', John Donne complained of the 'wantonness' of the Fathers and the 'wildness' of the schoolmen in their attempts to explicate this passage. He poured particular scorn on an author who 'afraid of admitting too great a hollowness in the Earth, lest then the Earth might not be said to be solid, pronounces that hell cannot possibly be above three thousand miles in compasse'.[49] The following year the Norwich minister Samuel Gardiner similarly castigated those who took it upon themselves to define the situation of hell 'in a hollow cave, or center of the earth, and so punctually doe describe unto us the space thereof, as if with a reed or metwand [measuring rod] in their hand they had taken the iust measure of it'.[50]

By the later sixteenth century English Catholic writers as well as Protestants seemed increasingly reluctant to pronounce definitively on the precise dimensions or location of hell. In 1529 Thomas More was quite certain that Hell 'nothynge ellys sygnyfyeth unto us . . . but ye habytacyons of sowlys byneth or under vs in ye low placys under ye ground'.[51] Half a century later, the Jesuit Robert Persons, while accepting that the consensus of the Fathers was that hell was under the earth, admitted that it was uncertain 'whether it be under ground or no'.[52] Such caution also increasingly characterized Catholic discussions on the location of purgatory. William Allen pronounced that 'it is better to be in doubt of these secretts, then to stande in contentious reasoning of thinges uncertaine'.[53] In the early seventeenth century, the Catholic controversialist Anthony Champney was prepared to commit himself no further than to state that 'after this life there is a purgatorie, or place where the soules of the faythfull . . . are detained untill they be wholly purged', while Sylvester Norris displayed a similarly minimalist attitude in 1622 by insisting 'we stand not upon the name, but uphold the thing, that is, a certaine penall estate, or cleansing . . . after this life'.[54] By the early part of the seventeenth century, right across the confessional spectrum, learned discussions of the whereabouts of hell, and in the case of Catholics, purgatory, seem to reflect a new sensibility, characteristically tempered by a kind of 'reverential agnosticism', a reticence about precise locations and (in contrast to the Middle Ages) a reluctance to define or situate the afterlife in geographical relation to the physical world.

This more guarded approach was equally evident in treatments of 'Abraham's bosom'. By the end of the Middle Ages, the dominant trend of Catholic theology was to identify this place (mentioned in Luke 16) with the *limbus patrum* harrowed by Christ, thus locating it within the macrocosm of the subterranean infernal world.[55] The reformers rejected this, but had difficulty knowing what to make of this unquestionably scriptural destination for dead souls. They refuted vehemently the suggestion that Abraham's bosom could be any part of hell (the rich man in hell was noted to have 'lift up his eyes' and seen Lazarus 'afar off'), but often they recognized that patristic writers had distinguished it from heaven, seeing it as a kind of atrium of paradise where the faithful did not yet enjoy that full blessedness which would be theirs at the final judgement.[56] Some Protestant authorities retained something of this outlook, Veron writing that Abraham's bosom was a paradise, 'but yet not so perfect as it was afterwards'.[57] Nonetheless, a desire to avoid needless speculation on the question was frequently expressed.[58] Without committing themselves to any precise cosmological location, however, the clear trend among Protestant writers was simply to affirm Abraham's bosom as a synonym for heaven. William Fulke averred, for example, that 'Abraham's bosome was a place of comfort. And other place of comfort then Heaven or Paradise, which is all one . . . I finde none in Scripture'.[59] In a devotional context, the identification of Abraham's bosom with heaven seems to have become almost entirely unexceptional. An early Jacobean funeral sermon by Robert Pricke stated it as certain that the souls of the faithful immediately 'meete with the Lord Iesus in Paradise: are gathered in the bosom of *Abraham*'.[60] A few years earlier, Nathaniel Gilby had told the dying earl of Huntingdon that 'angels attended to cary his soule to the bosome of Abraham'.[61] The deathbed declaration of faith which Philip Stubbes placed in the mouth of his teenage bride in 1591 included the comforting certainty that the blessed would recognize each other in the life to come, as 'the riche man lying in Hell, knewe *Abraham* and *Lazarus* in Heaven'.[62] The pastoral appeal of this elision of Abraham's bosom and heaven might also be adduced from the knowing solecism of Shakespeare's *Henry V*, where Hostess Quickly says of the deceased Falstaff, 'sure he's not in Hell, he's in Arthur's bosom, if ever man went to Arthur's bosom'.[63] To most Protestant Englishmen and women, the significance of Abraham's bosom probably lay in its familiarity and accessibility as a pledge of salvation and redemption, not in concerns over its theological nuances, or its positioning within a hierarchy of heavens. One early Stuart writer roundly attacked those who argued about the location of Abraham's bosom as 'rather producing scruples then instruction', adding that 'what ever they say, I take [it] to have been in Heaven, in which (we know) there are many stations, however they perplexe themselves in marshalling our lodging there'.[64]

In some ways equally perplexing, however, was the case of that other Lazarus of the Gospels, the brother of Martha and Mary, whom Christ raised to life after he had lain four days in the tomb.[65] In the Middle Ages, the case of Lazarus provided the inspiration for lurid evocations of the horrors that lay beyond the grave,[66] but in the Reformation period it could be made to serve a more overtly polemical purpose. Where had the soul of Lazarus resided while his body lay in the grave? It was inconceivable that Christ would have summoned back a soul from hell, and to have wrenched it from the enjoyment of eternal bliss in heaven would seem an act of injustice. As William Allen put it, 'it is sure and most certaine, that it had sum place of abyding after the separation from the fleshe', the implication being, of course, that this place could logically only be purgatory.[67] This was an objection that Protestant writers were obliged to take seriously. Calvinists such as the Englishman Andrew Willet, the Frenchman Pierre Du Moulin and the Scotsman William Guild could all agree that there was no compelling reason for thinking Lazarus was not in heaven. As Guild put it, 'private good must ever give place to the manifestation of Gods glorie'.[68] Yet Guild covered himself by assigning the question to 'the secret thinges [that] belong onely to God'.[69] This was the line taken earlier by Hugh Latimer, in the parallel case of the temporary location of the soul of Jairus's daughter: 'my own answer is this: I cannot tell, but where it pleased God it should be, there it was . . . other answer nobody gets at me, because the scripture telleth me not where she was'.[70] In his controversy with William Allen, Fulke reflected similar exasperation with

> foolish and unlearned questions . . . gendering strife rather than edificatio[n] . . . you shall never prove the common case of the departed

in Christ by these fewe peculiar cases. For when so ever and how so ever it pleased God, that their soules remained, it was determined of God that they should be restored to their bodies.[71]

The question, however, retained the capacity to perplex: the renowned Elizabethan preacher Henry Smith included it in a list of 'questions gathered out of his own confession . . . which are yet unanswered'.[72] Some years later, reflecting on his own 'catalogue of doubts', Sir Thomas Browne expressed a determination to believe 'that *Lazarus* was raised from the dead, yet not demand where in the interim his soule awaited'.[73]

IV

Thus far, this chapter has been describing developments that seem essentially endogenous, arising from the exigencies of theological debates between Catholics and Protestants, and among Protestants themselves, as they evolved over the century following the break with Rome. However, this may be to ignore the question of whether these changes in the discourse about the geography of the afterlife could have been linked to broader intellectual changes in this period, changes relating to improved physical knowledge of the earth, and of its place in the cosmos. According to Le Goff, the genesis of purgatory was intimately connected with the growing knowledge of the world in the high Middle Ages. The increasing concern with the spatiality of the other world mirrored developments in terrestrial cartography, the attempt to 'introduce realism into topographical representation' on maps which had previously been 'little more than an assemblage of topographical ideograms'.[74] If this is so, then it is at least arguable that the much greater advances in astronomical and geographical knowledge made in the sixteenth century may have stimulated an antithetical reaction. Any comprehensive discussion of the dual impact of the voyages of discovery and the Copernican revolution on early modern religious thought is well beyond the scope of this chapter. Yet it is fascinating to note the ways in which the imagery of cosmography, and the employment of cartographic and cosmological motifs, seeped into discussions of eschatology in late sixteenth- and early seventeenth-century England. Astronomical tropes are central to the humour of Donne's *Ignatius his Conclave*, which hinges upon the Jesuits' founder making good use of Galileo's telescope, and agreeing with Satan to found a new colony of hell on the moon.[75] In more sombre and elegiac mode, Donne's 1627 memorial sermon for Lady Danvers artfully deploys the language of terrestrial discovery as a mere simulacrum for man's understanding of the 'new Heavens and new earth' spoken of in St Peter's second epistle:

> in these discoveries . . . our *Maps* will bee unperfect. But as it is said of old *Cosmographers*, that when they had said all that they knew of a *Countrey* . . . they said that the rest . . . were possesst with *Giants*, or *Witches*, or *Spirits*, or *Wilde beasts* . . . yet wee must say at last, that it is a *Countrey* inhabited with *Angells*, and *Arch-angells*.

Donne concludes: 'Where it is *locally*, wee enquire not . . . Of these new Heavens, and this new earth we must say at last, that wee can say nothing.'[76] Here the signifiers of cartography are juxtaposed with the metaphorical promises of Scripture to suggest that the former can do no more than evoke the complete impermeability of the latter. Other Protestant writers were less subtle about it. In 1561 Jean Veron had scoffed that he didn't doubt that popish doctors 'could verye well make and compasse a Mappe or c[h]arte of those lowe and infernall regions'.[77] To Thomas Morton, purgatory and the limbos of fathers and of children were places 'without the horizons of mans wit'.[78] Hoby sneered that without Homer, Plato and Virgil

> you would never have knowne how to have set your compasse, for the discoverie of this new found world. And yet, if a man should aske the best navigator of you all, in what degree, & how many leagues *Purgatorie* is from the *Infernall Cape*, I think he would be put to his trumps.[79]

Similar motifs emerged in the exchanges of the Descensus Controversy. In 1607 Richard Parkes was stung by Andrew Willet's charge that he seemed to be encouraging belief in *limbus patrum*, and retorted that 'it should seeme you know in what clymate of your *Necrocosmus* it is sited: for how else can you judge of the aspect?' He went on to attack another Puritan opponent, Henry Jacob, as 'one of the skilfullest Cosmographers of this our age, in the description of New-found lands'.[80] What we are witnessing here seems a kind of epistemological dissociation, a growing perception that the categories appropriate to the pursuit of knowledge about this world were inadmissible in theological discourse about the world to come. It is revealing that Archbishop Ussher ascribed the eschatological fallacies of classical and early Christian writers to their imperfect knowledge of the shape of the world, specifically their belief that the horizon cut the world in half, and that the antipodes were an uninhabited, invisible kingdom of the dead.[81] The Scottish writer David Person mounted a comprehensive attack in 1635 on those who regarded the metaphysical world as a proper object for experimental investigation. Among his targets were 'curious *Ouranographers*' who applied meteorological criteria to determine the part of heaven into which Enoch and Elijah were assumed. He also condemned '*Topographers*' who wondered whether hell could be 'in the centre of this Terrestiall globe' and whether volcanoes might be 'the vents and chimneys of Hell'. Person castigated such enquiries as the product of frivolous and divisive curiosity, and warned that 'God disappointeth the expectations of the most curious'. Interestingly, however, he commended the 'practical curiosity' of Christopher Columbus.[82]

While most Protestant writers displayed a growing reluctance to specu-late on the locations of heaven and hell, an interesting counterpoint was the concern they increasingly displayed with the location of the earthly paradise described in the book of Genesis. As Jean Delumeau has shown, the early modern period witnessed a flood of conjecture on this issue, the question providing much of the impetus for the growing provision of maps in Protestant Bibles.[83] But the geographical issues here had more to do with biblical history than eschatology. In early modern Europe, both Catholic and Protestant authorities tended to reject the medieval idea that after the Fall the garden of Eden had been miraculously relocated to the heavens. Despite some enthusiastic interest in possible New World loca-tions, the most common conclusion was that reached by the Englishman John Salkeld in 1617: the earthly paradise had been destroyed by the flood and no longer existed.[84] With the expansion and mapping of the known world, the idea that hell and paradise could be situated in this world, under exotic volcanoes or on distant islands, was looking increasingly anachronistic, surviving only as self-consciously literary and philosophical conceits: More's *Utopia*, Bacon's *New Atlantis* or Harrington's *Oceana*.[85]

If in this period what we might call 'real space' was displacing 'eschato-logical space', this may be linked to a growing readiness in some quarters to assert that the quiddity of heaven and hell lay not in their locations, but in their psychological and existential meanings for the individual Christian. Such views are most readily associated with the 'Ranter' tracts of the 1650s, and have been linked with a continental tradition of mystical religious writings.[86] Yet language which stressed the immanence of heaven and hell was by no means the sole prerogative of a radical fringe. Once again, the Descensus Controversy was a factor here, as 'Puritan' writers sought to reconcile their acceptance of the Creed with their desire to exclude a grossly material conception of Christ's presence in hell. Andrew Willet declared 'that the place of Hell causeth not the torment, but the wrath and curse of God: for even out of hel God may make a man to

46

feele the torments of Hell'.[87] Henry Jacob likewise insisted that '*Hell* as we take it, (that is the sense of Gods wrath) is even in this life, found some-tyme'.[88] The topos was not an exclusively Puritan one. The 'avant-garde conformist' William Barlow allowed diverse interpretations of 'hell' which were not 'exorbitant from the Scriptures tacke'. These included the 'mis-erablest state which may befall a man'.[89] To John Donne, 'the Hell of hels, the torment of torments, was the everlasting absence of God'.[90] In 1631 the Catholic Richard Smith was able to claim (with some exaggeration) that 'Protestants expressly say, that hell is not place, no corporall place, no prison; that it is nothing but a wicked conscience'.[91]

In fact, the passages Smith provided in support of this charge were not as novel or heterodox as they might appear. The notion that devils always carried their hell around with them was a conventional one, sanctioned in the fifteenth century by that founding charter of witch-hunting and demonology, the *Malleus Maleficarum*.[92] Its most famous exposition is to be found in Marlowe's *Dr Faustus*, in Mephistopheles' declaration that

> Hell hath no limits, nor is circumscrib'd
> In one self place, but where we are is Hell,
> And where Hell is, there must we ever be.

Yet Mephistopheles also provides a more traditional affirmation of hell's location 'within the bowels of these elements'.[93]

To assert so volubly, however, that hell could be a condition in this life, that it had resonant symbolic meanings which could claim parity with, or even be prioritized over, its transcendent (and locational) reality, was to invite the speculation that it was no more than a condition in this life, that it had no existence beyond a symbolic or metaphorical one. As early as 1550 the Edwardian divine Roger Hutchinson had complained of 'Libertines' who taught that 'there is neither place of rest ne pain after this life; that Hell is nothing but a tormenting and desperate conscience'.[94] Such accusations of 'atheism' are of course notoriously problematic, and can, and should, be read as the constructions and projections of contemporary rhetorical discourse, rather than as objective socio-religious commentary. Yet by the early seventeenth century some in intellectual circles were clearly coming to regard any emphasis on the localized and spatial aspects of the afterlife as a vulgar misconception pertaining to the multitude. Thomas Browne thought that teaching the torments of a subterranean hell 'makes a noyse, and drums in popular eares', adding that 'though wee place Hell under earth, the Devills walke and purlue is about it; men speake too popularly who place it in those flaming mountaines, which to grosser apprehensions represent Hell'. To Browne, its true significance was that 'I feele sometimes a Hell within my selfe'.[95] In the mid-seventeenth century it became characteristic of the so-called 'Cambridge Platonists' to believe hell to be, in John Smith's phrase, 'rather a Nature then a Place'.[96] Most orthodox opinion would have balked at this phraseology, but something of this outlook had been presaged decades earlier in the writings of a considerable number of Elizabethan and Jacobean theologians, and perhaps also in those expressions of utter agnosticism about the conditions of the future life which in the later Elizabethan and early Stuart periods become a distinct literary topos. One thinks immediately of Hamlet's 'dread of something after death / The undiscovered country from whose bourn / No traveller returns', and also of Claudio's cri de coeur in *Measure for Measure*: 'to die, and go we know not where'.[97] Francis Bacon suggested that 'men fear death, as children fear to go in the dark'.[98] Thomas Browne later made a similar point, yet more graphically: 'a Dialogue between two Infants in the womb concerning the state of the world, might handsomely illustrate our ignorance of the next'.[99] In such rarefied intellectual circles at least, attitudes towards the afterlife seemed to be becoming, literally and metaphorically, dislocated.

V

If the argument of this chapter itself has a location, it might be seen as occupying the chronological and conceptual space between two influential books, Jacques Le Goff's *Birth of Purgatory* and D. P. Walker's *Decline of Hell*. Le Goff chronicles how the Christian afterlife achieved a kind of spatial integrity in the high Middle Ages with the formalization of beliefs about purgatory. Walker shows how over the course of the seventeenth century received ideas about hell and the eternity of infernal punishment came increasingly to be questioned. He notes that 'the Protestant rejection of Purgatory must be of great importance in attempts to discover why the doctrine of Hell began to be questioned when it did', but it is striking that he makes no real effort to follow up this insight.[100] Some other modern cultural studies of death in post-Reformation England make only passing mention of the 'absence', 'abandonment' or 'loss' of purgatory, almost as if the doctrine had been rather carelessly mislaid.[101] It has been a concern here to demonstrate that attacks on Catholic teaching on purgatory and the afterlife remained a commitment of Protestant theologians throughout the Tudor and early Stuart periods. This hostile attention often focused on the supposed locations of purgatory and limbo, and in the process it facilitated, even if it did not primarily intend, a process of 'despatializing' the afterlife, of abstracting or even internalizing it, of moving decisively away from a concern with its geographical configuration, and its vicinity to the physical world. There is, of course, a danger of overstating the case here: the concept of a localized hell was to have an extremely long shelf-life after 1600, implicitly underpinning many hellfire sermons over the decades and centuries to come. The Enlightenment itself was not an automatic solvent: in 1714 Tobias Swinden was to argue that the sun must be the site of hell, on the 'rational' grounds that the centre of the earth was too small to contain the enormous number of damned souls, and fire could not operate there without air. Three years later William Whiston trumped the proposition by asserting that the scientific and scriptural evidence proved hell to be contained within a comet.[102] In the 1860s an American clergyman, W. R. Alger, compiled a massive *Critical History of the Doctrine of a Future Life*, with the avowed intention of showing that 'the doctrine of a locall Hell . . . is plainly proved by historic evidence to be a part of the mythology of the world, a natural product of the poetic imagination of ignorant and superstitious men'. Yet as Alger was compelled to admit, 'most people still think [hell] is the interior of the earth'.[103] The diagnosis here, though, would seem to be a clear case of cultural lag. In England at least, the intellectual underpinnings of a literalist belief in a subterranean hell, and a cosmologically localized heaven, were already under strain two and a half centuries earlier.

VI

In a memorandum of 1536 the humanist Thomas Starkey warned of the effects of the radical preaching he saw going on around him: 'with the despising of Purgatory, [the people] began little to regard Hell, Heaven, or any other felicity hereafter to be had in another life'.[104] This was clearly an exaggerated fear, but in a certain sense it might have been allowed to stand as the epigraph to this chapter. The campaign against purgatory, *limbus patrum* and *limbus infantium* brought with it not merely a 'downsizing' of the afterlife, the smooth substitution of a binary for a tertiary model of the other world. Rather, it both effected and reflected the beginnings of a fundamental reconceptualization, a tectonic shift in accepted and permissible modes of representation. The repudiations that this involved may have been more acceptable in so far as they were seen to correspond with contemporary developments in exploration, cartography and cosmology. Before the Reformation, to elucidate the geography of the afterlife was the legitimate business of theologians, devotional writers and homilists. To attempt to do the same in post-Reformation England, however, was characteristically to engage not with a physical but with a metaphysical question, and increasingly, perhaps, a metaphorical one.

3

Judgement and repentance in Tudor Manchester: the celestial journey of Ellis Hall

I

Among the diversions for Londoners in the early summer of 1562 was the sight of a man confined in the pillory at Cheapside, bizarrely dressed in grey animal skins, and accompanied with the caption: 'For seducinge the people by publyshynge ffallce Revelations'. Ellis Hall had come to London from his home in Manchester with the intention of presenting to the Queen a 'greate booke' containing secret revelations written in verse. He went to the palace at Greenwich, but was denied his interview with Elizabeth. Instead, Hall was interrogated by the bishop of London, Edmund Grindal, on 12 June, and castigated in a sermon by the bishop of Durham, James Pilkington, two days later. On 18 June he was questioned by five members of the Privy Council, and on 26 June, after his spell in the pillory, he was sent on Grindal's orders to Bridewell, where he died three years later.[1]

From the records of the two interrogations an extraordinary autobiographical story emerges.[2] Hall was no youthful zealot, but a man of 60, born in 1502. As a child he claimed to have 'dyffred moche from all my fathers Children . . . geven to solitarynes abstinence and prayer'. But he turned his back on childhood piety, married at 27 and made a fortune as a draper, earning £500 'in the tyme of Kinge Edwarde the sixte when the great fale of money was'. One night in 1552, however, while poring over a set of accounts, he was interrupted by a voice, calling out three times, 'Elye thow Carpenters sonn . . . rise watche & praye for the daye drawethe nighe'. This was followed by a vision of 'a man clothed in white havinge fyve woundes bleadinge'. Believing this to be 'but a dream or phantasye', Hall continued in his 'covetous & worldly affayres', and in consequence was shortly afterwards struck down by a painful illness. As he lay tormented in his bed, the figure in white returned, telling Hall that he was 'electe & chosen of god to declare & pronounce unto his people his word',

51

that he was to write of a revelation that 'shalbe putt in to thy hed by the holye ghoste . . . & shew hit to the magistrates & rulers'. After this Hall was 'taken owt of my bed as it were in a tuft of fethers' and blown up into heaven where he beheld Christ seated in majesty, compassed about with angels, one of whom held a book in his hand. Then Hall was carried down into hell 'where I saw all the tormentes therof & also a place prepared for me, yf I wolde not amend my corrupte lyfe, & also a place prepared for me yn heaven if I wolde follow godes holy will'. Hall calculated that he was absent from his chamber two nights and a day, from 9 to 11 April 1552, 'in which tyme I was not sene of anye mann in the yearth lyvinge'. He was commanded to watch and pray for seven years, and then to write for a further three and a half, during the last year of which he would suffer persecution. Accordingly, at the end of Mary's reign he began to work on his book, but found no inspiration till he had distributed his goods to kinsmen and the poor, given up meat, fish and wine, and 'apparrelled myself thus as ye se'. He had also, he claimed, 'wrote everie worde of this booke on his knees'.

Between his second interrogation on 18 June and his commital to Bridewell on the 26th, Hall barely qualifies as a nine-day wonder. But he has retained a marginal claim on the attention of historians of the English Reformation since John Strype took notice of the case in the early eighteenth century. More recently, there have been passing mentions in surveys of early modern prophecy by Keith Thomas, Richard Bauckham and Alexandra Walsham, and in assessments of the early Elizabethan ecclesiastical scene by Norman Jones and Christopher Haigh.[3] The two latter scholars agree that he was evidently an irreconcilable Catholic opponent of religious reform. Jones comments that 'his revelation must have called the nation to repent its sins, probably including the Reformation', and Haigh, with tongue perhaps partially in cheek, observes that 'although Hall was clearly a madman, it is interesting that his mind was apparently unhinged under Protestant governments only'.

There are, it must be admitted, compelling reasons for approaching the case from this perspective. Having interrogated Hall, Bishop Grindal considered him to be 'of the popishe Iugement in Religion which verie manifestlye appeared by divers of his speaches'. Perhaps we should expect no less of an émigré from Lancashire, that notoriously intractable North-West Frontier of the Tudor Reformations. Though Hall's Manchester housed a Protestant presence, and was the venue for preaching by John Bradford in Edward's reign, Mancunians were regularly in trouble with the Elizabethan authorities for a variety of assertively conservative behaviours.[4] Moreover, and most suggestively, the alleged experience at the heart of Hall's claim to prophetic authority seems to belong securely in a recognizably Catholic and medieval genre. The otherworldly journey, in which a privileged visionary is able to travel, either in dream state or bodily, through the territories of the next life, and to return from them carrying cautionary messages for the living, is a much-studied phenomenon of late medieval popular religious culture.[5] In addition to their sheer entertainment value, such visions served to underscore conventional morality by advertising the fate awaiting the lecherous, the gluttonous and the proud. They confirmed, in a particularly flamboyant way, the truth of the Church's teaching about purgatory, limbo, heaven and hell, and they encouraged various forms of preparation for death, and intercession for the dead. They constituted, it has been aptly remarked, 'a folklore which had the imprimatur of the Church on it'.[6]

These traditions had by no means run their course by the generation into which Hall was born. Several well-established visionary accounts (*The Vision of the Monk of Evesham*, *The Pilgrimage of the Soul*, *The Gast of Guy*) were put into print in the last years of the fifteenth century, and some new ones continued to be written down.[7] In 1465 a Somerset gentleman, Edward Leversedge of Frome, lying sick with the 'plage of pestylence', felt his spirit to be 'raveschyd and departyd from my body'. His disembodied soul was then led by his 'good angell' through a valley filled with hostile demons, and up a high hill whence a ladder of crystalline stone led to a place of overpowering light. On the way he was admonished by the Virgin Mary about the perils of fashionable apparel and unchaste living.[8]

A similar 'vision in a trance' was experienced in 1492 by a man called John Newton, like Leversedge 'vesited with the plage of pestelence'. An unspecified 'leder' guided Newton through a wilderness where souls were being tormented in numerous horrific ways. This, he was informed, was not hell, but purgatory, though he also saw there a place beyond a wall of crystal whence joyful souls passed up to heaven. Newton believed 'that he was walkyng bodely upon the erth' for the space of three days, a little longer than Hall's physical removal from his chamber of 'two nights & one day'. Interestingly, Newton was, like Hall, a draper, and hailed from Congleton, just across the Cheshire border from Hall's Manchester.[9]

Such accounts surely constitute the genus of which Ellis Hall's is a late evolved species, a medieval dinosaur alive and well in the Lost World of Elizabethan Lancashire. But there are a number of departures from the conventional patterning which should give us pause for thought. In the first place, Hall's tour through the other world took in heaven and hell, but made no mention of purgatory, the focal point of the experiences of Leversedge, Newton and most other late medieval visionaries. Indeed, this omission seems to have struck Bishop Grindal as odd. Hall was pressed for his views on a number of doctrinal matters '& especially of purgatorie, for it is like that if he sawe heaven & helle he shulde have seene purgatorie also if there be anye'. Grindal's mocking tone echoed the Protestant polemic which regularly lambasted papists for their absurd and specious precision about the geography and topography of the next life – a theme much in evidence in a lively dialogue entitled *The Huntyng of Purgatorye to Death*, which Jean Veron, a prebendary of Grindal's cathedral of St Paul's, had published only the previous year.[10] The vivid descriptions of purgatory in late medieval visions often served a didactic purpose, inculcating the right understanding of the sacrament of penance and the importance of prayer for the dead. But doctrinal specifics of this kind are absent from the statements made by Hall. 'Beinge demaundett what his iugement is of the masse and of Transubstantiation', Hall refused to answer, saying he was commanded not to speak of those matters until he had delivered his book to the Queen.[11] Late medieval visionaries usually journeyed through the other world with the assistance of a spiritual guide, an angel, saint or other departed soul, but Hall was swept up into heaven and carried down into hell without any such companion. Hall's account also seems out of tune with the dominant late medieval English visionary tradition in its overtly apocalyptic refrain, the charge he received to preach 'repentaunce & amendment of lyfe' to people and magistrates alike because 'the daye drawethe nighe'.

There may be no great mystery here. The distinctive features and omissions of Hall's revelation are the product of his personal pathology, and of the fact that, unlike many medieval accounts, it comes to us relatively unmediated, without passing through the filter of scribal or clerical culture. But there is another possibility, and one which invites us to think again about the ways traditionally minded parishioners may have responded to the reforming initiatives of the Crown in the mid-sixteenth century. I wish to argue that Hall's revelations are difficult to fit unproblematically into a tradition of late medieval vision literature for the reason that they are closely patterned on the themes and phraseology of vernacular Scripture.[12] The proposition seems at first glance perversely counter-intuitive. Hall confessed to Bishop Grindal 'that he hath nott muche redde in the byble', and to the Protestant authorities his 'ffallce Revelacions' and 'Counterfet practyce' represented examples of the worst sort of unscriptural accretion to Christianity. But Hall's diffidence about his biblical knowledge may have been the proper humility of the acolyte, rather than the grudging concession of the illiteratus. He went on to claim 'that he is hable havinge penne yncke & paper to write, & to cite and allege authorities forthe of the scripture', and there are grounds for taking him at his word.[13]

<h1 style="text-align:center">II</h1>

My point of entry here is the injunction Hall received right at the outset of his supernatural experiences: 'watche and pray'.[14] This, of course, is the charge which in the Synoptic Gospels Christ gives to the weary disciples in the garden of Gethsemane on the eve of his Passion. He returns to repeat it three times, just as Hall heard a voice 'which spake these words unto me thre tymes havinge a lyttle dystance betwene them'. Immediately preceding the Passion narratives in Mathew, Mark and Luke is the set of verses which modern biblical scholars term the 'eschatological discourse' or the 'synoptic apocalypse', an exposition of a final judgement with eternal life for the righteous and endless punishment for the ungodly.[15] Here too Mark has Jesus urging his disciples to 'watche and praye for ye knowe not when the tyme is'.

Other passages in Hall's confessions suggest a close reflection on these signs of the impending end. Christ's warning that his disciples will be persecuted (Matt. 24.9) is given to Hall *ad hominem* in the vision of 1552: 'thowe shalte be trobled & falle into persecjution'. Hall's anxiety that 'yf I shuld preach wryte or teach the thinge which I could not prove, neytther weare agreable to the scryptures, I shulde not be beleved' is conceivably connected with the synoptic apocalypse's warnings about the appearance of false prophets and messiahs. But his vision of Christ 'syttinge in his royall seate compassed abowte wt aungels' surely evokes the promise of 'the sonne of man commynge in the cloudes of heaven, with power and greate glorye' in Matthew 24.30–31, sending forth his angels to 'gather together his chosen from the hyghest partes of heaven'. Indeed Hall had been assured that 'thow arte elect & chosen of god'. The revelation to Hall that 'the daye drawethe nighe' or 'draweth nere' evokes Christ's words in Matthew (26.45) that 'the houre is at hande', and in Luke that 'the tyme draweth neare' and that when the Son of Man comes in glory 'loke up, and lyfte up your heades; for your redempcion draweth nye' (21.8, 27–28). Hall may have been drawing on a wider range of biblical allusions, for there are echoes too in the epistle of James (5.8) – 'the commyng of the Lord draweth nye' – as well as in the prophetic warning of Ezekiel that 'the tyme commeth, the daye draweth nye' (7.12). Christ's injunction that Hall should 'aryse & mak thine accompte' is redolent of St Paul's monition (Rom. 14.10–12) that every person will have to stand before the judgement seat of Christ and 'geve accomptes of hymselfe to God'. The vision of an angel 'havinge a book in his hand' and another asking 'whether the tyme weare com' calls to mind the angel in Revelation (5.2), proclaiming 'Who is worthy to open the boke, and to lose the seales thereof?'

Ellis Hall may have been well into middle age before he had the opportunity to immerse himself in the Scripture in English. We do not know whether he owned a Bible, or whether he was one of those who went into his parish church to peruse the copy Henrician and Edwardian injunctions had compelled parishes to acquire.[16] We cannot even be certain that his scriptural awareness was not absorbed in a primarily oral/aural context, though he was clearly literate. The full inwardness of his response to the word of God in Scripture will always elude us, but it seems beyond question that it triggered an overpowering sense of personal vocation. Hall heard his name being called in the Scriptures, and perhaps rather literally. Before the councillors he termed himself 'Elye otherwyse called Ellys Hawle', while to Grindal he confessed that 'his name emong[est] the comon people is (as he sayethe) Elizeus Halle, but he writethe him selfe Ely the Carpenters sonne'. Hall's evident concern with these various redactions of his given name is interesting, and surely significant: the work of historians such as Scott Smith-Bannister and Stephen Wilson has made clear the importance that early modern people attached to personal names and the messages and meanings they were believed to carry.[17] Ellis, the name by which Hall seems to have been known in Lancashire, is an anglicization of Elias, the Greek transliteration of Elijah, while Eliseus is the latinate rendering of Elisha – both Elias and Eliseus were the forms used in early English translations of the Scripture.[18]

Between them, Ely-Elias-Eliseus-Elijah wove a spiritual identity for Hall criss-crossing the Old and New Testaments. Hall's career as a prophet and visionary began with an unseen voice calling out to him three times in the night. An obvious biblical prototype suggests itself here: God's threefold calling of Samuel, son of the priest Eli, against whose house God threatens judgement for the iniquity of Eli's sons.[19] The word 'Eli' appears more poignantly in the New Testament, in the anguished Hebrew of the crucified Christ: 'Eli, Eli, lama sabachthani?' – My God, my God, why hast thou forsaken me? (Matt. 27.46). The bystanders misunderstand, and remark 'this man calleth for Helias . . . let us se whether Helyas will come and delyver him'. But it may be that Hall too felt in some sense this was a call meant for him. 'Elye thow Carpenters sonn' is the appellation with which Christ greets him in the vision. Perhaps, as historians have assumed, Hall was indeed the son of a carpenter, but the phrase surely has more intimate and compelling associations. 'Is not this the carpenters sonne?' the crowd in Nazareth disparagingly ask when Jesus returns to teach there, a prophet without honour in his own country (Matt. 13.55).

But ultimately it is in the guise of the prophet Elijah that Hall understood the pattern of what he was being called to undertake. In almost the last words of the Hebrew Old Testament, Hall would have encountered God's promise in the mouth of Malachi (4.5): 'Behold, I will sende you Elias the prophet before the commynge of the daye of the great and fearful Lorde.' The New Testament abounds with references to the appearance of Elijah as the herald of the last days (Matt. 16.14; 17.10–12; Mark 6.15; 8.28; 9.11–13; Luke 9.8, 19; John 1.21, 25). Moreover, at the Transfiguration, the disciples were accorded a vision of Elijah/Elias, Peter foolishly offering to erect him a tabernacle (Matt. 17.2–5; Mark 9.3–7; Luke 9.29–34). Hall's vision of the glorified Christ is surely heavily indebted to the Transfiguration narratives, in its references to the appearance of a dazzling light, to 'a man clothed in white', and to a 'veale or courteyne drawn betwene me & the light' (in the Gospels, a cloud that overshadowed the disciples). We can only speculate as to whether Elijah's charge to convert King Ahab has any connection with Hall's mission as 'a mesenger sente from godde to the Quene & to all princes', or whether he used the name Eliseus to indicate that he, like the prophet Elisha, was Elijah's chosen successor. But the Manchester draper's close identification of himself with the Old Testament prophet and har- binger of the second coming must be considered settled by the manner of his bodily ascent to the judgement seat of Christ. 'Elias went up thorow the whyrlewynde into heaven.'[20] So too did Ellis Hall, 'taken owt of my bed as it were in a tufte of feathers with a worlewynde up into heaven'.[21]

III

There is then, I would argue, a close and complex pattern of scriptural 'self-fashioning' underlying the delusions of grandeur that impelled an obscure Lancashire draper to pursue his 15 minutes of fame on the national stage. But what in the end does this tell us? Was Bishop Grindal prejudicial and premature in declaring Hall to be 'of the popishe Iugement in Religion', and have historians like Christopher Haigh been too eager to see him as an extreme but yet somehow representative type, 'an anguished Catholic' taking a stand against the Reformation? Due to the non-survival of the 'greate booke' of Hall's revelations it is simply impossible to say for certain. In his two appearances before the authorities, the acknowledged themes are fasting and prayer, 'dewtye towardes god', 'vertuous lyvinge', 'baptisme repentaunce & amendment of lyfe', the forsaking of 'all thinges pleasante to the flesshe'. Stripped of their apocalyptic wrapping, these are the common denominators of early modern Christian morality. Hall's implicit advocation of a works-based soteriology, along with his allusion to the Five Wounds of Christ, seems to place him in a distinctly tradition-alist milieu, but on points of disputed doctrine, as on the question of his conformity to the established Church, he maintained a studied silence.

Was Hall a Catholic, a 'papist' even? The ambiguities of the case serve as a warning to Reformation historians that they should exercise caution before seeking to assign pristine confessional labels to their subjects, particularly in the case of those like Hall whose lives spanned the reigns of all five Tudor monarchs, and whose adult experience was thus of a bewildering succession of advances, reversals and false starts in ecclesias-tical policy. This hardly seems necessary advice. In recent years the work of David Cressy, Norman Jones, Alexandra Walsham, Tessa Watt and others has encouraged us to identify distinct traces of pre-Reformation religious culture in the private and public discourses of post-Reformation England, to see the lived cultural impact of the English Reformation as one of gradual accommodation rather than of rapid conversion or rabid resistance.[22] But the celestial journey of Ellis Hall invites us to look at these processes of religious inculturation through the other end of the telescope. It reveals not a slow and ameliorating acceptance of enforced change, but rather the capacity of a long-established cultural form – the revelation of an otherwordly journey – to appropriate, absorb and adapt elements of the 'new learning'. It also suggests how an acute interest in vernacular Scripture might be neither the mark nor the making of a predictably evangelical Protestant. In Ellis Hall we appear to have an example of that classic Reformation type: a mid-Tudor layman galvanized into thinking afresh about judgement and repentance, both personal and collective, through his encounter with the word of God in Scripture. Yet in this and perhaps other cases, the conjunction did not lead in the directions that contemporary reformers would have wished, or that modern historians have come to expect.

4

The Reformation of hell? Protestant and Catholic infernalisms *c*.1560–1640

It seems that historians will never tire of debating the impact of the Protestant Reformations on diverse aspects of the social, cultural and institutional structures of early modern Europe. To appropriate the titles of some recent books, the sixteenth and seventeenth centuries witnessed *The Reformation of the Parishes*, *The Reformation of Ritual*, *The Reformation of Community*, *The Reformation of the Image*, *The Reformation of the Keys* and *The Reformation of Feeling*.[1] Alongside these multiple transformations of social and community life was a crucial parallel development, one that Craig Koslofsky has dubbed *The Reformation of the Dead*. Rituals of the deathbed, funeral ceremonies, burial patterns, commemorative practices – all these were comprehensively remodelled across the Protestant world from the middle decades of the sixteenth century.[2]

Behind the reforms lay what was perhaps the single most audacious act of theological downsizing in the history of Western Christianity. The medieval Church had come to recognize five distinct places or states which defined the location and condition of the dead: in addition to heaven and hell, there was a purgatory for the souls of the moderately sinful, a limbo for unbaptized infants, and a second limbo for the righteous patriarchs and prophets who had died, of necessity non-Christians, before the incarnation of Jesus. This latter place was usually thought to be empty, since Christ had liberated its inhabitants in a kind of daring commando raid performed between his death and resurrection – the so-called harrowing of hell.[3] But Protestant reformers, Lutheran and Reformed alike, would have no truck with this. Purgatory and the limbos were declared unscriptural and therefore unreal, unhealthy fictions of the clerical imagination. The reformers recognized only two places in the hereafter: heaven and hell. Heaven has its own history.[4] But is it possible to speak meaningfully of 'the Reformation of hell' in this period? And if not, why not?

Despite an explosion of interest in the social history of death among scholars of the early modern period, the immediate and medium-term impact of Protestantism on teachings about and perceptions of hell has not attracted much attention as an object of study. D. P. Walker's seminal discussion of 'the decline of hell' has a firmly later seventeenth- and eighteenth-century focus.[5] Scholars who have considered the earlier period tend to conclude that continuity and traditionalism were the order of the day. Writing in the 1920s, the Anglican theologian Darwell Stone remarked that 'the widespread rejection of any kind of purgatory by members of the English Church in the sixteenth and following centuries was not accompanied by much modification of the corresponding ideas about hell'.[6] The literary scholar C. A. Patrides has even argued that Protestant writers 'transcended the bounds of their theological differences from Catholics' in writing about hell.[7] A similar argument is made by the French cultural historian Jean Delumeau, in his exhaustive survey of 'the emergence of a western guilt culture'. Hell features prominently in Delumeau's chapter on 'shared aspects of the Protestant and Catholic doctrinal programs'. Indeed, he questions whether historians have yet 'adequately underlined this penetration of Catholicism and Protestantism during a period of intense religious conflict'. To Delumeau, Catholic and Protestant sermons and treatises on hell and judgement from across Europe seem virtually interchangeable. They all hark on the same regulatory message: change your ways, or face the excruciating consequences. Indeed, he asserts that 'this pressing and constant plea makes any lengthy study of the Protestant hell unnecessary'.[8]

I am not entirely alone in wondering whether matters were really quite so straightforwardly monochrome. In an enlightening recent essay on 'the good side of hell' in early modern Spain, Carlos Eire suggests that 'more work is . . . needed on comparing the relative place of hell among early modern Catholics and Protestants, both literally and figuratively'.[9] This chapter seeks to take up the challenge, representing a tentative foray into the field of what one is tempted to call comparative infernalism. It concerns itself with English sources of the period *c.*1560–1640, the era and area in which Delumeau perceived a particularly marked convergence between Protestant and Catholic approaches, something he ascribed to a predilection for Augustinian pessimism among English theologians of divergent stripes.[10] The texts I have consulted include sermons, catechisms, instructional tracts, polemical writings and devotional manuals. Some are foreign works in translation, counted as English sources in this context, since my interest is in what was represented to and received by English readers. The sample is weighted towards the serious rather than the truly popular or recreational in vernacular print, and most of my authors are clergymen. Nor have I concerned myself with representations of hell in overtly fictive and literary sources. I have, as it were, stopped before Milton, and swerved around Marlowe and Shakespeare. Yet by examining images and tropes around hellfire and damnation from a variety of orthodox and rather mundane sources, I hope to bring into focus some significant questions about the dynamics of intellectual consensus and intellectual fragmentation in the later Reformation period.

I

An initial problem in setting out to study the Catholic–Protestant controversy over hell in later Reformation England is that there doesn't appear to have been one. Hell was not, formally and prescriptively, an object of religious disputation. Neither the existence nor the essential purpose of hell was ever at issue between Catholic and Protestant theologians. English Catholics would have had few problems accepting a definition like that of the Caroline minister Thomas Phillips: 'A place of infinite and extreame torment, created by God, and appointed for the punishment of the wicked after this life, to the glory and manifestation of his justice'.[11] It is not surprising therefore that hell does not appear as a topic in the seminary priest Anthony Champney's compendious *A Manual of Controversies* (Paris, 1614), nor in the Jesuit James Gordon's *A Summary of Controversies . . . now a dayes in dispute between Catholicks and Protestants* (St Omer, 1618). From the Protestant side, there was no need for any substantial discussion of hell in, for example, William Perkins' seminal work of quasi-courteous controversy, *A Reformed Catholike – A declaration shewing how neere we may come to the present Church of Rome in sundrie points of religion, and wherein we must for euer depart from them* (Cambridge, 1597).

In fact, far from aggressively diverging, Catholic and Protestant hells often drew on the same sources of inspiration. Some Protestant writing on the theme, for example, displays a remarkable indebtedness to medieval texts and motifs. Respectful citations of Aquinas pepper Protestant accounts, and a few authors unselfconsciously recycled the lurid descriptions of medieval vision literature, or, just like the eleventh-century Cluniac St Odilo, pointed to the roarings and flashings of volcanoes like Vesuvius and Etna as presages of the fate awaiting the damned. Such traditionalism was even more evident in the cheap print and ballad literature of post-Reformation England, where the Dante-esque notion of specific torments tailored to the particular sins of the damned was often wholeheartedly affirmed, and liars might expect to have molten lead poured down their throats. Such notions were decidedly not the sole preserve of a kind of Catholic survivalism. During his possession by the devil in 1596, according to the pamphlet printed about the case, the Puritan youth Thomas Darling had a vision of the 'place of torments where drunkards are hanged by the throats, swearers and filthy talkers by their tongues'.[12] In more sober and didactic sources, there are frequent reiterations of what was perhaps the most familiar of medieval tropes on hell: both Protestant and Catholic writers in our period regularly repeated St Augustine's striking suggestion that, in comparison to hellfire, earthly fire was but like a fire painted on a wall.[13]

Even more remarkably, Catholic texts with substantial amounts of material on hell were sometimes printed or reprinted in Protestant editions. That classic of fifteenth-century devotion, *The Imitation of Christ*, appeared in five Protestant translations between 1567 and 1639. Its eucharistic passages were heavily bowdlerized, but Protestants found nothing to object to in the chapter 'On judgment and the punishment of sinners', which emphasized how 'lovers of luxury and pleasure will be drenched in burning pitch and stinking sulphur, and the envious will howl in pain like mad dogs'.[14] An equally notorious case of pious appropriation was the Puritan Edmund Bunny's 1584 edition of the *Booke of Christian exercise* by the Jesuit Robert Persons. Bunny thoroughly edited and expurgated Persons' text, cutting, for example, all the material relating to purgatory and prayer for the dead. But he reproduced without any significant amendment all the sections on hell. Not long afterwards, the Lincolnshire gentleman Francis Meres produced a translation of the Spanish Dominican Luis de Granada's *Guía de pecadores*. This too contained a vivid chapter explaining how 'hell fire doth bind us to seeke after vertue'.[15] Another example of the process is the 1613 translation of Bernard of Clairvaux's *Dialogue betwixt the soule and the body of the damned* by the Puritan minister William Crashaw, an intensely physical vision of the yawning prospect of hell, with hideous demons dragging the damned soul off to perdition. Crashaw defended his endeavour on the grounds that his was 'an age that needs all helps to holiness'. Although the original was 'made in the mist of popery . . . yet it is not tainted with popish corruption, nor scarce smels of any superstition'.[16]

There is little suggestion, therefore, that the sometimes lurid physicality of traditional Catholic descriptions of hell failed to appeal to Protestants' sensibilities. Indeed, it often characterized their own writings. The Jacobean bishop Lewis Bayly, whose *Practise of pietie* was the bestselling homegrown devotional work of the period, unflinchingly enumerated the particular torments that would afflict the damned, stressing how dainty noses 'shall be cloyed with noysome stench of *Sulphur*'.[17] Protestant writers also vied with each other in their attempts to evoke the almost unimaginable horror of *eternal* torment. Arthur Dent invited his readers to imagine all the arithmeticians of the world spending a lifetime writing down the largest numbers they could think of, and then adding them all together: they could still 'never come any thing neere to that length of time wherein the wicked shall be tormented'. John Denison observed that if the damned had as many thousand years to endure as there were grains of sand on the shore, fish in the sea or stars in the firmament, then they could entertain some hope and comfort. But alas it was not so.[18]

There was much of the same in contemporary Catholic texts, though despite the impression given by some modern commentators, Counter-Reformation writers were fully capable of approaching the topic with caution and restraint. Cardinal Bellarmine, a favourite of the exiled English Catholic clergy, declared his intention of avoiding 'uncertaine or coniecturall points' in his treatment of hell's torments. He would deal only with what was clearly indicated in Holy Scripture, lest he be suspected of trying to arouse vain fears, and 'force teares from the eyes of the simple and ignorant'. The French Jesuit Nicholas Caussin, in the translation of the recusant gentleman and poet Thomas Hawkins, argued that silence was the only appropriate descriptor for the enormity of hell: 'I let passe this world of punishments figured by vultures, gibbets, tortures, snakes, burning pincers.' His contemporary, Bishop Jean Pierre Camus of Belley, advanced the virtues of brevity, in eschewing 'those vulgar similitudes or conceipts, which give to weaker wits slender ideas of eternitie'. Not for him the sands of the sea, or leaves on the trees, though he could not resist one such metaphor of immeasurable duration: a little immortal bird attempting to empty the ocean by drawing from it in its beak a drop of water once every hundred thousand years.[19]

II

In neither Protestant nor Catholic texts of the period is there very much sense of writers wallowing sadistically in descriptions of hellfire and torment for its own sake. On both sides of the confessional divide, the intent was much the same: such passages were a wake-up call for sinners, a counter-blast against what the Protestant preacher Henry Greenwood called 'the presumptuous security of this our age', and the Catholic Bishop Camus dubbed 'the lethargie of pleasures'.[20] Readers were to meditate on hell so that they would never have to come there. A speaker in one moralistic Protestant dialogue even dared his interlocutors to 'suppose there were no hell (as euery good christian doth beleeue there is one)'. Yet to think there was such a place would lead only to good, and 'cause us to shunne that evill, that otherwise we should doe'.[21] Historians will be tempted to call this social control; contemporaries, however, thought of it as a spur to repentance, something which was a primary concern of pastors on all points of the religious spectrum.

There were, of course, some distinctive dynamics to Catholic and Protestant understandings of repentance, underpinned as they were by radically different soteriologies or theories of salvation. Protestant authors were sometimes sensitive to the charge that the abolition of purgatory, along with the abrogation of mandatory auricular confession, had significantly weakened their arsenal of moral deterrence. The Jacobean court preacher George Hakewill, a fierce anti-papist, denied the necessity of lay-people having personal confessors, adding 'yet might and ought inferiors be kept in awe of hell fire by their preachers'. As for purgatory, William Tyndale had made the case years earlier, 'to fear men . . . Christ and his apostles thought hell enough'.[22] In a sense, then, hell was of necessity more central to the Protestant than Catholic scheme of moral regeneration because it was, ultimately, the only sanction available. Though at the same time it is possible, as Alexandra Walsham has intriguingly suggested, that the loss of purgatory may have sharpened a Protestant interest in the notion of retributive providences in this world.[23]

Moreover, Catholic and Protestant strategies of avoidance for hell could hardly be the same. Under the Catholic dispensation of free will and resistible grace, dying outside mortal sin was the key test. But for the orthodox Calvinist predestinarians who dominated the Elizabethan and early Stuart Church, no individual could presume to alter a divine decree of election or reprobation. A turning away from sin, spurred on by the fear of hell, was of course understood as part of the effectual 'calling' of the elect. But Protestant divines sometimes recognized that more tangible incentives were required for the entire body of humanity, whether saved or not. A partial solution was found in another characteristic of hell that Protestants could agree upon with their Catholic opponents: the notion that different degrees of punishment were to be experienced within it. So, for example, the editors of the Catholic Rheims New Testament of 1582 glossed Christ's words in Matthew 10.15 – 'Amen I say to you, it shall be more tolerable for the land of Sodom and Gomorrha in the day of judgment, than for that city' – to suggest that it is 'hereby . . . evident there bee degrees and differences of damnation in hell fire according to men's deserts'. Here the presbyterian controversialist Thomas Cartwright, though engaged in denouncing the translation, readily conceded that there is 'nothing material in the note to bee suspected'. For Calvinists, this actually meant that good works had a positive role to play after all, because they might ameliorate the situation of the damned in hell. George Abbot was thus able in 1600 to offer these words of dubious comfort: 'suppose that thou belong not to him . . . yet flie from sinne, and do moral vertues . . . that at least shall ease some part of the extremity of those torments, which thou shalt have in hell fire'.[24] By contrast, Abbot's Catholic opponents could tender a more absolute assurance that if the right steps were followed, without deviation or digression, hell could be avoided altogether.

Yet in many ways it is surprising how little an impact the rival theologies of grace seem to have made upon Reformed and counter-reforming discourses about hell. If we ask the question of where on the ecclesiological spectrum hell loomed largest in this period, it turns out to be unanswerable in any meaningfully statistical way. One of the striking features of the imagined obsession with hell in early modern sources is how relatively little of it there seems to have been about.[25] If one uses the subject term 'hell' to search the 25,000 or so volumes digitalized in Early English Books Online for the period 1560–1640, the exercise produces a mere 27 titles – all but four of which are concerned with the very discrete and rather technical controversy over the meaning of the phrase in the Apostles' Creed that Christ 'descended into hell'. Attention to the topic was of course diffused much more widely than this, and hell featured regularly in the homiletic and devotional writings of both confessions. It never seems, however, to have dominated or unbalanced them. Its treatment in both Catholic and Protestant catechisms of the period appears to have been similarly measured and limited, not usually attracting more than a few lines, and with Christ's descent into hell often once again the main focus of interest.[26] We should note too how regularly the context for discussion of hell was a parallel evocation of heaven, the descriptions of misery serving to underscore the felicity of the saved in works like Samuel Rowlands' *Hels torments, and heavens glorie* and John Denison's *Three-fold resolution . . . Describing earths vanitie. Hels horror. Heauens felicitie.* On the Catholic side, Thomas Everard, translator of Bellarmine's *Of the eternal felicity of the saints*, inserted into it a 'Discourse of the torments of hell' from another of the cardinal's works, on the Ramist grounds that 'the common axiome in philosophy is, that contraries compared one to the other, do afford a greater illustration'.[27] For both Catholics and Protestants, then, hell was an instrumental doctrine; an object of improving meditation, just as much or even more than it was a subject for systematic theology. Bearing this in mind probably helps to explain why some early modern discussions of hell can seem rather vague on apparently important points – for example, over whether they are describing hell as currently configured, or as it would be after the final judgement and resurrection of the dead.

One stimulus for meditation did change after the Reformation. In late medieval England, most parish churches were furnished with a prominent and striking image of the prospect of hell, part of the Last Judgement or 'doom' painted on the tympanum above the chancel arch. Protestant iconoclasm removed this visual dimension of catechesis, and also reduced the options for the mimetic representation of hell, as the traditional cycles of civic mystery plays were wound up across England in the 1580s. It has been suggested that the Protestant imagination compensated for these losses by developing habits of intense 'inner picturing', a substitutive real presence of the divine, which came into the mind on hearing or reading God's word. Thus, the Puritan Richard Bernard's 1610 volume of *Contemplative pictures* offered 'certain pictures, not popish and sensible for superstition, but mental for divine contemplation'. One of the themes of the volume was the contemplation of hell, and readers were left in no doubt that it offered a prospect 'wofull, dolefull, horribly fearefull, insufferably painefull'.[28]

Could it be then that the impoverishment of visual culture paradoxically made the imagining of hell more real and immediate for devout believers? Perhaps; though we should be careful not to exaggerate the contrasts here. For a start, Catholic writers, and not only Jesuits armed with Ignatian meditative techniques, were quite as capable of inducing internalized images as Protestants were.[29] Nor was the visual quite so thoroughly expunged from post-Reformation religious culture as it was once fashionable to think. Historians like Tessa Watt and Alexandra Walsham have modified Patrick Collinson's influential emphasis on the 'iconophobic' impulse of the later English Reformation by pointing to the survival of graphic material in Protestant literature of various kinds.[30] Hell (literally) fits the picture here. Illustrations depicting the flames and demons awaiting the damned accompanied several godly ballads, as well as pamphlets on witchcraft and possession. Samuel Rowlands' *Hels torments, and heavens glorie* of 1601 boasted an illustration of souls being dragged down by demons into a gaping hell mouth. In addition, a whole series of striking woodcuts itemizing the torments of hell continued to appear in editions of the popular late medieval work *The Shepherds kalendar* into the middle decades of the seventeenth century. The story of Lazarus in heaven and

Dives in hell was often depicted on domestic wall hangings in the later sixteenth century, and hell, as Dr Faustus and others were to discover, still had a secure place on the secular stage.[31]

III

Thus far, I have not made much, if any, progress towards establishing my initial contention: that Catholic and Protestant discourses about hell show some significant and revealing disparities. The broad parameters, the rhetorical strategies, the pastoral objectives; all look pretty much the same. But if we move from the general contours of the landscape to examine some specific features of the terrain, a few interesting fissures start to open up. In particular, we can compare and contrast approaches to the two questions that St Augustine had considered the most uncertain of all matters relating to hell, requiring for their resolution a special revelation from the Holy Spirit. These were the precise nature of hellfire, and the question of hell's location.[32] Taken together, attempts to address these questions do indicate some clear patterns of divergence along broadly confessional lines.

That hell was a place of fire seemed on the surface easily the most uncontentious of theological commonplaces. The Bible abounded with references to 'the fire that shall never be quenched', and to tormenting 'with fire and brimstone'.[33] The fire of hell belonged, in a distinction well understood by both Protestant and Catholic interpreters, to the torments of the senses, the *poena sensus*, rather than to the spiritual or psychological torment of being deprived of the sight of God, the *poena damni*.[34] But the precise nature of this fire had long been a source of puzzlement in Christian thought. Among the Fathers, Origen had argued that the fire spoken of in Scripture was merely figurative, a judgement shared by Ambrose, though many others disagreed.[35] In the high Middle Ages, Thomas Aquinas had posed the questions of 'whether the fire of hell will be corporeal' and of 'whether the fire of hell is of the same species as ours'. He had answered both cautiously in the affirmative, while conceding that the fire in hell most probably would subsist in a different kind of matter, and would exhibit different properties from earthly fire – such as giving out no light, and not requiring kindling to start it or fuel to keep it alive.[36] Similarly, in the period under discussion, it was characteristic of Catholic writers to insist upon the genuinely material nature of the fire to be found in hell, while conceding that the question inevitably threw up some tricky metaphysical issues. The Jesuit Persons ascribed the infinitely greater heat and power of hellfire over earthly fire to the fact that 'ours is out of its natural place and situation', abated by the coldness of the air, whereas 'that of hell is in the naturall and proper place wherein it was created'.[37] More commonly, however, Catholic authors reversed the emphasis and wondered how it was possible for a real and corporeal fire to rage eternally in hell. Nicholas Caussin admitted that 'libertines' would ask how a material fire could burn spiritual souls, a question that had earlier perturbed Aquinas. Caussin's answer was that the soul retained the same sensitive faculties as the body, and hence an ability to perceive pain. It was, he wrote, true that 'the soule separated from the body hath not a natural antipathy and disagreement from fire, but what this imperious element cannot have remaining within the limits of nature, it obtayneth by a particular ordinance and disposition of God'.[38] Cardinal Bellarmine also conceded that the issue of the affliction of spirits by a corporeal fire was 'a large disputation'. Again, an emphasis on the miraculous sustenance of Almighty God was the appropriate response to those who 'over curiously should demaund, from whence this continuall fyre doth receave its nourishment and supply'. Yet at the same time Bellarmine was inclined to take rather literally the scriptural allusions to brimstone or sulphur as the fuel for the fires of hell.[39] Luis de la Puente thought 'the eternal breathe of almightie God' would be sufficient to preserve the fire of hell, but he similarly did not rule out the presence of real brimstone, likewise preserved from depletion by the motion of God.[40]

In Protestant texts, by contrast, we find a much greater willingness to accept that details such as the brimstone should be understood as metaphor or allegory. We need to be clear about what we mean by allegory in this context. It was not that Protestant writers entertained doubts about the literal, physical reality of hell, or the certainty of its intense torments. In fact, its torments were unimaginably real, in the sense that analogies to familiar earthly phenomena were hardly adequate to describe them. The tone here had been set by Calvin, who argued in the *Institutes* that because 'language cannot describe the severity of the divine vengeance on the reprobate, their pains and torments are figured to us by corporeal things'.[41] The metaphorical nature of the worm that 'dieth not' (Mark 9.48), signifying the torment of conscience, was rarely contested by either Protestant or Catholic authors; this had been the common scholastic interpretation.[42] But, more controversially, some Protestant writers extended this line of interpretation to the fire of hell itself, as a figure for the literally indescribable torments awaiting the damned in hell. William Perkins gave his readers to understand 'that by hell fire is not meant any bodily flame, but it signifies the seazing of the fearful and terrible wrath of God'.[43] Perkins' disciple Thomas Tuke also discounted the possibility of a corporeal fire: 'if the fire of Hell bee corporall, it must bee fed by corporall fuell, which beeing once wasted it also must goe out'. Rather, Tuke suggested, 'it pleaseth the Holy Ghost by these words to point out, and as by similitudes to shew vnto vs the griefes and gripes of the damned'.[44] The Puritan minister of Dedham in Essex, John Rogers, similarly argued that as 'we cannot conceive nor utter the extremity of these torments . . . yet the Scriptures expresse them by the sharpest and most intolerable punishments we can know or can conceive; as fire, brimstone, darkenesse, weeping, &c . . .'.[45] As the Canterbury clergyman Thomas Wilson put it in his *Christian dictionarie* of 1612 – the first dictionary of the Bible to be published in English – 'fire being a most terrible element, is fittest to expresse the dreadfull state of such as be in hell'.[46] The most emphatic statement of this position came from the pen of the semi-separatist Puritan minister Henry Jacob, who in 1598 dismissed the very notion of a material fire in hell as a 'toyish fable'. One might as well say, he argued, that there was '*materiall brimstone* and *much wood* which the fire burneth upon'. Until very recently, he suggested, all Protestants had shared his view on this, and only papists had dared contradict it.[47]

That was not quite accurate. A number of Protestant writers had always positioned themselves somewhere on a spectrum between Calvin's portrayal of hellfire as a scriptural allegory for divine retribution, and a perceived Catholic insistence on its being, as Thomas Phillips put it, '*ejusdem speciei*, of the same kind with our fire both elementary and culinary'.[48] As Henry Greenwood suggested in a sermon published in 1615, 'the most and best of the learned' (including such luminaries as Heinrich Bullinger) held it to be a true and substantial fire, albeit not a material one.[49] Some Puritan writers of the early seventeenth century made reference to a 'spiritual fire' in hell, emphasizing its action on the internal sensation of the soul, while some more conservative or 'conformist' Protestants preferred to speak about a 'true', 'external' or 'sensible' fire.[50] Catholic observers like the lawyer James Anderton (alias John Brereley) could thus gleefully point to Protestant divisions over the issue.[51] But reformers of various stripes often agreed that the precise nature of hellfire was a 'curious' question into which there was no necessity to enquire closely.[52] The Essex minister John Smith, writing in 1632, lambasted the supercilious certainties of the papists, for 'it be not a point of faith, for a man to beleeve or know what a kinde of fire it is'. At the same time, he made short shrift of the notion that a material fire might miraculously endure in hell without spending fuel, without giving light or without finally consuming the bodies of the damned: 'hell', he sententiously pronounced, 'is no place for miracles'.[53]

The uncertainties about the exact nature of hellfire were linked to another 'curious' question exercising both Catholic and Protestant minds in the later Reformation period: that of where in the created universe the fires of hell were to be found. The nature of hellfire was more easily comprehended, for example, if it were supposed that hell was located in the proper sphere or element of fire. Scripture was decidedly unhelpful on this issue, and no formal pronouncement of the medieval Church had ever sought to resolve it. Such luminaries as Augustine and Gregory had been cautious about any categorical pronouncement on the matter. Nonetheless, a convention had long been established that the place of hell was under the earth, most likely in the very centre of the world. The Latin term for hell – *infernus* – seemed to imply a location below, and the notion fitted with a cosmology in which God inhabited an empyrean beyond the planetary spheres – as far as could be from a subterranean hell. Metaphysically, the medieval association of sin with weight and heaviness reinforced the connection.[54]

There is no doubt, however, that Catholic authors in our period held on to this tradition much more resolutely than Protestants, locating hell in the midst of the earth, as a place, in Bellarmine's words, 'furthest remote from the glorie of the blessed'. The cardinal believed that hell was 'certainly thousands of myles' under the earth's surface. Persons cited the authority of the old Fathers and of Augustine in favour of the proposition, and Camus, after weighing the patristic and scriptural evidence, pronounced that for anyone 'to doubt whether hell be in the center of the earth . . . seemes to me a thing impossible'. Some continental Catholic authors not translated into English in this period were even more precise in their determinations. The sixteenth-century Spanish priest Alejo Venegas, for example, calculated that hell was exactly 1,193 leagues beneath the surface of the earth. The presentation of the afterlife by the Jesuit Jerónimo Nadal, so Carlos Eire assures us, was 'as geologically precise as a *National Geographic* diagram'.[55]

Catholic convictions about the geographical location of hell also help to explain a feature of their descriptive writing which seems much less evident in Protestant sources: an emphasis on the 'straitness' of hell, on physical overcrowding as an anguish of the damned. According to Luis de la Puente, the number of people descending to hell would be so great that each would barely possess the space of a crowded grave: 'they shall bee crowded together like brickes in a fiery furnace'. In Bellarmine's opinion, the straitness of the place would be such 'as it shall scarce be able to take the multitude of the damned bodies'.[56] The Bavarian Jesuit Jeremias Drexel arrived at the conclusion that if hell had the dimensions of a square German mile, it would nonetheless have capacity for 100,000,000,000 of the damned, forced together 'like grapes in the press, or like sardines in the barrel'.[57]

Protestant writers, by contrast, were usually markedly reluctant to pronounce definitively on the question of where hell was to be found. In an anti-Catholic work of 1592, the Calvinist theologian Andrew Willet expressed no doubt 'that there is a locall place of torment'. But he took Bellarmine to task for asserting that 'the place where damned spirites are tormented . . . is about the center of the earth, the lowest of all places'. The scriptural texts Bellarmine cited simply did not prove the case.[58] 'As for the situation of hell', reflected Thomas Tuke, 'to say precisely where hell is, it is not easie.'[59] Some Puritan theologians drew attention to the passage in Ephesians 2.2 which seemed to imply that the devil's habitation was up in the air.[60] The Hebrew scholar Hugh Broughton even argued that 'they are much deceaved who thinke hell to be in this world, lowe in the earth'.[61] The majority of Protestant writers probably did think it likely that hell was under the earth, but they often expressed the opinion guardedly, and never reproduced in their writings the precise topographical calculations of some of their Catholic contemporaries.[62] Since Scripture did not pronounce definitively on the location of hell, 'curious' enquiry was best avoided.[63] In a sermon of 1626, John Donne mocked the Swiss cosmographer Sebastian Münster for pronouncing categorically 'that hell cannot possibly be above three thousand miles in compasse'.[64]

Protestant guardedness about affirming the precise whereabouts or dimensions of hell provided an opening for Catholic opponents to exploit. The Jesuit John Radford claimed in 1605 that some heretics 'stick not to confesse . . . that hell is only in the brest and but a darknes of the minde and conscience, or some biting of the same'. In 1631 the former vicar apostolic of English Catholics, Richard Smith, made the charge that 'Protestants expressly say, that hell is not place, no corporall place, no prison; that it is nothing but a wicked conscience'.[65] Such sentiments – imagining hell as a purely internal or psychological punishment – would in time be articulated by radical separatists of the Civil War era, but there were few real antecedents of this among the orthodox Calvinist theologians who were Smith's intended target. It is certainly true that inner, psychological torments had always figured prominently in Protestant enumerations of the pains of hell.[66] But in fact it was a devotional trope common to both Catholic and Protestant writers that a consciousness of the deprivation of God – the *poena damni* – would be a more intolerable punishment to the reprobate than sensory torments.[67] Ironically, the idea of a purely internal hell, a hell within oneself, in some ways made more sense within a Catholic theological framework. For Protestants, it was simply inconceivable that damned souls might ever come forth out of hell. Yet the Catholic teaching on ghosts allowed for the possibility in some exceptional circumstances. In such cases, noted Drexel, 'yet still he should carry an hell about him'.[68]

On the question of the location of hell, and on issues relating to the nature of its punishments, it appears therefore as if English Protestant commentators *can* be meaningfully distinguished from their English and continental Catholic counterparts. There was a greater reluctance to affirm the unknowable with certainty, a greater openness to the possibility of allegory and metaphor in making sense of the reality of hell. It looks as if we are on the curve of a familiar trajectory, along which Protestantism progresses more naturally and easily towards a concern with empirical verification, and ultimately, towards modernity itself. But we should exercise caution here. For in so far as the position of Protestants might sound more recognizably 'modern' on some of these issues than did that of Catholics, it was determined not so much by temperamental cousinage to ourselves as by the tactical demands of theological polemic. Hell, I will suggest by way of conclusion, was never quite so uncontroversially ecumenical a topic as it might at first appear.

IV

To start with, questions about the situation of hell could not easily be separated from speculations about the existence and location of that Protestant *bête noire*, purgatory. In the Catholic topography of the hereafter, the place of eternal punishment was one of a series of 'hells' which were generally understood as being in descending proximity to each other under the ground: *limbus patrum* or the limbo of the fathers; purgatory; *limbus infantium* or the limbo of unbaptized infants; and hell proper. The latter was sometimes glossed in Catholic sources as 'the hell of the damned' to distinguish it from these other subterranean regions.[69]

A professed Protestant agnosticism about the exact location of hell was in large measure intended to disrupt and disparage this eschatological system.[70] The trend towards the allegorization of hellfire, or at least to deny its strictly material nature, could similarly serve to unsettle medieval and scholastic speculations, such as the idea that the proximity of hell and purgatory allowed the very same fire to torment souls in both locales.[71]

One medieval conjecture about hell, still rehearsed in the sixteenth century by Catholic authorities like Bellarmine, but which seems to be largely absent from Protestant discussions, is the notion that part of the happiness of the souls in heaven derives from their contemplation of the torments of the damned – an idea which in the nineteenth century was christened 'the abominable fancy'. Noting the absence of this motif from seventeenth-century English sources, D. P. Walker ascribed the development to a changing attitude in society towards the suffering of others.[72] But it seems equally plausible to invoke a more tactical explanation. A key proof-text for the idea was Luke chapter 16, where the rich man in hell is able to see Lazarus ensconced in the 'bosom of Abraham', and begs Abraham to send Lazarus to warn his five brothers of the fate in store if they do not mend their ways. Protestant exegetes were made distinctly uneasy by this passage's apparent encouragement of the notion of traffic and communication between worlds, and they tended to emphasize its character as a parable and an allegory. Moreover, while Protestants generally regarded 'Abraham's bosom' as a circumlocution for heaven, Catholic tradition saw it as an alternative name for *limbus patrum*, that outer skirt of hell, and thus identified a literal proximity of Dives and Lazarus in the next life. As the Elizabethan Catholic controversialist Gregory Martin put it, not just Dives but 'Abraham and Lazarus also were in hell, but in a place of great rest and refreshing'.[73]

It was in fact controversy about the very meaning of the word 'hell' that proved the single most formative influence on late Reformation modifications of thinking about the place of the damned. Specifically, much of the discussion of the location of hell, the character of hellfire, and other related matters, was driven by debates over the proper interpretation of the clause in the Apostles' Creed which stated that Christ 'descended into hell' between his death and resurrection. The so-called 'Descensus Controversy', which ran from the early years of Elizabeth to the middle of the reign of James I, was a spirited three-way quarrel between Catholics, Puritans and those more establishment-minded Protestants best described as 'conformist'.[74] Catholics related the credal article to the 'harrowing of hell', the belief that during the three days his body lay in the ground, Christ descended to *limbus patrum* or Abraham's bosom to free the souls of the patriarchs and carry them triumphantly to heaven. This idea was anathema to Protestants of all stripes – *limbus patrum* was, perhaps literally, only a short step from purgatory – though reformers were far from united in putting forward an alternative explication. The article was interpreted literally by Jacobean conformists like Thomas Bilson or John Higgins, who insisted that Christ's soul did 'really and locally, actuallie and effectually descend into hell' in order to signify his triumph over the powers of evil.[75] The consensus of much Reformed theology, by contrast, was that there had been no local or spatial descent. Many English theologians endorsed Calvin's spiritual interpretation that Christ experienced the pains of hell on the cross. The debate took a decidedly philological turn, with Puritans emphasizing non-literal uses of 'hell' in the Bible, and arguing that the key Hebrew word *sheol* should be translated as 'death' or 'the grave'. 'Christ's locall descension', so Andrew Willet argued, 'was but to the grave.'[76] If it could be established that hell itself was not necessarily or demonstrably 'below', a subterranean abode of corporeal fire, then the proponents of a merely spiritual descent had moved the ground, as it were, from under the feet of their opponents.

V

The late J. H. Hexter famously observed that historians can be divided into 'lumpers' and 'splitters'.[77] This essay has undoubtedly been an exercise in splitting; perhaps, one might think, in splitting hairs. It has picked over the unpromising terrain of Catholic and Protestant writings about hell in a search for, if not the tyranny, then at least the existence, of small differences. It would be reckless to contend that arguments about such matters as the quality of hellfire and the geography of hell were more than side issues in the great confessional controversies and quarrels of the day. Nonetheless, these minor divergences presaged some larger transformations in religious thought, and paying attention to them adds a suggestive dimension to existing discussions of the 'decline of hell'. Jean Delumeau's 'evangelism of fear' was a collaborative Catholic–Protestant exercise, undergirded by a series of vast collective disasters stretching from the Black Death to the end of the Wars of Religion. It was, in his view, 'the alleviation of serious threats to daily life' from the end of the seventeenth century onwards which undermined the potency and persuasiveness of traditional threats about the punishments of the next world. D. P. Walker meanwhile attributed the waning of belief in the idea of eternal torment over the same period to inherent weaknesses in the scriptural and functional arguments for hell, and to the gradual advance of rationalist modes of religious thought.[78] However, a close reading of late sixteenth- and early seventeenth-century clerical discourses suggests that – for England at least – the beginnings of a process by which hell could become less emphatically 'real' for people can be detected in the polemical and strategic requirements of Reformation theology, as much as in the changing macro-environment, or in any inevitable triumph of reason.[79] On the surface, writings about hell were some of the most solidly consensual of all Christian doctrinal productions of the later Reformation period. Yet, almost in spite of themselves, they managed to play a discernible part in processes of group solidarity and identity-formation, and in laying some of the foundations for changed thinking about the essential relationship between this world and the next.

5

The company of heaven: identity and sociability in the English Protestant afterlife *c*.1560–1630

The English Reformation's dramatic changes to the liturgy, ritual and structures of the Church in this world were from the outset inextricably bound up with a revolutionary set of assumptions about the nature of the world to come. In place of the five locations which late medieval Catholic theology regarded as constituting the hereafter (heaven, hell, purgatory, the limbos of the fathers, and of children) the reformers accepted only two. All Christians upon their death went directly either to heaven or hell, depending on whether God had vouchsafed to elect them to eternal life. Purgatory was declared to be an unscriptural imposture perpetrated by an avaricious Catholic clergy, and the consequent dissolution of the chantries and proscription of all related forms of intercession precipitated a momentous social and cultural realignment in the association of the living and the dead. Thus we are told that the Reformation served to redraw 'the boundaries of human community', to do away with the dead's status as an 'age group' in society, 'to sever the relationship between the dead and the living', to allow each generation to become 'indifferent to the spiritual fate of its predecessor'.[1]

Of course, no one supposes that the Reformation in England inaugurated a state of total collective amnesia in the living's response to the dead. On the contrary, the reign of Elizabeth, and even more so that of James I, witnessed an extraordinary efflorescence of commemoration: increasingly elaborate funerals, an unprecedented number of tombs and monuments placed in parish churches, the emergence of the printed funeral sermon as a popular literary genre.[2] Nonetheless, cultural historians have been inclined to locate these developments within fundamentally altered patterns of meaning. The demise of the imperative to pray for the dead resulted in a kind of 'secularization' or at least 'naturalization' of their memory; the deceased were contemplated as exemplifications of past virtue rather than as persons with whom any kind of continuing relationship could be envisaged. The commemorative culture of post-Reformation England is presented as profoundly retrospective in its outlook, its nodal points the articulation of social hierarchy and the celebration of secular achievement.[3]

It is the intention of this chapter to suggest ways in which supposedly more 'secular' habits of thinking about the dead continued to be shaded by a decidedly prospective interest in their 'estate' in the next life. In particular, the focus will be on a set of themes that intrigued the religious imagination of late sixteenth- and early seventeenth-century Protestant England: the ontological status of the dead in heaven, the nature of the 'society' they would partake of there, and the conditions under which the living would be reunited with the dead in the life to come. Despite a general recognition that the abolition of purgatory signals one of the most profound disjunctures between medieval and modern mentalities, there has not been much detailed examination of Elizabethan and Jacobean belief about the nature of the future life, or of the idioms in which perceptions of the condition of the departed there were expressed. I will argue that Protestant divines often found these issues problematic, but that both theological and pastoral imperatives obliged them to engage with them. Further, I will suggest that the manner in which these themes were articulated and negotiated was an important aspect of the reconfiguration of the cultural and emotional nexus binding the living to the dead in Reformation England, and thus of the Reformation's impact on society more generally. One of the findings will be that Elizabethan and Jacobean Protestantism, rather in spite of itself, was less impeccably dogmatic and pastorally inflexible, more open to selective appropriation by the laity, than some influential accounts would have us believe.[4]

I

The commemoration of the dead in pre-Reformation England had been posited on a model of reciprocal prayer between living and dead, of mutual exchanges between the members of a tripartite Church: militant, suffering and triumphant. Seeking the intercession of the saints, or praying for souls in purgatory, struck reformers of all hues as a derogation of the all-sufficient sacrifice of Christ, and their determination to fracture this reciprocity resulted in a radically curtailed conception of the sensibility and consciousness of the souls of the dead. A recurrent and insistent refrain was that the dead did not listen to the prayers of the living, indeed could not hear them; on their own account they had no knowledge of what transpired in the created world. The Elizabethan homily on prayer invoked patristic authority on this very point:

> [the departed] have so little knowledge of the secrets of the heart, that many of the ancient Fathers greatly doubt whether they know any thing at all, that is commonly done on earth. And albeit some think they do, yet St Augustine, a Doctor of great authority and also antiquity, hath this opinion of them; That they know no more what we do on earth, than we know what they do in heaven.[5]

To suppose that the dead could know the thoughts of the living was to make them gods.[6] It also defied common sense: the Puritan Thomas Cartwright mocked papists for believing 'small and low voices to be heard of creatures removed . . . from other infinite spaces'.[7] The Catholic exile Richard Smith, whose *Conference of the Catholike and Protestante Doctrine* (1631) often caricatured or misconstrued his theological opponents, was for once strikingly accurate when he affirmed that 'Protestants expressely say, that saints know not what we doe, that they heare not our praiers, perceave not our necessities, know not our estate'.[8]

That the dead were unaware of the condition of the living was an idea which appeared to have strong scriptural endorsement: Ecclesiastes 9.5 ('the dead know not any thing'); Isaiah 63.16 ('thou art our father, though Abraham be ignorant of us'). Awkwardly, however, there were other passages in the Bible suggesting that Abraham's ignorance might not be total. The parable of Dives and Lazarus (Luke 16.19–31) implied that Abraham knew of the actions of the rich man and the beggar in their lifetimes, as he also knew of Moses and the prophets who had come after him. Another passage in Luke's Gospel (15.10) stated that the angels rejoiced whenever a sinner repented on earth. There did not appear to be complete radio silence between this world and the next.

To account for this apparent anomaly, Protestant exegetes were again prepared to follow the lead of St Augustine: the dead have no knowledge of our actions while we are committing them, but (God permitting) may hear of them afterwards, either from souls newly arrived in heaven, or from the angels who were present on earth when the actions were done, and who travel back and forth between the two worlds as executors of God's justice and mercy. To concede such a possibility, thought George Wither, did not amount to 'anie ordinarie knowledge of our affaires' by the saints in heaven.[9] Not all Protestants, however, were comfortable with this rather mechanistic model of how news might be transmitted between earth and heaven, William Fulke remarking that here 'Augustine wandreth in his imaginations'.[10]

The fact that the dead were by the nature of the divine order unable to perceive the needs of the living was not, however, intended to betoken an intrinsic lack of charity on their part, an extinction of their enduring 'humanity'. In considering the doctrinally sensitive question of whether the dead prayed for the living, the leading Elizabethan Calvinist William Perkins allowed that the saints

> doe in generall pray for the church militant upon earth . . . I say *in generall,* because they praie not for the particular conditions and persons of men upon earth considering they neither know, nor see, nor hear us: neither can they tell what things are done upon earth.[11]

This seems to have been a broadly consensual position among Elizabethan and Jacobean divines: the saints could be expected to evince an inclusive concern for the welfare and salvation of the elect in the world, but they did not pursue individual cases.[12] The minimalist position was stated by William Whitaker: 'whether the martyrs and heavenly saints pray unto Christ for us or no, we know not: but certaine it is, that they are ignorant of those things we doe'.[13]

Some Protestants argued that to suppose the saints in heaven cognizant of our affairs was not merely an insult to the majesty of Christ, but an injury to the dead themselves, for how could they enjoy that blessed rest promised by the Scriptures if they were distracted by the strivings of the living? In a treatise on the parable of Dives and Lazarus, the Jacobean preacher Robert Horne dismissed the popish interpretation that Dives' request for Abraham to warn his brothers to mend their ways meant that

> the blessed Saints in heaven have care of their friends on earth; that is, in special and carnall manner of those friends whom they knew familiarly . . . to say that the godly in peace should be troubled particularly, or in speciall manner about their friends affayres below; what were it, but much to derogate from their true rest.[14]

Preaching in 1601 at the exequies of the young Lancashire gentlewoman Katherine Brettargh, William Leygh posed the question,

> May we think them at quiet whom the troublesome sturs of this world may vexe? I trow no, for doe but suppose, that the saints in heaven did behold the miseries heere on earth; Princes the subversion of their kingdomes; Noblemen of their houses; Gentlemen of their lands, line, and families; did fathers see the sinnes of their sonnes, and mothers the shame of their daughters . . . I say, if saints in heaven had a sense and feeling of these miseries, woes, and calamaties, small were their rest, little were their ease, and heaven were no hold for happiness.[15]

The Norwich minister Samuel Gardiner envisaged the dead

> without any further regard or reckoning, sleep[ing] supinely in their lockers, careless and senseless of secular affaires; whether there be peace or war; be the pestilence never so ragious, or the famine grievous . . . whether their posterity be in prosperity, or suffer adversity, all is one to them.[16]

The layman and moralist writer James Cole similarly believed that when we are dead 'our wives and children will then move us no more, then if wee never had loved them'.[17] A work promising *The Cure of the Feare of Death* by the Jacobean preacher Nicholas Byfield advised readers that 'when thou diest, all will be forgotten, there is no more remembrance of former things, nor shall there be any rememberance of things which are to come, with those that shall come after'. In Timothy Oldmayne's 1636 funeral sermon for the young Suffolk gentleman Edward Lewkenor, forgetfulness similarly becomes a defining condition:

> when a man is dead, hee remembreth no more the worke and labour of his hands . . . Hee knoweth not what hee hath done: and if you tell him, hee will not regard. Friend or foe are all one to him: neither doth he care, whether his sonnes be honourable, or of low degree.[18]

In such accounts, death is presented as a radical and transformative dissociation of affinity: the living are obliterated from the consciousness of the dead.

Such assertions were engendered primarily by the polemical urge to deny saintly intercession, yet there was also a consolatory aspect to them, in so far as they were designed to bring home to survivors the calm and peace characterizing the experience of the elect in the next life. Nonetheless, there are scattered echoes in the sources to suggest this was sometimes felt to be emotionally unsatisfactory, even among those of impeccable Protestant orthodoxy. Writing to Peter Martyr in March 1551 to describe the recent exequies of Martin Bucer, and the honour done to him by the scholars and townspeople of Cambridge, Sir John Cheke allowed himself to hope that 'if there be any perception by those who rest in Christ of the transactions of this earthly scene, [he] may rejoice in the fruit of the labours which he bestowed in this world below'.[19]

Some funeral sermons stressed the obliviousness of the dead, but others employed an affective language to suggest their continuing tenderness towards the living. Thus the dedicatory epistle to John Wall's 1623 sermon for the Oxford student John Stanhope encouraged his parents to imagine that 'hee behold you from the top of heaven, and seeme to speake unto your hearts in that sweet and gracious voice of our blessed Saviour on the Cross, Woman, behold thy sonne.[20] Preaching at the funeral of John Downe in 1631, George Hakewill imagined that 'many a good soule now a saint in heaven, did they understand our actions and desires, and withall could make knowne their conceits to us', would be eager to confess that Downe had been the instrument of their conversion.[21] Another early Stuart funeral sermon, originally preached at the funeral of the wife of the English ambassador in Constantinople, went further. It depicted the souls in heaven, not in a state of complete emotional detachment from the living, but actively concerned for their salvation and in lively anticipation of seeing them again:

> an infinite number of acquaintance expect us there: our parents, our brethren and sisters, our children, our kindred, our friends, that are alreadie secure of their own immortalities, but yet sollicitous for our safetie, what ioy, what comfort will it be to see, to imbrace them.[22]

Here the depiction of heaven involved, in some clear if unspecific sense, the reconstitution of earthly bonds of affinity and sociability.

II

This deeply comforting concept surfaced repeatedly in contemporary discussions of the afterlife, yet it was an issue which for some Protestants raised extremely vexatious questions. The paradox of attempting to say anything meaningful about society in heaven (perhaps the paradox of theology itself) was that theologians had to shape a discourse which made clear that what they were describing was not a mere sequel to or reconstruction of human companionship, while being able to bring to the task of description only familiar human concepts: knowledge, recognition, networks of affinity and association. It was a theological axiom, as well as a social and cultural 'fact', that the dead were 'persons' with a past, a present and a future (corresponding to their mortal life, their soul's abode in heaven and their expectation of resurrection). But were the modes in which they could express desire, experience consciousness, or exercise will, in any way comparable to those of living persons?

The literary scholar Robert N. Watson has claimed that Protestant theology

> by its particular emphasis on individual interiority, on the sinfulness of that interiority, and on the lack of any purgatorial process that could winnow out that sinfulness, must have made it virtually impossible to imagine satisfactorily the survival of full selfhood in heaven.[23]

This seems on the face of it too extreme an assessment. Protestantism taught there was a specific judgement on persons at the point of their death, and its insistence on 'degrees of glory' in the afterlife, where souls in heaven would receive rewards according to their merits, implicitly affirmed the idea of the preservation of individual identity beyond death.[24] Moreover, the doctrine of the resurrection of the body was entirely predicated upon the physical manifestation of an individuated existence for the elect in eternity.[25]

Nonetheless, it is undoubtedly the case that much of the language used to delineate the situation of the saints in heaven was more eloquent on their unity of purpose, and their conformity to the will of God, than on their existential disaggregation from the mass of their fellows. A consensus seemed to be, not that individual identity was extinguished in heaven, but that heaven was a perfectly corporate and non-hierarchical society where 'the happinesse of one is the happinesse of the whole, as the happinesse of the whole is the happinesse of every one'.[26] In the more mystical language of John Donne, 'all soules shall be so intirely knit together, as if all were but one soule, and God so intirely knit to every soule, as if there were as many Gods as soules'.[27]

There seems to be little scope here for the expression of 'personality' or the enjoyment of 'relationships' in the sense with which we are familiar with the terms. Many Protestant writers clearly envisaged the pre-eminent activity in heaven as being one of rapt contemplation and adoration of the Godhead, and which left little scope for any other association. The Devon minister John Preston believed that 'although the soule thorough death doeth not loose his faculties, notwithstanding she doth not exercise her operations. The actions of the godly after this life is a perpetuall fruition of eternall happinesse, put in the contemplation of divine glory'.[28] In striving for the metaphor which best captured this face-to-face exaltation of the deity, writers evoked the congregational psalm-singing characteristic of Protestant worship: 'their time shall bee spent in singing the hymnes of prayses to the harpe of glory'; 'singing praise to God with the whole Church'; 'singing our ditty Allelujah, the quire Angels and Saints'.[29] It is no surprise to discover that for some Puritans the most pleasing analogy was that of a perpetual sabbath.[30] Another characteristic note was an emphasis on the stilling of individual desires. 'In heaven', observed the Jacobean preacher John Bowle, 'there is *Desideriorum quies*, the verie center and quiet of desiring, where our desires shall not be satiated, but they shall be *satisfied*'.[31] Christ had taught that there was to be no marriage in heaven; indeed some commentators denied that souls possessed any distinction of sex or gender.[32] The poignant vow of the marriage ceremony – 'till death us do part' – was glossed by some commentators to mean that there would be no companionship of former spouses in the next life. All in all, the English evidence broadly endorses the intuition of Colleen McDannell and Bernhard Lang that the Reformation preferred a 'theocentric model' of heaven.[33]

On the other hand, most authorities did not mean to give the impression that blessed souls were rapt in the contemplation of God to the extent that they were oblivious of the presence of others: the dominant model for activity in heaven was that of congregational worship, not private devotion. The question of whether we shall know one another in heaven was frequently posed, and invariably it was answered in the affirmative. The teaching of Scripture appeared to be definitive on this: Adam knew Eve in Paradise; the apostles recognized Moses and Elijah during the Transfiguration; Jesus promised that the faithful would sit down with Abraham, Isaac and Jacob in the kingdom of heaven; the rich man knew Lazarus in hell. This being so, concluded Lewis Bayly, 'much more shall the Elect know one another in heaven.'[34]

Such mutual recognition did not necessarily imply, however, any priority to the resumption of past relationships. The saints in heaven would know each other irrespective of whether they had ever met in this world: a number of accounts stressed the joys of continual conversation with saints, angels and prominent biblical figures, without much interest in the renewal of earthly bonds of sociability.[35] Indeed, some early seventeenth-century writers explicitly contrasted the social networks of this world with those of the next. In the view of Edward Vaughan, one of the reasons which should make people willing to die was

> of our companie; as when we change the societie, fellowship, and companie of men, for the company and societie of Angels; the company of whoremongers, drunkards, liers, swearers, oppressors, and such like, for the company of the saints; the company of children on earth, for the company of children in heaven, the company of husband or wife, for the company of Iesus Christe himself.[36]

To James Cole, the exchange seemed similarly straightforwardly beneficial: 'if heere wee depart from our earthly parents, we are entertained there of *our Heavenly father*. If here wee leave our chiefest friends and kindred, wee meete there with our brethren in Christ.'[37]

Some theologians, in fact, displayed a distinct unease about the anticipation of joyous reunions with the dear departed. William Fulke insisted that the love of the saints 'is not now carnal and special towards their friends in the flesh, brethren, kinsfolkes and other, but spiritual and generall toward all the elect of God'.[38] In the opinion of William Perkins, the question 'whether men shall knowe one another after this life or no' was 'oftener mooved by such as are ignorant, then by them that have knowledge'. He confirmed there would be recognition, 'but whether they shall know one other after an earthly manner, as to say, this man was my father, this was mine uncle, this my teacher &c. the word of god saith nothing: and therefore I will be silent'.[39]

Perkins' agnosticism over whether relationships among the elect included any awareness of consanguinity was reiterated by Samuel Gardiner, who regarded the question as 'curious', advising 'let our care be to knowe whether wee shal come to heaven, then to know whether we shall know one another in heaven'.[40] Another Calvinist luminary, Robert Bolton, expressed similar misgivings. While Bolton was in no doubt that there would be 'familiar acquaintance' in the life to come, he was also worried that the topic encouraged 'the curious *Quaere* of carnall people . . . feeding falsly their presumptuous conceipts with golden dreames, and vaine hopes of many future imaginary felicities in the world to come'. 'Our mutual knowledge one of another in heaven', Bolton insisted, 'shall not be in outward and worldly respects, but divine and spirituall.'[41] In such qualifications we encounter a familiar Puritan anxiety about the 'country divinity' of the common people, in their expectations of life after death looking merely for the reconstitution and amplification of the good and familiar things of this life, rather than reflecting on the utter transcendence of God and his kingdom.[42]

III

The issue of reunion with the dead was nonetheless a highly poignant one, and in addressing it Protestant writings were by no means univocal. In many pastoral works, consolatory treatises on death and printed funeral sermons, theological caveats of the sort espoused by Perkins or Bolton were largely missing. Bolton may have been concerned about the 'presumptuous conceipts' of the hoi polloi, but, according to his biographer Edward Bagshawe, as he lay on his deathbed he summoned his wife 'and bad her make no doubt but shee should meete him againe in heaven'.[43] It was a cliché of pious literature and of funeral sermons that the dead had 'gone before us', and we would follow after.[44] Theologically questionable though it may have been, preachers at Elizabethan and Jacobean funerals habitually presumed to familiarity with God's decree of predestination and declared the deceased to be a blessed soul in heaven.[45] They also encouraged their auditors to hope that they would meet with them again: as Richard Stock put it in his 1614 sermon for Lord Harington, 'lead the same life with him, and you shal soone enioy his holy and comfortable presence'.[46]

Some preachers, like Stock, envisaged a reunion of souls in heaven immediately consequent upon the death of the surviving friend, spouse or child. Many other divines, however, preferred to imagine a meeting-again which would take place at the end of time, when the Lord returned in glory, and the bodies of the dead rose from their graves to rejoin their souls upon a new earth. According to John Rogers, 'then we shall see and know one another, the King his subjects, the Pastor his people, the Parents, their children, the Husband his wife, the Master his servants, and they him'.[47] A similarly joyous scene was evoked by John Andrewes:

> fathers and mothers, husbands and wives, maisters and servants, brothers and sisters, parents and children, neighbours and friends, all shall meete together: what cryes and shouts will there be for ioy? What clapping of hands and sweete embracements one of another?[48]

John Donne reflected that 'though we part at divers daies, and by divers waies, here, yet wee shall all meet at one place, and at one day . . . the day of the glorious *Resurrection*'.[49]

Conversely, it was taught that one of the horrors awaiting the reprobate at the Day of Judgement was that they would be pulled from the presence of parents, spouses and friends 'who shall then justly and deservedly abandon them with all detestation and derision'.[50] The centrality of the Last Judgement and the resurrection of the body is a striking feature of the theology of Elizabethan and early Stuart Protestantism, and is of considerable significance for how that religious culture constructed its view of the afterlife, and articulated its relationship with the dead.

In the course of a funeral sermon in 1585, the Puritan minister Thomas Sparke broke off from his discussion of rewards in heaven to make clear that 'I would not have it hereupon inferred, that my meaning is, that soules departed in faith have straight their consummation & ful crown of glorie, that is prepared for them. For I know that shal not be before the general resurrection'.[51] Some years later, the Jacobean preacher Samuel Crooke tempered his fulsome account of the joyous state of elect souls with the tantalizing reflection that 'all this is but an *interim* of blessednes, a *morsell* to keepe the soule in appetite, till the great *day of the restitution of all things*'.[52]

This was fully consistent with a Reformed theology which envisaged the salvation of the elect as a process leading from initial justification, through sanctification to ultimate glorification. The justified sinner was sanctified in this lifetime to begin to conform himself or herself to the image of God, but this process was only finally consummated when the soul of the saint was reunited with its glorified body.[53] Thus John Denison's account of the steps of the godly into glory (starting with their sense of assurance in this life) could completely ignore the interim stage of enjoyment of heaven without the body.[54] Calvin himself depicted the post-mortem condition of the elect as one of happy anticipation: 'the souls of the righteous, after their warfare is ended, obtain blessed rest where in joy they wait for the fruition of promised glory'.[55] William Perkins was of the same mind:

> soules being once in heaven, remaine there till the last day of iudgement, where they partly magnifie the Name of God, and partly doe waite, and pray for the consummation of the kingdome of glorie, and full felicitie in body and soule.[56]

This of course begged the question posed in Elnathan Parr's catechism of 1614: 'if the soules of the Elect goe presently after their death to heaven, and the soules of the Reprobate to hell, what neede a generall Iudgement?' Parr's own answer was a rather juridical one:

> there must be a general Iudgement notwithstanding, both that the iustnesse of such particular Iudgement may bee made more manifest to the glorie of God, and that the whole man, consisting of body and soule, may receive the due reward.[57]

Other Protestant writers, however, preferred to emphasize the 'natural appetite and desire' the soul had to be reunited to the body.[58]

There was a fine line to be trod here. The condition of the elect in heaven might be considered imperfect by God's standards, but most Protestants had no wish to imply that it involved any actual sorrow or poignant longing on the part of souls who were still separated from their mortal bodies. In a Jacobean dialogue between the flesh and the spirit, flesh asks 'Doth not the soule then long for the body, seeing it knoweth it is rotten in the cold ground?' The spirit replies that souls rest in a place where there is no unquietness or desire, looking forward to the resurrection without sorrow, persuaded that no mischance can befall their bodies 'but that they pleasantly and softly sleep and rest' until rising again.[59]

This imagery of sleep is highly significant, and pervades the Protestant literature on death and commemoration of the dead to an extraordinary extent. Reformers were drawn to it for a number of compelling reasons. In the first place, it was or seemed to be profoundly scriptural. Both the Old and New Testaments abounded with references to the dead sleeping in the Lord.[60] The concept of the dead sleeping or resting was also believed to be inimical to the popish concept of purgatory: how could the blessed dead be said to be at rest if they were tormented with purgatory fire? To conceive of death and the state of being dead as a sleep was also regarded as a comforting doctrine for the dying and the bereaved. The congruences seemed to make the analogy a perfect one: 'nothing more like death than sleep;' 'nothing more like to the grave, then our beds;' 'nothing better resembleth death then our sleep.'[61] Indeed, it may be a measure of how deeply embedded in English religious culture the symbolism of sleep had become that by the 1630s a funeral sermon could feel obliged to labour the rather obvious point that people should not imagine death as 'properly to be asleep'; that death was called sleep 'in regard onely of a kinde of similitude and proportion that is betwixt them.'[62]

The notion of death as sleep had enormous utility as an instrument of pious consolation, particularly in the literature of *ars moriendi*, and in the printed funeral sermon. It was constantly reiterated that the godly should not fear to die, nor should their loved ones mourn excessively for them, since, to the godly, death was but a sleep.[63] According to Samuel Gardiner, the thought of the dead merely having put off their clothes and gone to bed allowed us to 'sucke comfort from the iuyce of this grape, against the bitter death of such, as while they lived, were most deare and neere unto us.'[64] In his *Anatomie of Mortalitie*, George Strode remarked that Scripture's designations of death as bed, peace, rest, sleep was for 'the singular comfort of all Gods children.'[65] The associations religious writers applied to the condition of the dead revolved around concepts of rest from wearisome labour, physical comfort, exemption from trouble and cares, refreshment and new starts. The frequency and enthusiasm with which the typology of sleep was adduced in these contexts attests to the importance of sleeping as a socially and culturally constructed experience in early modern England, a theme which has now been ably explored by Sasha Handley.[66]

However, for Protestants to make sleep the dominant image for death was not, in theological terms, an entirely risk-free strategy. To exhort the faithful to envisage their death as a falling-asleep might encourage them to give credence to the doctrine of 'soul-sleeping', the idea that the souls of the dead remained completely devoid of consciousness until the Last Judgement itself. Despite some early flirtations, mainstream English Protestantism had comprehensively repudiated this notion in the mid-Tudor period, largely due to its association with Anabaptism, the Edwardian articles of 1553 pronouncing that 'the souls of them that depart this life do neither die with the bodies, nor sleep idly'.[67] The article was withdrawn from the Thirty-Nine Articles promulgated in 1563, but a number of authors of death treatises and funeral sermons continued to take sideswipes at the 'sleepy-heads', and to emphasize that the scriptural promises of sleep related to the body only and not to the soul.[68] The etymology of the Greek-derived word 'cemetery', it was often rather pedantically noted, indicated a dorter or sleeping place.[69] To its exponents, the metaphor of the sleep of the body was a powerful one because it pointed to a fundamental Christian verity. According to Bullinger, it was to show that the body was not extinguished by death, that 'holy men are said in the scriptures to sleep, not to die, that thereby the mystery of the resurrection of our flesh may be signified'.[70] A Jacobean funeral sermon by the Devon pastor Richard Carpenter reached a triumphal yet conventional conclusion: 'it is but a sleep which is mis-called death, his grave is his bed, and he shall awake as sure as he lay downe, yea more fresh and glorious in the great day of resurrection'.[71]

IV

The doctrine of the resurrection of the body has, of course, always been a cornerstone of Christian faith, but it looks particularly prominent in the mindset of early modern English Protestantism.[72] To reformers of all types it was axiomatic, for example, that while funeral exequies and burial practices were of no spiritual help to the deceased, decent burial was meaningful as a token of faith in the resurrection.[73] The resurrected body itself exercised the imagination of Protestant theologians to a considerable degree.[74] Yet despite the enthusiasm with which they approached the subject, Protestant writers in the early seventeenth century regularly admitted that of all the doctrines of the faith, the resurrection of the body was the most difficult for people to accept, a consequence of 'our naturall incredulitie, and distrust in this point'.[75] To coin an unfortunate phrase, the devil was in the detail. Protestant writers on the Last Judgement imagined doubters rehearsing the kind of hypothetical objections familiar to their medieval scholastic predecessors: what if a man were eaten by a wolf, the wolf by a lion, the lion by birds, and the birds by other men; what of those eaten by cannibals?[76] The multiplication of detailed, practical questions about the mechanics of the operation was Satan's preferred strategy to make it 'bee thought a meere *dreame* and *fable*'.[77] Just as with the issue of post-mortem reunions, there was a concern in some quarters that ordinary people would miss the point, approaching questions about the resurrection in a grossly material way.

In a good many orthodox Protestant accounts of the life to come, there was a distinct emphasis on deferred gratification, a privileging of the imagery of sleep and of the joys to be experienced by the resurrected. Here was the ultimate revelation of God's majesty and infinite power. Rather less interest was displayed in the intermediate state, except in so far as reformers were concerned to steer a course between alternative egregious errors: the Scylla of popish purgatory, and the Charybdis of soul-sleeping and mortalism.[78] The obsession of the unreformed Church with nego-tiating the counterfeit demands of purgatory had engendered a crude foreshortening of the eternal perspective of Christianity. Many Protestant reformers refocused their own hopes on the end of time, an end which some at least did not believe to be so far away.[79] A more difficult question to assess is that of the extent to which this attitude took root in English religious culture more generally.

In his study of wills from sixteenth-century Madrid, Carlos Eire reflects on 'the nearly universal tendency of Western Christendom' to overlook the orthodox teaching that Christ redeemed the whole human person, body and soul:

> little mention is ever made of the promised resurrection of the body . . . It is the soul – and *only* the soul – that is created and redeemed by the blood of the Lord. The body simply dissolves into the earth and disappears.[80]

Mutatis mutandis, this characterization would seem to work just about as well for the testamentary evidence from later Reformation England. Ralph Houlbrooke's study of wills across the period 1558–1660 led him to conclude that 'the great majority of preambles were concerned with the destination of the soul rather than the ultimate fate of the body'. A rela-tively small number of testators expressed hopes of resurrection, and still fewer made explicit reference to the reunion of soul and body.[81]

Wills, of course, were concerned primarily with the immediate disposal of the goods of the deceased, and by analogy their spiritual concerns were with the imminent requirements of body and soul. One might expect the longer-term view to be more evident on tombs and monuments, struc-tures which their patrons and builders hoped would stand until the Last Judgement. Inscriptions and epitaphs which alluded to the resurrection began to appear with some regularity on brasses and stone monuments in Elizabeth's reign, particularly from the 1570s.[82] After 1600, the subject started to impinge on monumental sculpture. A handful of monuments in the second and third decades of the seventeenth century showed the body of the deceased rising from the grave, a fashion which reached its artistic apogee in Nicholas Stone's famous 1631–2 monument to John Donne in St Paul's Cathedral.[83]

Throughout this period, however, tombs and epitaphs which sought to focus the onlooker's attention on the resurrection to come were greatly outnumbered by those asserting that the soul of the deceased was dwelling in heaven now. Perhaps the most common formulation was that while the body lay here in the earth, the soul had gone to heaven.[84] Other epitaphs referred to the deceased being lifted into heaven,[85] called to heaven,[86] entering heaven's harbour,[87] going to God,[88] appearing before God in glory,[89] seated in glory,[90] crowned with a glorious crown,[91] inheriting heaven,[92] living with Christ for ever,[93] dwelling 'in endlesse blisse',[94] reigning with Christ and the just,[95] 'entombed in Abram's brest',[96] perpetually rejoicing in the company of saints,[97] 'sweetly paradis'd in Eternity',[98] or simply living or being with God or in heaven.[99]

Epitaphs which looked towards the reunion of loved ones after this life occasionally did so in the context of the resurrection; more commonly they envisaged a meeting in heaven immediately after the death of the survivor.[100] Sometimes these showed scant regard for the biblical teaching that there would be no marriage in the life to come. The brass of the widow Elizabeth Alfraye at Battle in Sussex (1590) referred to her soul seeking out that of her husband 'among the saints above / And there in endless blysse enioye her long desired love'. In the inscription to Dorothy Pytt at Ombury, Shropshire (1630), death divorces her from her husband, leaving him to grieve 'Till death, by striking him, weds her againe'.[101] These monuments do not suggest an outlook which regarded the soul's sojourn in heaven as merely an interim and provisional anticipation of full blessedness, nor one which consigned the dead to a realm beyond the limits of human knowledge, love or longing. As we have seen, the clergy of the Church of England did not always discourage these deeply human hopes and yearnings.

V

To return to our point of departure: blanket assertions that the English Reformation 'broke the bonds' linking the living to the dead are likely to obscure subtle and fluid processes of religio-cultural adaption and accommodation. Without any doubt, the abolition of purgatory was a huge cultural watershed, and other shifts of emphasis in the morphology of the afterlife served to reinforce the pre-eminent result of that abolition: a heightened sense of distance and separation between this world and the next, of the strangeness and 'otherness' of the dead.

Yet at the same time these developments created their own counter-currents: an impulse to affirm that the beloved dead were saints in heaven, and to express the expectation of meeting them again. Paradoxically, an insistence on the inability of the dead to know or care about living relatives may have added poignancy to the theme of post-mortem reunion. These themes found expression in diverse ways. Some theologians downplayed the immediate beatitude of the dead to concentrate upon the joys of all the elect following the Last Judgement. Other sources demonstrate greater concern with the society the saints would enjoy in the 'intermediate state'. The intention in this chapter has not been to suggest a crude dichotomy of 'elite' and 'popular' religion over these issues. All the sources available, from theological treatises to funeral sermons, epitaphs and wills, pertain to a fairly restricted social group. Rather, I have attempted to suggest that Protestant eschatology in the Reformation period had to function as an applied science, addressing legitimate concerns about the nature of life beyond the grave. In later sixteenth- and early seventeenth-century England, profoundly theological absolutes – the absence of purgatory, the inability of the living to ameliorate the condition of the dead – were necessarily processed in intimate and pastoral contexts. The ways in which this took place suggest a more complex and creative pattern of cultural change emanating from the Protestant reconfiguration of the afterlife than has often hitherto been recognized.

Part 2

ANGELS, GHOSTS AND FAIRIES: SPIRITS IN THE HUMAN WORLD

6

Angels around the deathbed: variations on a theme in the English art of dying

The conjunction in the last couple of decades between the new social history and the historiography of the English Reformation has had several happy outcomes. One of these has been the promotion of death (or 'mortality studies') to the status of a serious topic of historical enquiry. Thanks to the work of David Cressy, Eamon Duffy, Ralph Houlbrooke and numerous others, the history of death in the Reformation period has veritably come alive in recent years, and we have begun to recognize the importance of the deathbed as a seminal site of cultural and religious change.[1]

The theological revolution which in the mid-sixteenth century abolished the doctrine of purgatory and introduced the doctrine of predestination had immense consequences, both for the symbolic representation of death and for its practical management. It led, depending on one's point of view, either to sadly impoverished ritual support for the dying, or to enhanced opportunities for men and women to make inspiring public witness to their faith. But we have been made aware of continuities too. Above all, a persistent preoccupation with the importance of 'good death'. From the 1550s onwards, a flourishing genre of Protestant, and often distinctly godly, prescriptive literature adapted and transformed a pre-existing body of writing on the making of a good death, the *ars moriendi* or art of dying.[2] The recent scholarship on these themes has immeasurably improved our understanding of the ways in which religious reform was intended to touch the lives of ordinary people, and the extent to which it may actually have done so.

Yet there is a significant thematic gap in the current literature on the reform of the deathbed. Angels are ubiquitous in the mortuary culture of late medieval England, as of Western Europe generally, but Reformation historians have not sought to ask what happened to them when the theology of death underwent its Protestant makeover in the later Tudor and early Stuart decades. Even Ralph Houlbrooke's magisterial treatment of the theme in his *Death, Religion and the Family in England* has nothing to say on either the persistence or demise of angels in the Protestant *ars moriendi*.

One might suspect, of course, that there is no great issue or mystery here. Along with the invocation of saints, the anointing of the sick, and the use of crucifix, candles and holy water, angels simply had no role to play in the reformed understanding of what constituted a good death, and vanished from the cultural scene. As I will demonstrate, however, this is far from being the case. Despite the overhaul of liturgies for the visitation of the sick, and burial of the dead, in the prayer books of 1549, 1552 and 1559, and the subsequent ongoing revision of prescriptive advice about how to die well, angels continued to play a significant role in the imaginative representation and devotional management of death in post-Reformation England. Understanding the ways in which they did so not only restores a missing piece of the puzzle, as we observe reformers attempting to reassemble an acceptable and meaningful pattern from the fragmentation of traditional attitudes towards death. It also helps to illuminate in a broader sense the acculturation of Protestant reform in the first century of the English Reformation.

I

In his admirable survey of medieval angelology, David Keck has observed that 'perhaps the most common of angelic motifs in medieval Christianity was the presence of angels at the moment of death and in the life of the soul after its separation from the body'.[3] Evidence from late fifteenth- and early sixteenth-century England undoubtedly supports the contention. Two broad themes emerge from the sources. First, there was an expectation that angels would hover around the bed of the dying person, to strengthen their faith and help them resist the wiles of the devil. Second, after death had taken place, angels would convey the soul of the deceased to its resting place in the next life, a conception which derived ultimately from the parable of the rich man and Lazarus in St Luke's Gospel (16.19–31). When the beggar Lazarus died, 'portaretur ab angelis in sinum Abrahae' ('he was carried by angels to Abraham's bosom').

Mortuary angels manifested themselves both in the official liturgical forms for the care of the dying and commendation of the deceased, and in the pious meditations on them which issued in copious numbers from the early printing press. The medieval office for the visitation of the sick involved the priest praying that God would visit the ill person, as he visited Peter's mother-in-law, the centurion's servant, 'et Tobiam, et Saram, per sanctam angelum tuum Raphaelem' ('and Tobias and Sarah, by your holy angel Raphael'). The commendation of the soul in *articulo mortis*, which began the rite of extreme unction, called on Michael, Gabriel, Raphael, and all angels and archangels to intercede, invoking by name the traditional nine orders of angels. A further set of commendations was recited as soon the person had died: 'Subvenite sancti Dei, occurrite angeli Domini, suscipientes animam ejus. Offerentes eam in conspectu altissimi' ('Come to his aid, saints of God, meet him, angels of the Lord, receiving his soul, offering it in the sight of the Most High'). 'Suscipiat te Christus qui vocavit te, et in sinum Abrahae angeli deducant te' ('May Christ, who has called you, receive you, and may angels lead you to the bosom of Abraham'). These texts, *Subvenite* and *Suscipiat*, were reiterated throughout the extended funeral liturgy – at the preparing of the body, at its lifting and carrying to church, at the entry into the church, during the funeral office and as responses at the absolution. They were supplemented by other texts invoking angelic protection, including the deeply moving antiphon *In Paradisum*:

> In paradisum deducant te angeli in suum conventum, suscipiant te martyres et perducant te in civitatem sanctam Hierusalem. Chorus angelorum te suscipiat, et in sinu Abrahae collocet, ut cum Lazaro quondam paupere aeternam habeas requiem. (May the angels lead you into paradise in their assembly, may the martyrs receive you, and bring you into the holy city, Jerusalem. May the choir of angels receive you, and care for you in Abraham's bosom, and with Lazarus, once a beggar, may you have eternal rest.)[4]

Yet the central importance of angels to the successful negotiation of death is best seen not so much in the liturgy itself, as in the set of related texts going under the generic title of *ars moriendi*. These derived from an early fifteenth-century original, composed by the chancellor of Paris, Jean Gerson, and intended as a commentary on the *Ordo Visitandi*.[5]

Such handbooks on the art of dying enjoyed an extraordinary diffusion in fifteenth- and early sixteenth-century Europe. They portrayed the deathbed as the site of a cosmic struggle between forces of good and evil, a place where angels would encourage the dying person to overcome the temptations directed at him or her by the devil and his minions, and would contend with Satan's forces for custody of the soul. The popular appeal of the *ars moriendi* was undoubtedly strengthened by its sets of accompanying woodcuts, illustrating the various temptations to which the soul of the dying person would be subject, and sometimes depicting angels and devils in dramatic confrontations with each other across the enclosed space of the death chamber. In one such woodcut an angel assuages *moriens'* temptation to despair by assuring him that his sins are capable of forgiveness and reminding him of notorious sinners who had found sanctity and salvation in the Lord: St Peter (with the cock betokening his disowning of Christ), St Mary Magdalene, the good thief, St Paul, thrown from his horse by the blinding light of the Damascus road. A cowering demon bewails the expected victory being torn from his grasp.[6]

Such images encapsulated a central theme of the text. In the weakened state of the dying, the devil will come to 'lay before you the multytude of your sins'.[7] *Moriens* would be assaulted with five diabolical temptations of unprecedented force: against faith, towards despair, against patience, towards spiritual pride and towards an excessive concern with the things of this world. But to counter these, 'God gheuys to man 5 good inspuracyons send by ye angels for to resyst'. In delivering their 'inspyracyon and good monysyng', the angels address the sick person as 'my freynd', a poignant demonstration of their intimate fellow-feeling for suffering humanity.[8]

The collaboration of angels could be expected, but it should also be requested. Caxton's 1490 abridgement of the *ars moriendi* encouraged the protagonist at the point of death to

> calle on the holy angellys in sayeng, ye spirytes of heven angels moche gloryous, I byseche you that ye woll be assystete wyth me that now bigynneth to departe and that ye delyuer me myghtily from the awaytes and fallaces of my aduersaryes.

There was a special appeal to the guardian angel, 'my leder and my good angel wyche by our Lord art deputed to be my warden and keper'. It is he who, by implication at least, delivers the 'inspirations' and appears in the woodcuts of several *ars moriendi* texts.[9]

A particular role too was envisaged for the archangel Michael. The idea of a deathbed contest between angels and demons, visible only to the dying themselves, had scriptural roots in the epistle of Jude, verse 9, where Michael is described contending with the devil over the body of Moses. This helps to account for depictions of Michael in late medieval culture as the archetypal saint of the deathbed.[10] Those around the bedside were instructed to pray:

> Saynt Mychael, archaungel of God, socoure us now to fore the ryght hye iudge. O champyon inuyncyble, be thou present now and assyst to this, N. our brother, whiche strongly laboureth toward his ende, and defende hym myghtyly from the dragon infernal.

Michael was urged also to 'benygnely and swetely receyue his soule in to thy ryghte holy bosome . . . brynge hym in the place of refressynge of peas and reste'.[11] The successful accomplishment of such hopes is illustrated in the final block of the woodcut series, the soul issuing forth from the mouth of the expiring Christian into the arms of a waiting angel, to the consternation of devils robbed of their prey.[12]

Such devotions spilled out from the *ars moriendi* itself into the prayer books and primers of the late Middle Ages, texts which are replete with prayers calling on the guardian angel to be present at the hour of death and manifesting a special devotion to the archangel Michael as the weigher of souls. One prayer 'to the proper angel', from a 1531 Sarum primer, called on the guardian angel 'et post hanc miseram et caducam vitam perduc animam meam ad aeternam felicitatem' ('after this miserable and fallen life to lead my soul to eternal bliss'). Another prayer in a manuscript collection invoked the guardian 'at the hour of my deth be present, that my gostly enemy in me haue noo power. And after brynge me to the blysse, where euer with the I may lyue and prayse our saviour'.[13]

Medieval prayers for angelic assistance could manifest a tendency to slip across into overtly instrumental incantations for angelic protection.[14] The compilers of prescriptive guides about dying sometimes sought to impress on their readers that the effectual aid of the angels could not simply be taken for granted. In a popular text printed by Wynkyn de Worde entitled *The Deynge creature*, a man facing the summons of death remonstrates with his good angel:

> where be ye now? Me thynketh ye sholde be here now and answer for me, for the drede of death does troubleth me so that I can not answere for my selfe; here is my bad aungell redy and is one of my chefe accusers with legyons of fendes with hyme.

But the good angel refuses to speak up for him, protesting that during his life he had done everything in his power to turn him away from sin, but had found 'your natural inclynacyon more dysposed to be rewled by your bad aungell than by me'. In a telling reminder of the late medieval hierarchies of grace and divine favour, the Virgin eventually intercedes on the man's behalf.[15]

There was further food for thought in one of the sermons of the popular compilation of saints' lives, *The Golden Legend*. Sinners would discover that at the Day of Judgement, their guardian angel would be one of the witnesses called to testify, 'and the angel knowing everything he has done, will bring testimony against him'.[16] Such tableaux of the imagination were intended to remind Christians that at the hour of death, as throughout life, the angels cooperated with, but did not substitute for, human effort and soteriological free will.[17] In the last moments of life, when (so the wood-cuts strongly implied) normally invisible spiritual forces would manifest themselves perceptibly to the dying person, men and women were drawn with transfigured intensity into the fierce (but ultimately unequal) super-natural warfare which had rumbled on throughout their earthly lives. Any suggestion that they were now become mere spectators of the struggle waged between two otherworldly forces is wide of the mark.[18] Angels, like the other supernatural helpers, the saints, were both citizens and symbols of a single Christian society, encompassing earth and heaven. Their pres-ence and role at the deathbed encapsulated the Church's understanding of salvation: the limitless capacity of divine offer, and the absolute necessity of human response.

II

In all of this, there would seem to be little that the Protestant Reformation of the sixteenth century might want to preserve, and much that it would instinctively abhor. The doctrine of justification by faith alone, and the extrapolation from it of a doctrine of double predestination, which became normative for the English Church from the mid-sixteenth century onwards, rendered nonsensical the idea of the deathbed as a place of final ordeal where salvation could be won or lost. In mature Protestant soteri-ology, the grace of God was simply irresistible: the 'elect' could not fall away at the last moment, and did not require a panoply of ritual support to help them seize an offer of salvation which it lay in their power to refuse. In the course of the Tudor Reformations, therefore, the elaborate 'last rites' of the medieval Catholic Church were radically curtailed, and the process of dying was reconceived as an opportunity for giving expression to the effectual faith of a life well lived.[19] The clergy, neighbours and kin clustered around the deathbed were no longer expected to 'commend' the departed soul to its maker, nor to offer prayers in order to speed its progress through a purgatory which the articles of the Church had declared to be 'a fond thing, vainly feigned, and grounded upon no warrant of scripture'.[20]

Instead they were to seek to strengthen the faith of the departing, and to expect to be edified by them in their turn. The invocation of angels, so central to the Catholic 'management' of the deathbed, had no place in this schema. Directing prayers to angels, as to saints, rather than to Christ alone, was anathema to all shades of Protestant opinion.[21] The very existence of the traditional recipient of much of that prayer, the individual guardian angel, was doubted by many Protestants.[22] More generally, the ways that pre-Reformation approaches to dying articulated the wider cult of the angels seemed to exemplify many of the most egregious aspects of popular religious culture – a popular religious culture that was the most conspicuous casualty of the official English Reformation in its first phases. Angels are remarkable by their absence in two 'humanist' forays into the *ars moriendi* genre, published in England in the mid-1530s.[23]

Yet as scholars such as Alexandra Walsham and Laura Sangha have shown, English Protestant attitudes towards angels in the later sixteenth and early seventeenth centuries were anything but straightforward.[24] Unlike so many other props of medieval mortuary ritual, the care of humans by angels appeared to have sound biblical foundations. Angels were defined, in a text extremely popular among Protestant writers (Heb. 1.14), as 'ministering spirits, sent forth to minister for them who shall be heirs of salvation'. When might such ministry be more needful than when the heirs of salvation lay in the agonies of death? Intuition suggests, and the sources happily confirm, a potential for modulation between distaste and unease on the one hand, and enthusiasm and excitement on the other, an oscillation that was characteristic of Protestant approaches to ministering angels in general, and to angels around the deathbed in particular.

The pattern starts to become apparent if we turn to examine a set of liturgical and para-liturgical texts, the prayer books and primers produced in the mid-Tudor decades as successors to the *Horae* so lovingly described by Eamon Duffy.[25] Invocations of saints Michael, Gabriel and Raphael, ubiquitous in the Sarum primers, survived into the litany of the English primer of 1549, but no further.[26] By contrast, all the Tudor books of common prayer invited intending communicants to join 'therefore with angels and archangels' in praise of the 'holy, holy, holy Lord', a vernacular rendition of the way the *Sanctus* prayer had been prefaced in the pre-Reformation mass. Meanwhile, the resilience of Michaelmas as a marker of the agricultural, legal and academic year was matched by the retention of the feast of St Michael and All Angels in the official calendar. A resplendent collect for this day petitioned that 'they which always do thee service in heaven, may by thy appointment succour and defend us in earth'.[27]

The extent to which angels were envisaged as having a particular and distinctive ministry to the sick and dying is, however, a more elusive theme in these texts. The 1549 Order for the Visitation of the Sick, in a virtual straight translation from the corresponding passage in the Sarum rite, directed the minister to say: 'Visit him, O Lord, as thou didst visit Peter's wife's mother and the Captain's servant. And as thou preservedst Thobie and Sara by thy Angel from danger . . .' Yet in 1552 and subsequently, the reference to Toby and the angel (from an 'apocryphal' book of Scripture) was dropped.[28] The burial services of 1549, 1552 and 1559 included no mention of angels, and neither did the prayers 'to be said at the hour of death' in any of the Edwardian or Elizabethan primers. These acknowledged the need for aid against 'al the assaultes of the deueyll', but directed prophylactic attention solely to the Passion of Christ.[29]

Yet the marginalization of angels from their accustomed role of providing succour to the dying was not quite complete in these sources. The primer of 1553 contained a remarkable prayer 'For the help of God's holy Angels', reprinted in Thomas Becon's 1558 *Pomander of Prayer*, and in the primers of 1560 and 1568. This text acknowledged that 'an infinite number of wicked angels . . . without ceasing seek my destruction'. But against them God could be asked to send 'thy blessed and heavenly Angels, which may pitch their tents round about me, and so deliver me from their tyranny'. Thus Christians might 'with a joyful heart say: Death, where is thy sting? Hell, where is thy victory?' An additional prayer 'for the health of the bodye' in the primer of 1568 noted how the soul is constantly vexed with wicked assaults of the devil and is always in danger of being overcome by its enemies 'were it not preserved of thy goodnesse by the ministery and service doing of thy holy angels'.[30]

As Duffy has demonstrated, the Elizabethan primers were remarkably conservative texts in all sorts of ways, and it might be tempting to regard such emphases on angelic conflict with the devil as mere residues, random traces of a decaying religious culture.[31] A more pertinent question for our purposes is whether these themes made any impression on the extremely vibrant literary genre of the post-Reformation *ars moriendi*. Examination of an extensive sample of these works reveals an interestingly complex patterning. A handful of treatises, such as John More's *A lively anatomie of death* (1596) or William Cowper's *A defiance to death* (1610), simply made no reference whatever to angels in connection with the deathbed.[32] The Jacobean writer John Moore's *A mappe of mans mortalitie* mentioned them only to warn against trusting in the merits of angels and saints: 'if thou cry to Angels, they cannot comfort thee'.[33]

Such reticence was, however, the exception to prove the rule. At the very least, most writers gave due prominence to the biblical evidence that after this life, angels would bring the souls of the saved into the bosom of Abraham. As William Perkins put it, this was the moment when 'the body goes to the earth, and the soule is caried by the angels into heaven.[34] In a section on heaven in his 1629 work *Of Death a true description*, James Cole informed readers: 'On what maner our soules get thither, we may observe by the fore-named *Lazarus*, who was carried thither by the ministrie of Angels.'[35] Such laconic phrases might seem to imply a merely technical concern with how souls managed to make their way from this world across to the next. In a gloss on the Dives and Lazarus text, the influential *Decades* of the Swiss reformer Heinrich Bullinger offered the somewhat superfluous observation that 'angels therefore are swift and passing speedy'.[36]

But recurring references to angelic transportation were usually intended, not so much to assuage metaphysical curiosity, as to bring pastoral comfort to the dying and bereaved. The Jacobean preacher Thomas Adams encouraged his listeners to reflect on how a poor beggar that in life could neither stand nor sit would now be carried 'not on the shoulders of men, as the pope, the proudest on earth, but hee rides on the wings of angels. He is carried to a glorious port by gracious porters.'[37] Cole included in his treatise a prayer he had composed for a dying servant: 'if it seeme good unto thee, restore unto him his former health. If not, send thine angels unto him, that they in due time bring his soule into thy bosome.'[38]

Such consolation was available right across the social spectrum. Awaiting execution in 1601, the earl of Essex beseeched God to 'send thy blessed angels to be near me, which may convey [my soul] to the joy of heaven'. When the third earl of Huntingdon lay dying in December 1595, his chaplain Nathaniel Gilby urged him to remember that 'angels attended to cary his soule to the bosome of Abraham . . . At which wordes he seemed to be greatly comforted.'[39]

By the early seventeenth century, this was veritably the comfort of cliché. Robert Hill encouraged the sick to 'thinke that the angels stand at your beds head, to carrie your soule into Abrahams bosome'; Richard Brathwaite called on them to imagine 'angels coming forth to meet thee, the whole host of heaven to conduct thee to the palace of eternity'. George Strode envisaged 'holy angels (who are all ministring spirits, sent forth to minister for them who shall be heires of salvation) to carrie them into Abraham's bosom.' Christopher Sutton's prayer commending the dying man into the hands of God at the hour of death called upon the Lord to 'command thy angels to bring him to the land of everlasting peace'.[40] In a culture which has sometimes been described as 'iconophobic', there even remained possibilities for visual representation of the idea.[41] Angels escort the soul of the king in Rubens' painting of the reception of James I into heaven on the ceiling of the Whitehall Banqueting House. More prosaically, recurring marginal illustrations in Richard Day's 1578 *Book of Christian Prayers* depicted the souls of the faithful transported to heaven by angels, and those of the damned carried to hell by demons.[42]

III

All this discussion seems nonetheless to amount to an essentially passive role prescribed for the angels – they function as supernatural undertakers, waiting patiently for the death throes to end in order to collect the souls of the deceased and deliver them safely to their heavenly resting place. James Cole, for example, included several pages of advice on resisting the assaults of the devil, but made no suggestion that angels had any particular part to play in this process.[43]

Had the angels then finally relinquished their accustomed roles as supernatural allies in a momentous deathbed struggle? In a word, no. From the 1550s through the 1650s and beyond, this idea persists as a tremulous subtext of Protestant writing on the art of dying. Take, for example, what can be considered the first distinctively Protestant *ars moriendi* work of the English Reformation, Miles Coverdale's translation of a treatise on death by the Swiss reformer Otto Werdmüller. Employing the metaphor of a city under siege, Werdmüller portrayed devils compassing 'the soule of man wyth violence and subtiltie, to take possession of the pore soule'. But, almost in the manner of a column of relief, 'God commaundeth his aungels, that they wyth hym doe loke unto thee . . . the aungell of the Lorde pitcheth round about them that feare him, and delyvereth them'. At his last end the Christian should remember that 'in hys death he is not alone, but that very many eies loke unto him'. Something close to the traditional conception of a deathbed contest of spiritual forces shines through strongly here.[44]

More atavistic still was a poem affixed to a 1578 English translation of *The maner to dye well* by the Spanish Dominican Pedro de Soto. This envisaged a conflict between 'huge routes of uglye dreadfull divelles' and 'angels passing cleare', each clamorously presenting the sins and virtues of the dying.

> And in the midst betwixt them both,
> by iust and upright dome:
> Its clearly iudged to whether side,
> the wandring soule shall come.

A later reference in this text to 'my good angell unto whose custodye I am committed' strikes an equally old-fashioned note.[45] Guardian angels were usually conspicuous by their absence from the Protestant *ars moriendi*, though in 1624 the controversial Arminian cleric Richard Montagu did not scruple to assert that every Christian 'hath by God's appointment and assignation, an Angell Guardian to attend upon him at all assayes, in all his wayes, at his going forth, at his coming home'.[46] Guardian angels at the deathbed appear in the writings of another anti-Calvinist writer, Laud's protégé Jeremy Taylor, whose *Holy Dying* (published in 1651) is gener- ally considered an 'Anglican' classic of the good death genre. A recurrent theme is the role played by angels in helping the Christian 'to resist and to subdue the devils temptations and assaults'. When a good man dies, 'the angels drive away the devils on his death-bed'. Prayers for angelic assis- tance against 'the violence and malice of all . . . ghostly enemies' feature prominently in Taylor's schema for a revived clerical and sacramental ministry to the dying.[47]

Like much else in Elizabethan and early Stuart England, angels had the capacity to become a totemic marker between Calvinist and anti- Calvinist styles of divinity. The propagation of 'magical, suspicious and popish conceits of angels' was put to the charge of one of his fellows by the Puritan Master of St John's, Cambridge, in 1587, and accusations of having defended prayer to angels surfaced in the settling of scores against several Laudian ministers in the 1640s.[48] There were, of course, distinctively Puritan and non-Puritan approaches to the art of dying, as David Stannard, Ralph Houlbrooke and others have documented.[49] But a declared interest in angelic ministry at the deathbed, and in angelic protection against evil powers, does not really work as a diagnostic test of churchmanship in this period, and was by no means an exclusively 'high church' phenomenon. A thoroughly orthodox Calvinist writer like George Strode could equally well evoke an image of the angels, who 'willingly pitch their tents about thee; and refuse not (for thy safety) to beare thee in their hands . . . the divels of Hell by God's providence are kept off from thee, as with a strong hedge'.[50]

The theme makes an appearance even in the most theologically fas- tidious and low temperature of contemporary *ars moriendi* tracts, the Cambridge Calvinist theologian William Perkins' *Salve for a Sicke Man*. To Perkins, the deathbed assaults of Satan were real enough, but should be regarded as primarily spiritual and psychological. Ravings and convul- sions on the deathbed 'comes not of witchcraft and possessions, as people commonly thinke, but of choller in the vaines'. This sounds somewhat akin to the extreme position held by his contemporary Reginald Scot, who denied the corporeality of all spirits and the possibilities for their intervention in the created world. Yet Perkins was much more traditional than this. Like Luther before him, he advised the sick man tempted by Satan to 'commend thy cause to God . . . and then certenly Christ will come unto thee with all his angels'.[51]

There was noticeably less restraint in other godly advice-writing. In particular, we should consider what were far and away the two bestselling *ars moriendi* tracts of the period: Thomas Becon's *Sick Man's Salve*, first published in 1561, and in its twenty-fifth edition by 1632, and Philip Stubbes' *A Christal Glasse for Christian Women*, published in 1591 and reaching a remarkable 34 editions before the end of the sevententh century.[52] Becon's exposition of the textbook good death takes the form of a dialogue, at the climax of which the dying Epaphroditus is consoled by the minister Philemon:

> Fear not, brother Epaphroditus: God is your loving Father and most gentle Saviour . . . He hath sent his holy angels hither unto you, even into this your chamber . . . They have pitched their tents about you that they may keep you harmless and safe from the devouring teeth of Satan. They wait upon you diligently for your defence, and will never depart from you, till they receive your soul, and carry it up lovingly as a most precious relique into the kingdom of heaven.[53]

Stubbes' text differed from Becon's in purporting to be an accurate account of a real deathbed, that of the author's teenage bride, Katherine. It differed too in that 'Katherine' is a less conventional and restrained protagonist than the more overtly fictional Epaphroditus. Indeed, she takes the initiative in calling on God to 'sende thy holie angels to conduct my soule into the euerlasting kingdome of heauen', and she reports visions of 'infinite millions of angels attendant upon me, and watching ouer me'. Katherine engages in rumbustious conflict with Satan: 'avoid therefore, thou dastard . . . get thee packing'. And she threatens the devil with 'that valiant Michael, who beate thee in heaven, and threw thee downe to hell with all thy hellish traine'. When Satan departs defeated, she turns to the bystanders, asking 'do you not see infinite millions of most glorious angels stand about me, with firie charets ready to defend me . . .? These holy angels, these ministring spirits, are appointed by God to carrie my soule into the kingdome of heauen.'[54]

Katherine Stubbes was not the only dying person among the godly reported to have actually *seen* those angels, whose supernatural presence at every faithful Christian's end was so widely affirmed by the experts. The Protestant deathbed can to some extent therefore be considered a site of exception to the conventional wisdom of Elizabethan and early Stuart theologians that visible appearances of angels were not to be looked for in the post-apostolic age.[55] In London in April 1625, Mrs Joan Drake wrestled with a deathbed conviction that she was one of the reprobate, with no fewer than nine ministers attempting to convince her of the contrary. Eventually, she triumphed over despair and was said to have cried out 'Lo, Lo, the angels are come, they wait, they stay for mee'. Three quarters of a century later, nonconformist ministers were still reporting the incident as the climax of a famous deathbed conversion: 'she had her eyes lifted up, and fixed on the house-top, as if she had seen a vision of angels'.[56]

As the seventeenth century progressed, there are indications that the idea of a palpable angelic ministry to the dying and dead may have retained a particular hold in some nonconformist circles.[57] On her deathbed in 1647, the sectarian Sarah Wight told bystanders that 'the devil fights with me, as he did with Michael and his angels', and asked them, 'do ye not see him?'[58] A few years later John Bunyan can be found reiterating the traditional view that 'whereas the deathbed of the ungodly is surrounded by devils to take the soul to hell, the dying Christian is waited upon by angels to carry him to Abraham's bosom'. The devils around the deathbed of the ungodly were sometimes 'very visible to the dying party'. Conversely, though 'the glorious angels of God do not appear at the first, to the view of the soul', the godly could rely on the comforting assurance that 'the angels do alwayes appear at the last, and will not fail the soul'.[59] In the second half of the seventeenth century, accounts of exemplary deathbeds, from which the pious had announced to bystanders the sensible presence of angels, were eagerly recorded by Puritan angelologists such as Isaac Ambrose and Increase Mather.[60] Another thoroughly medieval idea – that angels would be needed 'to scour and cleer the passage for us', as the departed soul made its dangerous journey towards heaven through an upper air infested with demons – was also regularly rehearsed in nonconformist sources.[61]

Ironically enough, in insisting that spiritual forces at the deathbed might impress themselves sensibly upon the dying, seventeenth-century dissent found itself in agreement not only with pre-Reformation tradition, but with the approved templates of the Counter-Reformation. Richard Verstegan's 1603 translation of an *ars moriendi* tract by the Italian canon regular Pietro da Lucca approvingly cited the opinion of St Vincent, St Gregory and other doctors concerning 'devils that appeare at the tyme of death'.[62] The Jesuit Robert Persons' *First Booke of the Christian Exercise* also noted that 'often tymes God doth permit the visions of angels both good and euill, as also of other sayntes to men lyinge on their death beddes.' Yet there was no smooth confessional convergence on this question. In his famous adaptation of Persons' book for a Protestant readership, the Elizabethan Calvinist Edmund Bunny silently omitted the discussion of apparitions on the deathbed.[63]

IV

The most famous evocation of angels attendant upon a death in post-Reformation England has been held in reserve up to this point: 'Good night, sweet prince, / And flights of Angels sing thee to thy rest!'[64] Horatio's valediction for his deceased friend Hamlet focuses for us a number of issues about the acculturation of Protestant reform in the period under discussion. Critics have long recognized here an allusion to abrogated liturgical rites, either to the antiphon *In Paradisum* of the pre-Reformation funeral liturgy ('May the angels lead you into Paradise . . . May the choir of angels receive you'), or to the *commendatio animarum* (commendation of the soul) to be recited immediately after death ('may angels lead you to the bosom of Abraham').[65]

Without wishing to step into the interpretative minefields which continue to be planted around the question of Shakespeare's religious sympathies, one thing can safely be asserted. A willing recognition of the ministry of angels to humans, immediately before and immediately after their demise, is in and of itself no *prima facie* evidence of quasi-Catholicism in this period.[66] Nor does it seem quite appropriate, as one scholar has done, to characterize seventeenth-century interest in the visual perception of good and evil angels at the deathbed merely as 'the tag ends of medieval sentimentality and of fifteenth-century sensationalism'.[67]

In terms of the conventional metanarratives of continuity and change employed by historians of the English Reformation, the evidence set out in this chapter may well be difficult to read. It is clearly not a straightforwardly revisionist case-study in the resilience of traditional religious culture.[68] Yet neither does it quite fit the prescriptions of a cheerful post-revisionism, in which traditional motifs almost unconsciously seep through the topsoil of religious reform to create part of a 'distinctively post-Reformation' synthesis.[69]

The sources under discussion in this chapter were in the main composed and created by educated Protestants, men who knew quite clearly what they were about. Whether or not we can usefully conceive of angels in Protestant culture stepping forward to plug the devotional and functional interstices left by the demise of the saints,[70] an undue emphasis on 'continuity' is likely to obscure the extent to which the ministry of angels became a *less* prominent theme of English mortuary culture after the Reformation. As we have seen, the rich visual tradition of the *ars moriendi* block pictures was largely swept away, along with the tradition of offering prayers to the tutelary archangel Michael, or to one's own individual guardian. It would, of course, be foolish to deny that in some sense the persistent presence of angels at the deathbed does represent continuity, a cultural bridge between the experience of death in the fifteenth and seventeenth centuries. But this was not an unbroken or unproblematic connection.

That seminal moment in English cultural history, the rejection of purgatory, is of crucial importance here. As Catholic writers very occasionally admitted, the logic of their soteriology required them to recognize that angels often escorted the souls of the saved, not to immediate bliss, but to a fiery purgation.[71] Medieval theologians had tended to identify Abraham's bosom, the place to which the angels bore the soul of Lazarus, with *limbus patrum*, the limbo of the fathers and patriarchs which Christ had emptied after his crucifixion in the so-called 'harrowing of hell'.[72] But the overwhelming tendency of Protestant scriptural exegesis was to regard the bosom of Abraham as a straightforward synonym for heaven, and in the hands of reformers the motif of angels carrying Lazarus to the bosom of Abraham could thus become potent propaganda against the doctrines of purgatory and intercessory prayer. As Becon's protagonist Philemon expressed it, 'the papists heretofore have taught . . . that men's sins after their death be forgiven them through the sacrifice of that most wicked and abominable popish mass, and by pilgrimages-going'. But in fact each would receive his reward of everlasting life or eternal damnation immediately upon death: 'the history of the unmerciful rich man, and of the poor Lazare, painteth it out very lively'.[73]

In the minds and writings of reformers, then, an emphasis on angels was in the end not knowingly a concession to 'weak' brethren, an *adiaphoron* or indifferent thing to ease the transition from the old religious culture to the new. Drawing as ever on the deep well of Scripture, Protestant writers concerning themselves with death self-consciously reinvented the role of angels in order to help underwrite a crucial socio-religious change – from a pattern of dying inviting human effort and invocation, to one totally dependent on divine initiative. Yet in the process, and perhaps in spite of themselves, reformers often found themselves working with rather than against the grain of popular culture. In the context of a universal human experience, they emphasized the sometimes threatening, but more often comforting, proximity of a vibrant world of supernatural forces.

7

The guardian angel in Protestant England

The aim of this chapter is to listen in on an extended dialogue between the culture of English Protestantism and one of the keynote ideas of medieval religion, a conversation which was pursued sporadically but sometimes vigorously over the century and a half following the accession of Elizabeth I.

The suggestion that every Christian was watched over by an individual guardian angel was a patristic idea, and one that had become firmly rooted in both scholastic teaching and popular devotion of the high and later Middle Ages. From a Protestant perspective, its realization epitomized many of the worst aspects of pre-Reformation religion. In the first place, guardian angels were the focus of iconography and the object of votive masses; they were the recipients of a veneration which the reformers insisted could never be given to any created being. Like the saints, they were the gracious receivers of petition: prayers addressed to the guardian angel abound in late medieval primers and manuscript collections.[1]

Such invocation was anathema to Protestants: 'we must call neither upon Angel, nor yet upon Saint, but only and solely upon God' was the stern admonition of the Elizabethan homily on prayer.[2] Medieval guardian angels were not simply the distant object of veneration: they communicated with the humans in their charge, and intervened in many aspects of their daily lives. Occasionally, this could be through the direct agency of a vision, but more commonly it was by an unseen influence on the conscience and the will. Guardian angels could, for example, shape the decisions that averted personal folly or disaster, and more broadly they stepped in to help men and women choose good over evil.[3] In doing so, they did not override free will, but they did draw humans towards cooperation with the divine offer of grace – something which looked like a prop of that 'works righteousness' the inversion of which was the preferred theological definition of the Reformation itself. The prominent role allotted by late medieval texts to the guardian angel at the deathbed underlined the point. To Catholics this was a place where salvation could be won or lost through the exercise of the will, but to Protestants it was a site for the validation of a divine decree of election.[4]

A very great deal of the medieval understanding of angels in general was tarnished and tainted to the Protestant mind. But Protestants could hardly do without them. As one seventeenth-century English reformer pointed out, 'above 260 times are Angels mentioned in Scripture'.[5] Thanks to the work of Deborah Harkness, Joad Raymond, Laura Sangha, Alexandra Walsham and others, we have become aware that 'Protestant angelology' is very far from being a contradiction in terms.[6] The protective ministry of angels resonated in the reformed imagination. But Protestant theologians had few qualms about ditching whatever seemed to them to be unscriptural accretions. The ninefold angelic hierarchy of the sixth-century Pseudo-Dionysius, for example, an idea foundational to much medieval angelology, received extremely short shrift in nearly all Protestant surveys.[7]

What then of the Christian's guardian angel – was this a 'popish opinion' to be drummed out of the heads of the people, an invitation to idolatry? Or was it a notion that could be shown to be compatible with Scripture, and with Reformed theodicy and soteriology? In this chapter I seek to track some long-term responses to those questions through a range of vernacular Protestant texts. It will be a somewhat circuitous journey, but one which I hope will take us to some interesting places, and offer some fresh perspectives on patterns of religious and intellectual change.

I

Reformation begins with Martin Luther, and Luther, in so many ways a man of the late Middle Ages, was rather keen on guardian angels.[8] In Elizabethan England, however, the theological lodestar was not Luther, but John Calvin, and any survey of the place of the guardian angel in English Protestant thought would do well to start by considering what Calvin had to say about the matter. In his discussion of the issue in the *Institutes*, Calvin began from a position of studied scepticism: 'whether or not each believer has a single angel assigned to him for his defence, I dare not positively affirm'. Two passages from the New Testament had traditionally been seen as providing support for the doctrine: Christ's commendation of the children, whose 'angels do always behold the face of my Father' (Matt. 18.10), and the disciples' mistaking the escaped Peter for 'his angel' (Acts 12.15). But, Calvin suggested, the former might be read to imply a merely collective guardianship, and the latter could refer to 'any one of the angels to whom the Lord might have given the charge of Peter at that particular time, without implying that he was to be his perpetual guardian'. There were, moreover, several texts showing that 'each of us is cared for, not by one angel merely, but that all with one consent watch for our safety'. The angels in general rejoice for 'one sinner that repenteth' (Luke 15.7), and angels (plural) had carried the soul of Lazarus to the bosom of Abraham (Luke 16.22). Without closing the question down completely, Calvin concluded that those 'who limit the care which God takes of each of us to a single angel, do great injury to themselves and to all the members of the Church'.[9]

In the main, Elizabethan theologians borrowed this tone of agnostic aversion; their resolve was stiffened by the fact that the marginal annotations to the Catholic Rheims New Testament of 1582 resolutely upheld the doctrine of angelic guardianship. In their gloss on Matthew 18.10, the 'Rheimists' noted how it was

> a greate dignitie and a marvelous benefite that every man hath from his Nativitie an Angel for his custodie and Patronage . . . and the thing so plaine that Calvin dare not deny it, and yet he will needes doubt of it.

In one of several Protestant critiques of the Catholic translation, William Fulke protested that Calvin had no doubts about the protection of God's angels, but that there was nonetheless no place of Scripture to prove that 'every one hath a severall Angell'.[10] The presbyterian activist Thomas Cartwright was considerably more forthright, asserting that Calvin *had* rejected the notion, and that this passage of Scripture 'hath no one word, which tyeth the Angelicall attendance upon the faithful to one onely Angell'. Dismissively, Cartwright described the doctrine as one which 'coming first from Plato, afterward received some strength of the testimony of the Fathers'.[11]

Angelic guardianship was yet more explicitly identified as a papist error in the Puritan controversialist Andrew Willet's *Synopsis Papismi* (1592), a massive compendium of anti-popish argument. Willet considered in turn three passages of Scripture regularly deployed by the papists: Jacob's reference to 'the Angell that hath kept mee from my youth' in Genesis 48.16; the mistaking of Peter for 'his Angel' in Acts 12.15; and the children's angels of Matthew 18.10. Jacob's angel was in fact Christ himself, and 'other proper Angell Iacob had none'. The angels of the children of God exercised a collective rather than a particular commission, and if Peter was delivered from prison by one angel, 'it followeth not, that therefore he was his proper Angell'.

Like Calvin, Willet regarded Luke 16.22, the parable of the rich man and Lazarus, as a telling proof-text against angelic guardianship. Lazarus was carried by angels, not one angel, into the bosom of Abraham. Surely, Willet argued, 'if he had one Angel appointed to be the president of his life from his nativitie, it had beene also parte of that Angelles charge, to have conveyed his soule into Heaven'?[12] The argument was a shrewd one, not least because much pre-Reformation devotion to the guardian angel was predicated upon a central role in the negotiation of death, and prayers directed to the 'proper angel' often explicitly beseeched him to lead one's departed soul to paradise.[13] The fact that it was not 'one onelie angel' which transported the soul of Lazarus was similarly noted by the lay anti-papal writer, and notable sceptic, Reginald Scot. Scot's main concern was to ridicule reports of angelic apparitions, an absurdity which the belief in guardian spirits might potentially feed. Scot could find 'no reason in nature, nor authoritie in scripture' for the doctrine, though he was com-pelled to admit that 'it hath beene long, and continueth yet a constant opinion, not onelie among the papists, but among others also.[14]

In fact, the opinion that God 'hath appointed and given unto every one his Angell, which may protect and direct him, even from his mothers womb' was aired in a Protestant work first published just before Scot's *Discoverie* was: a translation of a sermon by the Saxon reformer Urbanus Rhegius.[15] Rhegius had died in 1541, so his might already seem like the voice of a past generation, as well as of a Lutheran religiosity that carried a limited charge with the opinion-makers of the Elizabethan Church. Yet even within the contemporary Reformed camp there was an important exception to the approach indicated by Calvin. The Heidelberg reformer Girolamo Zanchi posed, and answered in the affirmative, the question of 'Whether a created angel has been appointed to every man.[16] An aware-ness of divided opinion may have prompted the highly circumspect approach we can discern in some quarters. Remarkably, Elizabethan England's leading Calvinist theologian, William Perkins, managed to include an extended discussion of angelic protection in his *A golden chaine* of 1600, without addressing at all the question of whether when angels 'abase themselves to become guardians and keepers unto sinful men' they did so on the basis of individual allocation.[17] Here Perkins might have been taking his cue from the Reformed continental theologian who, alongside Calvin, enjoyed the greatest prestige in the Elizabethan Church. The Swiss reformer Heinrich Bullinger's collection of sermons known as the *Decades* contained a homily on 'the holy angels of God' and their ministrations towards mankind. Yet despite expounding one of the key texts for individual guardianship (Acts 12), Bullinger entirely evaded the issue itself.[18]

II

There was thus a broad functional consensus among Elizabethan theologians that belief in guardian angels was at best a very uncertain opinion; at worst a toxic relic of popery. This, however, was to be rudely disrupted in the following reign with the publication in 1613 of the first full-length work of English Protestant angelology. The title page of John Salkeld's *A Treatise of Angels*, dedicated to James I, announced its unusual provenance. The author was 'lately fellow of the Iesuites Colledges in the Universities of Conimbra, Corduba, and Complutum. Assistant in studies to the famous Iesuites Francis Suarius, and Michael Vasquez'.

Salkeld had fully conformed to the Church of England after his capture on the English mission the previous year. But the blazoning of this exotic pedigree, and in particular the linking of his name with the leading Counter-Reformation theologian, and renowned angelologist, Francisco Suárez, carried the implicit message that the proper study of angels was a Catholic specialism, and Salkeld's own text involved much discussion of the kind of scholastic subtleties that Protestants usually preferred to leave well alone. With respect to guardian angels, Salkeld began his discussion echoing the words of Calvin: 'whether every man hath his peculiar Angell, I dare not certainely affirme'. But the fact that he devoted the longest section of his treatise, nearly 30 pages of text, to amassing support for the doctrine from the Greek and Latin Fathers leaves little doubt about his own position. The provision of guardian angels seemed to Salkeld to be a natural expression of 'the bounty and love of God towards man', and he did not hesitate to point out that 'many, even Protestants, thinke the affirmative part to be the truth'. There was little effort on Salkeld's part to distinguish Protestant from papist approaches to the topic. He observed that 'in the Church of Rome this is ordinarily accounted as a thing so clearly deduced on the holy Scripture, as who should deny that every man hath his particular Angell, keeper, and guard, should be censured'. Among Protestants, 'it is not thought a matter of such moment and certaintie'. But there was no definite declaration that the latter had the right of it.[19]

Informed readers could hardly have been unaware that at the time Salkeld was writing, the Church of Rome was vigorously promoting the cult of the guardian angel. In 1608 Paul V instituted a universal feast and office dedicated to the 'Holy Guardian Angels'. The following half-century witnessed a renewed flowering of the devotion across the Catholic world, with widespread iconographic representation, numerous confraternity dedications, and a plethora of treatises on guardian angels emerging from counter-reforming, especially Jesuit, pens.[20] One of these, the *Horologium Auxiliaris Tutelaris Angeli* (1622) of Jeremias Drexel, was published in an English Catholic translation at Rouen in 1630.[21] In such a context, any expressions of enthusiasm for guardian angels might give pause for thought, and indeed did sometimes seem to emanate from suspicious-looking quarters. In 1616, for example, their importance was asserted in a printed sermon by a chaplain of the Catholic queen, Anne of Denmark. Godfrey Goodman bemoaned that 'we scarce heare any mention of the good Angels, of our guardian Angels . . . If any extraordinary good doe befall us, we will rather choake it up with unthankfulnesse, or attribute it to some secret and hidden cause in nature.' Although promoted to the bishopric of Gloucester in 1625, rumours of Goodman's conversion to Catholicism were circulating in the 1630s, and were eventually confirmed by his will of 1656.[22]

Still more of a splash was created by another cleric on the ceremonialist wing of the Jacobean Church. Guardian angels featured prominently in two works of 1624 by the pugnacious Arminian Richard Montagu: his notorious *New Gagg for an Old Goose* (which argued that Rome was a true, though flawed, Church) and his treatise on the invocation of saints. The latter was in part composed to refute claims being made by the Catholic-turned-Anglican-turned-Catholic again, Marcus Antonius de Dominis, that he had heard Montagu preach before the king that there was no reason why a man might not turn to his guardian angel and say 'Holy Angell keeper, Pray for me'. Yet Montagu went on to argue that the sentiment itself was not an absurd one, and in no way validated Romanist invocation of angels and saints. Such invocation was ridiculous because saints and angels simply could not hear the prayers of people on earth. But, Montagu added, 'the case of Angell Guardians is farre different, being ever in *procintu*, nigh at hand unto us, continually and never abandoning us all our dayes.' There could therefore be no more impiety in turning to say 'sancte Angele custos ora pro me', than in asking one's friend or brother to do the same.[23] Similar assertions were made in the *New Gagg*, where Montagu provocatively took as his starting point, not Calvin's judgement, but that of the Jesuit author Michael Vasquez: 'wee cannot deny without very great rashnes, that every man hath his Angell-keeper'. Montagu himself declared assent to the notion of angel-keepers, adding somewhat disingenuously, 'as most doo, as the Church of England doth'.[24]

To Montagu's critics – and they were many – this seemed like the thin end of a popish wedge, an invitation to resurrect full-scale veneration of saints and angels in the Church of England. Indeed, charges were later brought against a number of minor Laudian clergy that they had defended praying to saints and angels in the 1630s.[25] A collective denunciation of Montagu in 1629 by some self-styled 'orthodox ministers of the Church of England' accused him of promoting the false notion that it was no impiety to believe 'that some saints have a peculiar patronage, custody, protection and power, as angells also have over certain persons and countries by especiall deputation'.[26]

It would appear, then, that by the early Stuart period guardian angels had opened themselves to charges of guilt by association with the agenda of the Arminian faction within the Church. It is not surprising, therefore, to find some Jacobean Calvinists continuing to express the reserve or hostility characteristic of earlier Elizabethan discussions. Preaching in Cambridge, the Puritan minister Thomas Taylor insisted that God 'hath many good Angels to pitch about a godly man', and denied that 'the scripture speake[th] of one speciall Angel, assigned to every speciall man'.[27]

The issue was further addressed in a series of sermons published in 1616 by the London rector Thomas Adams, a conformist Calvinist and dedicated anti-papal controversialist. Adams mocked the Romanists for allotting 'a particular tutelar Angel to every Colledge and Corporation: yea to the generation of flies, fleas and ants'. Yet Adams could not but admit that whether every man had a particular angel for his guardian was 'a question much disputed', the case in favour having been made by many of the Fathers, most of the schoolmen 'and some Protestant Divines'. Adams announced that 'I will not dispute it, yet I must doubt it; because I see no cleare ground in the Scriptures to prove it'. Like earlier authors, he expounded the Matthean text to mean that 'all the Angels take care of all God's little ones'. The cognate passage in Acts usually proved trickier for opponents of the doctrine, but Adams took a no-nonsense approach to it: 'I answere that the Disciples amazed at the strange report, spake they knew not what'. Rather in contradiction to this, he went on to concede that they may have spoken 'after the common opinion of men in that age'. But his readers were to reflect that 'all are not Christian truths, that true Christians have spoken'.[28]

A similar note of cool circumspection was adopted in a sermon by the royal chaplain and renowned Calvinist theologian John Prideaux, who noted that many of the proofs brought forward in support of the doctrine were 'exceeding wavering'. Prideaux's view was that 'the Romanists dare say anything that may backe their worshipping of Angels, and make way for their Invocation of Saints'. Paul V's recent proclamation of a feast in honour of the guardian angel was an object lesson. Prideaux did not condemn the existence of guardian angels outright, aware that Zanchi had thought it agreeable to Scripture. He speculated, however, that, if there were such protectors, they might operate somewhat in the manner of royal ambassadors and 'be removed from one negotiation to another', rather than 'keepe alwaies to the same charge'. Ultimately, Prideaux would go no further than Calvin: 'I dare affirme nothing, for certainty'.[29]

III

In the end, however, positions with regard to guardian angels did not neatly arrange themselves along confessional lines, or simply mirror the main ideological fractures within the early Stuart Church. In the middle decades of the seventeenth century we can identify a strain of positive enthusiasm for the doctrine, not in crypto-Catholic but within godly Calvinist circles, and a growing number of texts directly addressing themselves to the theme. The first of these was a 1630 sermon on 'the Angell Guardian', published by the Oxford anti-Laudian cleric John Bayly.[30]

Bayly was the son of a famous father, the bishop of Bangor and best-selling devotional writer, Lewis Bayly. A dedicatory epistle to the bishop called on 'the Angell of God which hath hitherto protected your Lordship from many most knowne and imminent dangers, [to] tarry round about you'. Tackling the core question of 'whether there be one Angell Guardian only or more assigned to attend us', Bayly ranged widely, beginning with the ancient Platonist teaching that each man had three special angels of this kind: his *sacer demon* (inspiring good thoughts), his *genius* (with charge of his outward life) and his *spiritus professionis* (helping him in his particular trade or calling). While sensitive to the reservations expressed by Calvin, Bayly found it nonetheless 'not improbable' that every man had his particular angel, and indeed went so far as to claim that 'the moderne learned doe subscribe unto Zanchius his conclusion. That ther is one Angell ordinarily assigned unto every one man as a Tutor or protector of him in all his waies'.

Bayly was conscious, however, that this starting point raised some weighty subsequent questions – specifically, whether those who did not fear God had angels to protect them, and whether those who did fear him were invariably attended by their angels. These were conundrums with distinct implications for Calvinist teachings about election and assurance. Bayly followed traditional scholastic teaching in affirming that the ungodly did have their own guardian angels: to bridle their malice, and to restrain the power of the devil over them. But God had decreed this in order that 'their wickedness should not too much annoye the elect of God'. The guardian angels of the godly meanwhile never ceased to preserve them from the devil's malice 'and from those many casuall dangers wee are daiely subiect to'. But when good men fell into sin, as they do 'not once, but seaven times, not in a yeere, but in a day', it sometimes pleased God to withdraw their angels from them. Nonetheless, 'presently they come in againe to take us up', and would never finally forsake the righteous.[31]

If Bayly appeared here to be skirting around the relationship between angelic guardianship and the more existential aspects of Calvinist soteriology, other commentators were keen to tackle it head-on. In 1646, the layman Henry Lawrence, returning from Baptist exile in the Netherlands, and taking up a seat in the House of Commons, published *Of our Communion and Warre with Angels*. The first comprehensive work of Puritan angelology, Lawrence's treatise inevitably had to address the issue of whether Christians were assigned an individual guardian. Aware perhaps that this was a well-worn debate, Lawrence abbreviated the conventional discussion of authorities: 'not to trouble you with the dispute, some incline rather to the negative'. He recognized the occasions in Scripture – such as the conveyance of Lazarus's soul to paradise – where more than one angel was pressed into service. Nonetheless, and partly on the basis of a rather traditional and patristic reading of Matthew 18 and Acts 12, Lawrence came down firmly on the other side, remarking that attempts to suggest that Peter's angel was but one of a multitude attending to him 'lookes like an evasion'. There was, however, a crucial qualification, which had been implicit in much Protestant angelology up to this point, but was now made firmly explicit: 'the tutelage of the good Angells belongs only to the elect'. 'The wicked have no Angells to looke to them'.[32] From this perspective – stemming from a literalist reading of Hebrews 1.14's description of angels as ministering spirits to those 'who shall be heires of salvation' – Lawrence's understanding of guardian angels functioned as a veritable grammar of Puritan practical divinity.

Like Bayly, Lawrence wondered 'whether the Angell keepers doe ever leave men or no with whose guardianship they are . . . trusted?' His conclusion was that, though it was possible angels might withdraw to produce a time of affliction, they would always return, and never totally forsake their charge. This was powerfully indicative of orthodox Calvinist teaching on the perseverance and indefectability of the elect. Lawrence also considered an old and more scholastic conundrum, that of when the angelic guardianship actually started. Either because, or in spite, of his adherence to the concept of believers' baptism, Lawrence rejected the

idea that association with the guardian angel began at the time of chris-
tening; instead he inclined to the view that it started 'assoone as the soule
is infused'.[33]

Lawrence's emphasis on individual guardianship also served to delineate and circumscribe the scope of angelic knowledge and agency. His
text displayed a characteristic Protestant revulsion against the idea of
angelic omniscience, a refusal to affirm that angels 'know all the particular
actions, what ever is done, said, or suffered'. Yet while this applied to
angelic knowledge on the macrocosmic level, 'of those committed to their
charge there is no question'. This was not because angels could directly
know people's thoughts, affections and desires: 'God is onely the searcher
of the hearts'. But like skilled physicians assessing the outward symp-
toms of a familiar patient, 'they are extremely ingenious in guessing'.[34]
Moreover, guardian angels were able to influence the internal senses, 'to
wit, the fancy and imagination', by appearing in dreams or visions. Though
God alone could enlighten the understanding and determine the will,
angels were able, through the imprinting of internal impressions, to influence 'those sensitive passions which are in us'.

There were limits to this facility: angels could not 'put in new species
of things into the fancy, and such as the senses never had any knowledge
of': a man born blind could not be made to dream of colours, for example.
Nonetheless, 'they can in a very great measure know our mindes and
necessities, they can by the mediation of our fancies, and inward sences
speake to us, almost what ever they will'.[35]

These were deep waters indeed, and on them Lawrence might seem to
be drifting away from the conventional Protestant patterning of angels as
merely external protective agents, and sailing closer to the medieval and
scholastic conception of the guardian as a moral collaborator in the exercise of the will. Lawrence was aware that some of his readers might wish
matters of the spirit to be left to Christ alone, but he insisted this was a
false division of labour: 'if it be no prejudice to Christ that the Angells take
care of our bodies, which is also his care, what prejudice will it be that the
Angells should also have a care of our spirits'? Indeed, he did not scruple
to assert that 'things communicated to our inward man, is ordinarily the
administration of Angells'.[36]

Several of Lawrence's themes were recapitulated (and in fact plagiar-
ized) in a 1653 treatise by Robert Dingley, congregationalist minister on
the Isle of Wight: *The Deputation of Angels, Or, The Angell-Guardian*. This
was a considerably less subtle piece of work than *Of our Communion and
Warre with Angels*, but as the first full-length English treatise dedicated to

demonstrating the existence of guardian angels, it deserves admiration for its thoroughness. By the time Dingley declares that he has 'answered all the Objections that I ever yet met withall, or can possiby think of', the reader is in no mood to disagree.[37] In spite of Calvin, Dingley cited no fewer than 23 'godly and learned authors' in support of the doctrine, excluding 'such as are tainted with Romish interest'. His tone throughout was combative, warning critics that 'in slighting this Doctrine, take heed least yee be found among the slighters of Christ, who delivered it'.[38] Dingley's treatise proceeded in quasi-scholastic fashion, identifying and addressing 'twelve Questions or Objections to be resolved and untyed, that are (or may be) raised against this Point of Angellical Deputation'.

For Dingley, the question of why only one angel should be deputed, when so many attend on God, was conceived of as a kind of problem in celestial logistics. Angels could not be in more than one place at a time, and Scripture taught that most of them were in heaven. Moreover, the elect were scattered across the earth, and their number was so great 'as to passe alle the known rules of Arithmatick'. In asking rhetorically 'whether it bear a face of probability that each one of so great a company have many troops of Angels still to attend him?', Dingley came perilously close to saying that there were simply not enough angels to go around. Conversely, however, a problem of potential underemployment was easily resolved: when their human ward died, the guardian moved on to another assignment. Citing the authority of the twelfth-century theologian Peter Lombard, Dingley pronounced that 'wee may believe a Transmigration of guardian Angels'.[39]

Lombard was soon cited again, in support of the guardian angel's ability subtly to communicate with and influence the conduct of his earthly charge: 'Hortatur ad Bonum; He doth admonish and perswade us on all occasions to that which is good'.[40] In this tricky area, Dingley followed the lead of Lawrence, alleging the ability of guardian angels to plant impressions in the imagination during sleep, as well as their extraordinary ability to fathom our thoughts, affections and desires:

> if the Wife that hath been forty years in thy bosome is able in great measure to know thee, to guess at thy thoughts, and trace thee in thy wayes: And know when thy tongue and heart do not agree, how much more thy Angel Guardian that hath ever been with thee?[41]

Other queries Dingley set out to resolve included the questions of whether both Adam and Christ himself had guardian angels (yes, and yes), and the role of the guardian at death. In blithe disregard of the usual Protestant reading of the Dives and Lazarus story, he flatly affirmed that 'the Angel guardian conveys the believing soul into Abrahams bosom'.[42]

Inevitably, Dingley also pondered the issue, which had divided both the Fathers and the medieval schoolmen, of when precisely in the human life-cycle the guardian began his duties. It was clear to Dingley that the very youngest infants must have guardian angels: 'Were it not so, into how many dangers would they fall? They would be disfigured and lamed with bruises, and fearfull miscarriages'. Indeed, like Lawrence, Dingley inclined to the earliest possible assignment, at conception. There was, moreover, a specifically Calvinist rationale for this solution: 'it may be the Mother is not Elect, and so hath no angel to look to her'. Conversely, an elect woman carrying twins would most likely have three angels 'to attend her Motions and all Occurrences'.[43]

All these musings suggest how closely Dingley's theological and emotional investment in the concept of angelic guardianship was tied to a specifically predestinarian divinity. He was emphatic that only the elect had guardians, and that though their influence might at times be suspended, they never left the presence of God's chosen: 'as a shaddow followeth the body without leaving it or lagging behind, so do the Angels accompany Beleevers in all their walks and wayes'. This also enabled him to deal with an objection he anticipated hearing against the whole concept of angel guardianship – whether it were not 'a Popish and Antichristian point, maintained chiefly by Jesuites and Papists, and rejected by Protestants and sober men?' A fundamental error of the Romanist was to suppose that 'every man hath his Guardian-Angel from God'. Yet this did not stop Dingley from conjecturing (on the basis of no real scriptural evidence) that God might have permitted Satan to place an evil angel over each of the reprobate.[44] Through such refined speculations, the doctrine of angelic guardianship became nothing less than the certification of the decree of election itself.

IV

With the emergence by the 1650s of a fully-fledged Puritan angelology, configured around the concerns of experimental predestinarianism, it is tempting to see attitudes towards guardian angels shifting significantly again as a marker of variant forms of churchmanship. Yet the demarcations are not entirely straightforward. After all, Richard Montagu, no less, had berated the papists for teaching that 'every man living, good and bad . . . hath an Angel-guardian deputed to him'.[45] We can see similar cross-currents in the work of another unreconstructed Laudian polemicist, Peter Heylyn, who was emphatic as any Puritan angelologist that the privilege pertained only to God's elect.[46]

Although the passionate advocacy of Robert Dingley was decidedly unusual, a number of mid-seventeenth-century sources suggest that the belief in guardian angels could quite often be taken for granted, referred to in passing as if it were an unexceptional opinion. Robert Burton's *Anatomy of Melancholy*, for example, contains a brief allusion to the 'assisting Angells' of Christians, an analogue to the *Daemonium* of Socrates.[47] The relevant patristic sources were cited, briefly but approvingly, in Thomas Heywood's eccentric and hugely long poem of 1635, *The Hierarchie of the Blessed Angels*.[48] In a sermon of 1650, the London minister Robert Gell similarly endorsed 'the judgement of the ancient Fathers . . . that every particular person hath an Angel deputed to him.'[49] In another 1650s sermon, the earl of Leicester's chaplain, John Gumbleden, announced it to be 'not altogether improbable, that every particular faithfull Man, hath his particular tutelar Angel assigned him of God.'[50] The same conclusion had been arrived at a few years earlier by the mercurial physician and idiosyncratic philosopher Thomas Browne, who mused that 'I could easily beleeve, that not onely whole Countries, but particular persons have their Tutelary and Guardian Angels'. It seemed to him very likely that many prodigies, prognostications and premonitions, 'which more careless enquiries terme but the effects of chance and nature', were in fact the promptings of protective angels. If the doctrine was not manifestly defined in Scripture, 'yet it is an opinion of a good and wholesome use in the course and actions of a mans life'. Moreover, 'it is not a new opinion of the Church of *Rome*, but an old one of *Pythagoras* and *Plato*'. The pagan origins of the concept, which had seemed so objectionable to a previous generation of Protestant divines, now positively recommended it to the mind of this late Renaissance polymath.[51]

Not all English Protestants under the Commonwealth were swept along with an enthusiasm for the ministry of guardian angels. A notable sceptic, despite his interest in angelic ministry in general, was the Calvinist bishop Joseph Hall. In marked contrast to Browne, Hall was dismissive of 'this piece of Platonick Divinity'. Though the doctrine was 'perhaps well meant, and . . . seconded with much reverent antiquity', it seemed to Hall to represent 'some scanting of the bountiful provision of the Almighty'.[52] Similarly, the Church of Ireland minister Nicholas Bernard was convinced that the numbers of the elect being so few, and the numbers of angels so innumerable, 'it will not be necessary to limit each Christian to one tutulary Guardian'.[53] In a commentary on the Acts of the Apostles, the biblical scholar and Presbyterian sympathizer John Lightfoot was decidedly sceptical. If the task of angels was to attend individual human beings, what, he asked, 'did all the angells but Adams and Eves and a few more for many hundreds of yeers, till the world was full?'[54]

Despite the best efforts of Dingley and Lawrence, the doctrine of angelic guardianship was still associated with popery in some clerical minds. Towards the end of a cycle of sermons preached at St Clements, Eastcheap, and printed in 1652, Thomas Fuller told his auditors that he knew that 'if one of the Romish perswasion were in my place, he would particularly consigne you to the tutellage of such Guardian angels which he conceiveth most proper for your several professions'. But in order to 'shun all shadow of supervision', Fuller commended his congregation instead 'to the Tuition of the God of these Angels'.[55]

After the Restoration, a full spectrum of views about the probability of guardian angels, and the nature and scope of their ministry to mankind, continued to be expressed in print. The first angelological treatise to appear under the new dispensation was the work of the nonconformist minister Isaac Ambrose: *Ministration of, and Communion with Angels*, first published in 1661, and reprinted in 1673, 1682 and 1689. Ambrose upheld the standard Puritan position that angels were appointed to the elect only, and that their guardians were assigned to them in the womb. He confirmed that angels could work on the imagination, typically in dreams, helping to instil good motions and to prevent sin. In all of these areas he had little to add to what Lawrence had laid down a decade earlier.[56] Strikingly, however, Ambrose omitted any rehearsal of the scriptural, patristic and modern authorities for and against the existence of guardian angels. The soteriological centrality of angelical guardianship was further implicitly downplayed in a letter appended to the volume from the doyen of Presbyterian divines, Richard Baxter. In marked contrast to the celestial econometrics of Robert Dingley, Baxter asserted the number of angels to be 'incomparably more than all the men in the world'. This meant that 'every Christian, even the weakest, hath one or more Angels deputed by God to take a special care of him', though 'the same Angels may also take care of others'.[57]

The issue of whether God's plan involved an exclusive pairing of angel guardian and human charge was more directly tackled in the next substantial angelological treatise to be published in Restoration England. The Leicestershire rector Benjamin Camfield's *A Theological Discourse of Angels and their Ministries* addressed a subject the author considered all 'too suitable to that Atheistical and degenerate Age we live in.[58] In traditional, if slightly truncated fashion, Camfield reviewed the relevant scriptural and patristic texts, adopting a studiedly agnostic stance. He pointed out that the same angel could be found bringing messages to diverse persons, with Gabriel despatched to Daniel, Zacharius and the Virgin. Yet from such instances 'I dare not conclude, (as some have done) that it is contradictory to holy scripture, to assert some one Angel ordinarily attending every good man'. On the other hand, diversity of opinions about precisely when the guardian angel began his charge – to most earlier commentators a straightforward problem to be solved – seemed to Camfield simply to render the whole notion 'somewhat the more dubious'. In the end, he inclined cautiously to the view 'that every man [at least every pious and good man] hath his Tutelar or Guardian Angel'. The qualification was significant: there is no insistence here that the ministry of guardian angels must be confined exclusively to the elect. Indeed, Camfield's own anti-Calvinist convictions are not long in emerging: he was openly impatient with those arguing for 'the absolute and unconditional assurance of Salvation to any select number, or the absolute certainty of their perseverance in a salvable state'.[59]

A breaking of the linkage between the ministry of the angels and the indefectable perseverance of the elect is discernible in other sources from this period. In 1667 an Irish Anglican could unselfconsciously declare that God 'appoints an angel for the guard of every individual person'.[60] A few years later, the future archbishop of Canterbury, Thomas Tenison, regarded it as 'most probable that Angels are often absent from grown men, especially whilst they remain in ordinary circumstances'.[61] A similar conclusion was arrived at in an anonymous tract of 1695, attempting to prove 'both from nature and scripture the existence of good genii, or guardian-angels'. This took the view that God allotted to every infant a particular guardian to keep watch over him or her, 'at least so long till vitious Habits confirmed or increased, set this pure incorrupt Watcher at liberty to withdraw from his Charge'. The ministration of guardian angels was thus 'continued only to those who improve by it' – an emphatically un-Calvinist way of looking at things or representing the pathway to salvation.[62]

It seems fairly clear that the attempt, never uniformly adopted by the spokesmen of the godly, to make the guardian angel into an emblem of Calvinist group-identity had by the end of the seventeenth century largely run its course. Into the 1700s, English Protestants were as divided as ever about the very existence of guardian angels, with some deploying against them the arguments Calvin had adduced a century and a half before. Commenting on Acts 12, the ejected Presbyterian minister Matthew Poole described 'the opinion of tutelary Angels' as 'not certain or needful', though he conceded it was 'to this day thought probable'.[63] The 1701 *Angelographia* of Richard Saunders similarly rejected patristic interpretations of Matthew 18 and Acts 12. Although the angel of the latter might indeed have been Peter's, this did not mean that it was on permanent secondment. One might just as well refer to 'the King's Physician' or 'the King's servant' without denoting one particular person, 'because the King hath many'. It seemed to Saunders highly unlikely 'that usually 'tis the same Angel that attends a man from first to last'.[64] A series of sermons on angels by Thomas Shepherd, published in 1702, found no grounds for the opinion in either reason or Scripture, and regarded it as 'brought out of Plato's school into the Church by those, who when they were become Christians, could not easily forget that they had been Philosophers'.[65] The minister Edward Young, a chaplain in ordinary to William and Mary, likewise considered it 'too Nice to say that every distinct Man has his distinct Guardian Angel'.[66]

On the other side of the debate, self-consciously Anglican texts, like Robert Nelson's *Companion for the Festivals and Feasts of the Church of England*, envisaged guardian angels as 'ready at hand to do all good offices to good men', a decidedly unpredestinarian gloss on the ministry to 'heirs of salvation' spoken of in Hebrews 1.14.[67] At the same time, there were still those in the ranks of nonconformist Protestantism prepared to speak up loudly for the doctrine. The octogenarian ejected minister George Hamond published a short defence of it in 1702, ascribing opposition to those places 'where prejudice hath forestalled the Judgement, and confident ignorance incapacitated the Mind'.[68] Guardian angels also popped up in one of the more doleful ditties of Isaac Watts's *Hymns and Spiritual Songs*:

> And must my Body faint and die?
> And must this Soul remove?
> O for some guardian Angel nigh
> To bear it safe above![69]

Although some tropes about guardian angels were endlessly recycled in the period we have been surveying, speculation about their activities had taken some rather heterodox turns by the close of the seventeenth century. Hamond, for example, floated the suggestion that it was not necessarily the same angel who would continue with a man throughout his life, 'but that as by the sincere and constant Practice of Virtue, he asserts himself under a higher Providence, so there is an Angel of a higher rank and order appointed to preside over him.' He also took the view that tutelary angels could exercise their protective ministry 'not only by externally applying themselves to us, but by insinuating themselves into our very Bodies', just as 'the Imps of Witches actually Enter into and possess their Bodies'.[70] This latter conjecture was almost certainly taken from the writings of the Cambridge Platonist Henry More, whose idiosyncratic blend of natural philosophy, supernatural reportage and anti-atheistical advocacy exercised a magnetic appeal for certain sections of the clergy in the later seventeenth century. In addition to speculating about physical possession by guardian angels, More had mused over whether every human being was morally capable of 'consociation with these good Genii', before concluding, with admirable self-awareness, that an atheist reader might think he had 'run a long division upon very uncertain grounds'.[71]

V

So far, I have been tracing opinions about guardian angels through various 'magisterial' texts without much attention to the role beliefs about them may have played in wider religious culture. For some in seventeenth-century England, however, the guardian angel was far from being an abstract, dogmatic or merely assentient proposition. A belief in their active intervention, and in how they might overtly manifest themselves to their charges, seems, for example, to have been current in the circle gathered around the Berkshire minister John Pordage in the 1650s. During proceedings against him by the commissioners for ejecting scandalous ministers in October 1654, Pordage was accused of giving up preaching and the taking of tithes after claiming to receive a command to that effect by his angel. More dramatically, he had talked of being defended by 'his own angel . . . in his own shape and fashion' against a great dragon 'with a tail of eight yards long' that attacked him in his chamber. Richard Baxter later lambasted Pordage 'and his Family, who live together in Community, and pretend to hold visible and sensible Communion with Angels, whom they sometime see, and sometime smell'.[72]

The idea of 'sensible communion' with angels was alien to orthodox Protestant sensibilities, redolent of the promiscuous supernatural exchanges characteristic of the pre-Reformation world. In his epistolary 'afterword' to Isaac Ambrose's treatise, Baxter put forward an interestingly paradoxical claim: 'it serves to take off the inordinate desires of visible and extraordinary converse with Angels; when it is understood that they are appointed to be ordinarily, and invisibly serviceable to us'.[73] Yet Baxter himself was not immune to the temptation to believe that on occasion guardian angels might make their presence known. His *Certainty of the World of Spirits* (1691) included an account of a gentleman of his acquaintance, who had fallen into dissolute ways, and who used to hear a knocking at his bed's head every time he fell asleep drunk and slept himself sober. Baxter mused whether it might not be his guardian angel 'that hath such a Care of this Man's Soul'.[74]

Alleged interventions of guardian angels were by no means restricted to a radical fringe, but could emanate from the most orthodox Protestant circles. A much-repeated story, originating during the Irish Rebellion in early 1642, held that an angel had miraculously provided buttermilk for the starving infant of the godly Church of Ireland minister Faithful Teate, during the family's flight from the island.[75] The autobiography of the pious Anglican Alice Thornton, composed around 1669, was prefaced with expressions of gratitude to God for sending 'His angeles to keepe and guard little children'. In her own case, she was certain that 'God hath sent His guardian angell to watch over me and mine for my good preservation ever since I was borne', and went on to describe a dozen or so 'miraculous deliverances' from her childhood and youth.[76] Still further to the right of the theological spectrum, the Restoration biographer Izaak Walton, in his account of the death of Richard Hooker, reported how Hooker's 'Guardian Angel seem'd to foretell him, that the day of his Dissolution drew near'.[77]

Other stories concerning the proactive agency of guardian angels were collected and disseminated by the angelologists themselves. A favourite was an incident from Jean Bodin's *De la Démonomanie des sorciers* concerning a man (whom scholars now believe to have been Bodin himself) who desired the assistance of an angel, and was from the age of 37 continually accompanied by a spirit that offered him 'sensible manifestations' – for example striking his right ear to indicate disapproval, his left for approval.[78] Isaac Ambrose in particular liked to punctuate his expositions of angelic doctrine with illustrations of 'experiences of this truth'. In his section on the role of angels in conversion, for example, he recounted the experience of a man 'labouring in the pangs of his New-Birth' who had begun to contemplate suicide after despairing of his salvation. On his way to commit the act, the phrase 'Who knows?' shot suddenly into his mind. He took this to mean that no one in fact knew God's decree of predestination, and that he might have been saved after all. This seemed a classic instance of the guardian angel implanting formative impressions on the imagination.

Another case involving pain and self-doubt in the process of conversion was recounted to Ambrose directly by the woman concerned. In the process of bewailing her sins, she 'heard at last a voyce, plainly and distinctly saying to her . . . *If thou'l forget, I'le forget, If thou'l forget, I'le forget*'.[79] George Hamond could offer similar compelling second-hand testimony: a man of his acquaintance had been admonished by 'a small voice' to visit a dying friend, and ten years later he heard the same voice urging him to attend to a business affair in London. Hamond considered that if any man were to

> review and call to mind the several remarkable passages and more notorious
> Accidents that befel him in his past Life, wherein he either strangely escaped
> an imminent Danger, or met with some lucky hit . . . he will find reason
> sufficient to attribute these things to the watchful care of some Friendly and
> Tutelary Genius, which prevents those unlucky chances our heavy and dull
> mortality cannot forsee.[80]

Noting the ways in which medieval writers were apt to identify the unseen intervention of guardian angels in the aversion of crisis and in the exercise of apparently random human choice, David Keck has spoken of 'the Christianization of Fortune'.[81] In some ways, it might seem, little had changed in the course of half a millennium. But we should remember that the clergymen registering such interventions of guardian angels were not chroniclers but advocates. Belief in these ministrations could not be taken for granted. Writing in 1725, the Newcastle clergyman and proto-folklorist Henry Bourne dismissively described the belief 'that every Man has his Guardian Angel' as 'that old opinion' which the arrival of the feast of Michaelmas would invariably bring into the minds and discourse of 'country people'.[82]

Urban sophisticates, such as the readers of *The Athenian Mercury* in the 1690s, may have had an open mind on the issue. One correspondent wrote to the panel of self-styled 'Athenians' who ran the paper enquiring 'whether every man has a good and bad angel attending him?'[83] The editors replied that it was certain that children had a particular angel, and very likely that adults, 'tho' never so vicious', did so too. Hamond's treatise of 1702 was similarly composed in reply to a correspondent, who had written requesting 'my thoughts concerning this Question, *whether it may not be probable that every man hath his Guardian Angel*'.[84]

Like those of Ambrose before him, Hamond's anecdotes bring out a sense of extraordinary intimacy between guardian and charge. In a revealing phrase, he speaks about the 'charitable officiousness' which characterized their ministry.[85] This raises the question of whether, in the conscious or unconscious minds of ordinary laypeople, the unceasing attendance of a guardian angel was necessarily an unmixed blessing. Across the whole of our period, one of the most recurrent themes of applied guardian angelology was the insistence that Christians were never actually alone, that at all moments 'thy Angel stands by and beholds thee, and takes notice of thy behaviour either for Virtue or Vice'. There was an inescapably minatory aspect to this teaching, an intimation of the Panopticon. Robert Dingley warned that angels were 'exact and carefull observers, and eye-witnesses of our Behaviour and Deportment'. 'I ask thee', intoned Thomas Adams, 'when thou pollutest the marriage bed, attemptest an homicide, plottest a treason, forgest a writing, wouldest thou then have the Angels present with thee, or absent from thee?'[86]

VI

In the end, it is quite impossible to say how 'popular' the belief in guardian angels continued to be in seventeenth-century England, though it is revealing that few of the authors I have looked at ever supposed that it was in serious or terminal decline. What does seem safe to suggest is that through the seventeenth century, and into the eighteenth, it remained a ubiquitously familiar and proverbial concept, part of the cultural wallpaper of English society.[87] As in our own day, the protection of guardian angels could be no more than a joke. A humorous tract satirizing astrology, and containing 'infallible predictions for the year 1699', foretold that, if Mars proved ascendant over Venus, a young woman foolish enough to purchase a charm to protect her virginity might the next hour be 'cheated out of her Maiden-head, in spight of her Guardian Angel'.[88] At the beginning of the eighteenth century, even those clergymen to be found debating the issue didn't always consider it to be one of overweening importance. To Richard Saunders, the arguments in both directions seemed 'not very material'.[89] Henry Bourne thought that the balance of probabilities was against the existence of guardian angels, though he saw 'no fault in believing either the one or the other'.[90]

Yet, ironically, in some ways it is the very provisional and peripheral quality of the idea that gives it its considerable utility as a yardstick of religious and cultural change. Across a century and more the belief in individual guardian angels was that rare thing in a profoundly propositional and instinctively conformable age – a genuine matter of opinion. Even the most enthusiastic proponents of the idea, with rare exceptions, did not try to insist upon it as a matter of faith. As Richard Montagu had pointed out to a Catholic opponent, the belief in guardian angels was 'a thing not defined in any Councell; no not in that last Conventicle of Trent, because free, and in opinion every way'.[91] Its ultimately non-dogmatic character prevented it from ever becoming a fixed confessional shibboleth, and enabled it to function as a vehicle for the advancement or containment of a variety of individual and sectional concerns and agendas. Some aspects of this long conversation – such as the necessity and methods of scriptural exegesis – look remarkably constant over time. Yet over the period as a whole, we can also discern a broad pattern whereby discussions of the guardian angel were becoming less a matter of theological probity or doctrinal correctness, and more a means of exploring ideas about providence and fortune, human physiology and personal psychology. I will try to resist the temptation to say that guardian angels were 'good to think with' in early modern England. But they were certainly something that, implicitly or directly, people were often invited to think *about*. The space for relatively unfettered enquiry and speculation that they represented should be seen as a small but solidly placed milestone on the road from Reformation to Enlightenment.

8

Deceptive appearances: ghosts and reformers in Elizabethan and Jacobean England

Over the two generations or so during which the Protestant Settlement of 1559 put down roots in English society, few issues seemed to reformers to epitomize so clearly the link between the Catholics' false doctrine and their degenerate superstitious devotion as belief in the appearance of ghosts. Associated indelibly with the abrogated teachings on purgatory and intercessory masses, stories about ghosts encapsulated the ignorance, credulity and corruption of papists, whereas the rejection of them by Protestants was symptomatic of a sober, scriptural faith. In a sermon of 1552, Robert King contrasted the spirit, which relies on the unadorned word of God, with the flesh which 'sekethe the trueth at the deade . . . geveth credite to spirites'.[1] The Jacobean bishop Thomas Morton argued that Romanists displayed an 'infatuation' with 'ghostly apparitions, which Protestants dare not beleeve', making them 'speciall grounds for the defence of their doctrines of Purgatorie, power of *Indulgences*, and . . . praier for the dead'.[2] That Catholic authorities habitually and promiscuously appealed to the authority of ghosts to prop up their imaginary purgatory was a recurrent refrain throughout the period.[3] Indeed, it was commonly asserted that a belief in ghosts was not some accidental waste-product of the popish purgatory, but the foundation of the whole edifice. In a sermon of 1564, the bishop of London, Edmund Grindal, even alleged that the doctrine of purgatory was 'maintained principally by feigned apparitions'.[4] To the Elizabethan preacher Henry Smith, it was notorious that

> they had never heard of Purgatorie, but for these spirites which walked in the night, and tolde them that they were the soules of such and such, which suffred in fire till their masses, and almes, and pilgrimages did raunsome them out.[5]

Small wonder, then, that in his magisterial survey of popular belief in early modern England, Sir Keith Thomas asserted that belief in ghosts was 'a shibboleth which distinguished Protestant from Catholic almost as effectively as belief in the Mass or the Papal Supremacy'. He went on to suggest that in the first century of the Reformation, ghosts 'presented no problems' to reformers, who knew exactly what they thought about them.[6]

The emphasis in this chapter, however, will be on ghosts as a distinctly problematic feature in the mental landscape of late sixteenth- and early seventeenth-century English Protestantism. I will argue that the intellectual rationalization of ghostly experience was a somewhat uncertain exercise, which threatened to expose tensions within English Protestantism, and also that teaching the people what to believe about the nature of apparitions posed pastoral problems of considerable magnitude. It will further be argued that in engaging with these problems in a variety of genres and contexts, English Protestant writers sometimes remained closer to traditional ways of thinking than they would themselves have cared to recognize.

I

In their efforts to discredit popish visions of the dead, Protestant authors instinctively turned, not to reason, but to Scripture. While a huge array of texts could be deployed against purgatory,[7] there were fewer places in the Bible that seemed to have specific application to the question of ghosts. Mention was frequently made of the warnings to the Israelites in Deuteronomy and Isaiah not to consult with the dead,[8] but only two proof-texts were construed at any length, one from the Old Testament and one from the New. The latter was the parable of the rich man and Lazarus in Luke 16. The rich man in hell spies Lazarus afar off in 'the bosom of Abraham', and pleads with Abraham to send Lazarus to his father's house to warn his five brothers of the fate awaiting them if they do not mend their ways. Abraham replies that they have Moses and the prophets, and that if they will not listen to them they would not repent even if one were to rise from the dead. Here surely was an unambiguous assertion of the primacy of the word of Scripture as the sole source of revelation, over visions, apparitions and human traditions. In the words of the Elizabethan bishop of Exeter, William Alley, 'by this place it is most certaine, and evidently confuted that the soules have not, nor can not appeare after their death'.[9] A series of sermons on the rich man and Lazarus by the Jacobean preacher Robert Horne concluded that 'the doctrine of teaching man, by men from the dead, is a doctrine from hell'.[10]

More widely canvassed than the Lazarus parable, however, was a passage which was, from the Protestant point of view, rather less straightforward, the account in the first book of Samuel of Saul's encounter with the Witch of Endor. This described how Saul had asked God how he would fare in his battle with the Philistines, and, the Lord declining to answer him, how he had turned to 'a woman that hath a familiar spirit'. The witch then summoned up the spirit of the dead prophet Samuel, who correctly foretold Saul's death in battle. Aside from the miracles associated directly with Christ, this was the sole instance of the appearance of a dead soul attested to in Scripture, and a text that, as the bishop of Winchester, Thomas Bilson, put it in 1599, 'hath moved much question in the church of God, whether it were Samuel in deede that rose and spake, or whether it were the divell transforming himselfe into the likenesse of *Samuel* to drive Saul into dispaire'.[11]

With some qualifications, the former interpretation was upheld by Catholic exegesis in this period.[12] Bilson, along with virtually all shades of opinion in the Church of England, insisted on the latter. Thus in marginal annotations to verse 14 – 'And Saul perceived that it was Samuel' – both the Geneva and Bishops' Bibles explained, 'To his imagination, albeit it was Sathan in dede'.[13] As William Perkins helpfully put it, Scripture often speaks of things 'not as they are in themselves, but as they seeme to us'.[14] The delusion was called Samuel, explained Henry Smith, 'as the Bookes of Calvin are called Calvine . . . as he that playeth the King upon a stage, is called a King'.[15]

There were numerous reasons why the apparition could not be the soul of the prophet: the souls of the dead are at rest; the Lord had refused to answer Saul by 'ordinary means'; the true Samuel would have reproved Saul for resorting with witches, and could not have prophesied that Saul (a reprobate) would be with him the next day.[16] Moreover, commentators noted that Saul had bowed down before the apparition: a true prophet would not have suffered himself to be worshipped, whereas Satan desires his followers 'to adore him as a God'.[17] To Protestants, the message of 1 Samuel 28 was clear: it provided a confutation, in the words of the Coventry minister Thomas Cooper, of 'that which the *Church of Rome* doates concerning the *walking of dead men*'.[18] It was also, suggested Perkins, a caveat 'not easily to give credit to any such apparitions. For though they seeme never so true and evident, yet such is the power and skill of the devill, that he can quite deceive us.'[19]

Yet the text used to establish this point was itself an ambivalent and potentially deceptive one. In the first place, Catholic controversialists could point out that another book of the Bible, Ecclesiasticus, asserted unambiguously that Samuel prophesied after his death.[20] To Protestants, of course, Ecclesiasticus was not a canonical book: it was part of the para-scriptural Apocrypha, and therefore open to relativist readings. 'Most Jews of those times did imagin ther might be some conference with spirits and soules of men', remarked Henry Holland. The supposed congruence of Catholic and Jewish superstition about ghosts was itself a polemical trope.[21] Yet the Book of Common Prayer sanctioned the use of the apoc-ryphal books in public worship – a source of irritation and embarrassment to some Protestants of a more 'godly' bent. In December 1584 the issue was raised at a conference at Lambeth between Archbishop Whitgift and the Puritans Thomas Sparke and Walter Travers. Whitgift was compelled to admit that the relevant chapter of Ecclesiasticus was indeed appointed to be read in church, prompting Lord Grey to ask 'what error the people might be in daunger to learne by the hearing of this read, and by believing of it?' To this, in Travers' account, the archbishop had no satisfactory answer.[22]

At much the same time a yet more unsettling interpretative trajectory from 1 Samuel was discharging from the pen of the Kentish gentleman Reginald Scot. His explanation of the incident, in his *Discoverie of Witchcraft*, shockingly broke ranks with the orthodox Protestant one in arguing that there was no manifestation of the devil at all, but merely 'an illusion or cousenage practised by the witch'. 'Samuel' was an accomplice kept in the witch's closet, whose prophecies were provided by the ventrilo-quist skills of the witch herself 'speaking as it were from the bottome of hir bellie'. In an objection remarkably similar to those made by Catholic commentators, Scot argued that 'if it had beene a divell, the text would have noted it in the same place of the storie'.[23]

Scepticism about the appearance of the devil was crucial to Scot's broader argument that witches had no real power to harness or channel the powers of Satan. This was the central theme of his *Discoverie*, in which ghosts *per se* play a merely subsidiary role. Nonetheless, he had little hesitation in applying the template constructed for the Witch of Endor to subsequent reports of appearances of the dead: 'in all ages moonks and preests have abused and bewitched the world with counterfet visions'. The biblical prohibitions on seeking counsel of the dead, or attempting to raise them, did not signify that these things were actually possible, but that 'men beleeve they doo them, and thereby cousen the people . . . some one knave in a white sheete hath cousened and abused manie thousands that waie'.[24]

Scot's thoroughgoing disbelief in the intervention of any supernat-ural forces in the created world made him pretty much unique among contemporary authors.[25] Nonetheless, echoes of his attitude to ghosts were to be found in later writers, most notably in Samuel Harsnett's *Declaration of Egregious Popish Impostures* (1603), which drew heavily on Scot to argue that 'all these brainlesse imaginations of . . . house-hanting and the rest, were the forgeries, cosenages, Impostures, and legerdemaine of craftie priests and leacherous Friers'.[26] Harsnett's fellow bishop, Gervase Babington, accepted that devils might indeed assume the shape of the deceased. But he laid greater emphasis on the 'many a thousand times' that 'false iuggling hypocrites abused Gods people to establish their idolatry, superstition and error . . . such Monkish spirits did walke apace about other mens houses, when hypocritical holiness said they might have no wives of their own'.[27] There was a considerable tradition to draw on here. Fraudulent apparitions had featured in Erasmus's *Colloquies*, and monkish tricks of this sort were enthusiastically exposed by continental writers such as Johan Weyer and Ludwig Lavater.[28] Even the Catholic writers Pierre Le Loyer and Noel Taillepied accepted that many apparitions were the product of human ingenuity, albeit they blamed youthful practical jokers, not deceitful priests.[29]

If for Scot the encounter between Saul and the Witch of Endor was the pattern and precursor of popish knavery, for many other Protestants it was no less than the archetype of demonic witchcraft. It is a measure of how corrosive Scot's theory was to the prosecution of witchcraft that over the succeeding decades English demonological writers turned repeatedly to attack the idea of 'a meere cosenage of the witch'.[30] If the one scripturally attested ghost was in fact the devil, then it followed that any subsequent appearance of one must similarly serve a satanic agenda. Here, indeed, the devil took a more direct and personal role than in any other manifestation of popish superstition: he, or one of his demons, took on 'the similitude of some person, that was lately, or had been long dead' to deceive the ignorant.[31]

Deuteronomy 18.10–11 seemed to identify seeking counsel of the dead as a species of witchcraft, and while 'necromancy' in this period served as a loose synonym for demonic magic of all sorts, in the taxonomies elaborated by Elizabethan and Jacobean demonologists it retained its specific sense of a means of divining by attempting illicit communication with the dead.[32] To some, 1 Samuel 28 was the key unlocking the pattern of demonic heresy underpinning all popish devotions. That Saul had worshipped the apparition was particularly significant. As perhaps the most potent symbol of the inversion of all right religion, idolatry firmly fixed the link between feigned ghosts, demonic witchcraft and superstitious popish practice. In the influential *Christian Disputations* of the Swiss reformer Pierre Viret, translated into English in 1579, the ultimate indictment of Catholicism was that it had

> set up & erected a necrolatrie . . . an adoration and worshipping of the dead, and the most greatest Idolatrie that ever was upon the earth: And have made the bodies of men to serve ye divell, & have made him to be worshiped, under the name and title of them, even as Saul worshiped him under the name of Samuel.[33]

The theories that visitations of ghosts were elaborate frauds perpetrated by avaricious priests, and that they were personal appearances by the devil or one of his minions, were by no means mutually exclusive. Thomas Beard, for example, argued that all the 'strange stories . . . touching walking ghosts' found in old popish books fell into one of two categories: 'eyther they were jugling tricks of imposters to deceive the simple, or deceits of devils to delude the learned'.[34] Another Jacobean writer equally hedged his bets: 'if they be not popish which make such false apparitions for gaines sake, they are certain evil spirits'.[35] In a sermon preached at St Mary's in Cambridge towards the end of James's reign, Robert Jenison similarly asserted that many apparitions were fained popish miracles, but that 'many also have the devill, who is false and a lier, for the chiefe author of them; by which, the supposed miracle-workers his instruments, doe not only delude others, but are deluded themselves'.[36]

Papists were thus both perpetrators and victims of the delusions and of the falsehoods which apparitions fathered upon the world. In Elizabethan and Jacobean England, ghosts validated a spectrum of anti-Catholic views. To some, they did no more than epitomize the credulity and knavery of papists, though to others they conveyed more transcendent meanings. Papist endorsement of demonic apparitions (starting with that of 'feigned Samuel') could slot effortlessly into that system of antithesis, contrariety and inversion which permeated early modern intellectual thought, and by which popish religion as a whole could come to be associated with the anti-type of God, Satan, and with Satan's worship on earth, witchcraft.[37]

As the Puritan Richard Bernard remarked in 1627, Satan is ever ready 'to further popish Idolatry', and 'sorcery is the practice of that whore, the Romish synagogue'.[38] A rather different conclusion was drawn, however, in one of John Donne's sermons of the same year. Donne detected connections between 'the easiness of admitting Revelations . . . and Apparitions of spirits, and Purgatory souls' by papists on the one hand,

and the 'super-exaltation of zeale, and . . . captivity to the private spirit' characteristic of schismatics on the other.[39] Echoes of a conformist anti-Puritan rhetoric are also audible among the anti-Catholic trumpetings of Harsnett's *Declaration of Egregious Popish Impostures*.[40]

II

Ghosts were thus a very multivocal instrument of theological controversy and polemic. But on this issue reformers could not simply face back-wards towards the repudiated popish past, or outwards, towards Rome and the folly or heresy of her doctrines and adherents. Their gaze was also of necessity drawn inwards, onto the Church and people of officially Protestant England. How should they respond to appearances of 'dead souls' in a country which had abandoned purgatory and intercession; what were the people to be taught regarding them; and what did the reported sightings of such apparitions say about the progress of godly reformation itself?

From one perspective it could seem that these were questions which did not demand anguished or extended answers. A recurrent theme of English Protestant writing about ghosts was that they were simply no longer a problem. Ghosts were part of the superstitious dross which had clogged up the house of English Christianity, but had now been swept out by the new broom of the gospel. This opinion was voiced as early as 1543 by the Henrician reformer Robert Wisdom, who asserted that 'sowles departed do not come again and play boo peape with us'. He added that 'thankes to god, ever since the word of god cam in thei be nether herd nor senne'.[41]

Under Elizabeth, a number of authorities were keen to confirm Archbishop Sandys's encouraging assurance that 'the gospel hath chased away walking spirits'.[42] The theme was a recurrent one of the transla-tion of Lavater's ghost treatise: 'there were farre more of these kindes of apparitions and myracles seen amongest us, at such tyme as we were given unto blindnesse and superstition . . . The clere light of Gods word driveth away al such spirits'.[43] The narrator of the satirical *Greenes News both from Heaven and Hell* (1593) consciously evoked a *retardataire* ethos in his response to 'a most grislie ghost wrapt up in a sheete . . . I remembered my self how old Fathers were wont to say, that Spirits in such cases, had no power to speake to any man, untill they were first spoken to'.[44] Unsurprisingly, one of the most emphatic assertions that ghosts were now an infrequent occurrence came from Reginald Scot. Thanks to the preaching of the gospel, the sighting of apparitions was much reduced and would shortly vanish away completely. In Germany, he reported on good authority, spirits had ceased to appear since the time of Luther. In distinctly triumphalist mode, Scot propounded that

> through ignorance of late in religion, it was thought, that everie churchyard swarmed with soules and spirits: but now the word of God being more free, open, and knowne, those conceipts and illusions are made more manifest and apparent . . . Where are the soules that swarmed in times past? Where are the spirits? Who heareth their noises? Who seeth their visions? Where are the soules that made such mone for trentals, whereby to be eased of the paines in purgatorie?[45]

Scot was here again echoed by Samuel Harsnett, who scoffed that in the time of 'popish mist', children, old women and maids were afraid to cross a churchyard, and if tithes or Peter's Pence were unpaid, 'people walked in fear of spirits'.[46] The claim that sightings of ghosts were more usual when popery held sway was made by other early Stuart anti-Catholic writers, including John Donne, Richard Bernard and Edward Hoby, the latter referring contemptuously to those night-ghosts 'which the world hath now for many yeares since forgotten to believe.'[47]

The question of whether there were more spectral apparitions in 1500 than in 1600 is one which unfortunately does not lend itself to any kind of meaningful historical analysis. The vanishing of spirits was in any case less an empirical observation than a rhetorical and polemical trope in the campaign against Catholicism. In other contexts, Protestant writers were quite ready to affirm that the popular belief in ghosts was far from moribund. In 1571, for example, the preacher John Northbrooke can be found insisting that souls 'wander not abroade as foolishly is furnished'.[48] Such admonitions against superstitious survivalist beliefs were perhaps to be expected in the early years of Elizabeth's reign, but in fact they supplied a constant refrain throughout the period. A range of divines attributed belief in the apparition of souls to 'the unskilled multitude', 'the simple people', 'the common people' and 'many ignorant persons among us', finding it 'still in the mouth and faith of credulous superstition at this day'.[49] In the theophrastic dialogues beloved of Puritan writers, bucolic characters are sometimes made to confess their desire to communicate directly with the dead. In Jean Veron's *The Huntyng of Purgatorye to Death*, Didymus, 'a poore simple and ignoraunt person', confesses that he doesn't know what to think about purgatory 'except peradventure, I shoulde chaunce too mete with some of those spirits & soules, which (as our priests wil make folkes to believe) arte wont to appeare after their deathe, for to crave good deedes'.[50] Four decades later, in Arthur Dent's dialogue *The Plaine Man's Pathway to Heaven*, the character of Antilegon refuses to accept assurances about the small number of the elect, unless, 'there should come two soules, one from heaven, and another from hell, and bring us certaine newes how the case stood'.[51]

Didymus and Antilegon were of course straw men, literary stereotypes whose dialectical function was to underscore true doctrine by articulating objections that could easily be disposed of.[52] Taking Protestant writing on ghosts as a whole, however, it seems fairly clear that in expressing concerns about popular beliefs, many authors were not merely constructing an artificial 'other', an inversion of orthodoxy whose postulation provided the logical and philosophical basis for their own attitudes. Rather, they were speaking to and from experience, and directly confronting a pastoral reality. Underpinning the ghost treatise of the Swiss reformer Ludwig Lavater was his conviction that 'daily experience teacheth us that spirits do appear to men'.[53] The translator, Robert Harrison, justified turning the treatise into English on the basis of pressing pastoral need. Not only were there still superstitious persons who had been taught to believe that 'mens soules returne agayne on earth, cravyng helpe of the lyvyng', but there were also those 'otherwise well trayned up in religion' whose beliefs on the question of ghosts were confused and uncertain, and did not conform to those of orthodox Protestantism. Like Lavater, Harrison confirmed that 'there be many also, even nowe a dayes, which are haunted and troubled with spirites'.[54] Reginald Scot found it bitterly ironic that while his contemporaries gave no credit to tales of purgatory souls wandering the earth in pursuit of trentals and masses, 'we thinke soules and spirits may come out of heaven or hell, and assume bodies'.[55]

Some leading reformers were able to confirm from first-hand experience that this was the case. In around 1564 Bishop Pilkington of Durham wrote to Archbishop Matthew Parker about events at Blackburn where a young man had been conversing with a neighbour who died four years before. The curate, schoolmaster and other neighbours had seen the apparition also, and Pilkington despairingly commented that 'these things be so common here, and none of authority that will gainsay it, but rather believe and confirm it, that everyone believes it'.[56]

Despite (or perhaps because of) this unsettling experience, Pilkington does not seem to have been impelled to consider the question of ghosts at any length in his writings. But some who went into print on the issue clearly did so in response to actual sightings or affirmations among their parishioners. In a 1581 treatise on the *Nunc Dimittis*, the Puritan minister

Anthony Anderson included a long discursus 'beating down to death this error . . . that the soules of the dead depart not so from us, but that after buryall they walke in the earth, and appeare unto men'. His motive for doing so was that even as he composed the work 'a most slanderous report is raysed of an honest and vertuous Minister departed this lyfe, that hys soule nowe walketh at this daye in his Parsonage house'.[57] In a printed funeral sermon of 1619, John Preston took occasion to reprove the 'many who affirme that they have seene and heard dead men to walke and talke, to frequent their premises, and to say, I am the soule of this man, or of that woman'.[58] Preachers sometimes imaginatively anticipated (or perhaps just echoed) the scepticism of the people towards orthodox Protestant interpretations. 'Thou wilt say', remarked Anderson, 'what shall we say to this, there is much iumblyng in suche a house, and there is seene lyvely such a man walke before us, whome we cannot but say to be our friend departed, to all our sences judgement.' 'How then?', ventriloquized Henry Smith, 'what is this which I see in the night like such a man, and such a man?'[59] The renowned Elizabethan pastor Richard Greenham was asked by a parishioner if spirits might haunt a house, and replied that it was possible, but that 'it is not undoubtedly the soule of any departed'.[60]

Some reformers made serious efforts not merely to denounce, but to explain to the laity why apparitions could not be the souls of the dead. Smith patiently expostulated that such an entity could not be a soul, since souls are spirits and by definition invisible. Nor could it be a body, since a body cannot walk without a soul, and a look in the grave of a dead man would confirm his body to be still there. In short, the apparitions of the age are none other than that which appeared to Saul, a dangerous delusion of the devil 'to draw us from the word of God, to visions, & dreams, and apparitions, upon which manie of the doctrines of the papists are grounded'.[61] Gervase Babington proceeded in similarly syllogistic fashion. Such spirits could not come from hell, whence there is no escape, and if they came from heaven, 'who should send them there hence to wander on earth?' Not the devil, who has no rule in heaven; nor God 'for he hath thousands of Angels to doe his will'. If the dead were able to come back of their own volition, then they would seek to be with us always, 'they being not now deprived of love, and become cruel'. Like other commentators, Babington cited St Augustine's remark that if the dead were able to return, his loving mother Monica would never have left him alone.[62]

III

Protestant preachers and writers could thus with great confidence and clarity tell people what ghosts were not – they were not the souls of dead persons returning from heaven or hell, or from a non-existent purgatory. Rather more problematic was the task of accounting for what they actually were, and about this there was no certainty or infallible test. Very commonly, of course, ghosts were supposed to be devils, but this was not the only theory canvassed. Nor was it always clear with what aims and by whose authority such devils operated on earth. In the process of telling the people what to think about ghostly apparitions, reformers were in fact working it out for themselves, and they came up with a number of overlapping interpretative models.

To begin with the most esoteric of contemporary speculations, some reformers showed an awareness of the theory, propagated by the Renaissance magus Cornelius Agrippa, that apparitions of the dead represented a kind of temporary and natural projection from the body of the deceased, though generally they did so only to reject it.[63] Ironically, here the postulations of learned natural magic may have overlapped with a long-standing popular intuition that the souls of the dead lurked for a transitional period near the places where they had been buried.[64] For neither reason did the idea recommend itself to the proponents of godly reformation.

The explanation which some Protestants had used to account for the proliferation of visions and apparitions in medieval times, namely that they were frauds engineered by the duplicity of popish priests and monks, obviously had more limited application in accounting for the continued reporting of ghosts, though it was still periodically trotted out. A 1582 tract by Barnaby Rich described how a teenager in Flintshire in Wales, Elizabeth Orton, 'had been seduced by a ronegate priest, and how by his instructions she had feined to see certaine visions' including that of a recently deceased local girl.[65] In 1624, the pamphleteer John Gee accused the Jesuits of faking two recent ghostly appearances in London, for the purpose of conning gullible women to part with their fortunes and enter nunneries. One of the victims reportedly told Gee that she thought 'some of those things could not be done without witchcraft, or some strange helpe by the devill', but Gee's own conclusion was that the apparitions were 'some iugling tricke', adding sarcastically that 'apparitions from the dead might be seen farre cheaper at other Play-houses. As for example, the Ghost in Hamlet, Don Andreas Ghost in Hieronimo.'[66] The Jesuits, however, could not plausibly be blamed for all the walking spirits infesting Protestant England.

A rather different approach to the problem was to imply that many of these were not true apparitions at all, but rather the product of timorousness, overactive imaginations and that characteristic Elizabethan malady, melancholy. It was a cliché of contemporary commentators on spectres and apparitions, English and continental, that the groups most likely to believe they had seen a ghost were melancholics, madmen, cowards, those with guilty consciences, the sick, the aged, children, women (especially menstruating women).[67] As Babington remarked, 'many times the corrupt humours that are in our heads will make us thinke we see formes, and faces and shapes and shadowes that indeed are not at all there'.[68] There was, however, no necessary and intrinsic contradiction, and certainly no hard and fast dividing line, between the idea of subjective illusion and that of objective delusion, between 'natural' and 'supernatural' explanations for the phenomenon of ghosts. Melancholics, like sinners and papists, were expected targets for the devil to insinuate himself upon, a truism reflected in contemporary theories of suicide, as well as in Hamlet's poignant concern that the devil 'out of my weakness and my melancholy – as he is very potent with such spirits – abuses me to damn me'.[69] The *locus classicus* of early modern treatments of melancholia, Robert Burton's *The Anatomy of Melancholy*, cited it as axiomatic that 'melancholy men are most subject to diabolical temptations and illusions, and most apt to entertain them'.[70]

If the overwhelming consensus of commentators was that at least a proportion of apparitions possessed some kind of objective reality, did it follow that they were necessarily evil? As Michael MacDonald has observed, 'Elizabethans believed that the world was vibrant with supernatural forces and invisible beings'.[71] Many of these beings were God's servants, the angels; might they not on occasion manifest themselves visibly for the furtherance of God's purposes?

The possibility was admitted by the pre-eminent Protestant ghost authority of the age, Ludwig Lavater. Lavater began his treatise observing that spirits were 'not the souls of dead men . . . but either good or evill Angels', and he went on firmly to maintain that good angels sometimes appear. But Lavater was also quick to insist that since all that was necessary for salvation was contained in the word of God, 'good angels appeare to us more seldom in this oure tyme'.[72] Indeed, a number of Protestants raised the possibility of angels appearing in bodily form to human beings only immediately to dash it. Predictably, Reginald Scot took this view: the age of miracles was past, and God no longer sent his 'visible angels' to men and women on earth.[73] But Scot was here in good company. Elizabethan England's leading theologian, William Perkins, was of the opinion that angels 'appeare not nowe as in former times'.[74] The king of Scots, and soon to be king of England, agreed. In his *Daemonologie*, James denied that angels could appear in the forms of dead people, and insisted that 'since the comming of Christ in the flesh, and establishing of his Church by the Apostles, all miracles, visions, prophecies, & appearances of Angels or good spirites are ceased'.[75]

Despite this authoritative testimony, however, the isssue was not a closed one in Jacobean England, as some events at Hidnam House near Launceston in Cornwall make clear. The divine Daniel Featley was here house-guest to Sir Thomas Wise, who sounded him out on 'the truth of apparitions . . . and notes of difference betweene good angels and bad'. Wise then confessed that about a month earlier his household had been haunted. A ghostly vision of a woman appeared in the bedchamber of his maids, their screams waking the house. They told their master that 'they were frighted with a walking spirit'. Sir Thomas initially dismissed this as 'vaine fancy of womanly feare', but the following night the apparition appeared in his own chamber, standing at the foot of his bed for half an hour before gradually vanishing. Wise, previously 'ever of the opinion that there were no such apparitions', had by his own account behaved in an exemplary Protestant fashion. He had prayed fervently, confessing his heinous and grievous sins, and charged the apparition 'in the name of the God of heaven to come no nearer'. After the event he sought the counsel of an archdeacon who pronounced it 'an angellical apparition and not a diabolicall illusion', on the grounds that it did him no hurt, that he had the power to speak to it, and that it had appeared in white and shining raiment. Featley, however, judged 'rather it was an evill spirit'; first because 'miraculous revelations and angelicall apparitions are ceased', but also because an angel would have delivered a message, and because it was unheard of for an angel to appear in the form of a woman. He advised Sir Thomas not to enquire curiously about the apparition, 'but to examine his owne conscience, and give God thanks for his deliverance, but especially to sinne no more, lest a worse thing befell him'.[76]

The Hidnam haunting opens for us a range of perspectives on the same event: that of the terrified servants, of the educated Protestant layman Sir Thomas, and of the learned divines he subsequently consulted about the affair. Even when the latter had had their say, the happening remained numinous and uncertain. The remaining part of this chapter will attempt to explore how cultural constructions of the ghost in Protestant England were refracted through dialogues between elite and popular culture (albeit less literal ones than at Hidnam) and how in the process traditional ideas helped to shape, and to some extent mitigate, the demonic apparition of Protestant orthodoxy.

IV

A useful point of departure here is the recognition that to Protestants, no less than to Catholics, ghostly apparitions might serve didactic and exemplary purposes. It was a commonplace of Protestant rhetoric that the devil and his minions 'can do us no harme be they never so desirous, excepte God give them leave thereto', and that they might on occasion be directly employed to execute the judgements of God.[77] Ghosts, therefore, might be subsumed into that mindset of providentialism, which, as Alexandra Walsham has demonstrated, saturates the discourses of early modern England.[78]

This could lead to the expression of a certain amount of ambivalence about the status and nature of ghosts, even in rather surprising places. In the 1563 edition of his *Acts and Monuments*, for example, John Foxe retold a story from the medieval chronicle of Mathew Paris. Pope Innocent IV had excommunicated the bishop of Lincoln, Robert Grosseteste, for rebuking the pope's corruption, and two years after his death the bishop appeared in the night to Innocent and beat him up with his staff. In the second, 1570 edition, Foxe repeated the story in much greater detail, though this time adding 'a note to the reader concerning the appearing of dead men' to the effect that though images of things unseen through the permission of God can come to people in their sleep, 'certaine it is, that no dead man materially can ever rise againe, or appeare, before the judgement day'.[79] Despite this delayed disclaimer, the moral and dramatic force of the story clearly lay in the idea of the dead as instruments of God's justice avenging wrongs committed against themselves, an idea commonly found in the popular sermon collections of the late Middle Ages.[80]

A 1581 pamphlet by the moralist Philip Stubbes told a similar, if more homely, cautionary tale. An avaricious Leicestershire woman, who refused to remit the debt of a dying poor man, was visited by the devil in the guise of the pauper, who struck her and turned her body black as pitch.[81] Stubbes at least was clear that the visitant was the devil in appropriate disguise. The issue was less clear-cut in another providential pamphlet, *A Strange and Fearful Warning to all Sonnes and Executors*, which appeared in 1623. As the title suggests, this concerned a dutiless son, the heir of John

Barefoote, a tailor of Sunning in Wiltshire, who held back some legacies intended for his sisters. In consequence, his house and belongings were repeatedly wrecked by a poltergeist until he finally relented. In rehearsing these events, the pamphlet displayed considerable ambiguity about the identity of the supernatural force at work. It is described initially as the work of the devil and an 'evil spirit', but later as 'Gods Angel and no evill'. Moreover, the author reported that certain children of the town had seen old Barefoote 'walke in the churchyard in a most strange and fearefull manner'. The pamplet offered a somewhat convoluted hypothesis here:

> it may be, that they might see some vision or representation of him, for some spirit (through Gods sufferance) might assume an apparant likeness of him: a thing only appointed to make men know and beleeve, that he was shewed in the likenesse of a Spirit, as a cause of all these present evils, in regard that he being wronged, that all these things (for his sake) happened to the wronger.[82]

Remarkably, there were some Protestant tellers of providentialist anecdotes who didn't even go this far in conforming to orthodox doctrine about the spirits of the dead. A work by the Scottish writer David Person, published in London in 1635, unselfconsciously related the tale of a man who broke his promise to bury his wife in the churchyard. As a result, 'this woman's ghost . . . did so incessantly both haunt and affright, both him, his children, and family, that there was no resting for them at any time'.[83]

In these exemplary cases of spirits (in the likeness of identifiable dead individuals) haunting malefactors of various kinds, it is possible to see Protestantism involved in a kind of dialogue with more perdurable elements of popular beliefs about the behaviour and rationale of ghosts. This is a pattern for which we have been prepared by the work of Walsham on providential literature more generally, of Peter Lake on murder pamphlets, and of Tessa Watt on cheap print and godly ballads.[84] In the field of ghost lore, however, it is possible to suggest that the writings of reformers not only engaged with popular belief, but were themselves structured by it, that English Protestant typologies of the demonic apparition were in fact substantially shaped by traditional expectations about the ghostly revenant.

In the first place, there was the question of what was considered to be the characteristic, even defining, activity of apparitions and spirits. In attacking Catholic traditions and superstitious popular beliefs about ghosts, reformers overwhelmingly typified them as 'walking' or 'wandering' spirits.[85] These rather aimless-sounding activities seem somewhat at odds with official Catholic teaching, which held that ghosts appeared by special permission of God for highly specific reasons, but they undoubtedly reflected a widespread popular sense about the restless, troubled spirits of some of the dead. It seems highly likely too that this was how people in Reformation England continued to represent to themselves the nocturnal behaviour of spirits, whether malevolent or benign. As we have seen, the maidservants of Sir Thomas Wise were 'frighted with a walking spirit'.[86] Looking back from the later seventeenth century, the antiquarian John Aubrey remembered how 'when I was a child (and so before the Civill Warres) . . . the fashion was for old women and mayds to tell fabulous stories nightimes of Sprights and walking of Ghosts'.[87] Protestants knew of course that the souls of the dead did not walk; that it was the devil who simulated this to deceive the unwary. The logical corollary of this, however, was that in Protestant demonology one of the most direct and overt forms of satanic activity in the world was patterned after the folk beliefs of medieval Catholicism. As Sir Thomas Browne put it, writing in the 1630s,

> those apparitions, and ghosts of departed persons are not the wandring soules of men, but the unquiet walkes of Devils, prompting and suggesting us unto mischiefe, bloud, and villany, instilling, & stealing into our hearts, that the blessed souls are not at rest in their graves, but wander solicitous of the affaires of the world.[88]

A similar structural congruence between learned Protestantism and unlearned opinion relates to the places where this walking was most likely to take place. John Bossy argued that the traditional ghost 'was personal not real; he haunted people not places'.[89] In fact, this is probably only half-true. The leading authority on medieval ghosts, Jean-Claude Schmitt, asserts that 'countless tales of apparitions' were linked to parish cemeteries.[90] Reginald Scot sarcastically noted that in the past 'every churchyard swarmed with souls'.[91] There was no particular reason in Catholic theology why souls from purgatory should have manifested themselves pre-eminently in churchyards. That ghosts were seen there was probably linked to a more naturalistic popular conception of the dead, which associated their spirits with the places where their bodies were buried. 'The common people deem that the spirits and ghosts of the dead walk at their graves and relics, and are most conversant in churchyards', noted John King in a sermon at York in 1594.[92]

Nor was there an obvious rationale for the devil to make the churchyard his base of operations, other than the fact he appeared to do so. Inventive reasons were sometimes advanced by Protestant writers to account for this. Thomas Nashe stated that 'if anie aske why [the devil] is more conversant and buysie in churchyards and places where men are buried, than in anie other places', it was because he wanted to make us believe that 'the bodies & soules of the departed rest entirely in his possession', adding that 'the boanes of the dead, the divell counts his chiefe treasure, and therfore is he continually raking among them'.[93] Thomas Browne adduced a similar explanation: the reason that phantoms 'doe frequent Cemiteries, charnall houses, and churches, it is because those are the dormitories of the dead, where the Devill like an insolent Champion beholds with pride the spoyles and Trophies of his victory in Adam'.[94]

Some echoes of genuine popular concerns are also faintly audible in discussions of whether the *bodies* of the dead were ever disturbed from their rest. As Nancy Caciola has demonstrated, a belief in the power of the malevolent dead to reanimate their corpses was characteristic of some strands of non-learned culture in medieval northern Europe. It was a particularly prominent feature of the series of ghost stories recorded by a monk of Byland Abbey in Yorkshire in the early fifteenth century.[95] Whether or not the devil had the power to assume and automate the bodies of the dead was a question that genuinely divided Protestant divines and demonologists in the sixteenth and early seventeenth centuries. Some authors, including Lavater, denied it outright.[96] Others were more agnostic, but thought it unlikely that the devil could do so.[97] The champion of the contrary view was James VI & I, who argued that if demonic possession of the living was permitted by God, appropriation of corpses certainly would be. As a consequence, the devil could become visible to human beings 'and as it seemes unto them naturallie as a man converses with them'.[98] Significantly, the Jacobean witchcraft statute of 1604 added to the list of capital offenders those who dug up the bodies of the dead to use for any kind of sorcery.[99]

In his 1596 treatise *The Divell Conjured*, Thomas Lodge agreed that evil angels can 'appeare in assumpted bodies, appropriat to their intents'. Furthermore, Lodge appeared to subscribe to the popular (and erroneous) belief that the hair, beards and nails of the recently dead could continue to grow.[100] It is certain that these were issues that resonated outside the world of theological polemic and demonological scholarship. In the popular drama *The Vow Breaker* (1636), by the provincial playwright William Sampson, the ghost of a scorned lover returns to haunt his false sweetheart. However, the apparition is considered by one of the other characters to be the result of sorcery:

Hell can put life into a senseless body,
And raise it from the grave, and make it speake;
Use all the faculties alive it did,
To worke the Devill's hellish stratagems![101]

As *The Vow Breaker* reminds us, ghosts in Reformation England were not just a topic of theological discourse, or an occasional and disturbing facet of genuine experience. They were also a cultural type affording the opportunity for imaginative representation. Ghosts, of course, made regular appearances on the Elizabethan and Jacobean stage. It has been calculated that in the period 1560–1610, 51 ghosts were featured in 26 plays.[102] They were also a mainstay of the genre of 'news' or 'letters from hell' which was in vogue in the 1590s and early 1600s, the ghosts here usually acting as mouthpieces for satire or social criticism.[103] Occasionally, representations of ghosts in literary works might carry rather self-conscious health warnings. When the ghost of the actor Richard Tarleton appears to the narrator at the start of the late Elizabethan burlesque *Tarleton's News out of Purgatory*, the latter starts back, crying '*In nomine Jesu*, avoid, Satan, for ghost thou art none, but a very devil. For the souls of them which are departed (if the sacred principles of theology be true) never return into the world again till the general resurrection.' The ghost, however, is decidedly unimpressed, responding, 'Oh there is a Calvinist'.[104]

Many dramatists who employed ghosts did not agonize unduly over their precise ontological status, or they evaded sensitive theological issues by rationalizing them as spirits from Hades in the Senecan tradition. A good number of critics have noted too that Shakespeare's *Hamlet* is highly unusual among Elizabethan and Jacobean plays in explicitly addressing the question of whether the apparition is really the spirit of Hamlet's father, or a demonic illusion, and making it central to the action of the play.[105] It does not by any means follow that authors of works employing ghosts necessarily rejected the orthodox view that the souls of the dead could not appear again to the living: even so fervent an opponent of walking spirits as John Donne could in verse imagine himself returning as a ghost to haunt a faithless lover.[106] Rather, it points to the decidedly limited utility of the Protestant demon-ghost as an embodiment of dramatic meaning. The literary ghost, whether seeking revenge, showing solicitude for a loved one or tormenting a guilty conscience, usually implied some direct association with the dead person whose likeness it bore. The cultural patterning of the ghost in English Renaissance theatre was a compounded one: it certainly recognized the ideas of the Reformation, and generally contained no hint

(*Hamlet* is a possible exception) of Catholic notions of purgatory and intercession. Nonetheless, its emotive and imaginative energy was predicated on assumptions other than the doctrinally sound one that the dead had no interest in the state of affairs they left behind them, or the obligations and deserts of the living.

V

It is no new discovery that the Reformation in England failed to eradicate a widely held belief in the possibility of the dead making contact with the living. In 1659, a full century after the Elizabethan Settlement, it could be asserted that examples of people returning as ghosts after their deaths were 'numerous and frequent in all mens mouths'.[107] This failure was not, I think, as Ronald Hutton has argued, because of an 'instinctive assumption on the part of Protestants' that folk beliefs about wandering spirits were 'essentially harmless', and a wise pastoral decision was to leave the subject well alone.[108] The evidence cited in this chapter suggests that the continuing propensity of people to believe they had had, or potentially might have, encounters with the souls of the dead was of concern not just to a handful of Puritan zealots, but to a broad spectrum of English Protestant opinion. Although writers and preachers construed ghosts and their significance in diverse ways, there was a clear bottom line. In the words of Henry Smith, he that departeth from this life 'hath no more societie with them that live upon the earth'.[109] Yet this was a message mediated through a culture which unashamedly continued to employ quasi-traditional ghost-figures in its literature and drama, and in which, as Thomas and others have shown, ghosts continued usefully to embody a set of sanctions for upholding social and moral norms.[110] It was a message at times problematized by Protestant authorities themselves, as they attempted to press-gang ostensible appearances of the dead into a framework of providentialist justice. Ghosts and apparitions might seem to represent a clear marker between popular and learned religious cultures, between 'superstitious' and transcendent understandings of the ordering and operation of the supernatural world. But as the reformers themselves well knew, appearances can be deceptive.

9

Piety and poisoning in Restoration Plymouth

Can we identify any pre-eminent physical location for the encounter between elite and popular religious mentalities in seventeenth-century England? A once fashionable, and almost typological, identification of 'elite' with the church, and 'popular' with the alehouse, is now qualified or rejected by many historians. But there has been growing scholarly interest in a third, less salubrious, locale: the prison. Here, throughout the century and beyond, convicted felons of usually low social status found themselves the objects of concern and attention from educated ministers, whose declared purpose was to bring them to full and public repentance for their crimes. The transcript of this process is to be found in a particular literary source: the murder pamphlet, at least 350 of which were published in England between 1573 and 1700.[1]

The last few decades have witnessed a mini-explosion of murder-pamphlet studies, as historians and literary scholars alike have become aware of the potential of 'cheap print' for addressing a range of questions about the culture and politics of early modern England. The social historian James Sharpe has led the way here, in an influential article characterizing penitent declarations from the scaffold in Foucauldian terms, as internalizations of obedience to the state.[2] In a series of studies, Peter Lake has argued that the sensationalist accounts of 'true crime' which were the pamphlets' stock-in-trade also allowed space for the doctrines of providence and predestination, providing Protestant authors with an entry point into the mental world of the people.[3] Lynn Robson has built on this approach, portraying the murder pamphlet as a fundamentally Protestant form, rooted in the theologies of original sin and justification by faith, and identifying its close cousinage to devotional writings on the art of dying.[4]

This chapter focuses upon a single, previously unexamined murder pamphlet, though hardly a typical one. *Hell Open'd, or, The Infernal Sin of Murther Punished* was written in 1676 by the Presbyterian minister John Quick. The declaration of authorship was unusual – the overwhelming majority of murder pamphlets were anonymous. Also unusual was Quick's voluminous treatment: at 96 pages the work is one of the longest, perhaps the very longest, of the entire genre. As with all such sources, we are not hearing a genuine conversation: the voices of the felons are reported, if not ventriloquized, for us by the clerical author. Nonetheless, a close reading of Quick's text reveals much about ministerial strategies for reaching the most wretched of the populace, and about the responses they might evoke. It tells us something about relations between Church and Dissent in one part of the south-west, and, more generally, it helps us to take the temperature of a religious culture which, even in godly circles, is often supposed to have cooled a degree or two in the post-Restoration decades. John Sommerville has argued that the characteristic features of popular religion in the Restoration were 'a decline of confidence, a contracting sphere for God's agency, and a lowering of affective tone'.[5] A foray into the world of John Quick suggests a rather different picture, and reveals how an active interest in the supernatural remained close to the heart of some forms of both lay and clerical Protestantism in the later seventeenth century.

I

John Quick was a native of Plymouth and resident there in the spring of 1676: it was a local *cause célèbre* which prompted the writing of *Hell Open'd*. On 23 August 1675, the family of Mr William Weeks, a Plymouth dyer, were seized with 'frequent vomitings and violent purgations . . . accompanied with grievous pains and swellings in their stomacks'.[6] Weeks and his granddaughter survived, though his wife Elizabeth and daughter Mary did not. A coroner's jury concluded that they had been poisoned, and two suspects were soon arrested: Mrs Weeks's maidservant, an orphan named Anne Evans, and the granddaughter's nurse, Philip[pa] Cary. Between 25 August and 22 September, Evans and Cary were held in Plymouth while the magistrates pieced together a sorry tale from the depositions of no fewer than 19 separate witnesses.

Elizabeth Weeks was a hard mistress: it was reported that Evans was made to rise at four in the morning on the Sabbath, and she was supposed to have said that she would run away with the mountebanks rather than endure more of her treatment. Meanwhile there had been a falling out between Cary and Mistress Weeks 'concerning the frying of pilchards'. But there was more to it than this: Elizabeth had called the nurse 'whore', and said 'that she was her husband's whore'. Cary secretly swore revenge, and persuaded the hapless Evans to place ratsbane (arsenic) in a dish of pottage she was preparing for the family, telling her that 'when the old woman was gone, that we should live so merry as the days were long'.[7] The girl eventually admitted doing so, though she protested she had not thought it would cause death. Cary strenuously denied any part in the affair.

At the end of September, the pair were despatched to the prison at Exeter to spend six months awaiting the assizes. At the trial, Evans was found guilty of petty treason and murder, and sentenced to be burned; Cary was to hang. A petition for changing the punishment into one of transportation was denied, and an attempt by Cary to claim 'benefit of belly' was dismissed after a jury of matrons found her not to be pregnant. Upon the request of Master Weeks, the judge designated Plymouth the place of execution, and a crowd variously reported to be between 10 and 20,000 turned out to see the grisly event on 29 March 1676.[8]

While Quick provides his readers with a full circumstantial account of the crime, and of the 'rare spectacle' of the double execution, the real drama of his narrative is played out in the temporal and psychological space between the two events, as he and other ministers 'discoursed' with the two women, first in Exeter gaol, and again in Plymouth on the eve of their executions. Sharpe is inclined to see clergymen engaged in this sort of activity as 'agents of the state' and 'embodiments of the secular power'.[9] But these labels hardly apply to Quick, a dissenting minister who had been deprived of his living at nearby Brixton under the oppressive Clarendon Code.[10] Nor was Quick in any sense a hack writer specializing in this kind of sensationalist reportage, such as the chaplain or 'Ordinary' of Newgate was to become in the eighteenth century.[11] His other publications comprise a smattering of funeral sermons, a catechism, a tract condemning marriage to a deceased wife's sister, as well as a learned history of the Huguenot Church, the work for which he is chiefly remembered today.[12]

Nonetheless, Quick took to the task in distinctly writerly fashion, with vocative appeals to his 'Reader', and demonstrating a lively facility for scene-painting.[13] What he offered his readers was a compelling psychodrama, a tale of two sinners – the young misguided maid, and the older, more conniving nurse. It opens with Quick undertaking an early morning visit to Exeter gaol, and making a collective address to those condemned at the recent assizes: 'You are here judged of man, and you must die; but what also if you are condemned of God, and must to Hell for ever?' How did they expect to escape God's dreadful wrath? The prisoners offered what they clearly thought was the right answer – by repenting – but Quick made short work of this: 'you think to put off Gods wrath with your pittiful repentance?' A great and terrible God demanded satisfaction, full amends and a ransom; if they could not bring it, 'they must expect as soon as they had died, to be damned for ever'. This, of course, was only phase one of a classic evangelical conversion strategy: the bringing of sinners to their lowest point before starting to raise them up again. Quick went on to offer his listeners 'a discourse made of Christ, adapted to their capacities', emphasizing that his death was the price of redemption to all penitent believers, 'and that this was now offered unto them upon these terms of confessing and abhorring their sins'.[14]

Quick was armed with a sense of vocation that was ministerial in both a pastoral and a clericalist sense. He styled himself God's 'ambassador', and wrote elsewhere in condemnation of 'sorry mechanicks' who 'take upon them to over-rule and correct their pastors'.[15] There was, he later opined, 'not a Minister of the Gospel, who doth not by vertue of his office lie under an indispensable obligation to destroy sin and save sinners'.[16] It was to be achieved in this case by using the threat of hellfire to break the women's spirits, and bring them to an unfettered acknowledgement of their utter sinfulness; a prelude to accepting the free offer of Christ's atoning sacrifice. In a series of subsequent interviews, Evans responded by becoming, at least in Quick's representation of it, the model of penitence. 'She fell a trembling and weeping, and desired my help and direction'.[17]

This took the form of an instruction to review her life, remembering that 'by every sin that you have been guilty of, you have crucified Christ afresh'. She was to exercise herself in continual prayer, until God 'do make your hard heart wax soft within you'. At first this led her to believe that she was damned, but Quick endeavoured to persuade her 'she was nearer Heaven than she was aware of'. By the eve of execution she was ready to acknowledge that she would not despair of mercy, for had not the good thief found it at the last hour? As she was bound to the stake, Quick sought to comfort her, and edify the spectators, with a long extempore prayer, calling on God to remember that 'she is the purchase of thy Son's blood, Oh, let him not loose her! . . . 'Tis late indeed that she comes unto thee, but not too late . . . Late repentance is seldom true, but yet true repentance is never too late'. Quick assured Anne that God would send his angels in a fiery chariot to convey her soul to heaven, and she wept, thanking him for his labour of love on her behalf.[18]

The nurse's tale offers a stark contrast to this satisfying, if heart-wrenching, denouement. Through several interviews with Quick, Philippa Cary stuck to protesting her complete innocence, placing all the blame on Evans, and accusing the judge and jury of convicting her unjustly. In the process she withstood very considerable psychological pressure from Quick and other ministers, working almost in shifts to get her to confess.

Cary was variously told that she was 'one of the most bloody women, that ever came into this gaol'; 'that she was drowned over and over in blood-guiltiness'; 'that she was a brazen impudent hypocrite, thus to dissemble with God and man'; 'that in the day of Judgment, I should be a witness against her, and it would be a fearful thing, that God Almighty should tell her; did I not send minister upon minister to convert, reconcile and save thee?'; 'that she was going into a lake of fire and brimstone there to be tormented for ever and ever; and when she was in the midst of those eternal torments, she would remember that I had told her of it'.[19]

Yet Cary would not budge, and was even prepared to contradict the minister on points of faith. When Quick insisted that she could not get to heaven without confession, 'being a main and principal ingredient into repentance', she retorted 'that it was enough to confess to God, and why should she confess unto men?' Quick hoped that she would not follow the example of her brother, a professional thief hanged the previous year, who had delayed any admission of guilt till he was about to be turned off the ladder. 'To which she rejoyned, that her brother had made a godly end, and she was sure he was now in Heaven, and did wish she might make as good an end'. In the face of repeated assertions of her certain damnation, she wept, 'but she hoped it would not be so bad with her as I spake'.[20]

The usual fallback in cases of convicts protesting their innocence was to persuade them that their sentence of death was nonetheless just, either for other capital crimes they might have committed, or for their general sinfulness.[21] But Cary would not collaborate here either, only admitting at the very end to having been a liar, swearer and Sabbath-breaker, and to once having received stolen money from her brother. As the halter was placed around her neck, she defiantly exclaimed the words of Psalm 43, 'Judge and revenge my cause, O Lord!' At the last Cary was asked if she would have anyone pray for her, and she pointed wordlessly to Quick. But because she would not confess her sin of murder, 'he durst not take the name of God in vain for her sake'. Instead, 'Mr R. the minister conceived a pithy and pertinent prayer'.[22]

II

This tragic moment of refusal, with an Anglican minister stepping forward to observe the formalities, points up the distinctively nonconformist character of Quick's narrative. It is shot through with that subjectivity, interiority and attention to the autobiographical which N. H. Keeble has seen as characteristic features of nonconformist culture.[23] Generically, it seems to belong to what Peter Lake has termed 'Puritan appropriations of the murder pamphlet'. This is not to say that *Hell Open'd* is a work of overt confessional propaganda.[24] The text gives no indication of Evans' or Cary's denominational allegiances, and it displays a noticeably respectful attitude towards the conformist Anglican clergy ('the reverend and learned ministers of Plymouth')[25] who cooperate with Quick and other dissenters in their ministry to the condemned. This seems to confirm the intuition of some recent historians that the 'sober' nonconforming ministers often remained on good terms with Church of England clergy in the Restoration period.[26]

Yet there is no mistaking the distinctively godly dynamic of Quick's conversion narrative. As Anne Evans is fastened to the stake, he is able to contain any impatience he may have felt that it was 'thought requisite that the established Order of the Church should be observed'.[27] But when two unnamed persons proceed 'to instruct her in the nature of Faith, that it was to take Christ as Lord and King, and to submit unto all his Laws, to be governed by them, and in particular to this of suffering the punishment inflicted on her for her sin' (they had clearly read their Foucault), Quick's patience gives out. 'Gentlemen; do not trouble her, 'tis unseasonable now to catechize her in doctrinals; she stands in need of some sovereign cordials to revive and support her drooping spirits.'[28]

An assessment of the respective strengths of nonconformist and Anglican piety in meeting the spiritual needs of the most vulnerable and wretched in English society is well beyond the compass of this chapter. But the ways in which the nonconformist outlook might operate in demotic mode is worthy of some further consideration. Let us return to our starting point: the prison as a site of encounter between popular and elite. It was the considered view of John Bunyan, one gathered from personal experience, that 'God sometimes visits prisons more / than lordly palaces'.[29] Quick did not appear to share this sacralizing gaze. The prison, he remarks, is 'the very suburbs of Hell . . . a seminary of all villanies, prophaneness, and impieties'.[30] On his first meeting with the condemned, Quick asks them if they know who or what Jesus Christ was, and what he had done for them. Predictably, they could not tell. 'None that knows a gaol will conceive this a fable. Hardly any but atheists, and the most ignorant wretches in the whole county are clapt up there.'[31] Yet these were not just contemporary platitudes. Like Bunyan, Quick knew about prisons, and about Exeter gaol in particular, having been incarcerated there for three months in 1663–4 for continuing to officiate at Brixton after his ejection. In 1673 he was imprisoned again, in the Plymouth Marshalsea, after the collapse of the crown's second declaration of indulgence. Quick's prison ministry thus had deeply personal resonances. After one of his conferences with Anne Evans, he delivered a mini-sermon to the prisoners flocking about him in the court of the gaol, telling them that 13 years before, 'I was confined unto this place, but blessed be God for no evil that I had done.' However, the experience had taught him 'to compassionate all prisoners. And the mercies (being a stranger and prisoner), I found by the good providence of my God in this house, have made me pay yearly some vows and thank-offerings to Him within these walls.'[32]

It seems legitimate to propose here that Quick and his fellow casualties of the Anglican purge of 1662, the victims of 'Black Bartholomew', could bring to their ministry in the gaols a level of empathetic insight that their conforming colleagues could not.

Quick's reference to divine providence suggests another way in which the barriers of understanding might be breached, or at least punctured. The work of Alexandra Walsham has persuasively presented an interest in providential occurrences as a form of 'cultural cement' between the Protestant clergy and the people. But both she and others detect a waning interest in providentialism in elite circles after the civil wars. In the Puritan murder pamphlets he has studied from the 1650s and 1660s, Lake finds a spiritualized or moralized emphasis on providence, but 'no pseudo-miraculous providentialism'.[33] Yet in Quick's text, this more traditional variety is never far below the surface. He rehearses, for example, the case of a young criminal 'whose curled black locks upon the gallows instantly turned white'[34] – an evident declaration by God that he would have lived long enough for this to happen naturally, had he obeyed his superiors. Quick's description of the Plymouth executions displays distinctly Foxean touches. Despite 'all the skill and diligence' of the executioner, he found himself unable to light the pyre until well after Anne had expired from strangulation. The wind then shifted to blow the smoke from the fire into the face of the nurse, 'as if God had spoken to her, the smoke of my fury, and flames of my fiery vengeance are now riding upon the wings of the wind towards thee'. When Cary is finally turned off the ladder, 'she went out like the snuff of a candle, leaving a stench behind her'.[35]

Alongside such portents, ghosts and apparitions make several appearances in Quick's text. Anne Evans was reported to have said that she would not lie one night in the house after Mistress Weeks was buried, 'for that she was sure she would appear again as a spirit'.[36] Interestingly, Quick presents this as an understandable fear of judgement, rather than as a popular superstition to be reproved. Murderers characteristically presumed upon secrecy, and yet, Quick observed, 'how miraculously have they been detected? Dreams, apparitions, and meer circumstances have detected and convicted them'.[37]

Again, this was a conviction born of experience. As a minister in rural Devon, Quick had heard, and later assembled in manuscript, various local traditions about Mrs Leakey, the mother-in-law of John Atherton, a Somerset rector, and subsequently bishop of Waterford in Ireland. She had returned from the grave to expose his crimes – incest and infanticide – and to warn him (unsuccessfully) to mend his ways: Atherton was hanged for sodomy in 1640.[38] Quick's interest in apparitions was such that he speculated whether the perplexing refusal of Cary to confess to her crime might have been due to the threatening presence of a ghost; he had heard of a similar case from a minister in Cornwall.[39]

III

From one perspective, the discourses in the gaols of Exeter and Plymouth seem to represent the most starkly confrontational encounter of elite and popular culture and religion, involving a total asymmetry of power and resources. But from another, we can identify more complex processes at work here, in the activities (or at least the representational strategies) of a minister whose priorities were not identical with those of the state Church or the law, who shared something at least of the mental world of the prison inmates and who knew their experience of the powerlessness of incarceration at first hand. Nor should we forget that the genre in which he chose to express himself – the news or murder pamphlet – was itself a thoroughly hybrid cultural form, designed to appeal to a plebeian popular readership.

In his seminal 1985 article on 'The Godly and the Multitude in Stuart England', Eamon Duffy sought to overturn the stereotyped view that Puritan clergy were simply unremittingly hostile to the mass of the population, and he suggested that many ejected nonconformist ministers in particular can be shown to have had an abiding concern for the evangelization and instruction of the poor.[40] Quick's prison ministry can be regarded as a sub-specialism of that larger project.

But we should pause before lauding too much the pastoral achievement of what is, after all, a study in failure. Writers of murder pamphlets typically did not dwell overlong on the intransigently unrepentant.[41] Quick was unusual in making the centrepiece of his narrative Philippa Cary's complete failure to respond to his call for conversion, something he was patently puzzled and challenged by.[42] Remarkably, Quick resisted the temptation to make the maid and the nurse into straightforward emblems of election and reprobation.[43] He refused to speculate on whether Cary was indeed damned, observing that 'God can come in, if he please, between the bridge and water, the cup and the lip'.[44] Moreover, he was clearly troubled by the nagging suspicion that she might indeed be telling the truth, something which made him rehearse all the counter-arguments at considerable length. Dying persons were to be credited, but only if they were persons of credit. Cary was known to be of bad character: 'a man might with a wet finger, prove her guilty of foul and frequent adulteries'.[45] A truly innocent person would have been less concerned for her own life, knowing that she was assured of salvation. Or, alternatively, her innocence would surely have 'ingaged her to a more curious and exact scrutiny into her life past, to have found out the true cause of Gods anger in shortning her days'.[46]

Quick's narrative, in other words, points both to the potential and the limitations of the affective 'heart-religion' which was the bedrock of non-conformist piety. It confirms what Duffy, Margaret Spufford and others have long insisted upon, that Puritanism was no respecter of social boundaries, and that it could evoke a heartfelt response on the lowest rungs of the ladder of society.[47] But where the high-octane tactics failed, there was simply bafflement, and an absence of any adequate pastoral response.

10

Transformations of the ghost story in post-Reformation England

I

Ghosts are creatures of the imagination, traditionally the stuff of story-telling rather than of history. Indeed, the social history of ghosts – or rather, the social history of ghost beliefs – is a relatively recent scholarly development, achieving some measure of respectability only in the 1970s and 1980s, with the turn towards cultural history. The pioneering work here, as for many other aspects of pre-modern popular belief and culture, was Keith Thomas's *Religion and the Decline of Magic* (1971), a book which, though principally concerned with witchcraft, devoted a chapter to the 'allied belief' in ghosts and fairies. It was to be another decade, however, before a full-length scholarly history appeared, in the shape of the 1982 book *Appearances of the Dead* by Ronald Finucane, a medievalist with an eclectic set of historical interests.[1] A few decades on, there is now a thriving cottage industry of academic interest in the ghost as a historical construct, and in the ghost story as a species of historical discourse.[2]

Historians working in this field are deeply conscious of how much of the groundwork for their endeavours was laid by literary scholars of the early and mid-twentieth century, more often than not trying to establish the cultural and religious context for the ghosts of Renaissance drama, in particular, the enigmatic presence at the heart of Shakespeare's *Hamlet*. Even now, the articles by Leeds University English professor F. W. Moorman in the *Modern Language Review* for 1906 on 'The Pre-Shakespearean Ghost' and 'Shakespeare's Ghosts' remain exceptionally useful points of departure for the cultural historian.[3]

It may be time for historians to return the favour, and attempt to say something historically helpful about the genealogy of the modern English ghost story, the cultural confluences and long-term antecedents under-lying its extraordinary popularity and remarkable versatility as a literary form.[4] This is a history whose broad outlines we may feel we already know. In an important study, Emma Clery has examined 'the rise of supernatural fiction', or rather 'the emergence of the supernatural *into* fiction'. The modern ghost story was born in the eighteenth century as an aspect of a consumer revolution which placed a premium on sensation. Fear became valued and desired aesthetically; by the end of the century, literary tales of horror occupied 'an autonomous realm of the aesthetic', detached from concerns of social or religious utility.[5]

The unlikely godparents of this emergent genre were the avid collectors and publishers of supernatural incidents in the latter part of the seventeenth century, English clergymen like Henry More, Joseph Glanvill and Richard Baxter, or the Scot George Sinclair. Such writers publicized what they emphatically insisted were not mere stories, but 'true relations' of preternatural encounters. They aimed to confound a perceived rise of atheism and religious indifference with irrefutable proofs of the existence of a spirit world. Authentication, rather than titillation or literary embellishment, was their goal. Indeed, in their concern to attest and verify, to provide, in Glanvill's phrase, 'sensible proof of spirits', the Restoration demonologists and ghost collectors reflected the very spirit of the Scientific Revolution, even as they seemed to protest against it.[6]

Yet the aspiration to demonstrate empirically the reality of the supernatural, it has been suggested, was ultimately bound to collapse under the weight of its own contradictions.[7] In the end, and despite insisting on the veracity of witnesses, and enumerating circumstances of place and time, the campaigning anti-atheistical authors had to fall back on rhetoric and crafted narrative, on the compelling techniques of literary persuasion. Several of them were astute enough to recognize the temptation of didacticism slipping into entertainment, and to protest, at times too much, against it. Thus, Glanvill could write, a touch disingenuously, that 'I never had any faculty in telling of a story'.[8] Richard Baxter, too, betrayed anxiety about the exercise on which he was engaged, writing in the preface to his *The Certainty of the World of Spirits* (1691) that his aim was to confirm readers in the 'faith of supernatural revelation', and not 'to please men with the Strangeness and Novelty of useless Stories'.[9] George Sinclair, a Glasgow professor of philosophy, wrote indignantly that his relations were 'matters of fact' and 'no old wives trattles about the fire'.[10]

Yet entertainment value undoubtedly contributed to the success of works like Glanvill's *Saducismus Triumphatus*, Sinclair's *Satan's Invisible World Discovered*, or Richard Bovet's *Pandaemonium, or the Devil's Cloister* (1684). In Clery's phrase, 'the stringently factual stories . . . could not contain their affective dimension'.[11] The moralists were storytellers in spite of themselves, and the end of the seventeenth century witnessed 'a

shift from propaganda to pastime, from indoctrination to literary entertainment'.[12] By general agreement, the midwife at the birth of the modern
ghost story was the journalist and novelist Daniel Defoe, whose writings
on the supernatural combined Protestant moralizing with vivid writing
and literary artifice, and accelerated a tendency towards the self-conscious
fictionalizing of ghost stories.[13] It is also possible to inject a note of sober
economic and political determinism into the discussion of textual shifts
and readerly appropriations. In 1724, the British parliament passed a
Stamp Act which imposed a higher rate of taxation on pamphlets dealing
with 'publick news, intelligence or occurrences' than on those containing
history, biographies or literature. This created an obvious incentive for
apparition narratives to relocate from the former category to the latter, and
to confess finally to their essentially imaginative character.[14]

II

This account of the circumstances surrounding the birth of supernatural
fiction is sound in its essentials. But a longer perspective needs to be taken
into account. In this chapter, I want to re-examine the role played by the
Protestant Reformation in creating a context for the eventual emergence
of the fully fictive ghost story. This role was largely one of failure and dere-
liction. The Reformation, I will argue, neither thoroughly suppressed nor
effectively appropriated the apparition narrative. It did, however, bring
about a series of dislocations – theological, social, textual – which created
the conditions for a freer exercise of the imagination in relation to the
supernatural.

To talk so freely about the history of the ghost story, however, begs
some important questions. It assumes that we can identify a genre of
spoken or written narrative whose development is traceable over time. But
what in the pre-modern context was a 'ghost story'? Michael Cox and R.
A. Gilbert, editors of the *Oxford Book of English Ghost Stories*, employed
five criteria for inclusion. The narrative should, first, 'reveal to the reader a
spectacle of the returning dead, or their agents and their actions'; second,
'there must be a dramatic interaction between the living and the dead,
more often than not with the intention of frightening or unsettling the
reader'; third, the story must have clear literary quality; fourth, it must
possess a definable Englishness; and finally, somewhat bathetically, it must
be relatively short.[15]

Only the last of these really works as an almost invariable characteristic of early modern apparition narratives. Even Englishness was hardly

a defining characteristic, as many of the best-known tales were imported ones, such as the account of a poltergeist's haunting of a Huguenot minister in the French town of Mâcon.[16] Literary quality was often mixed, and 'a spectacle of the returning dead' falls short as a definition, as the ontological status of the apparition was often a matter of doubt and debate. We can, however, adopt and adapt Cox and Gilbert's second criterion, and define the early modern ghost story as an account of a dramatic interaction between the living and a supernatural agent claiming to be, or potentially interpretable as, a manifestation of the dead.

There is also, of course, the not-so-small matter that the great majority of sixteenth- and seventeenth-century ghost stories purported to be accounts of real incidents. This raises an issue, unproblematic from the perspective of Cox and Gilbert, but lying at the heart of the construction and character of the pre-modern ghost story: the question of authorship. Occasionally, compilers of manuscript or printed ghost stories wrote autobiographically, claiming themselves to have been the percipients of a supernatural visitation. But more commonly, they described their accounts as relations, and themselves as relators, of episodes that had happened to someone else in the recent or more distant past. In other words, there was already a story in existence, possessing some narrative shape, and having been received by an audience or audiences. We cannot ever recover that ur-narrative. Instead, what we usually have is a composite, layered artefact, in which an original experienced or imagined event has been mediated or filtered through the perceptions and preoccupations of educated recorders, something which is true even of evidence presented and recorded in courts of law.[17] In some ways this represents a serious evidential problem, but in others it presents a potentially instructive vantage point. The recorded ghost story stands squarely at the intersection of two of the classic binaries of pre-modern culture: between the oral and the literate, and between the elite and the popular. This was to be of the greatest significance for its later literary development.

The collaboration of the demotic and the learned in the construction of ghost stories was not an innovation of the sixteenth and seventeenth centuries. The leading historian of ghost traditions in the Middle Ages, Jean-Claude Schmitt, has observed that though the great majority of medieval ghost stories appear in clerical texts, they were also the 'product of a more or less lengthy chain of informants who referred to an earlier visionary experience of a third party'.[18] Medieval ghosts are found in didactic visions of the afterlife and as exempla in sermon collections, with occasional circumstantial accounts in chronicles or other sources. At times, curious folkloric elements manage to appear through a thick gloss of ecclesiastical propriety. This is particularly the case with a vivid collection of accounts of local hauntings, compiled in the early fifteenth century by a Cistercian monk of Byland in North Yorkshire. These spirits are often robustly physical, buffeting and wrestling with the living, and sometimes assuming bird or animal shape.[19] In a few other sources as well, as Ronald Finucane has noted, 'supernatural beings assume bizarre forms and take to frightening people for no apparent reason'.[20]

But the majority of medieval ghost stories evinced reason and order, lying relatively comfortably within a coherent, and pastorally explicable, theological framework. Discounting apparitions of saints, and the occasional visitations of damned souls from hell, encounters with the dead in the Middle Ages followed an established pattern. Ghosts were souls on temporary release from purgatory. They appeared to the living either for their own benefit – to request the masses and prayers that would ease their passage through purgatorial pains – or they carried didactic and improving messages for the percipient: repent of your sins before it is too late; maintain the sanctity of your vows; avail yourself of the grace of the sacrament of penance. The medieval Church managed, with a remarkable degree of success, to appropriate and integrate the popular ghost traditions of pre-Christian Europe into orthodox ecclesiastical understandings of sin and sanctity.[21] In Britain and Ireland, at least, this was probably facilitated by the fortuitous proximity of the commemorations of All Saints and All Souls (1–2 November) to the ancient Celtic festival of *Samhain*. The onset of winter is a classic moment of liminality, when unseen spiritual forces might be expected to break through the barrier between worlds and enter the habitats of the living. But the propensity of ghosts to appear around Halloween caused few difficulties for the medieval church authorities. For when were the souls of the departed more likely to appear and beg piteously for succour than during the Church's great annual festivals of intercessory prayer?

III

The Protestant Reformation of the sixteenth century had no room for such accommodations and rationalizations, being virtually predicated on an absolute rejection of the assumption that had granted house room to ghosts and ghost stories in medieval Christianity. From Martin Luther's protest against indulgences onwards, Protestantism had a violent antipathy towards the notion of purgatory. Protestants hated purgatory as unscriptural, as supporting a parasitic superstructure of chantry chaplains and massing priests, devouring alms that should have gone to the poor, and as contradicting their theology of justification by faith alone, implying that Christ's sacrifice was insufficient and that human striving somehow contributed towards salvation. In the Thirty-Nine Articles of the Elizabethan Church of England, purgatory is 'a fond thing vainly invented' – fond meaning stupid or harebrained rather than affectionate.[22] The vain invention is significant too. As Stephen Greenblatt has emphasized, a recurrent and resonant refrain in Tudor polemics against purgatory is the supposedly fictive quality of the doctrine, its special relationship to fantasy and the imagination, the frequent charge that purgatory was 'poetry'.[23]

No purgatory, no ghosts. The doctrine of post-mortem purgation and the belief in walking spirits were inextricably connected in the minds of early Protestants. It was because the faithful dead were received straight away into the hands of God that the author of a mid-Tudor treatise against unscriptural 'unwritten verities' (possibly Thomas Cranmer) insisted that the soul, 'after it be departed from the body, cannot wander here among us'. Claims to the contrary were 'old wives' fables, the words of liars, and fraybugs of children'. Stories of walking spirits, 'of ugly and fearful ghosts', were, claimed the Elizabethan court preacher William James, props for 'the insufferable pains of purgatory' and the illusionary teachings of the popish Church.[24]

Ghosts were a cynical Catholic marketing device, to shore up a money-making system which sharp-witted Protestant satire christened 'purgatory pickpurse'.[25] With the abolition of purgatory, the apparitions would cease. Already in the reign of Henry VIII, the reformer Robert Wisdom was giving (as it turned out, premature) thanks that 'ever since the word of God cam in thei be nether herd nor senne'.[26] 'The gospel hath chased away walking spirits', exulted Archbishop Sandys of York in 1585. A year earlier, Reginald Scot sarcastically suggested that the ghosts were 'all gone into Italie, bicause masses are growne deere here in England'.

Protestants conceded the theological possibility that souls of the dead might appear. God was sovereign, and could do as he pleased. But there was no persuasive testimony in Scripture that God had ever allowed this, and no evident reason why he should. The souls of the damned were reaping their reward in hell, and those of the saved were enjoying the beatific vision of God in heaven, deaf to the concerns of a world they had left behind them.

And yet the ghosts had certainly not all departed for Italy, and, to paraphrase Mark Twain, reports of their death had been greatly exaggerated.

Protestant pastors soon found that people continued to see ghosts and to circulate stories about them. Such tales were 'so common here . . . that everyone believes them', complained the bishop of Durham in 1564. Nearly a century later, the Cambridge scholar Henry More could report tales of revenant spirits of the dead to be 'numerous and frequent in all mens mouths'.[27]

In the view of Protestant reformers, those who believed they had experienced an encounter with the dead, or those spreading reports of such encounters, were committing what in modern philosophical parlance would be called a category error. Correcting it called for new paradigms to make sense of apparitions' unexpected persistence. Visionaries might simply be confused, mistaking natural phenomena for a manifestation of the supernatural. As Scot put it, on a dark night 'a polled sheepe is a perillous beast, and many times is taken for our fathers soule'.[28] Fraud and trickery – so often ascribed to the medieval Catholic clergy – remained possibilities. A pamphlet of 1624 accused Jesuits of faking a series of ghostly appearances in London, for the purpose of conning gullible young women into parting with their fortunes and entering nunneries.[29]

But even the most paranoid anti-papist clergyman could hardly credit the Catholic missionary priests with the authorship of all reported apparitions. Most Protestant commentators conceded that preternatural apparitions did occur, but the spirits were of a different order and character than the ignorant believed: they were either angels or demons. The former possibility was entertained usually for purposes of cautious rejection. Protestant orthodoxy insisted that angels were active in the world, as agents of God and secret guardians of human welfare, but visible manifestations were thought highly unlikely, centuries after the 'age of miracles' had ended.[30] God's revelation to humanity was complete in Christ, and manifest in Scripture. New revelations were inconceivable – the message carried by any angel sent by God would simply confirm scriptural teaching.

But few attested apparitions conformed to these strict criteria. The possibility of an angelic vision was entertained by one Cornish clergyman, asked for his opinion by the Jacobean gentleman Sir Thomas Wise, after a ghostly vision of a woman appeared and stood wordlessly at the foot of Wise's bed for half an hour in the night. But a more on-message minister, the Puritan Daniel Featley, soon put Sir Thomas right: the spirit could not have been an angel as, first, 'miraculous revelations and angelicall apparitions are ceased'; second, angels were always sent with a message, and third – this the apparent clincher – it was unheard of for an angel to take the form of a woman. 'Rather', it seemed clear to Featley, 'it was an evill spirit'; he evidently shared the view expressed a few years earlier by the Oxford scholar Randall Hutchins that it was impossible 'that a good spirit has been seen in woman's form'.[31]

An incident in Yorkshire in 1621 seemed to confirm the intuition that visible apparitions of all kinds were deeply suspect. Helen Fairfax, daughter of a Yorkshire gentleman, had visions of an angelic young man, clad in shining white. At first suspicious, she was then inclined to believe his protestations that he had come to offer her comfort. But after family members persuaded her it must indeed have been an evil spirit, she challenged it on its next appearance, and watched 'many horns begin to grow out of its head'.[32]

If not an angel, then a demon. This – somewhat depressingly – was the closest to an agreed orthodox Protestant position on ghosts and ghost stories. If a clergyman were asked, as the renowned Elizabethan pastor Richard Greenham once was, about the nature of a spirit haunting a house, he might be expected to reply 'it is not undoubtedly the soule of any departed, but the evil spirits in the ayer'.[33] This raised an obvious question: why would a devil, or even *the* devil, take on the form of a deceased person, more often than not, the form of a neighbour, kin-sperson or loved one? The Elizabethan pamphleteer Thomas Nashe had his answer ready:

> No other reason can bee given of it but this, that in those shapes which hee supposeth most familiar unto us, and that wee are inclined to with a naturall kind of love, we will sooner harken to him than otherwise.

It was, remarked the earl of Northampton in 1583, the cruel deception of Satan to 'set snares for the living' by 'lurking under the names and title of the dead'.[34]

There was, moreover, a crucial biblical prototype for this demonic strategy: the passage in the first book of Samuel where, at Saul's request, the Witch of Endor summons up the soul of Samuel to prophesy about Saul's fate in battle with the Philistines. This Old Testament story was virtually the sole biblical reference to post-mortem appearance. Catholic sources interpreted it as proof that 'soules sometimes appear after death'. But, almost without exception, Protestant exegetes insisted this was no true appearance of Samuel but a delusion of the devil to lead Saul to damnation.[35] The story supplied, in the words of the Coventry minister Thomas Cooper, a confutation of 'that which the *Church of Rome* doates concerning the *walking of dead men*'.[36] It was also, suggested the Calvinist divine William Perkins, a caveat to us 'not easily to give credit to any such apparitions. For though they seeme never so true and evident, yet such is the power and skill of the devill, that he can quite deceive us.'[37]

IV

The Reformation should, then, have led, not so much to the abolition of stories about ghosts, as to their literal demonization. A whole area of numinous experience, of interaction with preternatural forces, was reassigned to the category of the unambiguously demonic. Within a Protestant frame of understanding, narratives of encounters with supposed ghosts should have functioned as clear-headed cautionary tales, of the dangers of satanic temptation and of practical instruction on how to overcome it.

But despite this apparent clarity, the Protestant position on ghosts appears to have been conveyed to the populace in the later decades of the sixteenth century and early decades of the seventeenth in what can only be described as muffled tones. Discussion of the proper interpretation of spirits is a theme conspicuous by its absence from the key didactic instruments of pastoral Protestantism, printed catechisms and the official book of homilies.[38] Judging from surviving examples of printed sermons, it does not appear that ghosts were spoken about much from the pulpit: scattered, occasional references were apparently provoked by local gossip or rumour, such as when the Puritan minister John Preston, in a funeral sermon of 1619, reproved the 'many who affirme that they have seene and heard dead men to walke and talke'.[39] With the exception of Thomas Nashe's eccentric 1594 meditation on *The Terrors of the Night*, no treatise on the nature of ghostly apparitions was composed and printed in England prior to the middle of the seventeenth century. Two foreign works were translated, but in neither case did the initiative lie with the orthodox establishment. In 1572, the Swiss minister Ludwig Lavater's *Gespensterbuch* was rendered into English as *Of Ghostes and Spirites Walking by Night*.[40] The translator was the religious radical and separatist Robert Harrison, whose motivation, revealingly, was that even people 'otherwise well trayned up in religion' were thoroughly confused and uncertain about what to believe regarding ghosts.

The second text, appearing in 1605, had a still less respectable provenance. *A Treatise of Specters or Strange Sights, Visions and Apparitions appearing Sensibly unto Men* was an English translation of *IIII Livres des spectres* by Lavater's French Catholic opponent Pierre Le Loyer. The translator, Zachary Jones, was most probably, like some dramatists of the time, attempting to cash in on the new king's known interest in the supernatural, and he dedicated the book to James I. Jones may indeed have started his translation before reading all the way through the original. *A Treatise* comprises only the first of Le Loyer's four books, dealing with demonic and delusory apparitions. When the text turned to consider the phenomenon of real ghosts from purgatory, Jones ended his translation with an abrupt 'Finis'.[41]

Why did Protestant writers and clergymen not do more to disseminate the new orthodoxy about ghosts? There was a recognized need for popular re-education, as well as a surely golden opportunity to score points about papist credulity, and the demonic underpinning of popish doctrine itself. Yet the response was patchy and tentative. In part, I suspect, this was to do with the frankly flimsy scriptural evidence available. In explicating the appearance of Samuel, or rather, the devil, to Saul, Protestant authors were obliged to forgo their usual hermeneutic instincts for the clear, literal sense of the text. Scripture described the apparition as 'Samuel', and for once it was Catholic exegetes who could accuse their opponents of strained and over-elaborate interpretations. Moreover, another Old Testament book, Ecclesiasticus, asserted unambiguously that Samuel had prophesied after death. Protestants could retort that Ecclesiasticus was an apocryphal text. But it was nonetheless appointed to be read in the Book of Common Prayer – a source of acute irritation to many on the more godly wing of the Church.[42]

There may too have been a recognition, consciously or not, that an inflexible emphasis on the demonic character of all apparitions was a difficult sell at the pastoral level. In stripping away the sacramentals and apotropaic rituals of the old Church, the Reformation had left ordinary people relatively exposed and defenceless against the machinations of the devil, and the discovery that Satan had opened a new front in his war against humanity was simply a further piece of bad news for the beleaguered faithful. It was an unpalatable teaching that the apparitions claiming to be one's father, mother or neighbour were nothing but the most insidious of delusions.

Furthermore, despite its coherent fit with reformed doctrines of justification and salvation, the official understanding of ghosts simply mapped badly on to the world of practical experience. Where ghostly apparitions urged people to kill themselves, or to commit murder, theft or adultery, their construal as demonic was relatively unproblematic. But far more often, ghosts seem to have been concerned with the exposing of murder, infanticide and other crimes; with directing people to the whereabouts of buried treasure; with protecting the interests of legatees cheated of their inheritances; with warnings against sin of various kinds; and with reassuring loved ones about the fate of the deceased's soul. Of course, not all ghosts made their aims and wishes clear, and, as Owen Davies has rightly warned us, there is a built-in bias in the written sources towards 'purposeful' ghosts, rather than the silent, baffling, haunted presences which are a feature of popular culture from medieval through to modern times.[43]

Nonetheless, if ghosts were either primly moralistic or frankly inexplicable, then what the devil was the devil up to? In time, some Protestant authors became more candid about the nature of the problem. Writing in the 1650s, the Cambridge philosopher Henry More remarked that since everybody knew ghostly priorities lay in 'detecting the murderer, in disposing their estate, in rebuking injurious executors, in visiting and counselling their wives and children, in forewarning them of such and such courses', it was odd work 'for a devil with that care and kindness to promote'.[44] Similar conclusions were arrived at in the following century by Edmund Jones, a nonconformist minister who collected apparition stories from across Wales. One of his tales concerned a Carmarthenshire man riding home from Pembrokeshire, whose horse was repeatedly frighted by a spirit, keeping it running till he reached his destination. Jones commented, 'this was an odd turn made by an evil spirit of the night, not easy to be accounted for. I would have thought it was the spirit of a dead relation who (Dives-like) wished well to his brethren, even out of hell'.[45]

In fact, long before this, there are examples of Protestant clergymen apparently less than convinced by the doctrine they were supposed to uphold. In 1584–5, the vicar of Lostwithiel in Cornwall, Henry Caesar, was in trouble for maintaining the 'apparition of souls after their departure out of this life'.[46] Caesar was suspected of crypto-Catholicism. But the belief was apparently shared by solid Protestants in the West Country. In a case from early Stuart Somerset (Minehead) one of the witnesses affirming the appearances of the ghost of 'old Mother Leakey' was the curate, John Heathfield.[47] The theologian and hymn writer Isaac Watts struggled with the passage in the Acts of the Apostles where the Pharisees wonder 'what if a spirit or an angel hath spoken to this man [St Paul]?' Since this seemed to imply that spirits and angels were distinct, it was hard to see what might be meant 'but an apparition of a human soul that has left the body'.[48]

In theory, a Protestant clergyman should have advised any parishioner visited by a spirit to pray fervently and to refuse to interact with the apparition in any way at all. But it is likely that in this, as in other respects, a fair number of ministers went with, rather than against, the grain of popular cultural expectation. In the West Country apparition stories studied by the folklorist Theo Brown, a recurrent motif involves local parsons 'conjuring' or laying the ghosts.[49] Nor does it seem that deviation from strict orthodoxy was the preserve of less educated, rural clergy. A leading Puritan divine, William Twysse, ascribed his conversion to godliness to a schoolboy experience in the 1590s, when the ghost of a dead schoolfellow appeared to tell him he was now a damned soul.[50] A story about a ghostly revenant circulating in Oxford in 1627 led to dispute among the fellows of Queen's College 'whether spirits really and substantially appear, i.e. the ghosts of the deceased'.[51]

While the fellows of Queen's struggled to make up their minds, ghosts and their stories continued to be seen and told across the nation. In the face of clerical hesitation, the narrational initiative was seized by the laity. Early to mid-seventeenth-century ghost stories have left only scattered evidential traces, but enough to suggest a deeply rooted habit of turning individuals' purported supernatural experiences into emplotted narratives for wider social consumption. Ghost stories occasionally came to the attention of ecclesiastical or secular courts, or appear in diaries and letters. Undoubtedly, they often served pragmatic and particular interests. In the village of Middlezoy in Somerset in 1622, Thomas Whyn was avidly spreading reports of the appearances of Christian Godfrey's spirit. Christian allegedly told Thomas's daughter that she was a soul from hell, a place where several inhabitants of the village would soon be joining her, while she added, somewhat superfluously, 'that it was a good thing to go to heaven'. Yet the real reason Christian could not be at rest, it turned out, was that a plank of wood belonging to Thomas was being detained unlawfully in someone's buttery.[52] Not all popular ghost stories were as transparently self-serving as this, but even the most blatant characteristically folded their concerns into expected cultural frames and recognized storytelling traditions.

It would be quite wrong to suggest that popular beliefs about ghosts, along with the narratives that both reflected and reconstituted those beliefs, were somehow impervious to the teachings of the Reformation. To take the most obvious example, virtually all overt traces of purgatory and intercessory prayer had disappeared from English ghost stories outside explicitly Catholic circles by the early part of the seventeenth century. There was also an evident popular awareness of the Protestant conflation of the traditional ghost and the demonic spirit. When Mrs Leakey of Minehead threatened in 1634 to haunt her family after her death, her quick-witted daughter-in-law retorted, 'What, will you be a divell?' But it was the same daughter-in-law who later orchestrated claims that the soul of Mrs Leakey had really returned.

A parallel dilemma is of course fictionalized in Shakespeare's *Hamlet*, whose protagonist must stake all on an agonizing gamble as to whether the apparition urging him to action is a 'spirit of health or goblin damned'. London theatre audiences at the turn of the seventeenth century were surely familiar with the religious debate over this question, or the play's great emotional and dramatic power simply ebbs away.[53] Many seventeenth-century ghost tales can perhaps be described as Protestant in that broad, cultural, non-dogmatic sense that the English people themselves became Protestant over the course of two to three generations. But it is equally the case that during those decades ghost stories never effectively served any kind of agenda of Protestant evangelization nor acted as a vehicle for the transmission of key Protestant doctrines.

V

In the later seventeenth century this started to change, up to a point. As anxieties about residual belief in purgatory started to recede in clerical circles, a more open-minded attitude towards the character of apparitions started to gain ground. The Restoration saw, by the standards of the preceding century, an explosion of ghost stories into print. In part, this was a function of a growing consumer demand for cheap reading material of all kinds, with ghost stories forming a discernible subcategory of the topical 'Strange News from . . .' genre. But there was also a conscious effort on the part of a loosely linked network of clerical and educated lay writers, some Anglican, some nonconformist, to make common cause with popular beliefs about apparitions and to publicize accounts of them for partisan ends.

These men – Glanvill, Baxter, Sinclair, More and others – employed such narratives, as they used accounts of witchcraft and other supernatural phenomena, to combat what they perceived as a growing tide of religious disbelief, stereotyped by contemporaries as Sadducism (after the Jewish Sadducees who denied the resurrection of the body), or as Hobbism (after Thomas Hobbes, the English philosopher who interpreted angels and spirits of all kinds in solely metaphorical terms). There was also, particularly as the century approached its close, a perception that traditional belief in spiritual forces was susceptible to a wave of fashionable ridicule, in which Sinclair detected 'an affected humour in many to droll, scoff and mock at all such relations.'[54]

The defenders of orthodoxy compiled their relations of spectres, apparitions and witchcraft because they were convinced that rejection of such phenomena was the thin end of an atheistical wedge. 'No spirit, no God' was Henry More's aphoristic view of the matter.[55] As Glanvill wrote, 'these things hang together in a chain of connection'.[56] His contemporary, the Leicestershire rector Benjamin Camfield, was convinced people's antipathy to the existence of spirits 'hath carried them on (and naturally doth so) to the dethroning of God, the supreme Spirit and Father of Spirits'.[57] As far as the spirits of the dead were concerned, a moral panic over scepticism and atheism now trumped earlier fears about popular popery. Respectable Protestant clergymen were prepared to stake their reputations on the credibility of spectral phenomena, even when it was often far from clear that the devil was the author of the spectacle.

Had, then, the wheel come full circle, with Protestantism finally prepared to appropriate and shape popular ghost stories for exemplary and theological ends, in much the same way as the medieval Church had done? It is sometimes suggested so, but the picture is more muddied and more interesting. In the first place, there was no clerical consensus about the ontological and theological status of ghosts, with some authorities sticking doggedly to the older line that the souls of the dead never appeared to the living. Writing in 1698, the Reverend John Roe sought to persuade readers that apparitions of the dead were 'directly contrary to the sense of the scripture', 'useless and unnecessary' and 'inconsistent with common reason'.[58]

Even among enthusiastic aficionados of spectral narratives, the precise status of the apparition was often a matter of doubt and uncertainty. Glanvill suggested a spectrum of possibilities. His spirits came under the collective heading of an 'intelligent Creature of the invisible World', but this could make them either evil angel or devil, 'inferior daemon, or a wicked soul departed'.[59] Richard Baxter frankly conceded that ''tis hard to know by their words or signs, when it is a Devil, and when it is a Humane Soul'. He also noted instances where 'it is uncertain to us, whether it be a good Angel, or the Soul of some former dear friend'.[60] When it came to individual cases, it was indeed often difficult to tell. One of Glanvill's relations, a story sent over from Ireland to Dr Henry More, involved a man, a kind of Hibernian Hamlet, unsure whether to pass on a message confided to him by a ghost 'since, though it was a real apparition of some spirit, yet it was questionable whether of a good or a bad'.[61]

In a good number of cases, in fact, musings as to the identity of the spirit were integral to the relation of the narrative, and to the sense of wonder it was supposed to evoke. One of Sinclair's stories involved the malevolent apparition of Isabel Heriot, a minister's former servant. Sinclair ended his account by asking 'what could her apparition be?' He concluded, tentatively, that 'it behoved, either to be her reall Body informed and acted by the Devil . . . or only the Devil taking upon him her shape and form, acting and imitating her to the life'. The latter he thought more probable, noting parenthetically that 'her soul could not be brought back'. Yet this nugget of solid Protestant orthodoxy was compromised by the numerous other ghost stories Sinclair related, some of them drawn from Glanvill, in which no theological caveats of the kind were expressed.[62]

A Glanvillesque compilation of 1688, *The Kingdom of Darkness: or history of daemons, specters, witches, apparitions, possessions, disturbances, and other wonderful and supernatural delusions . . . of the Devil*, belied its title with its account of an evidently benign spirit which guided the conduct of a correspondent of the French jurist Jean Bodin. The author pondered whether in such cases 'they be Angels that are uncapable of assuming humane shapes . . . [or] the souls of the deceased who have more affinity with Mortality and humane frailty'.[63] A similar case of an invisible but apparently benevolent knocking spirit came to the attention of Richard Baxter. It haunted the elder brother of a member of Baxter's congregation, making clear its disapproval of his habitual drunkenness. Baxter reflected:

> Do good spirits dwell so near us? Or are they sent on such messages? Or is it the soul of some dead Friend, that suffereth, and yet, retaining love to him, as *Dives* to his Brethren, would have him saved? God yet keepeth such things from us, in the dark.[64]

This indeterminacy reflected a genuine theological perplexity on the part of Baxter and his ilk, as well as an impulse deep in the Protestant psyche to let God be God and not to enquire too closely into his transcendent ways.[65] But at the same time, a quality of narrational uncertainty, doubt or ambiguity was intrinsic to the modus operandi of the anthologies. There was a strategic determination on the part of compilers not to over-editorialize, or to compromise the pledge to readers that these stories were unvarnished true relations. Thus, in editing for publication one of the manuscripts sent to Glanvill, Henry More made a point of noting that 'I have retained the Scotch Dialect here . . . for the more Authentickness of the matter'.[66]

The printed ghost stories of later Stuart England were replete with circumstances of time and date, with names of the principals involved, and of witnesses who had passed on the relation, with full assurances of their credibility. Letters from informants were often reproduced verbatim, especially if they were people of social standing and unimpeachable credit. There was little attempt to impose any approved and coherent theological framework on the material, beyond vague assurances that the circumstances were manifest instances of God's providence. Wonder and reverence were the responses the authors were looking to elicit, rather than precise doctrinal understanding.

Certainly, the philosophical and intellectual convictions of the learned compilers are occasionally on show: Henry More's determination, for example, to refute the Paracelsian notion that sightings of dead persons were manifestations of the deceased's 'astral spirit', or Joseph Glanvill's adherence to the notion of 'aerial vehicles' for the migration of souls.[67] But such Neoplatonic reveries did not impinge much on the retelling of the spirit narratives themselves. There was, of course, the ever-trumpeted need to confound atheism. But the requirements here were fairly minimal, and usually fulfilled adequately by the mere assertion and attestation of a supernatural event. The fulminations against atheism themselves were generally confined to title pages and prefatory epistles, rather than threaded closely into the narratives. In the case of the short, anonymous ghost pamphlets of the London press, with which the grander anthologies co-existed in uneasy symbiosis, one suspects that such title-page and dedicatory formulae as 'enough to convince the greatest atheist' might function more as marketing tags than as declarations of any serious theological intent.[68]

In short, the ghost and apparition tales circulating in late Stuart England had the capacity to operate as narratives independently of the polemical and didactic purposes to which the clerical anthologizers wished to put them. The ghosts themselves manifested an ability, one is tempted to say an uncanny ability, to evade authoritative meaning and definition. One of Henry More's narratives concerns the appearances of the spirit of James Haddock to Francis Taverner, a servant of the earl of Donegal, at Drumbeg near Belfast, at Michaelmas 1662. The ghost's declared concern was with a lease, of which his son had been wrongly deprived by his new step-father, and Taverner was instructed to declare the deceased's wishes in the matter to the boy's mother. The matter came to the attention of the earl of Donegal's chaplain, who persuaded Taverner to seek the advice of the minister of Belfast.

Within a day, in an ascending chain of clerical interventions, Jeremy Taylor, bishop of Down, Connor and Dromore, was interrogating Taverner, and reportedly 'satisfied that the Apparition was true and real'. The matter was patently too important to be left to the resources of a young serving man, and so Bishop Taylor supplied Taverner with an approved list of questions to put to the ghost on next appearance: 'Whence are you? Are you a good or a bad spirit? Where is your abode? What station do you hold? How are you regimented in the other World? And what is the reason that you appear for the relief of your son in so small a matter, when so many widows and orphans are oppressed in the World, being defrauded of greater matters, and none from thence of their Relations appear, as you do, to right them?' When the spirit appeared again to him in a courtyard that night, Taverner dutifully began to reel off the bishop's ghostly catechism. The spectre, however, 'gave him no answer, but crawled on its hands and Feet over the wall again, and so vanisht in white, with a most melodious Harmony'.[69]

It seems, then, that the exemplary and religious characteristics of ghost stories might be only uneasily aligned with other social and narrative functions, and that this left them open to various kinds of appropriation. In the last decades of the seventeenth century, in fact, we can begin to see among the educated elites themselves some slippage in the motives for collecting ghost stories, a shift from providentialist piety across into connoisseurship, an antiquarian and folklorist enjoyment of the story for its own sake. A key figure here was the antiquary and biographer John Aubrey. An associate of Glanvill and More in the Royal Society, Aubrey cooperated with them in the publicizing of apparition narratives, a genre which represents a significant strand of his *Miscellanies* of 1696, and his earlier unpublished *Remaines of Gentilisme and Judaisme*. Aubrey's stance was often one of apparent credulity, yet he did not embellish his narratives with the didactic or providential spin that came naturally to other writers. Rather, Aubrey placed distance, both chronological and cultural, between himself and the supernatural events he described. His habit was to introduce some popular belief or custom with phrases like 'when I was a boy, before the civil wars'. It was a fashion of his childhood, he recalled, 'for old women and maids to tell fabulous stories night times, of sprites, and walking of ghosts'.[70] Aubrey was probably wrong to think this habit was in decline at the end of the seventeenth century, but his apparent willingness to reclassify the status of ghosts, from being matters of reportage, whether true or false, into the stuff of an acknowledged storytelling tradition, is very revealing.

VI

What then has this cultural-historical excursus told us about the origins of the modern short ghost story? The trail has ended some considerable way short of Horace Walpole and Walter Scott, not to mention M. R. James or Algernon Blackwood, and it leaves a good many dots to be joined. Nonetheless, I hope to have identified a kind of evolutionary association between Reformation history and the developmental prospects of a venerable English literary genre. In spite of itself, the effect of the English

Reformation was to de-theologize the ghost story, leaving it open to a range of creative and functional rereadings and retellings.

Writing about Shakespeare and *Hamlet*, Stephen Greenblatt has suggested that Reformation debates about the afterlife 'unsettled the institutional moorings of a crucial body of imaginative materials and therefore made them available for theatrical appropriation'.[71] The argument can I think be expanded, generically and chronologically. But in the end, a kind of abnegation of interpretation was perhaps more significant than sustained polemical debate. Liberated from doctrinal obligation, sixteenth- and seventeenth-century ghost stories were remarkably diverse and creative. In their introduction to the *Oxford Book of English Ghost Stories*, Cox and Gilbert write dismissively about 'the conventional patterns of behaviour demanded from the ghosts of oral tradition'.[72] But early modern ghosts were far from being creatures who dutifully conformed to any approved template of conduct. There were benevolent ghosts and malevolent ones, angels, demons, unquiet souls and a whole host of 'questionable shapes'. Some spirits manifested in fully human form, some as animals or invisible poltergeists. Some brought with them shocking revelations about this life, others carried news about the next. Some were unbidden and unexpected, others came fulfilling the conditions of a pre-mortem pact. Some of the stories were religiously edifying, but others were merely piquant or picaresque. Many of the accounts were genuinely frightening, or at least had the potential to become so in the telling.

We should not exaggerate the control and consistency in apparition narratives before the Reformation, or in Catholic circles afterwards.[73] But there is no doubt that, for Catholics, ghosts were signifiers and certifiers of dogmatic orthodoxy in a way they could never be for English Protestants. Clarity of doctrinal meaning, however, may be inimical to literary and creative experiment. There is no or little fictional mileage in the apparition of a saint to its devotees. It is thus perhaps not too much to suggest that an essential precondition for the emergence of the short ghost story in post-Reformation England was for the Protestant religion, quite literally, to lose the plot.

11

Ann Jeffries and the fairies: folk belief and the war on scepticism in later Stuart England

I

In 1696 a short but remarkable pamphlet was published in London, its subject matter extraordinary even by the permissive and eclectic standards of the later Stuart press. Its author was the printer and bookseller Moses Pitt, and the tract billed itself as *An Account of one Ann Jefferies, Now Living in the County of Cornwall, who was fed for six Months by a small sort of Airy People call'd fairies. And of the strange and wonderful cures she performed with Salves and Medicines she received from them, for which she never took one Penny of her Patients.*[1]

Ann Jeffries was a girl from a poor family, apprenticed as a domestic servant to a substantial yeoman family in the parish of St Teath, on the western edge of Bodmin Moor. Pitt recounted that when she was 19 years old, and sitting one day knitting in a garden, there had hopped over the garden hedge to her 'six persons of a small stature, all clothed in green, which she call'd *Fairies*'. As a consequence of this visitation, she fell into a lingering sickness, and a succession of fits and convulsions, which made the rest of the household fear for her life. At other times she was so enervated 'that she became even as a Changling' – the weak and sickly creatures fairies were popularly believed to leave in exchange for human babies they stole from their parents.

But as Ann's strength recovered, she began to display great devotion, going constantly to church to hear the word of God read and preached, and memorizing large parts of the sermons, though she herself was illiterate. Then she began to discover she had powers of healing. Her first patient was the mistress of the house, who had hurt her leg in a fall. Jeffries had prior knowledge of the accident from the fairies, who after the incident in the garden had continued to appear to her, 'never less than 2 at a time, nor never more than 8' (and always in even numbers). She insisted that her mistress place the leg on her lap, and eased the pain by gentle stroking. According to Pitt, this cure, combined with the stories Ann Jeffries was telling about the fairies,

> made such a noise over all the county of Cornwall, as that it had the same effect [as] St Paul's healing of Publius's father of a fever and a blood Flux at Malta, after his shipwreck there, as related [in] Acts 28.8, 9.

She began to be resorted to by sick people with all manner of distempers and agues, from as far afield as Land's End in the one direction and London in the other. Several days before her patients reached St Teath, she would know their identity, and the manner and time of their arrival. In the meantime, she gave up the consumption of ordinary victuals, and from harvest time to Christmas was nourished solely on special bread given to her by the fairies. She was also seen dancing in the orchard among the trees. Invisible to other onlookers, the fairies danced with her.[2]

Beyond its colourful detail and extravagant claims, the pamphlet was remarkable in a number of ways. It was, so far as we can tell, the only English publication of the second half of the seventeenth century devoted primarily to the subject of fairies. It was also noteworthy for the distinctive perspective of its author. Pitt's account was partly autobiographical, for the family with whom Ann Jeffries was in service was his own, and her duties included attending to the young Moses, who at the time of the alleged fairy visitations in 1645–6 was no more than seven years old. Pitt's account was thus part personal reminiscence, part historical curiosity, a picturesque incident from the first half of the seventeenth century, retold at the very end of the second.

But Pitt's motivation in publishing this story – which had 'made so great an impression on me from my childhood hitherto' – was in fact a matter neither of public antiquarianism nor of private nostalgia. He believed the material to be both topical and valent in 1696, and to make the point Pitt affixed to his title page a quotation from a sermon which Samuel Barton, chaplain to the House of Commons, had preached before the members at St Margaret's Westminster earlier that year: 'all the works of Providence are not alike. Sometimes for wise and good Reasons God has been pleased quite to alter the course of Nature, as it were, to shew himself to have a Power above it.'[3]

Divine providence was frequently invoked in the last decade of the seventeenth century; it had after all just removed one king from the English throne and provided the nation with a reliably Protestant replacement.[4] But in some circles, the most pressing felt need was for providences which demonstrably surmounted the accustomed course of nature, and which could be held up in order to stem a perceived tide of atheism, scepticism and unbelief sweeping the nation. Pitt offered his account of Ann Jeffries' fairy-given powers to the public as evidence that 'the Great God has done as great and marvellous Works in our Age, as he did in the days of old'. It was, he considered, the duty of all who knew of such extraordinary works or providences of the Almighty to publish them to the world, so that 'the greatest Atheist may be convinc'd, not only of the Being of a God, but also that his Power and his Goodness are as manifest now as of old'.

Another voice was being ventriloquized here: that of the pamphlet's dedicatee, Edward Fowler, bishop of Gloucester. Pitt had first told the tale to Fowler 15 or 20 years before, over Sunday dinner, but during an encounter at Christmas 1695 the bishop had seized Pitt's hand and refused to let it go until he had promised to write and publish the account of Ann Jeffries.[5] Fowler had a long-standing reputation as an aficionado of the miraculous and the supernatural. As a young curate in the 1650s, he had made the acquaintance of the Cambridge Platonist Henry More, who shared his interest in apparitions and remarkable providences. Many of the stories which More included in his edition of Joseph Glanvill's compilation of supernatural phenomena, the *Saducismus Triumphatus* of 1681, were supplied by Fowler. A solid churchman, the Latitudinarian Fowler nonetheless enjoyed good relations with the famous dissenting minister Richard Baxter, whose *Certainty of the World of Spirits* (1691) was, like the publications of Glanvill and More, intended to assert the existence of an interventionist Deity through attested incidents of witchcraft and hauntings. The dissenting minister and medical doctor Henry Sampson wrote approvingly of Fowler as 'a great collector of such storys & others of like importance to prove the Being of Spirits'.[6]

'No Spirit, No God' was the prevailing view in these circles.[7] Far from being a backwards-looking obscurantism, entirely inimical to the outlook of the 'Scientific Revolution', modern scholarship has taught us to recognize that attempts to verify the existence of spirits in the Restoration period were often predicated upon the experimental method. Natural philosophers and Royal Society members like Robert Boyle hoped to place knowledge of the supernatural on a firmer empirical foundation, and collaborated with clerical collectors of spirit stories in the hope of confounding 'Hobbism' and 'Saduceeism'.[8]

But only slight attention has been paid to one, decidedly anomalous, strand in this discourse in the second half of the seventeenth century: discussion of the existence and nature of fairies.[9] Fairies were anomalous because, unlike other denizens of the spirit world (ghosts, demons, angels), they had never found a secure place in any orthodox Christian cosmology, Catholic or Protestant. In the eyes of learned writers, belief in fairies had long exemplified vulgar ignorance and superstition, and as a result was always particularly prone to ridicule and disparagement. Its apparent endorsement by one section of the educated elite thus brings into focus a particularly interesting cultural moment. It points to the possibilities for creative exchange between elite and popular cultures, as well as to the dangers and limitations. Positioned as it is, either side of the Restoration divide, Pitt's memoir of the adventures of Ann Jeffries invites us to track, and to consider the significance of, the changing valency of the world of fairy in seventeenth-century England.

II

Central to the claims to veracity of Pitt's pamphlet account was the announcement that its protagonist was still 'Living in the County of Cornwall', now 70 years of age, and married to a man called William Warden. Frustratingly for Pitt, however, Ann Jeffries flatly refused to cooperate in the writing of the account. In 1691 Pitt had asked his nephew, an attorney, to visit her and question her about 'those several strange passages of her life', but she could or would not tell him anything, 'it being so long since'. Two years later, Pitt prevailed on his brother-in-law, Humphrey Martin, to repeat the approach, and though Martin spent the greater part of a day with Jeffries, reading out to her for her comments a full account which Pitt had supplied, 'she would not own any thing of it as concerning the Fairies, neither of any of the cures she then did'.

Jeffries' reticence, and her evident suspicion of the renewed interest among her betters in these matters, was understandable, for half a century before, the fairies had got her into serious hot water with the authorities. That trouble had begun with an examination by local magistrates and ministers, and culminated in a three-month spell in Bodmin gaol, on the orders of a justice of the peace, John Tregeagle, who also summoned the young Moses and his mother to give evidence at a sessions. Jeffries was denied victuals in the gaol, and also afterwards, when she was kept as a prisoner in Tregeagle's house, but the fairies continued to feed her during this time. Upon her eventual release, she was ordered not to return to the Pitt family, and went instead to a sister of Moses' father, near Padstow. For a time, she continued to perform striking cures there, but when it was that the fairies finally forsook Ann Jeffries, Pitt was not able to say.[10]

Pitt's account of Jeffries' sufferings at the hands of her 'great persecutor', Tregeagle, was heartfelt, but it was also remarkably partial and incomplete, as can be demonstrated from a pair of contemporary letters of intelligence making reference to the affair. These show that Ann Jeffries' curative and prophetic powers had a decidedly political cast. One letter, sent from Bodmin in February 1647, told how after her encounter with 'small people clad in greene', she had been summoned in front of the County Committee established by the parliamentary authorities, and had brazenly bade its members to 'be good in theyr office, for it will not last long'. Since being housed under guard at the mayor's house in Bodmin, 'she prayes very much, & bids people to keepe the old forme of prayer. She says the King shall shortly enjoye his owne, & be revenged of his enemyes.' A second newsletter in April of that year reported that there was

> much discourse here of the Prophesies of a Maide in Cornwall, who heales the Kings Evill, broken Joynts, Agues &c by touch only. She foretells the Kings restoracion suddenly in a straing way. She is under custody & hath been long concealed, least her discourses (which are all on behalfe of the King & strangely saucy against the parliament) should trouble the Peoples mindes, who are apt to revolt from the Parliament's obedience.

In the meantime, the leading royalist Sir Edward Hyde was requesting his friend John Earle to find out more information for him 'of your prophetess of Bodmyn'.[11] Ann was a cheerleader for the defeated king, in a notoriously royalist part of the south-west of England. It was undoubtedly the overt politicization of this particular manifestation of Cornish folk belief about fairies that provoked the heavy-handed intervention of the authorities.[12]

Ann Jeffries' royalism and Anglicanism are striking features of the case: scholarly studies of female prophets and visionaries in this period tend to give the impression that they were almost always to be found in radical and sectarian circles.[13] Her experiences lend support to the insightful suggestion of Bernard Capp (commenting on another case of miraculous fasting within a non-sectarian household) that 'female visionaries of the period represent an extreme manifestation of religious emotions and sensibilities more widely spread'.[14] Pitt, however, entirely ignored the political dimension – his sole, and very oblique, reference to Jeffries' royalism concerns her breaking her fast and eating roast beef on Christmas Day 1645.[15]

Over and beyond its political dynamics, the Jeffries case neatly encapsulates some key themes in official and popular attitudes towards fairies, as they had developed in the decades following the English Reformation. Although a few of the more familiar folkloric tropes are missing – such as the association of fairies with gifts of money and hidden treasure, or with household cleanliness – several of the motifs in Jeffries' accounts of her dealings with the little people can be paralleled in other cases of direct or reported plebeian testimony from the Elizabethan and early Stuart periods. These include the association with the colour green, the diminutive stature, the appearance in groups or 'troops', the penchant for dancing. In particular, several village cunning folk in these decades attributed healing or divinatory powers to the gift of the fairies.[16] At the same time, Ann Jeffries' claims seemed to confirm a number of official expectations and stereotypes which had accumulated around the figure of the fairy by the early decades of the seventeenth century. In the first place, fairy belief was often heavily gendered in elite discourse: not only were fairies frequently associated with domestic settings and the female sphere, but the giving of credence to them was quintessentially a weakness of women, and ridiculing fairies often represented a validation of respectable masculinity. When fairies were mentioned in controversial or didactic sources the derisive expression 'old wives' tales' was seldom far away.[17]

Second, fairies were strongly associated with Catholicism. Somewhat implausibly, belief in them was frequently said to have been a form of superstitious delusion which the Romish clergy had foisted upon the laity of pre-Reformation England. Protestant authors differed over the extent to which fairy beliefs had withered in the pure light of the gospel. Some Elizabethans (like Thomas Nashe) consigned them wholesale to 'idolatrous former daies', while others, more convincingly, conceded that they 'sticketh very religiously in the mindes of some'.[18] Ann Jeffries was not, of course, a Catholic.[19] Yet the godly ministers who examined her would have been already primed to link credulity about fairies to cultural conservatism and religious recidivism.

A further early Stuart elite presumption about fairies is firmly imprinted on the Jeffries case. Along with ghosts of the dead (another incongruous presence in the post-Reformation metaphysical world) fairies could only retain their place as a *sometimes* objectively real phenomenon by submitting to a course of theological reprocessing and reclassification. The ministers who examined Ann (said by the February 1647 newsletter to be 'three able divines') tried hard to persuade her that 'they were evil spirits that resorted to her, and that it was the Delusion of the Devil'.[20] The identification of fairies as demons allowed the Protestant clergy to reconcile the beliefs and experiences of parishioners with their own macrocosmic understanding of the universe, and at the same time it accounted for the apparently greater prevalence of fairylore in Catholic times (when the devil's delusions held more sway). Several historians of witchcraft have noted a tendency on the part of legal authorities to hear narratives that probably reflected popular belief in household fairies or brownies like 'Robin Goodfellow', and interpret them as tales of demonic familiars.[21] Jeffries herself was perhaps lucky not to be charged with witchcraft.

The demonic pedigree of the fairies was reinforced by the sole (and oblique) reference to them Protestant exegetes could find in Scripture: Isaiah 13.21, a prophecy of the ruin of Babylon, and of the strange creatures that would come to dwell where its glory once stood. The Authorized Version stated that 'wild beasts of the desert shall lie there; and their houses shall be full of doleful creatures; and owls shall dwell there, and satyrs shall dance there'. For 'wild beasts' and 'doleful creatures' the Geneva Bible of 1560 preferred to leave untranslated the Hebrew words *Ziim* and *Ohim*, adding in a marginal note that this implied those wicked spirits 'whereby Satan deluded man, as by fairies, goblins and such like fantasies'.[22] The text also mentioned 'satyrs', and the tendency among learned commentators to link the fairies and elves of folklore with classical and pagan spirits and deities further underlined the diabolical association. A 'digression of devils' in Robert Burton's 1621 *Anatomy of Melancholy* explained that what people called fairies and Robin Goodfellow were simply those '*Lares, Genij, Faunes, Satyrs . . .* that kept the Heathen people in awe'.[23] James VI wrote in his *Daemonologie* of 1597 about a 'kinde of spirites, which by the Gentiles was called Diana, and her wandring court, and amongst us was called the Phairie . . . or our good neighboures'.[24] In a treatise on witchcraft published the same year that Ann Jeffries came to the attention of the authorities in Cornwall, the Huntingdonshire clergyman John Gaule identified the creatures of Isaiah 13.21 as devils, assuming a shape for witches to worship them. The same grim reality was to be found in 'the Fawnes, Satyrs, Sylvanes or Syrens, that the poets sing of . . . or in the plebeian-traditions of Fairies, Elfes and changelings'.[25]

But even as fairies were being slotted into the conventional categories of the demonologists, an alternative interpretative tradition was taking shape. For writers sceptical of the reality of witchcraft, or the powers claimed for witches, fairies were an extremely useful tool of decon-struction. Plebeian fairy traditions are, for example, frequently invoked by Reginald Scot in his 1584 *Discoverie of Witchcraft*, with the aim of establishing a kind of absurdity by association. To Scot it seemed highly significant that 'heretofore Robin Goodfellow, and Hob gobblin were as terrible, and also as credible to the people, as hags and witches be now'. The implication was that just as the former were losing their hold among persons of good sense, so, inevitably, must the latter.[26] The theme was echoed by seventeenth-century disciples of Scot such as Samuel Harsnett, and the medical doctor Thomas Ady, who included in his list of 'Causes of upholding the damnable Doctrin of Witches power', 'Old Wives Fables, who sit talking, and chatting of many false old Stories of Witches, and Fairies, and Robin Good-fellow'.[27] Another physician, John Webster, was similarly frustrated by the propensity of ignorant people to adhere to 'those fictions of Spirits, Fairies, Hobgoblins'. Conceding that people did believe they saw such things, Webster hypothesized that strange yet entirely natural animals were sometimes mistaken for spirits, and rendered into 'old wives fables of Apparitions and Goblins'. The creatures which for centuries had been called satyrs, for example, were in reality most likely a rare kind of ape.[28] To another, and more notable sceptic, Thomas Hobbes, fairies were of considerable polemical value. The *Leviathan* contains not only an extended and celebrated comparison of the Romish religion with 'the kingdom of fairy', but pronounces at the outset that 'the Religion of the Gentiles in time past, that worshipped Satyres, Fawnes, Nymphs, and the like; and now adayes the opinion that rude people have of Fayries, Ghosts, and Goblins' was simply the result of an inability to separate 'dreams and other strong Fancies, from Vision and Sense'.[29]

III

It was this increasingly clear link between the casual disparagement of fairies and other spirits, and the philosophical outlook of 'Hobbism', which encouraged some soi-disant defenders of Christian orthodoxy in the second half of the seventeenth century to begin to reappraise what had once been almost universally denigrated as 'old wives' tales'. That fairies might be the thin end of an atheistical wedge was something implicitly recognized in 1679 by the influential Cambridge Platonist Ralph Cudworth. Having dismissed all belief in spirits as mere imaginations, atheists had reached the conclusion that 'the Chief of all which affrightful *Ghosts* and *Spectres* . . . is the *Deity*, the *Oberon*, or *Prince* of *Fairies* and *Phancies*'.[30]

The rehabilitation of fairies took several forms. Their conflation with the mythological fauna of the classical world had served to collapse these creatures into the ranks of Satan's army. But it could work equally well to argue for their independent existence, by providing a venerable heritage of educated observation and classification. The mystical poet Samuel Pordage warned his readers to 'Laugh not at Fairies, Pigmies, Gnomies . . . At Nymphs, Penates, Durdales, Undenae, / For name them what you will . . . there such Spirits are as these.'[31] In a piece of remarkable textual subversion, a second *Discourse concerning Devils and Spirits*, appended to the 1665 edition of Scot's *Discovery of Witchcraft*, argued that the terrestrial spirits known to the ancient heathens as nymphs, satyrs, Lares and Penates were simply none other than the fairies and goblins of familiar folk belief.[32] The tireless scourge of atheism, Henry More, also associated the 'Aereall *Genii*' of ancient historians with the 'frequent fame of the dancing of Fairies in Woods and desolate places'.[33]

It must be admitted that, compared to the number of relations of witches, ghosts and poltergeists, there were few stories identified unambiguously as fairy apparitions in the compilations of men such as Glanvill and Richard Bovet.[34] But at times it was the very oddness of fairies, their position outside of the conventional Christian taxonomies, which appealed to the empiricist mindset of English natural philosophy, and drew the attention of practitioners of the new science and their clerical allies. It was widely known, for example, that the great Renaissance philosopher and physician Paracelsus had postulated the existence of a race of elusive terrestrial spirits, 'non-Adamic' creatures of a middle nature between human beings and angels.[35] One compiler of a celebrated anti-atheistical work, the Puritan clergyman Richard Baxter, indeed speculated whether the aerial regions 'have not a third sort of Wights, that are neither Angels . . . nor Souls of Men, but such as have been there placed as Fishes in the Sea . . . And whether those called *Fairies* and *Goblins* are not such.'[36]

In the 1690s, aficionados of the Royal Society like John Aubrey and Robert Boyle solicited accounts from clerical correspondents in Scotland about the experiences local people had had with fairies.[37] It may have been at Boyle's instigation that a Highland minister, Robert Kirk of Aberfoyle in Perthshire, completed in 1692 the only seventeenth-century British treatise devoted to the nature of fairies, a manuscript known as *The Secret Common-Wealth* and intended 'to suppress the impudent and growing Atheisme of this age'.[38] Kirk's extraordinary essay was a kind of ethnographic survey of the physiology, customs and social organization of these elusive creatures, who manifested themselves to humans possessed of the 'second sight'. Its modern editor describes it as 'a slightly strange book, which combines what is effectively reportage of folklore with erudite speculation and biblical exegesis'.[39]

Kirk had been contemplating the work during a visit to London in 1689–90, in the course of which he debated the utility and reality of apparitions over dinner with Edward Stillingfleet, the newly appointed bishop of Worcester. Kirk wrote afterwards in his diary that he considered it 'not repugnant to Reason or Religion to affect ane invisible polity, or a people to us invisible, having a Commonwealth, Laws and Oeconomy, made known to us but by some obscure hints of a few admitted to their converse'. It was, he thought, worth remembering that the very first reports of the lands and inhabitants of America had been 'lookt on as a fayrie tale, and the Reporters hooted at as inventors of ridiculous Utopias'.[40] It was Kirk's conviction that the fairy inhabitants of the invisible world were themselves courteously endeavouring 'to convince us (in opposition to Sadducees, Socinians and Atheists) of a Dietie, of Spirits'.[41]

In this context, therefore, Moses Pitt's attempt to put forward the appearance of fairies to a Cornish serving girl as evidence of the existence and providence of Almighty God does not seem quite so unique or eccentric as at first it might. Within months of its publication, Pitt sent a copy of his tract to a Sussex clergyman, William Turner, who was just then compiling a *Compleat history of the most remarkable providences* as 'one of the best methods that can be pursued against the abounding Atheism of this Age'. Turner printed the account in its entirety, with prefixed letters from Pitt's kinsman in the south-west, William Tom, affirming that 'all in it is very true', and from Pitt himself, adding some details he had forgetfully omitted from the original: '(viz.) that those Fairies are distinguished into Males and Females; and that they are about the bigness of Children of Three or Four Years of Age'.[42]

The appropriation of traditional fairylore, and its supposed amenability to the new spirit of scientific enquiry, represents a striking exception to the historical rule that elite and popular cultures were drawing inextricably away from each other in the latter part of the early modern era.[43] Folk knowledge about fairies – whether or not it was becoming, as Keith Thomas has claimed, 'primarily a store of mythology rather than a corpus of living beliefs' – continued to be a domain that the educated, particularly clergymen, had access to, and one they could adopt and adapt for their own purposes.[44]

IV

The contest over the reality of fairies was only a minor campaign in the larger war against scepticism, yet it proved in the end to be a battle fought by the anti-sceptics on ground of their opponents' choosing. In the late seventeenth century, belief in fairies was simply a step too far for most educated and respectable opinion. Robert Kirk expected and experienced incredulity and ridicule on this matter in London society, and Moses Pitt prefaced his pamphlet with a ready confession that 'the great Part of the

World will not believe the Passages here related.[45] It is possible in fact to suggest that fairies were somewhere near the tipping point in that 'tilting of a balance' which Alan McFarlane has put forward as a better explanation for the transition from a 'magical' to a 'modern' worldview than any radically paradigmatic shift.[46]

Fairies were mentioned, passingly but tellingly, in two key texts published the same year as Pitt's pamphlet. One of these was a lightning rod of orthodox ire: the deist John Toland's *Christianity not mysterious*, which argued for reason rather than revelation as the basis of religious faith. In his discussion of miracles, Toland applied the rule that none could be considered in any way credible 'unless for some weighty design . . . some special and important end'. By this token, 'the celebrated Feats of Goblins and Fairies, of Witches, of Conjurers, and all the Heathen Prodigies, must be accounted fictitious, idle, and superstitious'.[47] The other, an abridgement of John Locke's *Essay Concerning Human Understanding*, invoked fairies to lodge a fundamental epistemological objection to discussions about the spirit world. Since human senses could not certainly discover them, it was impossible to know with certainty that there were such things as spirits,

> for we can no more know that there are Finite Spirits really Existing, by the Idea we have of such Beings, than by the Ideas any one has of Fairies or Centaurs, he can come to know that Things answering those Ideas, do really Exist.[48]

In both cases, fairies are quite evidently the *reductio ad absurdum* of supernatural belief.

We also have one delayed but significant reaction to Pitt's pamphlet itself. In 1708 the aristocratic philosopher Anthony Ashley Cooper, earl of Shaftesbury, published *A Letter Concerning Enthusiasm*, in response to the activities in London of the so-called 'French prophets', a trio of Huguenot refugees from the Massif Central, who had become notorious for their histrionic displays of prophecy and religious ecstasy. In his dedicatory epistle, Shaftesbury took the opportunity for a side-swipe against the dedicatee of Pitt's pamphlet of 1696, Bishop Fowler of Gloucester, complaining of those who thought it necessary to improve on Scripture with 'a solid system of old wives' stories'. Why, he knew of one 'eminent, learned and truly Christian prelate . . . who could have given you a full account of his belief in fairies', being 'so great a volunteer in faith . . . beyond the ordinary Prescription of the Catholick Church' (Catholic here meaning orthodox or universal). It was in the *Letter Concerning Enthusiasm* that Shaftesbury enunciated his famous, or infamous, principle: that ridicule should be allowed to operate as a test of verity, the truth being able to withstand the scrutiny of raillery.[49]

By the end of the seventeenth century, it was to ridicule, rather than to reasoned philosophical argument, questions of observational method, or close scriptural exegesis, that fairies, and by extension the entire spirit world, were becoming particularly vulnerable.[50] 'Polite' and coffee house society was learning to scoff at 'enthusiasms' of all kinds, with essays in the burgeoning periodical press lumping together 'Fairies, Witches, Magicians, Demons and departed Spirits' as the detritus of discarded belief, and yawning that 'the World is already wearied with Stories of Witches, Fairies, &c.'[51] In August 1712 the godly Yorkshire antiquary Ralph Thoresby found himself on a visit to London having to argue late into the night against 'some who would be thought the only wits, and glory in the style of Free-thinkers, who deny the existence of spirits'.[52] In such a climate, the long-standing associations of fairies with the 'vulgar' people, with child-hood, and with tales told by old wives, placed severe limits on their utility for the vindication of orthodox Christianity. As Adam Fox has ably demonstrated, it was in the nurseries of gentry and middling-sort households that the cultural formation of elite males was, for a time at least, directly influenced by the outlook of illiterate females, maidservants and child-minders of a variety of ages.[53] This aspect of personal memory probably helps to explain both the enduring literary fascination with matters such as omens, ghosts and fairies among writers in early modern England, and also the periodically intense disparagement to which they were subject.

V

A careful reading of Moses Pitt's pamphlet of 1696 reveals the extent to which, albeit unconsciously, it presents us with a view of reality filtered through the eyes and understanding of a child, one punctuated by halcyon memories of Christmas dinners, and riding on horseback for the first time. There is a revealing remembered incident. During the time of her supposed fast, the young Moses came seeking for his nursemaid at her chamber door. She told him to 'have a little patience and I will let you in presently'. But looking through the keyhole 'I saw her eating; and when she had done eating, she stood still by her Bed-side as long as Thanks to God might be given, and then she made a coursey (or Bow) and opened the Chamber-door'. Ann Jeffries gave the child a piece of her bread, 'the most delicious Bread that ever I did eat either before or since'. The incident is offered by Pitt as evidence of Jeffries' miraculous sustenance by the fairies, rather than of her surreptitiously feeding herself in private. When Pitt remarks of the fairies that, unlike his sister Mary, 'I confess to your lordship, I never did see them', it is said in a genuine spirit of poignant regret.[54]

A more conscious sense of the inability of fairylore to transcend the worlds of childhood memory and nostalgic recollection can be detected even among some authors who were generally sympathetic to the project of confounding scepticism by the recording of remarkable providences. The antiquarian polymath and proto-folklorist John Aubrey avidly collected accounts of the appearances of fairies, and seemed periodically to adopt a stance of belief in respect of them. Yet at the same time, he refrained from explicitly presenting such narratives as either didactic or providential, and he tended to put distance, both cultural and chronological, between himself and the supernatural events which he recorded. In a typical authorial aside, he noted that 'when I was a Boy, our Country people would talke much of [fairies]'.[55]

Like Moses Pitt, Aubrey had had a childhood brush with the fairies at close second hand. In notes for his natural history of Wiltshire, Aubrey recounted how in 1633–4, while a schoolboy at Yatton Keynell in the northern part of the county, his curate, Mr Harte, had stumbled across a fairy ring while crossing the downs by night. The unfortunate Harte was buffeted and held prisoner by the fairies till they released him at sunrise the following day. Impressed by the story, Aubrey and a school friend set out after dark to dance upon the downs, but the fairies never appeared to them, as 'it is saide they seldom appeare to any persons who go to seeke for them'. As an adult, Aubrey inclined towards a thoroughly naturalistic explanation for the phenomenon of fairy rings in grassland: 'I presume they are generated from the breathing out of a fertile subterraneous vapour'.[56] Aubrey's reflections on these matters point to the potential for meaningful exchanges involving elite piety and emergent 'science' on the one hand, and customary folk belief on the other, as well as to the inherent fragility of any alliance between them.

The last words should go to Ann Jeffries herself. In the course of her interview with Humphrey Martin in early 1693, the old lady showed an astute understanding of the cultural and economic connectedness, as well as of the gulf, between her world and that of a successful London author and printer. She said that if she disclosed anything of what had transpired all those years ago, she knew that Moses Pitt 'would make either Books or Ballads of it', and she added 'That she would not have her Name spread about the Country in Books or Ballads of such things, if she might have five hundred pounds for the doing of it'.[57] Her wishes in this matter were to be ignored, but the result of her reticence, as so often, is that we hear her voice only in the accent and cadences of her betters.

Notes

Introduction

1 See J. Le Goff, *L'Imaginaire médiéval* (Paris, Gallimard, 1985): English translation by A. Goldhammer, *The Medieval Imagination* (Chicago and London, University of Chicago Press, 1988).

2 E. P. Thompson, *The Making of the English Working Class* (London, Victor Gollancz, 1963), 12.

3 This, more or less, was the approach of A. G. Dickens, *The English Reformation* (London, B. T. Batsford, 1964), with very few substantive changes to a second edition in 1989.

4 Seminal revisionist accounts of the Reformation include J. J. Scarisbrick, *The Reformation and the English People* (Oxford, Blackwell, 1984); E. Duffy, *The Stripping of the Altars: Traditional Religion in England 1400–1580* (New Haven and London, Yale University Press, 1992); C. Haigh, *English Reformations: Religion, Politics, and Society under the Tudors* (Oxford, Clarendon Press, 1993).

5 Review of Alexandra Walsham, 'Providence in Early Modern England', *English Historical Review*, 115 (2000), 964–5.

6 Among the most impressive examples of post-revisionist scholarship on the cultural impact of the Reformation are: C. Marsh, *Popular Religion in Sixteenth-Century England* (Basingstoke, Macmillan, 1998); T. Watt, *Cheap Print and Popular Piety 1550–1640* (Cambridge, Cambridge University Press, 1991); R. Hutton, 'The English Reformation and the Evidence of Folklore', *Past and Present*, 148 (1995), 89–116; A. Walsham, *Providence in Early Modern England* (Oxford, Oxford University Press, 1999); A. Walsham, *The Reformation of the Landscape: Religion, Identity, and Memory in Early Modern Britain and Ireland* (Oxford, Oxford University Press, 2011).

7 C. Lloyd (ed.), *Formularies of Faith* (Oxford, Clarendon Press, 1825), 16–17, 376; H. Gee and W. Hardy (eds), *Documents Illustrative of English Church History* (London, Macmillan, 1896), 328; J. Ketley (ed.), *The Two Liturgies . . . in the Reign of King Edward VI* (Cambridge, Cambridge University Press, 1844), 532.

8 Duffy, *Stripping of the Altars*, 8.

9 See P. Marshall, 'Fear, Purgatory and Polemic in Reformation England', in W. G. Naphy and P. Roberts (eds), *Fear in Early Modern Society* (Manchester, Manchester University Press, 1997), 150–66.

10 Thomas Starkey, *Life and Letters*, ed. S. J. Herrtage, Early English Text Society, 57 (Oxford, Oxford University Press, 1878), liii.

11 See D. P. Walker, *The Decline of Hell: Seventeenth-Century Discussions of Eternal Torment* (London, Routledge & Kegan Paul, 1964).

12 See in particular P. Collinson, *The Religion of Protestants: The Church in English Society 1559–1625* (Oxford, Clarendon Press, 1982); N. Tyacke, *Anti-Calvinists: The Rise of English Arminianism, c.1590–1640* (Oxford, Clarendon Press, 1987). In an earlier essay, Tyacke claimed that Calvinist teaching on predestination supplied a 'common and ameliorating bond' between clergy and educated laity: 'Puritanism, Arminianism and Counter-Revolution', in C. Russell (ed.), *The Origins of the English Civil War* (London, Macmillan, 1973), 121.

13 P. Marshall, *Beliefs and the Dead in Reformation England* (Oxford, Oxford University Press, 2002), 196–7.

14 D. Oldridge, *The Supernatural in Tudor and Stuart England* (Abingdon, Routledge, 2016), quote at ix.

15 A. Walsham, 'Invisible Helpers: Angelic Intervention in Early Modern England', *Past and Present*, 208 (2010), 85.

16 Walsham, 'Invisible Helpers'; L. Sangha, *Angels and Belief in England, 1480–1700* (London, Pickering & Chatto, 2012), esp. ch. 7.

17 On this, see in particular J. Raymond, *Milton's Angels: The Early-Modern Imagination* (Oxford, Oxford University Press, 2010).

18 See, for example, J. Shaw, *Miracles in Enlightenment England* (New Haven and London, Yale University Press, 2006).

19 Max Weber, *The Protestant Ethic and the Spirit of Capitalism*, tr. Talcott Parsons (New York, Scribner; London, Allen & Unwin, 1930).

20 S. Clark, *Thinking with Demons: The Idea of Witchcraft in Early Modern Europe* (Oxford, Clarendon Press, 1997); R. Scribner, 'The Reformation, Popular Magic, and the "*Disenchantment* of the World"', *Journal of Interdisciplinary History*, 23 (1993), 475–94; Walsham, *Providence in Early Modern England*; A. Walsham, 'The Reformation and "the Disenchantment of the World" Reassessed', *Historical Journal*, 51 (2008), 497–528. For an excellent overview, see Oldridge, *The Supernatural*.

1 After purgatory: death and remembrance in the Reformation world

1 C. Daniell, *Death and Burial in Medieval England* (London, Routledge, 1997), p. 69.

2 C. M. Koslofsky, *The Reformation of the Dead: Death and Ritual in Early Modern Germany, 1450–1700* (Basingstoke, Macmillan, 2000), 34–9.

3 P. Marshall, *Beliefs and the Dead in Reformation England* (Oxford, Oxford University Press, 2002), 55–6; S. E. Ozment, *The Reformation in the Cities* (New Haven and London, Yale University Press, 1975), 111–16.

4 Koslofsky, *Reformation of the Dead*, 90–1; P. Benedict, *Christ's Churches Purely Reformed: A Social History of Calvinism* (New Haven and London, Yale University Press, 2002), 494; B. Roussel, '"Ensevelir hinnestement les corps": Funeral Corteges and Huguenot Culture', in R. A. Mentzer and A. Spicer (eds), *Society and Culture in the Huguenot World, 1559–1685* (Cambridge, Cambridge University Press, 2002), 200.

5   William Allen, *A Defence and Declaration of the Catholike Churchies Doctrine touching Purgatory* (Antwerp, 1565), 169v; J. Pollmann, *Religious Choice in the Dutch Republic: The Reformation of Arnoldus Buchelius, 1565–1641* (Manchester, Manchester University Press, 1999), 86.

6   See, for example, D. Cressy, *Birth, Marriage and Death: Ritual, Religion and the Life-Cycle in Tudor and Stuart England* (Oxford, Oxford University Press, 1997), 396; E. Duffy, *The Stripping of the Altars: Traditional Religion in England, c.1400–1580* (2nd edn, New Haven and London, Yale University Press, 2005), 475; S. Karant-Nunn, *The Reformation of Ritual: An Interpretation of Early Modern Germany* (London, Routledge, 1997), 187.

7   O. H. Oexle, 'Die Gegenwart der Toten', in Herman Braet and Werner Verbecke (eds), *Death in the Middle Ages* (Leuven, Leuven University Press, 1983), 19–77. See also T. van Bueren and A. van Leerdam (eds), *Care for the Here and the Hereafter: Memoria, Art and Ritual in the Middle Ages* (Turnhout, Brepols, 2005); R. Weijert, K. Ragetli, A. Bijsterveld and J. van Arenthals (eds), *Living Memoria: Studies in Medieval and Early Modern Memorial Culture in Honour of Truus van Bueren* (Hilversum, Verloren, 2011).

8   C. Koslofsky, 'From Presence to Remembrance: The Transformation of Memory in the German Reformation', in A. Confino and P. Fritzsche (eds), *Work of Memory: New Directions in the Study of German Society and Culture* (Urbana, IL, University of Illinois Press, 2002), 31. See also P. Sherlock, 'The Reformation of Memory in Early Modern Europe', in S. Radstone and B. Schwarz (eds), *Memory: Histories, Theories, Debates* (New York, Fordham University Press, 2010), 30–40.

9   E. Panofsky, *Tomb Sculpture: Its Changing Aspects from Ancient Egypt to Bernini* (London, Thames & Hudson, 1964), 62–76.

10 C. Gittings, *Death, Burial and the Individual in Early Modern England* (London, Croom Helm, 1984); J. Finch, 'A Reformation of Meaning: Commemoration and the Parish Church c.1450–c.1550', in D. Gaimster and R. Gilchrist (eds), *The Archaeology of Reformation c.1480–1580* (Oxford, Oxbow, 2003); C. Eire, *A Very Brief History of Eternity* (Princeton, Princeton University Press, 2010), 151–2. See also the broader comments on connections between the modern sense of individualism and the Reformation's rejection of communal strategies of salvation in C. Taylor, *Sources of the Self: The Making of the Modern Identity* (Cambridge, Cambridge University Press, 1989), 215–30.

11 Koslofsky, *Reformation of the Dead*, 29.

12 N. Llewellyn, *Funeral Monuments in Post-Reformation England* (Cambridge, Cambridge University Press, 2000); O. Meys, *Memoria und Bekenntnis. Die Grabdenkmäler evangelischer Landesherren im Heiligen Römischen Reich Deutscher Nation im Zeitalter der Konfessionalisierung* (Regensburg, Schnell & Steiner, 2009); I. Brinkmann, *Grabdenkmäler, Grablegen und Begräbniswesen des lutherischen Adels* (Berlin, Deutscher Kunstverlag, 2010).

13 Cited in Marshall, *Beliefs and the Dead*, 276.

14 L. C. Attreed, 'Preparation for Death in Sixteenth-Century Northern England', *Sixteenth Century Journal*, 13 (1982), 65; C. J. Somerville, *The Secularization of Early Modern England: From Religious Culture to Religious Faith* (Oxford, Oxford University Press, 1992), 88; M. Neill, *Issues of Death: Mortality and Identity in English Renaissance Tragedy* (Oxford, Clarendon Press, 1997), 3, 38–40, 48, 306.

15 Eire, *Brief History of Eternity*, 153.

16 See C. M. N. Eire, *From Madrid to Purgatory: The Art and Craft of Dying in Sixteenth-Century Spain* (Cambridge, Cambridge University Press, 1995), 168–231; S. Nalle, *God in La Mancha: Religious Reform and the People of Cuenca, 1500–1650* (Baltimore, Johns Hopkins University Press, 1992), 202–5; E. Tingle, 'Purgatory and the Counter-Reformation: Perpetual Chantries in Southern Brittany, 1480–1720', *Journal of Ecclesiastical History*, 60 (2009), 464–89.

17 Marshall, *Beliefs and the Dead*, 210–15.

18 Koslofsy, *Reformation of the Dead*, 40–78; Karant-Nunn, *Reformation of Ritual*, 178–9.

19 N. Leroux, *Martin Luther as Comforter: Writings on Death* (Leiden, Brill, 2007), 259–65.

20 J. Beyer, 'A Lübeck Prophet in Local and Lutheran Context', in B. Scribner and T. Johnson (eds), *Popular Religion in Germany and Central Europe, 1400–1800* (Basingstoke, Macmillan, 1996), 166–82.

21 Eire, *Brief History of Eternity*, 23.

22 J. M. González, 'Sleeping Bodies, Jubilant Souls: The Fate of the Dead in Sweden 1400–1700', *Canadian Journal of History*, 40 (2005), 209; M. Todd, *The Culture of Protestantism in Early Modern Scotland* (New Haven and London, Yale University Press, 2002), 338–9.

23 V. Harding, 'Choices and Changes: Death, Burial and the English Reformation', in Gaimster and Gilchrist (eds), *Archaeology of Reformation*, 386–98.

24 Daniell, *Death and Burial*, 87–115; Marshall, *Beliefs and the Dead*, 295–6; Doreen Zerbe, 'Memorialkunst im Wandel: die Ausbildung eines luterischen Typus des Grab- und Gedächtnismals im 16. Jahrhundert', in J. Staecker and C. Jäggi (eds), *Archäologie der Reformation. Studien zu den Auswirkungen des Konfessionswechsels auf die materielle Kultur* (Berlin, De Gruyter, 2007), 118; A. Spicer, '"Rest of Their Bones": Fear of Death and Reformed Burial Practices', in W. G. Naphy and P. Roberts (eds), *Fear in Early Modern Society* (Manchester, Manchester University Press, 1997), 174–8; A. N. Burnett, *Teaching the Reformation: Ministers and Their Message in Basel, 1529–1629* (Oxford, Oxford University Press, 2006), 247.

25 D. MacCulloch, *Reformation: Europe's House Divided 1490–1700* (London, Allen Lane, 2003), 579.

26 H. Colvin, *Architecture and the Afterlife* (New Haven, Yale University Press, 1981), 296–303; A. Spicer, '"Defyle Not Christ's Kirk with Your Carrion": Burial and the Development of Burial Aisles in Post-Reformation Scotland', in B. Gordon and P. Marshall (eds), *The Place of the Dead: Death and*

Remembrance in Late Medieval and Early Modern Europe (Cambridge, Cambridge University Press, 2000), 149–69.

27 Spicer, 'Development of Burial Aisles'; K. Brown, *Noble Society in Scotland: Wealth, Family and Culture from Reformation to Revolution* (Edinburgh, Edinburgh University Press, 2000), 269; Todd, *Culture of Protestantism*, 333–4, 336.

28 Koslofsy, *Reformation of the Dead*, 90–4; Karant-Nunn, *Reformation of Ritual*, 181–4.

29 Gittings, *Death*, 161–4; Karant-Nunn, *Reformation of Ritual*, 181.

30 Marshall, *Beliefs and the Dead*, 151–3; R. Houlbrooke, *Death, Religion and the Family in England, 1480–1750* (Oxford, Clarendon Press, 1998), 277–8.

31 B. Gordon, *Calvin* (New Haven and London, Yale University Press, 2009), 336–7.

32 Benedict, *Christ's Churches*, 506–7.

33 Marshall, *Beliefs and the Dead*, 162–8; Benedict, *Christ's Churches*, 507; Todd, *Culture of Protestantism*, 340.

34 Benedict, *Christ's Churches*, 507; Todd, *Culture of Protestantism*, 340–1; Houlbrooke, *Death, Religion and the Family*, 277, 295–330.

35 Todd, *Culture of Protestantism*, 341; A. N. Burnett, '"To Oblige My Brethren": The Reformed Funeral Sermons of Johann Brandmuller', *Sixteenth Century Journal*, 36 (2005), 38.

36 E. Winkler, *Die Leichenpredigt im deutschen Luthertum bis Spener* (Munich, Kaiser, 1967); C. N. Moore, *Patterned Lives: The Lutheran Funeral Biography in Early Modern Germany* (Wiesbaden, Harrassowitz, 2006); M. J. Haemig and R. Kolb, 'Preaching in Lutheran Pulpits in the Age of Confessionalization', in R. Kolb (ed.), *Lutheran Ecclesiastical Culture, 1550–1675* (Leiden, Brill, 2008).

37 S. R. Boettcher, 'Late Sixteenth-Century Lutherans: A Community of Memory?', in M. Halvorson and K. Spierling (eds), *Defining Community in Early Modern Europe* (Aldershot, Ashgate, 2009), 121–41; R. Rast, '*Animo grato vovit*: Early Modern Epitaph Altars in Estonia', *Studies on Art and Architecture*, 20 (2011), 159–185.

38 P. L. Hughes and J. F. Larkin (eds), *Tudor Royal Proclamations* (3 vols, New Haven, Yale University Press, 1964–9), II, 146–9.

39 Marshall, *Beliefs and the Dead*, 174–5; J. Staecker, 'A Protestant Habitus: 16th-Century Danish Graveslabs as an Expression of Changes in Belief', in Gaimster and Gilchrist (eds), *Archaeology of Reformation*, 419.

40 S. Tarlow, 'Wormie Clay and Blessed Sleep: Death and Disgust in Later Historical Britain', in S. Tarlow and S. West (eds), *The Familiar Past? Archaeologies of Later Historical Britain* (London, Routledge, 1998), 187; S. J. Rosie, *Saints and Sinners: Memorials of St Magnus Cathedral* (Kirkwall, Orkney Media Group, 2015), 69, 79–80.

41 Cf. C. Bartram, '"Some Tomb for a Remembraunce": Representations of Piety in Post-Reformation Gentry Funeral Monuments', in R. Lutton and

E. Salter (eds), *Pieties in Transition: Religious Practices and Experiences, c.1400–1640* (Aldershot, Ashgate, 2007), 129–43.

42 Ø. Ekroll, 'State Church and Church State: Churches and Their Interiors in Post-Reformation Norway, 1537–1705', in A. Spicer (ed.), *Lutheran Churches in Early Modern Europe* (Farnham, Ashgate, 2012), 295–6; N. Pounds, *A History of the English Parish: The Culture of Religion from Augustine to Victoria* (Cambridge, Cambridge University Press, 2000), 496.

43 Marshall, *Beliefs and the Dead*, 229–30; P. Sherlock, *Monuments and Memory in Early Modern England* (Aldershot, Ashgate, 2008), 110–11; Staecker, 'Protestant Habitus', 421–2; González, 'Fate of the Dead', 206–7; Zerbe, 'Memorialkunst im Wandel', 140.

44 Haemig and Kolb, 'Preaching in Lutheran Pulpits', 131.

45 Cressy, *Birth, Marriage and Death*, 385–6; González, 'Fate of the Dead', 217.

46 For example, Deut. 31.16; 1 Kings 2.10, 11:43, 15.8; Ps. 4.8; Isa. 28.20; Dan. 12:2; John 11.11; Acts 7.60; 1 Cor. 15.6; 1 Thess. 4.13; Rev. 14.13.

47 See below, Ch. 5.

48 Sherlock, *Monuments and Memory*, 63.

49 Eire, *Madrid to Purgatory*, pt I; Tingle, 'Purgatory and the Counter-Reformation'; C. Göttler, *Die Kunst des Fegefeuers nach der Reformation. Kirchliche Schenkungen, Ablass und Almosen in Antwerpen und Bologna um 1600* (Mainz am Rhein, Philipp von Zabern, 1996).

50 P. Cockerham and A. L. Harris, 'Kilkenny Funeral Monuments 1500–1600: A Statistical and Analytical Account', *Proceedings of the Royal Irish Academy: Section C*, 101 (2001), 168–9.

51 Zerbe, 'Memorialkunst im Wandel', 127–35; Staecker, 'Protestant Habitus', 421.

52 Marshall, *Beliefs and the Dead*, 205–10.

53 B. Kaplan, *Divided by Faith: Religious Conflict and the Practice of Toleration in Early Modern Europe* (Cambridge, MA, Harvard University Press, 2007), 94–6; A. Eurich, 'Between the Living and the Dead: Preserving Confessional Identity and Community in Early Modern France', in Halvorson and Spierling (eds), *Defining Community in Early Modern Europe*, 43–62.

54 P. Marshall, 'Confessionalization and Community in the Burial of English Catholics, c.1570–1700', in N. Lewycky and A. Morton (eds), *Getting Along? Religious Identities and Confessional Relations in Early Modern England* (Farnham, Ashgate, 2012), 57–75; R. Gillespie, 'Godly Order: Enforcing Peace in the Irish Reformation', in E. Boran and C. Gribben (eds), *Enforcing Reformation in Ireland and Scotland, 1550–1700* (Aldershot, Ashgate, 2006), 184–201; C. Tait, *Death, Burial and Commemoration in Ireland, 1550–1650* (Basingstoke, Macmillan, 2002), 81.

55 R. Po-chia Hsia, *Society and Religion in Münster, 1535–1618* (New Haven, Yale University Press, 1984), 129–36; David Luebke, 'Confessions of the Dead: Interpreting Burial Practice in the Late Reformation', *Archive for Reformation History*, 101 (2010), 55–79.

56 K. Luria, *Sacred Boundaries: Religious Coexistence and Conflict in*

Early-Modern France (Washington, The Catholic University of America Press, 2005), 106–18.

57 W. Frijhoff, *Embodied Belief: Ten Essays on Religious Culture in Dutch History* (Hilversum, Verloren, 2002), 140.

58 Kaplan, *Divided by Faith*, 93–4.

59 Koslofsky, *Reformation of the Dead*, 115–32; Luebke, 'Confessions of the Dead'.

60 A. Walsham, 'Beads, Books and Bare Ruined Choirs: Transmutations of Catholic Ritual Life in Protestant England', in B. Kaplan, B. Moore, H. Van Nierop and J. Pollmann (eds), *Catholic Communities in Protestant States: Britain and the Netherlands, c.1570–1720* (Manchester, Manchester University Press, 2009), 112.

61 P. Roberts, 'Contesting Sacred Space: Burial Disputes in Sixteenth-Century France', in Gordon and Marshall (eds), *The Place of the Dead*, 131–48.

62 J. Cope, *England and the 1641 Irish Rebellion* (Woodbridge, Boydell Press, 2009), cover ill.; Tait, *Death, Burial and Commemoration*, 82–3; N. Canny, *Making Ireland British 1580–1650* (Oxford, Oxford University Press, 2001), 514–15.

2 'The map of God's word': geographies of the afterlife in Tudor and early Stuart England

1 See C. Carozzi, 'La Géographie de l'au-delà et sa signification pendant le haut moyen âge', *Popoli e Paesi nella Cultura Altomedievale*, Settimani di Studio del Centro Italiano di Studi sull'alto Medieoevo, 29 (Spoleto, Presso la Sede del Centro, 1983); J. Le Goff, *The Birth of Purgatory*, tr. A. Goldhammer (Chicago, University of Chicago Press, 1984); H. A. Kelly, 'Hell with Purgatory and Two Limbos: The Geography and Theology of the Underworld', in I. Moreira and M. Toscano (eds), *Hell and Its Afterlife: Historical and Contemporary Perspectives* (Farnham, Ashgate, 2010), 121–36; P. C. Almond, *Afterlife: A History of Life after Death* (London, I. B. Tauris, 2016), ch. 2.

2 C. McDannell and B. Lang, *Heaven: A History* (New Haven and London, Yale University Press, 1990), 352; A. Turner, *The History of Hell* (New York, Harcourt Brace, 1993), 238.

3 K. Thomas, *Religion and the Decline of Magic* (new edn, London, Weidenfeld & Nicolson, 1997), 170–1; C. Hill, *The World Turned Upside Down* (Harmondsworth, Penguin, 1975), 151–83, 185, 214, 221–2, 228, 339, 397; N. Smith, 'The Charge of Atheism and the Language of Radical Speculation 1640–1660', in M. Hunter and D. Wooton (eds), *Atheism from the Reformation to the Enlightenment* (Oxford, Clarendon Press, 1992), 136–7, 139, 158.

4 D. P. Walker, *The Decline of Hell: Seventeenth-Century Discussions of Eternal Torment* (London, Routledge & Kegan Paul, 1964).

5 P. C. Almond, *Heaven and Hell in Enlightenment England* (Cambridge, Cambridge University Press, 1994), 43; Smith, 'Language of Radical

Speculation', 134; Thomas, *Religion and the Decline of Magic*, 169–71; Hill, *World Turned Upside Down*, 26–7, 175.

6   D. Cressy, *Birth, Marriage, and Death: Ritual, Religion, and the Life-Cycle in Tudor and Stuart England* (Oxford, Oxford University Press, 1997), 396.

7   On medieval vision literature, see T. Wright, *St Patrick's Purgatory: An Essay on the Legends of Purgatory, Hell, and Paradise, current during the Middle Ages* (London, John Russell Smith, 1844); H. R. Patch, *The Other World According to Descriptions in Medieval Literature* (New York, Octagon Books, 1970); J. Le Goff, 'The Learned and Popular Dimensions of Journeys in the Otherworld in the Middle Ages', in S. Kaplan (ed.), *Understanding Popular Culture: Europe from the Middle Ages to the Nineteenth Century* (Berlin, Mouton, 1984); A. Gurevich, *Medieval Popular Culture: Problems of Belief and Perception*, tr. J. M. Bak and A. Hollingsworth (Cambridge, Cambridge University Press, 1988), ch. 4; E. Gardiner (ed.), *Visions of Heaven and Hell before Dante* (New York, Italica Press, 1989); A. Morgan, *Dante and the Medieval Other World* (Cambridge, Cambridge University Press, 1986); D. W. Pasulka, *Heaven Can Wait: Purgatory in Catholic Devotional and Popular Culture* (Oxford, Oxford University Press, 2015).

8   Gurevich, *Medieval Popular Culture*, 132–3.

9   Le Goff, *Birth of Purgatory*, quotes at 32, 228.

10 R. A. Bowyer, 'The Role of the Ghost Story in Medieval Christianity', in H. R. Ellis Davidson and W. M. S. Russell (eds), *The Folklore of Ghosts* (Cambridge, D. S. Brewer, 1981), 183.

11 Le Goff, *Birth of Purgatory*, 205–8, 252, 310–15.

12 Aquinas, *Summa Theologica*, cited in M. Joseph, 'Discerning the Ghost in Hamlet', *Publications of the Modern Language Association of America*, 76 (1961), 497.

13 Cited in R. L. White, 'Early Print and Purgatory: The Shaping of an Henrician Ideology', Australian National University PhD thesis (1994), 53.

14 *Here begynneth a Lytel Boke that speketh of Purgatorye* (London, 1531), A2v.

15 A. Kreider, *English Chantries: The Road to Dissolution* (Cambridge, MA, Harvard University Press, 1979); E. Duffy, *The Stripping of the Altars: Traditional Religion in England 1400–1580* (2nd edn, New Haven and London, Yale University Press, 2005); P. Marshall, *Beliefs and the Dead in Reformation England* (Oxford, Oxford University Press, 2002).

16 J. Belfield, 'Tarleton's News out of Purgatory (1590): A Modern-Spelling Edition, with Introduction and Commentary', University of Birmingham PhD thesis (1978), quote at 285; *Greenes Newes both from Heaven and Hell*, ed. R. B. McKerrow (London, Sidgwick and Jackson, 1911).

17 John Donne, *Ignatius his Conclave*, ed. T. S. Healy (Oxford, Oxford University Press, 1969), 5–7.

18 Donne, *Ignatius*, 9; John Donne, *Essays in Divinity*, ed. E. M. Simpson (Oxford, Clarendon Press, 1952) 27; Pierre Viret, *The Christian Disputations*, tr. J. Brooke (London, 1579), 225v–226r; Anthony Wooton, *An Answere to*

a Popish Pamphlet (London, 1605), 49; Edward Hoby, *A Letter to Mr T. H.* (London, 1609), 79; Thomas Beard, *A Retractive from the Romish Religion* (London, 1616), 9.

19   S. Rappaport, *Worlds within Worlds: Structures of Life in Sixteenth-Century London* (Cambridge, Cambridge Press, 1989), 11, 86, 213; I. Archer, *The Pursuit of Stability: Social Relations in Elizabethan London* (Cambridge, Cambridge University Press, 1991), 12–13, 185–6.

20   John Jewel, *Works*, ed. J. Ayre (4 vols, Cambridge, Cambridge University Press, 1845–50), IV, 845.

21   Thomas Morton, *A Catholike Appeale for Protestants* (London, 1609), 198, 197.

22   Jean Veron, *The Huntyng of Purgatorye to Death* (London, 1561), 159v.

23   William Fulke, *Two Treatises written against the Papistes* (London, 1577), 170.

24   William Barlow, *A Defence of the Articles of the Protestants Religion* (London, 1601), 138; Thomas Rogers, *The Catholic Doctrine of the Church of England*, ed. J. S. Perowne (Cambridge, Cambridge University Press, 1854), 215; Christopher Carlile, *A Discourse concerning Two Divine Positions* (London, 1582), 93r–v, 99r–100v, 160r–161v; William Fulke, *The Text of the New Testament of Iesus Christ translated out of the vulgar Latine by the Papists of the Traiterous Seminarie at Rhemes* (London, 1589), 119; Andrew Willet, *Synopsis Papismi, that is, a generall viewe of papistry* (London, 1592), 312; Henry Smith, *Sermons* (London, 1592), 534–5; Richard Field, *Of the Church: Five Bookes* (London, 1606), 95; Joseph Hall, *The Peace of Rome* (London, 1609), 48; William Leigh, *The Soules Solace agaynst Sorrow* (London, 1612), 32.

25   James Ussher, 'An Answer to a Challenge by a Jesuit in Ireland', in *The Whole Works of the Most Rev. James Ussher* (17 vols, Dublin, Hodges and Smith, 1829–64), III, 278–9.

26   Pierre Du Moulin, *The Waters of Siloe*, tr. I. B. (Oxford, 1612), 35.

27   Robert Bellarmine, 'Liber de Purgatorio', in *De Controversiis Christianae Fidei Adversus Huuis Temporis Haereticos* (5 vols, Ingolstadt, 1601), II, 793.

28   Randall Hutchins, 'Of Specters', tr. and ed. V. B. Heltzel and C. Murley, *Huntingdon Library Quarterly*, 11 (1947–8), 423; Andrew Willet, *Testrastylon Papisimi* (London, 1599), 180; Morton, *Catholike Appeale*, 198–9, 429; Du Moulin, *Waters of Siloe*, 35.

29   James I, *An Apologie for the Oath of Allegiance* (London, 1609), 43.

30   The best survey of this controversy is N. T. Burns, *Christian Mortalism from Tyndale to Milton* (Cambridge, MA, Harvard University Press, 1972), ch. 3.

31   D. D. Wallace, 'Puritan and Anglican: The Interpretation of Christ's Descent into Hell in Elizabethan Theology', *Archiv für Reformationsgeschichte*, 69 (1978); David Bagchi, 'Christ's Descent into Hell in Reformation Controversy', in P. Clarke and T. Claydon (eds), *The Church, the Afterlife and the Fate of the Soul*, Studies in Church History, 45 (Woodbridge, Boydell Press, 2009).

32   Burns, *Christian Mortalism*, 101; Marshall, *Beliefs and the Dead*, 223–5.

33   John Hooper, *Later Writings*, ed. C. Nevinson (Cambridge, Cambridge University Press, 1852), 63. See also Heinrich Bullinger, *The Decades: The Fourth Decade*, ed. T. Harding (Cambridge, Cambridge University Press, 1851), 389–90; Thomas Becon, *Prayers and Other Pieces*, ed. J. Ayre (Cambridge, Cambridge University Press, 1844), 182; Veron, *Huntyng of Purgatorye*, 1r.

34   William Tyndale, *Expositions and Notes*, ed. H. Walter (Cambridge, Cambridge University Press, 1849), 185; John Frith, *Work*, ed. N. T. Wright (Oxford, Sutton Courtenay Press, 1978), 192.

35   John Calvin, *The Institutes of the Christian Religion*, tr. H. Beveridge (2 vols in 1, repr. Grand Rapids, Eerdmans, 1989), II, 267.

36   William Allen, *A Defence and Declaration of the Catholike Churchies Doctrine touching Purgatory* (Antwerp, 1565), 117r.

37   Hoby, *Letter to Mr T. H.*, 79.

38   John Floyd, *Purgatories Triumph over Hell* (St Omer, 1613), 125. See also Theophilus Higgons, *The First Motive* (Douai, 1609), 155.

39   [Edward Hoby], *A Curry-combe for a Coxe-combe* (London, 1615), 205.

40   For a broad outline of the issues, see Turner, *History of Hell*; R. Hughes, *Heaven and Hell in Western Art* (London, Weidenfeld & Nicolson, 1968), ch. 4. The relevant scriptural texts are usefully collated by J. Delumeau, *Sin and Fear: The Emergence of a Western Guilt Culture, 13th–18th Centuries*, tr. E. Nicholson (New York, St Martin's Press, 1990), 374–5.

41   Viret, *Christian Disputations*, fo 290r; Carlile, *Discourse concerning Two Divine Positions*, 137v; Henry Jacob, *A Treatise of the Sufferings and Victory of Christ* (London, 1598), 122–3; Du Moulin, *Waters of Siloe*, 32.

42   Carlile, *Discourse concerning Two Divine Positions*, 105v–107r; Jacob, *Sufferings of Christ*, 146; Andrew Willet, *Loidoromastix* (London, 1607), 25–6.

43   Hugh Broughton, *Declaration of Generall Corruption of Religion . . . wrought by D. Bilson* (Middelburg, 1603), unpaginated.

44   William Whitaker, *A Disputation on Holy Scripture*, tr. and ed. W. Fitzgerald (Cambridge, Cambridge University Press, 1849), 538; William Perkins, *A golden chaine* (Cambridge, 1660), 372–3; Andrew Willet, *Limbo-mastix* (London, 1604), 55 (quote).

45   Thomas Bilson, *The Survey of Christs Sufferings for Mans Redemption* (London, 1604), 619; Adam Hill, *The Defence of the Article: Christ descended into Hell* (London, 1592), 10; Richard Parkes, *The Second Booke containing a Reioynder to a Reply* in *An Apologie: of Three Testimonies of Holy Scripture* (London, 1607), 4; John Higgins, *An Answer to Master William Perkins* (Oxford, 1602), 21–2.

46   Veron, *Huntyng of Purgatorye*, 155r–v; Carlile, *Discourse concerning Two Divine Positions*, 105v; Viret, *Christian Disputations*, 28v; Jacob, *Sufferings of Christ*, 153; Willet, *Synopsis Papismi*, 607–8; Perkins, *Golden chaine*, 373; Donne, *Essays in Divinity*, 36.

47   Ussher, *Answer to a Challenge*, 378.

48   Hill, *Defence of the Article*, 62; Higgins, *Answer to Perkins*, 19–20.

49   John Donne, *Sermons*, ed. E. M. Simpson and G. R. Potter (10 vols, Berkeley and Los Angeles, University of California Press, 1953–62), VII, 137. The allusion is to Sebastian Münster, *Cosmographiae Universalis* (Basle, 1550), 11–12.

50   Samuel Gardiner, *The Devotions of the Dying Man* (London, 1627), 332.

51   Thomas More, *The Supplication of Souls*, ed. F. Manley et al., *Complete Works of St Thomas More*, vol. 7 (New Haven and London, Yale University Press, 1990), 186.

52   Robert Persons, *The Christian directory* (St Omer, 1607), 229–30.

53   Allen, *Defence and Declaration*, 117r.

54   Anthony Champney, *A Manual of Controversies* (Paris, 1614), 76–7; Sylvester Norris, *An Antidote or Treatise of Thirty Controversies* (1622), 299. Norris thought it most likely, however, that purgatory was under the earth: *An Antidote or Treatise*, 302.

55   Le Goff, *Birth of Purgatory*, 157–8; Paul Binski, *Medieval Death: Ritual and Representation* (London, British Museum Press, 1996), 210; Allen, *Defence and Declaration*, 275v; Richard Bristowe, *A Reply to Fulke* (Louvain, 1580), 154.

56   Binski, *Medieval Death*, 183; Ussher, *Answer to a Challenge*, 291; Hoby, *Curry-combe for a Coxe-combe*, 153; Beard, *Retractive from the Romish Religion*, 414–15.

57   Veron, *Huntyng of Purgatorye*, 314v.

58   Heinrich Bullinger, *Decades: The First and Second Decades*, ed. T. Harding (Cambridge, Cambridge University Press, 1849), 139; Bilson, *Survey of Christs Sufferings*, 541.

59   William Fulke, *A Reioynder to Bristows Replie* (London, 1581), 149. See also Fulke, *A Defence of the Sincere and True Translations of the Holy Scripture*, ed. C. H. Hartshorne (Cambridge, Cambridge University Press, 1843), 285.

60   Robert Pricke, *A Verie Godlie and Learned Sermon treating of Mans Mortalitie* (London, 1608), E1r.

61   M. C. Cross, 'The Third Earl of Huntingdon's Death-Bed: A Calvinist Example of the *Ars Moriendi*', *Northern History*, 21 (1985), 102.

62   Philip Stubbes, 'A Christal Glasse for Christian Women', in *The Anatomie of Abuses*, ed. F. J. Furnivall (London, N. Trubner & Co., 1877), 204.

63   *Henry V*, II.iii.9–19. For other references to Abraham's bosom used in this sense in Shakespeare, see *Richard III*, IV.iii.38; *Richard II*, IV.i.94–5.

64   David Person, *Varieties: or a Surveigh of Rare and Excellent Matters* (London, 1635), 183.

65   John 11.1–44.

66   Wright, *Patrick's Purgatory*, 167; Duffy, *Stripping of the Altars*, 81–2, 340–1, pl. 127–8; C. Daniell, *Death and Burial in Medieval England 1066–1550* (London, Routledge, 1997), 10–11, 82; G. England and A. W. Pollard (eds), *The Towneley Plays*, Early English Text Society, 71 (Oxford, Oxford University Press 1987), 387–93.

67   Allen, *Defence and Declaration*, 277r; Bellarmine, *Liber de Purgatorio*, 798.

68   Willet, *Synopsis Papismi*, 307; Du Moulin, *Waters of Siloe*, 307; William Guild, *Ignis Fatuus or the Elf-fire of Purgatorie* (London, 1625), 41.

69   Guild, *Ignis Fatuus*, 41.

70   Hugh Latimer, *Sermons*, ed. G. E. Corrie (Cambridge, Cambridge University Press, 1844), 550.

71   Fulke, *Two Treatises*, 442.

72   *The Sermons of Mr Henry Smith* (2 vols, London, William Tegg, 1866), II, 420.

73   Thomas Browne, 'Religio Medici', in *Major Works*, ed. C. A. Patrides (Harmondsworth, Penguin, 1977), 87–8.

74   Le Goff, *Birth of Purgatory*, 229–30.

75   Donne, *Ignatius his Conclave*, 79–81.

76   Donne, *Sermons*, VIII, 81–2.

77   Veron, *Huntyng of Purgatorye*, 161r.

78   Morton, *Catholike Appeale*, 197–8.

79   Hoby, *Letter to Mr T. H.*, 79.

80   Parkes, *The Second Booke*, 4.

81   Ussher, *Answer to a Challenge*, 373–7.

82   Person, *Varieties*, 183–5, 188, 194, 199.

83   J. Delumeau, *History of Paradise: The Garden of Eden in Myth and Tradition*, tr. M. O'Connell (New York, Continuum, 1995), esp. ch. 7. See also C. Delano-Smith and E.M. Ingram, *Maps in Bibles 1500–1600: An Illustrated Catalogue* (Geneva, Librairie Droz, 1991), xvi, xxv–xxvi.

84   Delumeau, *History of Paradise*, 149, 152–7; John Salkeld, *A Treatise of Paradise and the Principall Contents thereof* (London, 1617), 39.

85   Gurevich describes the idea of an island location for hell and paradise as 'rooted in the consciousness of the inhabitants of the European North' in the Middle Ages: *Medieval Popular Culture*, 131. On island utopias, see J. C. Davis, *Utopia and the Ideal Society: A Study of English Utopian Writing 1516–1700* (Cambridge, Cambridge University Press, 1981).

86   Almond, *Heaven and Hell*, 46–7.

87   Willet, *Synopsis Papismi*, 609.

88   Jacob, *Sufferings of Christ*, 79.

89   Barlow, *Defence of the Articles*, 172. The classification of Barlow is Anthony Milton's: *Catholic and Reformed: The Roman and Protestant Churches in English Protestant Thought, 1600–1640* (Cambridge, Cambridge University Press, 1995), 23.

90   Donne, *Sermons*, V, 226.

91   Richard Smith, *A Conference of the Catholike and Protestante Doctrine with the Expresse Words of Holie Scripture* (Douai, 1631), 510. See also John Radford, *A Directorie teaching the Way to Truth* (England, secret press, 1605), 459–60.

92   Cited in R. H. West, *The Invisible World: A Study of Pneumatology in Elizabethan Drama* (repr. New York, Octagon Books, 1969), 82. See Bilson,

Survey of Christs Sufferings, 633; Browne, *Religio Medici*, 125; C. A. Patrides, 'Renaissance and Modern Views of Hell', *Harvard Theological Review*, 57 (1964), 228–9.

93 *Doctor Faustus*, II.i.122–6.

94 Burns, *Christian Mortalism*, 59.

95 Browne, *Religio Medici*, 125.

96 C. A. Patrides, *Milton and the Christian Tradition* (Oxford, Clarendon Press, 1966), 280, 176.

97 *Hamlet* III.i.80–2; *Measure for Measure*, III.i.118–27.

98 Francis Bacon, *Essays* (London, Dent, 1965), 6.

99 Browne, 'Hydriotaphia or Urne-Buriall', in *Works*, ed. Patrides, 302–3.

100 Walker, *Decline of Hell*, 59.

101 N. L. Beaty, *The Craft of Dying: A Study in the Literary Tradition of the Ars Moriendi in England* (New Haven and London, Yale University Press, 1970), 154; C. Gittings, *Death, Burial and the Individual in Early Modern England* (London, Croom Helm, 1984), 155; N. Llewellyn, *The Art of Death: Visual Culture in the English Death Ritual c.1500–c.1800* (London, Hale, 1991), 79.

102 Walker, *Decline of Hell*, 39–40, 100–1; Almond, *Heaven and Hell*, 125–30.

103 W. R. Alger, *The Destiny of the Soul: A Critical History of the Doctrine of a Future Life* (10th edn, New York, W. J. Widdleton, 1878), 698–9.

104 Cited by Kreider, *English Chantries*, 115.

3 Judgement and repentance in Tudor Manchester: the celestial journey of Ellis Hall

1 *The Diary of Henry Machyn*, ed. J. G. Nichols, Camden Society, 42 (London, J. B. Nichols and Son, 1847), 284; John Strype, *Annals of the Reformation and Establishment of Religion* (4 vols in 7, London, 1824), I/1, 433–5; I/2, 196; British Library, London, Lansdowne MS 24, no. 81; London Guildhall MS 33011/1, 222r.

2 The National Archives, London, SP 12/23/39; Bodleian Library, Oxford, MS Tanner 50, 16r–17r. The latter was edited in *English Historical Review*, 37 (1922), 256–7, by W. M. Kennedy as 'A Declaration before the Ecclesiastical Commission', though it seems more likely to have been an ad hoc grouping of available councillors: cf. *Acts of the Privy Council of England*, ed. J. R. Dasent (46 vols, London, HMSO, 1890–1964), VII, 105.

3 K. Thomas, *Religion and the Decline of Magic* (new edn, London, Weidenfeld & Nicolson, 1997), 133; R. Bauckham, *Tudor Apocalypse* (Appleford, Sutton Courtenay Press, 1978), 187–8; A. Walsham, *Providence in Early Modern England* (Oxford, Oxford University Press, 1999), 204; N. Jones, *The Birth of the Elizabethan Age* (Oxford, Blackwell, 1993), 41–2; C. Haigh, *Reformation and Resistance in Tudor Lancashire* (Cambridge, Cambridge University Press, 1975), 144–5.

4 Haigh, *Reformation and Resistance*, 168–9, 209, 219–20; R. Hollingworth, *Mancuniensis* (Manchester, W. Willis, 1839), 75–6.

5 H. R. Patch, *The Other World According to Descriptions in Medieval Literature* (New York, Octagon Books, 1970); J. Le Goff, 'The Learned and Popular Dimensions of Journeys in the Otherworld in the Middle Ages', in S. Kaplan, ed., *Understanding Popular Culture* (Berlin, Mouton, 1984); A. Morgan, *Dante and the Medieval Other World* (Cambridge, Cambridge University Press, 1986); A. Gurevich, *Medieval Popular Culture*, tr. J. Bak and Hollingsworth (Cambridge, Cambridge University Press, 1988), ch. 4; G. M. Walters, 'Visitacyons, Prevytes, and Deceytys: The Vision in Late Medieval English Popular Piety', University of Cambridge PhD thesis (1992). For a bibliographic overview, A. Claasen (ed.), *Handbook of Medieval Studies* (3 vols, Berlin, De Gruyter, 2010), I, 511–14.

6 Walters, 'The Vision in Late Medieval Piety', 21.

7 Peter Marshall, *Beliefs and the Dead in Reformation England* (Oxford, Oxford University Press, 2002), 8.

8 E. M. Thompson (ed.), 'The Vision of Edmund Leversedge', *Notes and Queries for Somerset and Devon*, 9 (1904–5), 19–35.

9 Bodleian Library, Oxford, MS Lat. Misc. c. 66, 21r–23v. See D. Marsh, 'Humphrey Newton of Newton and Pownall (1466–1536)', Keele University PhD thesis (1995), 311–17.

10 Bodleian Library, Oxford, MS Lat. Misc. c. 66, 155r–176r. See Ch. 1, above.

11 SP 12/23/39.

12 *Pace* the view of A. Walsham, 'Hall, Elizeus (1502–1565)', *Oxford Dictionary of National Biography*, online edn, that Hall's revelations 'showed little knowledge of the Bible'.

13 The most frequently printed version in the period before 1552 was the 'Great Bible', a 1541 edition of which (STC 2075) has been used for explicating Hall's statements, employing modern chapter and verse divisions.

14 Tanner MS 50, 16r, has the alternative 'faste and pray' – conceivably a mis-transcription, though this linkage too has scriptural resonances: Matt. 17; 21; Mark 9.29; Luke 2.37; Acts 10.30, 13.3, 14.23; 1 Cor. 7.5.

15 B. M. Metzger and M. D. Coogan (eds), *The Oxford Companion to the Bible* (New York and Oxford, Oxford University Press, 1993), 193; *The Jerusalem Bible: New Testament* (London, Darton, Longman & Todd, 1967), 69.

16 Haigh, *Reformation and Resistance*, 114, argues that 'it is very unlikely that vernacular Bibles reached the county in any number'. The one surviving set of churchwardens' accounts (Prescot) gives no sign of a purchase until after the 1547 royal visitation (Haigh, *Reformation and Resistance*, 115).

17 S. Smith-Bannister, *Names and Naming Patterns in England 1538–1700* (Oxford, Oxford University Press, 1997); S. Wilson, *The Means of Naming: A Social and Cultural History of Personal Naming in Western Europe* (London, UCL Press, 1998).

18 E. G. Withycombe, *The Oxford Dictionary of English Christian Names* (3rd edn, Oxford, Oxford University Press, 1977); P. Hanks and F. Hodges, *A Dictionary of First Names* (Oxford, Oxford University Press, 1990). 'Elys Hall' was junior constable of Manchester in 1557: J. Harland (ed.),

Manchester Court Leet Records, Chetham Society o.s., 63 (Manchester, 1864), 170.

19 1 Kings 3.1–18 = 1 Sam. in Authorized Version (AV).

20 4 Kings 2.11 = 2 Kings in AV.

21 Tanner MS 50, fo 16v. Strype, *Annals*, I/2, 196, suggested that the gown of skins worn in the pillory was 'perhaps in mockery to him, calling himself Elias, and going in camel's hair, in imitation of that prophet'. For later examples of soi-disant prophets claiming to be Elijah, see Bauckham, *Tudor Apocalypse*, 187; Walsham, *Providence*, 204.

22 D. Cressy, *Bonfires and Bells: National Memory and the Protestant Calendar in Elizabethan and Stuart England* (Berkeley, University of California Press, 1989); N. L. Jones, *The English Reformation: Religion and Cultural Adaption* (Oxford, Blackwell, 2002); A. Walsham, *The Reformation of the Landscape: Religion, Identity, and Memory in Early Modern Britain and Ireland* (Oxford, Oxford University Press, 2011); Walsham, *Providence*; T. Watt, *Cheap Print and Popular Piety 1550–1640* (Cambridge, Cambridge University Press, 1991).

4 The Reformation of hell? Protestant and Catholic infernalisms *c.*1560–1640

1 A. Pettegree (ed.) (Manchester, Manchester University Press, 1993); S. C. Karant-Nunn (London, Routledge, 1997); C. H. Parker (Cambridge, Cambridge University Press, 1998); J. L. Koerner (London, Reaktion Books, 2004); R. K. Rittgers (Cambridge, MA, Harvard University Press, 2005); S. C. Karant-Nunn (Oxford, Oxford University Press, 2010).

2 (Basingstoke, Macmillan, 2000). For a broad overview, see P. Marshall, 'Leaving the World', in P. Matheson (ed.), *Reformation Christianity* (Minneapolis, Fortress Press, 2007), 168–88. See also Ch. 1, above.

3 See R. V. Turner, '*Descendit ad infernos*: Medieval Views on Christ's Descent into Hell and the Salvation of the Ancient Just', *Journal of the History of Ideas*, 27 (1966), 173–94.

4 C. McDannell and B. Lang, *Heaven: A History* (New Haven and London, Yale University Press, 1990); J. B. Russell, *A History of Heaven: The Singing Silence* (Princeton, Princeton University Press, 1997).

5 D. P. Walker, *The Decline of Hell: Seventeenth-Century Discussions of Eternal Torment* (London, Routledge & Kegan Paul, 1964). See also P. C. Almond, *Heaven and Hell in Enlightenment England* (Cambridge, Cambridge University Press, 1994).

6 Darwell Stone, *The Faith of an English Catholic* (London, 1926). Online at <http://anglicanhistory.org/england/stone/faith/14.html>.

7 C. A. Patrides, '"A Horror beyond Our Expression": The Dimensions of Hell', in his *Premises and Motifs in Renaissance Thought and Literature* (Princeton, Princeton University Press, 1982), 182–99, quote at 184.

8 J. Delumeau, *Sin and Fear: The Emergence of a Western Guilt Culture,*

13th–18th Centuries, tr. E. Nicholson (New York, St Martin's Press, 1990), 505–22, quotes at 506, 512.

9   C. M. N. Eire, 'The Good Side of Hell: Infernal Meditations in Early Modern Spain', *Historical Reflections / Réflexions Historiques*, 26 (2000), 286–310, quote at 307.

10 Delumeau, *Sin and Fear*, 505–6.

11 Thomas Phillips, *The Booke of lamentations, or Geenologia a treatise of hell* (London, 1639), 10.

12 D. Oldridge, *The Devil in Early Modern England* (Stroud, Sutton Publishing, 2000), 66–8; P. C. Almond, *Demonic Possession and Exorcism in Early Modern England* (Cambridge, Cambridge University Press, 2004), 181.

13 Henry Greenwood, *Tormenting Tophet: or a terrible description of hel* (London, 1615), 17, 60, 63; [Samuel Rowlands?], *Hels torments, and heavens glorie* (London, 1601), C6v, D3v –5v; Robert Bolton, *The foure last things* (London, 1632), 100; Arthur Dent, *The Plaine Mans Pathway to Heaven* (London, 1601), 390; Phillips, *Booke of lamentations*, 32, 33–5; Luis de la Puente, *Meditations upon the mysteries of our holy faith*, tr. John Heigham (St Omer, 1619), I, 143; Robert Persons, *The Christian directory* (St Omer, 1607), 236. Cf. Jacobus de Voragine, *The Golden Legend*, tr. W. Ryan (2 vols, Princeton, Princeton University Press, 1993), II, 280; P. Sheingorn, '"Who Can Open the Doors of His Face?" The Iconography of Hell Mouth', in C. Davidson and T. H. Seiler (eds), *The Iconography of Hell* (Kalamazoo, Medieval Institute, 1992), 2–3; G. Cigman (ed.), *Lollard Sermons*, Early English Text Society, 294 (Oxford, Oxford University Press, 1989), 231. Descriptions of hell in popular ballads and chapbooks could be even more strikingly atavistic: T. Watt, *Cheap Print and Popular Piety 1550–1640* (Cambridge, Cambridge University Press, 1991), 110–12, 171, 238–9, 312; M. Spufford, *Small Books and Pleasant Histories* (London, Methuen, 1981), 200–7; Oldridge, *Devil in Early Modern England*, 66–7.

14 Delumeau, *Sin and Fear*, 505–6. Thomas à Kempis, *The Imitation of Christ*, tr. B. I. Knott (London, Collins, 1963), 76.

15 Edmund Bunny, *A booke of Christian exercise appertaining to resolution . . . by R. P. perused, and accompanied now with a treatise tending to pacification* (London, 1584), ch. 11; Luis de Granada, *The sinners guyde*, tr. Francis Meres (London, 1598), 104. Cf. B. Gregory, 'The "True and Zealouse Service of God": Robert Parson, Edmund Bunny, and *The First Book of the Christian Exercise*', *Journal of Ecclesiastical History*, 45 (1994), 244–68. On Protestant translations and reception of Catholic works in general, see H. C. White, *English Devotional Literature (Prose) 1600–1640* (Madison, University of Wisconsin Press, 1931), 98–115; J. R. Yamamoto-Wilson, 'The Protestant Reception of Catholic Devotional Literature in England to 1700', *British Catholic History*, 32 (2014), 67–90.

16 Bernard of Clairvaux, *Querela, sive, dialogus animaae et corporis damnati . . . The dialogue betwixt the soule and the body of the damned man*, tr. William Crashaw (London, 1613), epistle dedicatory.

17   Lewis Bayly, *The practise of pietie directing a Christian how to walke that he may please God* (London, 1613), 125–6.

18   Dent, *Plaine Mans Pathway*, 392; John Denison, *A three-fold resolution, verie necessarie to saluation. Describing earths vanity. Hels horror. Heauens felicitie* (London, 1608), 426. For more of the same, see Martin Day, *A monument of mortalitie* (London, 1621), 68–9; Thomas Tuke, *A discourse of death, bodily, ghostly, and eternall* (London, 1613), 99; Samuel Gardiner, *The Devotions of the Dying Man* (London, 1627), 336–7; Delumeau, *Sin and Fear*, 519; Almond, *Heaven and Hell*, 81–7.

19   Robert Bellarmine, *Of the eternal felicity of the saints*, tr. Thomas Everard (St Omer, 1638), 419; Jean Pierre Camus, *A draught of eternitie*, tr. Miles Carr (Douai, 1632), 151–2; Nicholas Caussin, *The holy court in three tomes*, tr. Sir T[homas] H[awkins] (Rouen, 1634), III, 178–9.

20   Greenwood, *Tormenting Tophet*, 20; Camus, *Draught of eternitie*, 117. For further explicit discussion of the deterrent value of hell, see Rowlands, *Hels torments*, B1v; Denison, *A three-fold resolution*, 431; Dent, *Plaine Mans Pathway*, 393; Richard Greenham, *The workes of the reuerend and faithfull seruant af Iesus Christ M. Richard Greenham* (London, 1612), 695; Thomas Wilson, *A commentarie vpon the most diuine Epistle of S. Paul to the Romanes* (London, 1614), 559; Robert Bellarmine, *The art of dying well*, tr. Edward Coffin (St Omer, 1622), 210. For a similar linkage of hell to the themes of salvation and redemption in Spanish sources, see Eire, 'Good Side of Hell'.

21   Thomas Lupton, *A dreame of the diuell and Diues* (London, 1589), D6v.

22   George Hakewill, *An ansvvere to a treatise vvritten by Dr. Carier* (London, 1616), 266; William Tyndale, *An answer to Sir Thomas More's dialogue*, ed. H. Walter (Cambridge, Cambridge University Press, 1850), 28.

23   A. Walsham, *Providence in Early Modern England* (Oxford, Oxford University Press, 1999), 16.

24   Emma Disley, 'Degrees of Glory: Protestant Doctrine and the Concept of Rewards Hereafter', *Journal of Theological Studies*, 42 (1991), 82–5. See also Tuke, *Discourse of death*, 102; de la Puente, *Meditations*, I, 143.

25   In contrast to the impression given by works such as P. Camporesi, *The Fear of Hell: Images of Damnation and Salvation in Early Modern Europe*, tr. L. Byatt (Cambridge, Polity Press, 1990).

26   On catechisms, see I. Green, *The Christian's ABC: Catechisms and Catechizing in England c.1530–1740* (Oxford, Clarendon Press, 1996), 316–9, 342–5; Laurence Vaux, *A Catechism of Christian Doctrine*, ed. T. G. Law, Chetham Society, n.s. 4 (Manchester, 1885), 13; Eire, 'Good Side of Hell', 305, and 306–7 on hell's limited place in continental Counter-Reformation preaching. Delumeau concedes, *Sin and Fear*, 519, that even among Puritans hell was not the preferred theme for sermons.

27   Bellarmine, *Of the eternal felicity of the saints*, 410.

28   W. A. Dyrness, *Reformed Theology and Visual Culture: The Protestant Imagination from Calvin to Edwards* (Cambridge, Cambridge University

Press, 2004), 138–40; Richard Bernard, *Contemplative pictures with whole-some precepts* (London, 1610), epistle dedicatory, 107–29, quote at 115.

29 See Eire, 'Good Side of Hell', 292–8; Camporesi, *Fear of Hell*, 56–7.

30 Watt, *Cheap Print*, ch. 4; Walsham, *Providence*, 250–66.

31 Oldridge, *Devil in Early Modern England*, 67; Rowlands, *Hels torments*, B1r; post-Reformation editions of the *Shepherds kalendar: Revised Short Title Catalogue* 22415–23; Watt, *Cheap Print*, 194, 202, 205–9; C. W. Cary, '"It Circumscribes Us Here": Hell on the Renaissance Stage', in C. Davidson and T. H. Seiler (eds), *The Iconography of Hell* (Kalamazoo, Medieval Institute, 1992), 195.

32 St Augustine, *The City of God*, tr. M. Dods (New York, Random House, 1950), 735.

33 Mark 9.43–48. See also Isa. 66.24; Luke 3.17; Jude 1.7; Rev. 14.10–11; 21.8.

34 For the almost universal adoption and retention of this twofold scheme, see Patrides, 'Dimensions of Hell', 185–7. Almond's suggestion, *Heaven and Hell*, 93–4, that Protestants applied the *poena sensus* only to the resurrected body after the Last Judgement, while Catholics envisaged both types of punishment for the disembodied soul in its 'intermediate state', does not seem to hold up for the pre-Civil War period.

35 W. Addis and T. Arnold, *A Catholic Dictionary*, rev. T. B. Scannell and P. E. Hallett (15th edn, London, Routledge & Kegan Paul, 1954), 389.

36 St Thomas Aquinas, *Summa Theologica*, tr. Fathers of the English Dominican Province, New York, Benziger Bros, 1947, suppl. q. 97 (online at <www.ccel.org/a/aquinas/summa/home.html>). Aquinas argued that the property of giving light did not belong to the essential nature of fire, noting, for example, how its brightness could be obscured by thick smoke. See also J. M. Steadman, 'Milton and Patristic Tradition: The Quality of Hell-Fire', *Anglia*, 76 (1958), 116–28.

37 Persons, *Christian directory*, 236.

38 Caussin, *The holy court*, III, 175.

39 Bellarmine, *Art of dying well*, 206; *Eternal felicity of the saints*, 424–5, 429–30.

40 de la Puente, *Meditations*, I, 136.

41 John Calvin, *The Institutes of the Christian Religion*, tr. H. Beveridge (2 vols in 1, repr. Grand Rapids, Eerdmans, 1989), I, 146–7. See also Calvin, *Harmony of the Gospels*, ed. T. Torrance (3 vols, Edinburgh, St Andrew Press, 1972), II, 275.

42 Compare Dent, *Plaine Mans Pathway*, Phillips, *Booke of lamentations*, 41, with Camus, *Draught of eternitie*, 136; St Philip Howard, *A foure-fould meditation, of the foure last things* (London, 1606), stanza 67; de la Puente, *Meditations*, I, 137; Bellarmine, *Eternal felicity of the saints*, 432–3.

43 William Perkins, *An exposition of the symbole or creed of the apostles* (Cambridge, 1595), 392.

44 Tuke, *Discourse of death*, 100.

45 John Rogers, *A discourse of Christian watchfulnesse* (London, 1620), 334.

46 Thomas Wilson, *A Christian dictionarie opening the signification of the*

chiefe words dispersed generally through Holy Scriptures of the Old and New Testament (London, 1612), 224.

47   Henry Jacob, *A Treatise of the Sufferings and Victory of Christ* (London, 1598), 81, 87–8.

48   Phillips, *Booke of lamentations*, 20.

49   Greenwood, *Tormenting Tophet*, 53–62, quote at 54.

50   Andrew Willet, *A Catholicon, that is, a generall preservative or remedie against the pseudocatholike religion* (Cambridge, 1602), 40; John Smith, *An exposition of the Creed* (London, 1632), 467; Thomas Bilson, *The Survey of Christs Sufferings for Mans Redemption* (London, 1604), 40, 46 (and at 47 unusually suggesting the possibility of material brimstone); Phillips, *Booke of lamentations*, 31. See also Richard Parkes, *A Briefe Answere unto certain obiections and Reasons against the descension of Christ into hell* (Oxford, 1604), 8.

51   John Brereley [James Anderton], *Sainct Austines Religion* (n.p., 1620), 161.

52   Perkins, *Exposition of the creed*, 392; Tuke, *Discourse of death*, 101; Greenwood, *Tormenting Tophet*, 59; Phillips, *Booke of lamentations*, 31.

53   Smith, *Exposition of the Creed*, 467. Though for examples of more literalist approaches, see Abraham Fleming, *The footepath of faith, leading the highwaie to heauen* (London, 1581), 141–2; John Moore, *A mappe of mans mortalitie* (London, 1617), 63.

54   For a fuller discussion of the 'geography' of the afterlife in Protestant thought, see Ch. 2, above.

55   Camus, *Draught of eternitie*, 128; Persons, *Christian directory*, 229–3 (though with the qualification, 'whether it be underground or no'); Bellarmine, *Art of dying well*, 205–6; *Eternal felicity of the saints*, 424 (quote); de la Puente, *Meditations*, I, 136; Eire, 'Good Side of Hell', 288–9.

56   de la Puente, *Meditations*, I, 139; Bellarmine, *Art of dying well*, 207. Persons, *Christian directory*, 238, also emphasizes 'the most severe straitness therof'.

57   Camporesi, *Fear of Hell*, 62. Camporesi regards an emphasis on congestion and restriction as characteristic of the 'Baroque hell', which he contrasts with the 'wide spaces' of the medieval hell: *Fear of Hell*, ch. 5, quote at 69.

58   Andrew Willet, *Synopsis Papismi* (London, 1592), 607–9.

59   Tuke, *Discourse of death*, 102.

60   Christopher Carlile, *A Discourse concerning Two Divine Positions* (London, 1582), 105v–107r; Jacob, *Sufferings of Christ*, 146; Andrew Willet, *Loidoromastix* (London, 1607), 25–6.

61   Hugh Broughton, *Declaration of Generall Corruption of Religion . . . wrought by D. Bilson* (London, 1603), unpaginated.

62   Bilson, *Survey of Christs Sufferings*, 619; Adam Hill, *The Defence of the Article: Christ descended into Hell* (London, 1592), 10, 62; Richard Parkes, *The Second Booke containing a Reioynder to a Reply*, in *An Apologie: of Three Testimonies of Holy Scripture* (London, 1607), 4; John Higgins, *An Answer to Master William Perkins* (Oxford, 1602), 19–20, 21–2; Phillips, *Booke of lamentations*, 14–21.

63 Carlile, *Two Divine Positions*, 105v; Pierre Viret, *The Christian Disputations*, tr. J. Brooke (London, 1579), 28v; Jacob, *Sufferings of Christ*, 153; William Perkins, *A golden chaine: or the description of theologie* (Cambridge, 1600), 373; John Donne, *Essays in Divinity*, ed. E. M. Simpson (Oxford, Clarendon Press, 1952), 36; James Ussher, 'An Answer to a Challenge by a Jesuit in Ireland', in *The Whole Works of the Most Rev. James Ussher* (17 vols, Dublin, Hodges and Smith, 1829–64), III, 378.

64 John Donne, *Sermons*, ed. E. M. Simpson and G. R. Potter (10 vols, Berkeley and Los Angeles, University of California Press, 1953–62), VII, 137.

65 John Radford, *A Directorie teaching the Way to Truth* (England, secret press, 1605), 460; Richard Smith, *A Conference of the Catholike and Protestante Doctrine with the Expresse Words of Holie Scripture* (Douai, 1631), 510.

66 Arguably, Patrides, 'Dimensions of Hell', 193–9, makes too much of this in asserting the genealogy of the concept of 'inner hell'.

67 Howard, *Foure-fould meditation*, stanzas 78–9; Camus, *Draught of eternitie*, 132; de la Puente, *Meditations*, I, 146; Bellarmine, *Eternal felicity of the saints*, 422–3; Bolton, *Foure last things*, 95–6; Patrides, 'Dimensions of Hell', 193–4. George Benson, *A sermon preached at Paules Crosse the seauenth of May, M.DC.IX.* (London, 1609), 54, was unusual in suggesting that the *poena sensus* was more to be dreaded than the *poena damni*.

68 Jeremias Drexel, *The considerations of Drexelius vpon eternitie*, tr. Ralph Winterton (London, 1632), 29. See also de la Puente, *Meditations*, I, 139. The 'ubiquitarian' views of the sixteenth-century Swabian Protestant Johannes Brenz (1499–1570), that the damned roamed around carrying their torment with them, did not catch on in Reformed English circles in this period: L. Paine, *The Hierarchy of Hell* (London, Hale, 1972), 21.

69 A. C. Southern, *English Recusant Prose 1559–1582* (London, Sands, 1950), 255.

70 See above, Ch. 2.

71 Aquinas, *Summa Theologica*, Appendix II, q. 1, a. 2.

72 Walker, *Decline of Hell*, 29–30.

73 Gregory Martin, *A discouerie of the manifold corruptions of the Holy Scriptures by the heretikes of our daies* (Rheims, 1582), 108–9. For Protestant insistence on the inability of the dead to have any awareness of the circumstances of the living, see P. Marshall, *Beliefs and the Dead in Reformation England* (Oxford, Oxford University Press, 2002), 210–15.

74 See D. D. Wallace, 'Puritan and Anglican: The Interpretation of Christ's Descent into Hell in Elizabethan Theology', *Archiv für Reformationsgeschichte*, 49 (1978), 248–87, though the interpretation here is coloured by a rather anachronistic attempt to isolate a distinctly 'Anglican' theology. For an illuminating discussion of contemporary continental debates, see David Bagchi, 'Christ's Descent into Hell in Reformation Controversy', in P. Clarke and T. Claydon (eds), *The Church, the Afterlife and the Fate of the Soul*, Studies in Church History, 45 (Woodbridge, Boydell Press, 2009).

75 Higgins, *Answer to Perkins*, 7. Bilson's *Survey of Christs Sufferings*, A1v,

attacks those that 'outface Christes *Descent to Hell* with phrases and figures, when it is plainly professed in the Creed'.

76 Viret, *Christian Disputations*, 290r; Carlile, *Discourse concerning Two Divine Positions*, 137v; Jacob, *Sufferings of Christ*, 122–3; Pierre Du Moulin, *The Waters of Siloe*, tr. I. B. (Oxford, 1612), 32; Andrew Willet, *Limbo-mastix* (London, 1604), 55.

77 See W. G. Palmer, 'The Burden of Proof: J. H. Hexter and Christopher Hill', *Journal of British Studies*, 19 (1979), 122–9.

78 Delumeau, *Sin and Fear*, 556; Walker, *Decline of Hell, passim*.

79 There is a parallel here with work suggesting that the decline of traditional views of the supernatural and witchcraft in late seventeenth-century England was not so much a consequence of scientific rationalism as polemically driven, reflecting the desire of Anglican controversialists to discredit the partisan propaganda of sectaries. See I. Bostridge, *Witchcraft and Its Transformations, c.1650–c.1750* (Oxford, Oxford University Press, 1997); J. Crawford, *Marvellous Protestantism: Monstrous Births in Post-Reformation England* (Baltimore and London, Johns Hopkins University Press, 2005).

5 The company of heaven: identity and sociability in the English Protestant afterlife *c.*1560–1630

1 E. Duffy, *The Stripping of the Altars: Traditional Religion in England 1400–1580* (New Haven and London, Yale University Press, 1992), 475; N. Z. Davis, 'Ghosts, Kin, and Progeny: Some Features of Family Life in Early Modern France', *Daedalus*, 106 (1977), 87–114, quote at 95; D. Cressy, *Birth, Marriage, and Death: Ritual, Religion, and the Life-Cycle in Tudor and Stuart England* (Oxford, Oxford University Press, 1997), 398; K. Thomas, *Religion and the Decline of Magic* (new edn, London, Weidenfeld & Nicolson, 1997), 603.

2 On funerals, see Cressy, *Birth, Marriage and Death*, ch. 19; R. Houlbrooke, *Death, Religion and the Family in England 1480–1750* (Oxford, Clarendon Press, 1998), ch. 9; on tombs, N. Llewellyn, *Funeral Monuments in Post-Reformation England* (Cambridge, Cambridge University Press, 2000); P. Sherlock, *Monuments and Memory in Early Modern England* (Aldershot, Ashgate, 2008). The definitive guide to the development of the funeral sermon is now Houlbrooke, *Death, Religion, and the Family*, ch. 10.

3 For suggestions to this effect, see C. Gittings, *Death, Burial and the Individual in Early Modern England* (London, Croom Helm, 1984), 144–9; R. Rex, 'Monumental Brasses and the Reformation', *Transactions of the Monumental Brass Society*, 14 (1990), 376–94; N. Llewellyn, *The Art of Death: Visual Culture in the English Death Ritual c.1500–c.1800* (London, Reaktion Books, 1991), 28, 46–9; M. Neill, *Issues of Death: Mortality and Identity in English Renaissance Tragedy* (Oxford, Clarendon Press, 1997), 38–42, 48.

4 For a survey of recent debates about the ability of Protestant reform to

respond creatively to popular culture, see P. Marshall, *Reformation England 1480–1642* (2nd edn, London, Bloomsbury, 2012), ch. 6.

5   *Sermons, or Homilies, Appointed to be read in Churches* (London, Prayer-Book and Homily Society, 1833), 223. The view of Augustine (*De cura pro mortuis*, ch. 13) was also appealed to by Jean Veron, *A stronge battery against the Idolatrous invocation of the dead Saintes* (London, 1562), 27r; Peter Martyr, *The Common Places*, tr. A Marten (London, 1583), pt I, 75; Andrew Willet, *Synopsis Papismi, that is, a generall viewe of papistry* (London, 1592), 338; William Leygh, *The Soules Solace agaynst Sorrow* (London, 1612), 25–8; Samuel Gardiner, *The Devotions of the Dying Man* (London, 1627), 302.

6   Heinrich Bullinger, *The Decades: The Fourth Decade*, ed. T. Harding (Cambridge, Cambridge University Press, 1851), 211; Willet, *Synopsis Papismi*, 337; T. Bell, *The Survey of Popery* (London, 1596), 340.

7   Thomas Cartwright, *A Confutation of the Rhemists Translation, Glosses and Annotations on the New Testament* (London, 1618), 192.

8   Richard Smith, *A Conference of the Catholike and Protestante Doctrine with the Expresse Words of Holie Scripture* (Douai, 1631), 153. For other statements that saints in heaven have no knowledge of events on earth, see Jean Veron, *The Huntyng of Purgatorye to Death* (London, 1561), 207v, 240v; William Perkins, *A Reformed Catholike* (Cambridge, 1598), 247, 250–6; *A golden chaine: or the description of theologie* (Cambridge, 1600), 503, 656; Matthew Sutcliffe, *An Abridgement or Survey of Poperie* (London, 1606), 175; John Vicars, *A prospective glasse to looke into heaven* (London, 1618), C6r; John Denison, *Heavens Ioy, for a sinners repentance* (London, 1623), 11–12; Francis White, *A replie to Iesuit Fishers answere* (London, 1624), 319.

9   Andrew Willet, *Testrastylon Papisimi* (London, 1599), 158; Bell, *Survey of Popery*, 338–41; George Wither, *A View of the Marginal Notes of the Popish Testament* (London, 1588), 73-4.

10 William Fulke, *The Text of the New Testament of Iesus Christ, translated out of the vulgar Latine by the Papists of the Traiterous Seminarie at Rhemes* (London, 1589), 117.

11 Perkins, *Golden chaine*, 503.

12 Willet, *Synopsis Papismi*, 334–5; Richard Field, *Of the Church, Five Bookes* (London, 1606), 111; Samuel Crooke, *Death Subdued or, the Death of Death* (London, 1619), F7r; Robert Horne, *Certaine Sermons of the Rich Man and Lazarus* (London, 1619), 121: 'Christian charity abides in the Saints in glory, not by speciall rememberance of one more then another; for, such charitie in them extendeth it selfe indifferently and generally to all here, living, or yet unborne, whom they love as themselves.'

13 William Whitaker, *An answere to the Ten reasons of Edmund Campian the Iesuit*, tr. R. Stocke (London, 1606), 106.

14 Horne, *Certaine Sermons*, 121.

15 Leygh, *Soules Solace agaynst Sorrrow*, 28–9. Leygh proceeded to launch a polemical sally against the invocation of saints: 'They see you not; they heare you not; nor have they feeling of your miseries. Your *ora pro nobis* is out at

doores' (30). The death of the godly Katherine (sister of the iconoclast John Bruen) was a minor *cause célèbre*, with local ministers determined to counter papist claims that she had died despairing of her salvation: R. N. Watson, *The Rest Is Silence: Death as Annihilation in the English Renaissance* (Berkeley and Los Angeles, University of California Press, 1994), 306–15.

16 Gardiner, *Devotions of the Dying Man*, 156.

17 James Cole, *Of Death a true description* (London, 1629), 54.

18 Nicholas Byfield, *The Cure of the Feare of Death* (London, 1618), 109–10; Timothy Oldmayne, *Lifes brevitie and deaths debility* (London, 1636), 71. There is an echo of these assertions in the (highly unusual) 1619 epitaph of Elizabeth Leigh at Arreton, Isle of Wight: 'What friends, what children, what blest Marriage, / Dead I forgette . . .' T. F. Ravenshaw, *Antiente Epitaphs (from A.D. 1250 to A.D. 1800)* (London, Joseph Masters & Co., 1878), 64.

19 G. C. Gorham (ed.), *Gleanings of a Few Scattered Ears, during the Period of the Reformation in England* (London, Bell and Daldy, 1857), 238–41.

20 John Wall, *A Sermon preached at Shelford in Nottinghamshire* (London, 1623), A5r. See also J. C., *A Handkercher for parents wet eyes, upon the death of children* (London, 1630), 64, advising a bereaved father to rejoice at his son's felicity: 'He sits aloft, and smiles at this *Emmet*-hill of Earth.'

21 George Hakewill, 'The funerall sermon on behalfe of the author', in John Downe, *Certaine Treatises* (Oxford, 1633), 49.

22 William Ford, *A Sermon preached at Constantinople, in the Vines of Perah, at the funerall of the vertuous and admired Lady Anne Glover* (London, 1616), 61.

23 Watson, *The Rest Is Silence*, 6.

24 E. Disley, 'Degrees of Glory: Protestant Doctrine and the Concept of Rewards Hereafter', *Journal of Theological Studies*, 42 (1991), 77–105.

25 Cf. C. W. Bynum, 'Material Continuity, Personal Survival and the Resurrection of the Body: A Scholastic Discussion in its Medieval and Modern Contexts', in her *Fragmentation and Redemption: Essays on Gender and the Human Body in Medieval Religion* (New York, Zone Books, 1991), 239–97.

26 William Drummond, *A midnights trance: wherin is discoursed of death, the nature of the soules, and estate of immortalitie* (London, 1619), 91. See also William Walker, *A sermon preached at the funerals of . . . William Lord Russell* (London, 1614), 29; Gardiner, *Devotions of the Dying Man*, 361.

27 John Donne, *Sermons*, ed. G. R. Potter and E. M. Simpson (10 vols, Berkeley and Los Angeles, University of California Press, 1953–62), VII, 139.

28 John Preston, *A Sermon Preached at the Funeral of Mr Arthur Upton Esquire in Devon* (London, 1619), 32. See also Perkins, *Golden chaine*, 142; Thomas Tuke, *The high-way to heaven* (London, 1609), 189; Walker, *Sermon at the funerals of . . . William Lord Russell*, 29; Ford, *Sermon preached at Constantinople*, 56; John Andrewes, *A celestiall looking-glasse: to behold the beauty of heaven* (London, 1621), 24.

29 John Denison, *A three-fold resolution, verie necessarie to saluation. Describing earths vanitie. Hels horror. Heauens felicitie* (London, 1608), 473; Robert

Pricke, *A Verie Godlie and Learned Sermon treating of Mans Mortalitie* (London, 1608), E4v; George Strode, *The Anatomie of Mortalitie* (London, 1632), 333.

30 Lewis Bayly, *The practise of pietie directing a Christian how to walke that he may please God* (London, 1619), 154–5; Gardiner, *Devotions of the Dying Man*, 383.

31 John Bowle, *A Sermon Preached at Flitton in the Countie of Bedford, at the Funerall of the Right Honourable Henrie Earle of Kent* (London, 1615), B3v. See also Bartholomew Robertson, *The crowne of life, containing the combate between the Flesh and the Spirit* (London, 1618), 359; Cort Aslakssøn, *The description of heaven*, tr. R. Jennings (London, 1623), 73.

32 Matt. 22.30; Robertson, *Combate between the Flesh and the Spirit*, 375; C. McDannell and B. Lang, *Heaven: A History* (New Haven and London, Yale University Press, 1990), 24–32; Hannibal Gamon, *The praise of a godly woman. A sermon preached at the solemne funerall of . . . Ladie Frances Roberts* (London, 1627), 3. The question of the gender of souls does not seem to have been much discussed, perhaps because it was widely accepted that the resurrected body would retain its sexual characteristics (if not habits).

33 R. Targoff, 'Burying Romeo and Juliet: Love after Death in the English Renaissance', in B. Jussen and R. Targoff (eds), *Love after Death: Concepts of Posthumous Love in Medieval and Early Modern Europe* (Berlin, De Gruyter, 2015), 149–51; McDannell and Lang, *Heaven*, 178.

34 Gen. 2.23; Matt. 17.4; John 20.20; Matt. 8.11; Luke 13.28; 16.23. See *The Sermons of Mr Henry Smith* (2 vols, London, W. Tegg, 1866), II, 420; Perkins, *Golden chaine*, 518; Gardiner, *Devotions of the Dying Man*, 363; Donne, *Sermons*, VII, 139; R. Bolton, *Foure last things* (London, 1632), 146–8; Bayly, *Practise of pietie*, 157 (quote).

35 Alexander Hume, *A treatise of the felicitie of the life to come* (London, 1594), 32–4; Robert Harris, *Samuels funerall. Or A sermon preached at the funerall of Sir Anthonie Cope* (London, 1618), 12; Crooke, *Death Subdued*, H4v; Donne, *Sermons*, VII, 139.

36 Edward Vaughan, *A Divine Discoverie of Death* (London, 1612), 47.

37 Cole, *Of death a true description*, 145. See also Crooke, *Death Subdued*, F6v; Charles Fitz-Geffry, *Elisha his lamentation . . . a sermon, preached at the funeralls of the Right Worshipfull Sir Anthony Rous* (London, 1622), 30; Downe, *Certaine Treatises*, 53.

38 Fulke, *Text of the New Testament*, 119.

39 Perkins, *Golden chaine*, 518.

40 Gardiner, *Devotions of the Dying Man*, 364–5; *Doomes-Day booke: or, An alarum for atheists* (London, 1606), 108–9.

41 Bolton, *Foure last things*, 144–50.

42 The attitude is epitomized in George Gifford, *A briefe discourse of certaine points of the religion, which is among the common sort of christians which may be termed the countrey divinitie* (London, 1581).

43 Edward Bagshawe, 'The Life and Death of Mr Bolton', prefixed to *The foure last things*, C6r.

44 Christopher Sutton, *Disce Mori: Learne to Die* (London, 1600), 275–6; Gabriel Powell, *The resolved Christian* (London, 1603), 59; Robert Welcome, *The State of the Godly both in this life and in the life to come* (London, 1606), 68; Daniel Price, *Spirituall odours to the memory of Prince Henry* (London, 1613), 49; Bowle, *A Sermon Preached at Flitton*, F4v; Stephen Denison, *The monument or tombe-stone: or, A sermon preached . . . at the funerall of Mrs. Elizabeth Iuxon* (London, 1620), A5r; Samson Price, *The two twins of birth and death. A sermon preached in Christs Church in London . . . Upon the occasion of the funeralls of Sir William Byrde* (London, 1624), 34.

45 Houlbrooke, *Death, Religion, and the Family*, 317–20.

46 Richard Stock, *The churches lamentation for the losse of the godly* (London, 1614), 102. The theme also figured prominently with a number of German preachers: S. Karant-Nunn, *The Reformation of Ritual: An Interpretation of Early Modern Germany* (London, Routledge, 1997), 186; B. Gordon, 'Malevolent Ghosts and Ministering Angels: Apparitions and Pastoral Care in the Swiss Reformation', in B. Gordon and P. Marshall (eds), *The Place of the Dead: Death and Remembrance in Late Medieval and Early Modern Europe* (Cambridge, Cambridge University Press, 2000).

47 John Rogers, *A discourse of Christian watchfulnesse* (London, 1620), 238.

48 Andrewes, *A celestiall looking-glasse*, 27.

49 Donne, *Sermons*, VIII, 62. Other writers whose discussion of post-mortem reunion focused on the resurrection include Perkins, *Golden chaine*, 518; Robert Hill, *The path-way to prayer and pietie* (London, 1609), 260; Thomas Playfere, *The pathway to perfection* (London, 1611), 222; Richard Parr, *The end of the perfect man. A sermon preached at the buriall of . . . Sir Robert Spencer* (London, 1628), A4r; J. C., *Handkercher for parents wet eyes*, 65; John Gaule, *A Defiance of Death being the Funebrious Commemoration of . . . Baptist Lord Hickes* (London, 1630), 46; Bolton, *Foure last things*, 144–5.

50 Bolton, *Foure last things*, 94. See also Arthur Dent, *The Plaine Mans Pathway to Heaven* (London, 1605), 367.

51 Thomas Sparke, *A sermon preached at Cheanies at the buriall of the . . . Earle of Bedford* (London, 1585), 85–6.

52 Crooke, *Death Subdued*, H4v–5r.

53 E. S. Hebblethwaite, 'The Theology of Rewards in English Printed Treatises and Sermons (*c.*1550–*c.*1650)', University of Cambridge PhD thesis (1992), 175.

54 Denison, *A three-fold resolution*, 439 ff.

55 John Calvin, *Institutes of the Christian Religion*, tr. H. Beveridge (2 vols in 1, Grand Rapids, Eerdmans, 1989), II, 267.

56 Perkins, *Golden chaine*, 142.

57 Elnathan Parr, *The grounds of divinitie* (London, 1614), 237. See also Henry Greenwood, *A treatise of the great and generall daye of iudgement* (London,

1606), 66–7; Thomas Draxe, *An alarum to the last iudgement* (London, 1615), 1–8.

58 Drummond, *A midnights trance*, 68–9; Playfere, *The pathway to perfection*, 230; John Donne, *Devotions upon Emergent Occasions*, ed A. Raspa (Montreal and London, McGill-Queen's University Press, 1975), 96.

59 Robertson, *The crowne of life*, 358–60.

60 A selection only: Deut. 31.16; 1 Kings 2.10; 11.43; 15.8; Ps. 4.8; Isa. 28.20; Dan. 12.2; John 11.11; Acts 7.60; 1 Cor. 15.6; 1 Thess. 4.13 (a key text); Rev. 14.13 (an important proof-text against purgatory).

61 Henry Bull, *Christian Prayers and Holy Meditations* (Cambridge, Cambridge University Press, 1842), 76; John Norden, *A Progress of Piety* (Cambridge, Cambridge University Press, 1848), 157; Francis Rodes, *Life after Death* (London, 1622), 21; John Moore, *A mappe of mans mortalitie* (London, 1617), 233.

62 Oldmayne, *Lifes brevitie*, 71.

63 John Jewel, *Works*, ed. J. Ayre (4 vols, Cambridge, Cambridge University Press, 1845–50), II, 866; Hume, *Felicitie of the life to come*, 21; Perkins, *Golden chaine*, 141; Sutton, *Disce Mori*, 120; Denison, *A three-fold resolution*, 479; Richard Kilbye, *A sermon preached in Saint Maries Church in Oxford . . . at the funerall of Thomas Holland* (London, 1613), 11; Gaule, *Defiance of Death*, 30.

64 Gardiner, *Devotions of the Dying Man*, 160.

65 Strode, *Anatomie of Mortalitie*, 203–5.

66 S. Hadley, *Sleep in Early Modern England* (New Haven and London, Yale University Press, 2016). In addition to the references already cited, see Thomas Sparke, *A sermon preached at Whaddon in Buckinghamshire . . . at the buriall of the Right Honorable, Arthur Lorde Grey of Wilton* (Oxford, 1593), 81–2; Pricke, *Godlie and Learned Sermon*, D3r; Thomas Tuke, *A discourse of death, bodily, ghostly, and eternal* (London, 1613), 63; William Cowper, *A defiance to death* (London, 1610), 91–2; Richard Brathwaite, *Remains after Death* (London, 1618), E7r; Byfield, *Cure of the Feare of Death*, 34; Bayly, *Practise of pietie*, 113; Denison, *The monument or tombe-stone*, 12, 74; Charles Fitz-Geffry, *Deaths sermon unto the living* (London, 1620), 11; William Stone, *A curse become a blessing* (London, 1622), 57; Bolton, *Foure last things*, 6. Further encouragement to compare death to a sleep was provided by the funeral service, which prescribed the reading of 1 Cor. 15: J. E. Booty (ed.), *The Book of Common Prayer 1559* (Charlottesville, University Press of Virginia, 1976), 310–12.

67 J. Ketley (ed.), *The Two Liturgies . . . in the Reign of King Edward VI* (Cambridge, Cambridge University Press, 1844), 537. The fullest study of soul-sleeping beliefs is N. T. Burns, *Christian Mortalism from Tyndale to Milton* (Cambridge, MA, Harvard University Press, 1972).

68 Bullinger, *Fourth Decade*, 389–90; Veron, *Huntyng of Purgatorye*, 31r; Thomas Becon, *The Catechism*, ed. J. Ayre (Cambridge, Cambridge University Press, 1844), 182; Anthony Anderson, *The Shield of our Safetie Set Foorth* (London,

1581), G3r-v; Sparke, *A sermon preached at Cheanies*, 90–1; *A sermon preached at Whaddon*, 83; Perkins, *Golden chaine*, 515; Welcome, *The State of the Godly*, 53; Walker, *Sermon at the funerals of . . . William Lord Russell*, 35; Robertson, *The crowne of life*, 370-1; Crooke, *Death Subdued*, F6v; Nicholas Guy, *Pieties pillar: or, A sermon preached at the funerall of mistresse Elizabeth Gouge* (London, 1626), 34; Cole, *Of Death a true description*, 34.

69 Veron, *Huntyng of Purgatorye*, 31r; John Whitgift, *Works*, ed. J. Ayre (3 vols, Cambridge, Cambridge University Press, 1851-3), I, 535; James Cleland, *A Monument of Mortalitie* (London, 1624), 36-7; Strode, *Anatomie of Mortalitie*, 94. See also Cressy, *Birth, Marriage, and Death*, 385-6.

70 Bullinger, *Fourth Decade*, 390.

71 Richard Carpenter, *The Soules Sentinel . . . A Sermon preached at the funerall Solemnities of the Right Worshipfull Sir Arthur Ackland* (London, 1612), 110. See also Horne, *Certaine Sermons*, 74; Richard Chambers, *Sarah's Sepulture, or a Funerall Sermon, preached for the Right Honourable and vertuous Lady, Dorothie Countess of Northumberland* (London, 1620), 25; Strode, *Anatomie of Mortalitie*, 94, 203-4.

72 Allusions to the resurrection in mid-sixteenth-century wills seem to be an indicator of Protestant sympathy: C. Litzenberger, *The English Reformation and the Laity: Gloucestershire, 1540–1580* (Cambridge, Cambridge University Press, 1997), 42, 75, 79, 120, 153.

73 James Pilkington, *Works*, ed. J. Scholefield (Cambridge, Cambridge University Press, 1842), 320; Thomas Draxe, *The earnest of our inheritance* (London, 1613), 60; Ford, *Sermon preached at Constantinople*, 71; Rodes, *Life after Death*, 214; Gervase Babington, *Workes* (London, 1622), 124; Richard Hooker, *Of the Laws of Ecclesiastical Polity*, ed. C. Morris (2 vols, London, J. M. Dent, 1907), II, 401, 404; Martin Day, *Doomes-Day: or, A Treatise of the Resurrection of the Body* (London, 1636), 16.

74 C. A. Patrides, *Milton and the Christian Tradition* (Oxford, Clarendon Press, 1966), 283-4; Houlbrooke, *Death, Religion, and the Family*, 42-3.

75 Moore, *Mappe of mans mortalitie*, 246. See also Draxe, *Earnest of our inheritance*, A2r; Drummond, *A midnights trance*, 94; Cole, *Of Death a true description*, 38.

76 John Barlowe, *Hierons last fare-well. A sermon preached at Modbury in Devon* (London, 1618), 25; Gardiner, *Doomes-Day booke*, 47, 54. Cf. Bynum, 'Material Continuity', 243-4, 260, 282, 288.

77 Day, *Doomes-Day*, 192.

78 I dissent here from the conclusion of Houlbrooke, *Death, Religion, and the Family*, 41, that most reformers were reluctant to dwell on the fact that the happiness of the saved would not be complete till after the resurrection, 'probably fearing that to do so might encourage a reopening of the question of the existence of purgatory'.

79 On this theme, see B. W. Ball, *A Great Expectation: Eschatological Thought in English Protestantism to 1660* (Leiden, Brill, 1975); R. Bauckham, *Tudor Apocalypse* (Appleford, Sutton Courtenay Press, 1978); P. Christianson,

Reformers and Babylon: English Apocalyptic Visions from the Reformation to the Eve of the Civil War (Toronto, University of Toronto Press, 1978); K. R. Firth, *The Apocalyptic Tradition in Reformation Britain 1530–1645* (Oxford, Oxford University Press, 1979).

80   C. Eire, *From Madrid to Purgatory: The Art and Craft of Dying in Sixteenth-Century Spain* (Cambridge, Cambridge University Press, 1995), 80–1.

81   Houlbrooke, *Death, Religion, and the Family*, 124.

82   Ravenshawe, *Antiente Epitaphs*, 36, 38, 44, 57, 59, 75; E. W. Badger, *The Monumental Brasses of Warwickshire* (Birmingham, Cornish Bros, 1895), 4, 38; H. W. Macklin, *The Brasses of England* (3rd edn, London, Methuen, 1913), 274; H. R. Mosse, *The Monumental Effigies of Sussex (London, 1250 to 1650)* (2nd edn, Hove, Combridges, 1933), 24, 29; F. A. Greenhill, *Incised Effigial Slabs: A Study of Engraved Stone Memorials in Latin Christendom c.1100 to c.1700* (2 vols, London, Faber, 1976), I, 333, 337; D. MacCulloch (ed.), *The Chorography of Suffolk*, Suffolk Records Society, 19 (Ipswich, Boydell Press, 1976), 90, 92; A. White, 'Church Monuments in Britain *c.*1560–*c.*1660', University of London PhD thesis (1991), 405, 406, 408.

83   White, 'Church Monuments', 416–21.

84   Greenhill, *Incised Effigial Slabs*, I, 337, 344; Badger, *Monumental Brasses of Warwickshire*, 36, 44; John Stow, *A Survey of London*, ed. C. L. Kingsford (2 vols, Oxford, Oxford University Press, 1908), II, 357; Ravenshaw, *Antiente Epitaphs*, 38, 41, 45, 55, 58, 59, 69, 70, 78; M. Norris, *Monumental Brasses: The Memorials* (2 vols, London, Phillips & Page, 1977), I, 239; Houlbrooke, *Death, Religion, and the Family*, 352.

85   Ravenshaw, *Antiente Epitaphs*, 29.

86   Badger, *Monumental Brasses of Warwickshire*, 22.

87   Ravenshaw, *Antiente Epitaphs*, 64.

88   Ravenshaw, *Antiente Epitaphs*, 46; Macklin, *Brasses of England*, 280.

89   Badger, *Monumental Brasses of Warwickshire*, 44.

90   G. Isherwood, *Monumental Brasses in the Bedfordshire Churches* (London, Elliott Stock, 1906), 32.

91   Macklin, *Brasses of England*, 274; Greenhill, *Incised Effigial Slabs*, I, 341.

92   Ravenshaw, *Antiente Epitaphs*, 63.

93   Greenhill, *Incised Effigial Slabs*, I, 333, 338.

94   Ravenshaw, *Antiente Epitaphs*, 60, 34.

95   Ravenshaw, *Antiente Epitaphs*, 27; Greenhill, *Incised Effigial Slabs*, I, 340.

96   Isherwood, *Monumental Brasses*, 18; Norris, *Monumental Brasses: The Memorials*, I, 240.

97   Badger, *Monumental Brasses of Warwickshire*, 59.

98   Ravenshaw, *Antiente Epitaphs*, 74.

99   Ravenshaw, *Antiente Epitaphs*, 27, 42, 47, 52, 53, 55, 59, 60, 69; Stowe, *Survey*, I, 212, 283; Mosse, *Monumental Effigies of Sussex*, 169; Greenhill, *Incised Effigial Slabs*, I, 343; MacCulloch (ed.), *Chorography of Suffolk*, 100.

100 Ravenshaw, *Antiente Epitaphs*, 28, 34, 55, 69.

101 Mosse, *Monumental Effigies of Sussex*, 25; Ravenshaw, *Antiente Epitaphs*, 77. See also Greenhill, *Incised Effigial Slabs*, I, 340–1, 342.

6 Angels around the deathbed: variations on a theme in the English art of dying

1 D. Cressy, *Birth, Marriage, and Death: Ritual, Religion, and the Life-Cycle in Tudor and Stuart England* (Oxford, Oxford University Press, 1997); E. Duffy, *The Stripping of the Altars: Traditional Religion in England 1400–1580* (New Haven and London, Yale University Press, 1992), esp. 299–378, 474–5; R. Houlbrooke, *Death, Religion, and the Family in England 1480–1750* (Oxford, Clarendon Press, 1998). Other works addressing the impact of the English Reformation on patterns of dying include R. Wunderli and G. Broce, 'The Final Moment before Death in Early Modern England', *Sixteenth Century Journal*, 20 (1989); L. M. Beier, 'The Good Death in Seventeenth-Century England', in R. Houlbrooke (ed.), *Death, Ritual, and Bereavement* (London, Routledge, 1989); C. Marsh, '"Departing Well and Christianly": Will-Making and Popular Religion in Early Modern England', in E. J. Carlson (ed.), *Religion and the English People 1500–1640* (Kirksville, MO, Thomas Jefferson University Press, 1998); D. Tankard, 'The Reformation of the Deathbed in Mid-Sixteenth-Century England', *Mortality*, 8 (2003); H. Cleugh, '"At the Hour of Our Death": Praying for the Dying in Post-Reformation England', in E. Tingle and J. Willis (eds), *Dying, Death, Burial and Commemoration in Reformation Europe* (Farnham, Ashgate, 2015).

2 Despite its teleological tone, and concern with 'literary' merits, the most useful guide to the scope of this literature remains N. L. Beaty, *The Craft of Dying: A Study in the Literary Tradition of the Ars Moriendi in England* (New Haven and London, Yale University Press, 1970). See also D. W. Atkinson, 'The English Ars Moriendi: Its Protestant Transformation', *Renaissance and Reformation*, n.s. 6, o.s. 18 (1982).

3 D. Keck, *Angels and Angelology in the Middle Ages* (New York and Oxford, Oxford University Press, 1998), 203. The topos was often incorporated into tomb design, a theme there is no opportunity to pursue further here: R. M. Frye, *The Renaissance Hamlet: Issues and Responses in 1600* (Princeton, Princeton University Press, 1984), 272–3; C. Daniell, *Death and Burial in Medieval England* (London, Routledge, 1997), 40.

4 W. Maskell (ed.), *Monumenta Ritualia Ecclesiae Anglicanae* (3 vols, 2nd edn, Oxford, Oxford University Press, 1882), I, 87, 123, 128, 130, 131–2, 137, 144, 147. See P. Sheingorn, '"And flights of angels sing thee to thy rest": The Soul's Conveyance to the Afterlife in the Middle Ages', in C. G. Fisher and K. L. Scott (eds), *Art into Life: Collected Papers from the Krege Art Museum Medieval Symposia* (East Lansing, MI, Michigan State University Press, 1995), 155–82.

5 On the genesis of the *ars moriendi* and its relation to the Office of the sick, see M. C. O'Connor, *The Art of Dying Well: The Development of the Ars Moriendi*

(New York, Columbia University Press, 1942); Beaty, *Craft of Dying*, ch. 1; E. Mâle, *Religious Art in France: The Late Middle Ages* (5th edn, Princeton, Princeton University Press, 1986), 348–55; P. Binski, *Medieval Death: Ritual and Representation* (London, British Museum Press, 1996), 33–46; Duffy, *Stripping of the Altars*, 314–17.

6   *The book intituled The art of good lywyng [and] good deyng* (Paris, 1503), tr. Thomas Lewington, P2v.

7   Richard Whytforde, *A dayly exercyse and experyence of deth* (London, 1537), D1v.

8   *Art of good lywyng*, O3v, Q2v–3r; *The crafte to lyue well and to dye well*, tr. Andrew Chertsey (London, 1505), Bb1r.

9   *Here begynneth a lityll treatise shorte and abredged spekynge of the arte & crafte to knowe well to dye* (London, 1490), A7v.

10 Keck, *Angels and Angelology*, 205; Duffy, *Stripping of the Altars*, 270, 325; Mâle, *Religious Art in France*, 355.

11 *Here begynneth a lityll treatise*, B3v–4r.

12 *Art of good lywyng*, R1v.

13 Duffy, *Stripping of the Altars*, 269–70; Maskell, *Monumenta Ritualia*, III, 289–92.

14 P. Marshall and A. Walsham, 'Migrations of Angels in the Early Modern World', in Marshall and Walsham (eds), *Angels in the Early Modern World* (Cambridge, Cambridge University Press, 2006), 12–13.

15 *The Deynge creature* (London, 1514), A2r–3v. Cf. here the popular iconographic motif depicting the Virgin decisively tilting the scales of justice in which Michael weighs the souls of the dead by placing her rosary in the pan: Duffy, *Stripping of the Altars*, 318.

16 Jacobus de Voragine, *The Golden Legend*, tr. W. Ryan (2 vols, Princeton, Princeton University Press, 1993), I, 12.

17 For scholastic discussion of this point, see H. Mayr-Harting, *Perceptions of Angels in History: An Inaugural Lecture Delivered in the University of Oxford on 14 November 1997* (Oxford, Oxford University Press, 1998), 19–20; Keck, *Angels and Angelology*, 161.

18 This is asserted by A. Tenenti, *La Vie et la Mort à travers l'art du Xve siècle* (Paris, A. Colin, 1952), 55, and implied by Beaty, *Craft of Dying*, 28–30; correctives supplied by Duffy, *Stripping of the Altars*, 317–18; P. Ariès, *The Hour of Our Death*, tr. H. Weaver (London, Allen Lane, 1981), 108–9.

19 See Houlbrooke, *Death, Religion, and the Family*, chs 6–7.

20 J. Ketley (ed.), *The Two Liturgies . . . in the Reign of King Edward VI* (Cambridge, Cambridge University Press, 1844), 532. For the Protestant campaign against purgatory, see P. Marshall, *Beliefs and the Dead in Reformation England* (Oxford, Oxford University Press, 2002), chs 2–4.

21 For example, Hugh Latimer, *Sermons and Remains*, ed. G. E. Corrie (Cambridge, Cambridge University Press, 1845), 87; Alexander Nowell, *A Catechism written in Latin . . . together with the same catechism translated into English by Thomas Norton*, ed. G. E. Corrie (Cambridge, Cambridge

University Press, 1853), 184–5; Heinrich Bullinger, *The Decades: The Fourth Decade*, ed. T. Harding (Cambridge, Cambridge University Press, 1851), 344.

22 Marshall and Walsham, 'Migrations of Angels', 15–16. But see below, Ch. 7.

23 Thomas Lupset, *A compendious and a very fruteful treatyse, teachynge the waye of dyenge well* (London, 1534); Desiderius Erasmus, *Preparation to deathe. A book as deuout as eloquent* (London, 1538).

24 A. Walsham, 'Angels and Idols in England's Long Reformation', in Marshall and Walsham (eds), *Angels in the Early Modern World*, 134–67; A. Walsham, 'Invisible Helpers: Angelic Intervention in Early Modern England', *Past and Present*, 208 (2010), 77–130; L. Sangha, *Angels and Belief in England, 1480–1700* (London, Pickering & Chatto, 2012). See also D. Oldridge, *The Supernatural in Tudor and Stuart England* (Abingdon, Routledge, 2016), ch. 5.

25 Duffy, *Stripping of the Altars*, chs 6–8.

26 *This prymer of Salisbury use* (Paris, 1535), 119v; Maskell, *Monumenta Ritualia*, III, 233; *The primer in English* (London, 1539), K1v; *The primer, set foorth by the Kynges Maiestie* (London, 1545), G7r; *The primer in Englishe [and] Latin* (London, 1548), E5v; [*Primer in English*] (London, 1549), H7r–v. Named archangels and all angels reappear (unsurprisingly) in the Marian *Primer in English for children after the use of Sarum* (London, 1556), K2v–3r.

27 Ketley (ed.), *Two Liturgies*, 74, 87, 263, 278, 453; J. E. Booty (ed.), *The Book of Common Prayer 1559* (Charlottesville, University Press of Virginia, 1976), 262, 301.

28 Ketley, *Two Liturgies*, 136, 312.

29 *The primer set furth by the Kinges maiestie* (London, 1547), Ff4v–Gg2r; W. K. Clay (ed.), *Liturgies and Occasional Forms of Prayer set forth in the Reign of Queen Elizabeth* (Cambridge, Cambridge University Press, 1847), 256–7.

30 Ketley, *Two Liturgies*, 474–5. There is no mention of angels in the 'prayer for them that lie in the extreme pangs of death', 481–2. Thomas Becon, *The Pomander of Prayer*, in *Prayers and Other Pieces*, ed. J. Ayre (Cambridge, Cambridge University Press, 1844), 84; *A primer of boke of private prayer* (sic) (London, 1560), X2r–v, and *A primer or booke of private prayer* (London, 1568), X2r–v, U7r.

31 E. Duffy, 'Continuity and Divergence in Tudor Religion', in R. N. Swanson (ed.), *Unity and Diversity in the Church*, Studies in Church History, 32 (Oxford, Blackwell, 1996), 171–205.

32 John More, *A lively anatomie of death* (London, 1596), D8r noted only that the soul after death goes to 'the celestiall Ierusalem, to the companie of innumerable Angels . . .' Cf. William Cowper, *A defiance to death* (London, 1610), 89: we should be comforted that our brother or sister is going to 'the company of innumerable angels'.

33 John Moore, *A mappe of mans mortalitie* (London, 1617), 74.

34 William Perkins, *A Salve for a Sicke Man* (Cambridge, 1595), 20.

35 James Cole, *Of Death a true description* (London, 1629), 141.

36 Bullinger, *Fourth Decade*, 335. Calvin cited the passage as evidence against the existence of guardian angels: 'It is also said that the angels (meaning more than one) carried the soul of Lazarus into Abraham's bosom.' *Institutes of the Christian Religion*, tr. H. Beveridge (2 vols in 1, Grand Rapids, Eerdmans, 1989), I, 141.

37 Thomas Adams, *The Happiness of the Church* (London, 1619), 44.

38 Cole, *Of Death a true description*, 162.

39 Frye, *The Renaissance Hamlet*, 271; M. Claire Cross (ed.), 'The Third Earl of Huntingdon's Death-Bed: A Calvinist Example of the *Ars Moriendi*', *Northern History*, 21 (1985), 102.

40 Robert Hill, *An instruction to die well*, in *The path-way to prayer and pietie* (London, 1617), 176–7; Sheingorn, 'Flights of Angels', 175; George Strode, *The Anatomie of Mortalitie* (London, 1618), 137; Christopher Sutton, *Disce Mori: Learne to Die* (London, 1600), 263. See also the instance of a minister seeking to persuade convicted felons in Exeter gaol that 'it was as easie going to heaven from the stake and gallows, as from their beds; and when their souls were departing out of their bodies, God's holy angels would convey them into Paradise': John Quick, *Hell Open'd, or The Infernal Sin of Murther Punished* (London, 1676), 49.

41 For the concept of Elizabethan and Jacobean 'iconophobia', see P. Collinson, 'From Iconoclasm to Iconophobia: The Cultural Impact of the Second English Reformation', in P. Marshall (ed.), *The Impact of the English Reformation 1500–1640* (London, Arnold Press, 1997). The idea is substantially modified by T. Watt, *Cheap Print and Popular Piety 1550–1640* (Cambridge, Cambridge University Press, 1991), chs 4–6.

42 Richard Day, *A book of Christian prayers* (London, 1578), 79.

43 Cole, *Of Death a true description*, 126–9. Bullinger, *Fourth Decade*, 340–4, expounded the ministry of angels in the care of mankind without any specific reference to a deathbed role.

44 Otto Werdmüller, *A moste frutefull, pithye and learned treatise, how a christen man oughte to behave himself in the daunger of death*, tr. Miles Coverdale (Wesel?, 1555), 18, 86–7.

45 Pedro de Soto, *The maner to dye well* (London, 1578), 4v, 23. The remarkable conservatism of attitudes towards death in post-Reformation ballads is noted by Watt, *Cheap Print*, 104–15. One of the most enduringly popular ballads, *The Clarke of Bodnam*, included references to angels having the soul in keeping while the body lay in the grave.

46 Richard Montagu, *Immediate addresse vnto God alone* (London, 1624), 97.

47 Jeremy Taylor, *Holy Dying*, ed. P. G. Stanwood (Oxford, Oxford University Press, 1989), 51, 65, 67, 133, 148, 174, 214, 219, 220, 221.

48 P. Lake, *Moderate Puritans and the Elizabethan Church* (Cambridge, Cambridge University Press, 1982), 172; C. Haigh, 'The Taming of Reformation: Preachers, Pastors and Parishioners in Elizabethan and Early Stuart England', *History*, 85 (2000), 577; A. Milton, *Catholic and Reformed:*

The Roman and Protestant Churches in English Protestant Thought 1600–1640 (Cambridge, Cambridge University Press, 1995), 207.

49 D. Stannard, *The Puritan Way of Death: A Study in Religion, Culture, and Social Change* (Oxford, Oxford University Press, 1977); R. Houlbrooke, 'The Puritan Death-Bed, *c.*1560–*c.*1660', in C. Durston and J. Eales (eds), *The Culture of English Puritanism 1560–1700* (Basingstoke, Macmillan, 1996).

50 Strode, *Anatomie of Mortalitie*, 251.

51 Perkins, *Salve for a Sicke Man*, 16, 109–11. For Scot's unusual scepticism, see S. Anglo, 'Reginald Scot's *Discoverie of Witchcraft*: Scepticism and Sadduceeism', in S. Anglo (ed.), *The Damned Art: Essays in the Literature of Witchcraft* (London, Routledge & Kegan Paul, 1977), 106–39. Perkins explicitly refuted Scot's views (in the context of the spirit summoned by the Witch of Endor) in *A Discourse of the Damned Art of Witchcraft* (Cambridge, 1608), 118.

52 These statistics derive from the calculations of Ian Green, *Print and Protestantism in Early Modern England* (Oxford, Oxford University Press, 2000), Appendix I, s.v. 'Becon', 'Stubbes'. Perkins' *Salve for a Sicke Man* reached an impressive 11 editions, and Sutton's *Disce Mori*, 10.

53 Thomas Becon, *The Sick Man's Salve*, in Becon, *Prayers and Other Pieces*, 126.

54 Philip Stubbes, *A Christal Glasse for Christian Women*, in Stubbes, *The Anatomie of Abuses: Part I*, ed. F. J. Furnivall (London, N. Trubner, 1877), 201–2, 205, 206–7. For divergent perspectives on the extent to which Stubbes should be considered a 'Puritan' writer, see A. Walsham, '"A Glose of Godliness": Philip Stubbes, Elizabethan Grub Street and the Invention of Puritanism', in S. Wabuda and C. Litzenberger (eds), *Belief and Practice in Reformation England* (Aldershot, Ashgate, 1998); Peter Lake with Michael Questier, *The Antichrist's Lewd Hat: Protestants, Papists and Players in Post-Reformation England* (New Haven and London, Yale University Press, 2002), 563–76. Within his godly moralizing, Stubbes displayed a marked affinity for reworking medieval themes. See, for example, his *Two Wunderfull and Rare Examples of the Undeferred Judgement of God* (London, 1581).

55 Marshall, *Beliefs and the Dead*, 250–1, noting some dissident contemporary views. Recent work on the cultural history of Protestantism has done much to unsettle the perception that the Reformation unambiguously rejected the miraculous, or created a 'disenchanted world'. For a broad overview, see U. Rublack, *Reformation Europe* (Cambridge, Cambridge University Press, 2005), ch. 4.

56 John Hart, *The Firebrand Taken Out of the Fire* (London, 1654), 140. Cf. George H. Williams, 'Called by Thy Name, Leave Us Not: The Case of Mrs. Joan Drake', *Harvard Library Bulletin*, 16 (1968), 111–28, 278–300; John Quick, *The Triumph of Faith* (London, 1698), 31.

57 The apparent affinity between some strands of nonconformity and a heightened interest in the supernatural world is further explored in Ch. 9 below. For the considerable potential for overlap between 'Puritan' and 'popular' religious mentalities in the preceding generation, see T. S. Freeman,

'Demons, Deviance and Defiance: John Darrell and the Politics of Exorcism in Late Elizabethan England', in P. Lake and M. Questier, (eds), *Conformity and Orthodoxy in the English Church, c.1560–1660* (Woodbridge, Boydell Press, 2000); P. Lake, 'Deeds against Nature: Cheap Print, Protestantism and Murder in Early Seventeenth-Century England', in K. Sharpe and P. Lake (eds), *Culture and Politics in Early Stuart England* (Basingstoke, Macmillan, 1994); A. Walsham, '"The Fatall Vesper": Providentialism and Anti-Popery in Late Jacobean London', *Past and Present*, 144 (1994).

58 B. R. Dailey, 'The Visitation of Sarah Wight: Holy Carnival and the Revolution of the Saints in Civil War London', *Church History*, 55 (1986), 447.

59 John Bunyan, *Grace Abounding to the Chief of Sinners* (Grand Rapids, Baker, 1978), 63; *A Few Sighs from Hell: Or, The Groans of a Damned Soul* (London, 1658), 27–9.

60 Isaac Ambrose, *Ministration of, and Communion with Angels* (London, 1673), 146–9; Increase Mather, *Angelographia, Or A Discourse Concerning the Nature and Power of the Holy Angels* (Boston, 1696), 92–3.

61 Sheingorn, 'Flights of Angels', 177; Robert Dingley, *The Deputation of Angels, Or, The Angell-Guardian* (London, 1653), 128 (quote); Ambrose, *Communion with Angels*, 143; Mather, *Angelographia*, 91; Richard Baxter, *The Certainty of the Worlds of Spirits* (London, 1691), A5r.

62 Pietro da Lucca, *A dialogue of dying wel*, tr. Richard Verstegan (Antwerp, 1603), 45v–46r.

63 Beaty, *Craft of Dying*, 187. Cf. B. Gregory, 'The "True and Zealouse Service of God": Robert Parson, Edmund Bunny, and *The First Book of the Christian Exercise*', *Journal of Ecclesiastical History*, 45 (1994), 244–68.

64 William Shakespeare, *Hamlet*, v.ii.373.

65 Brother Baldwin Peter, '*Hamlet* and *In Paradisum*', *Shakespeare Quarterly*, 3 (1952), 279–80; Frye, *The Renaissance Hamlet*, 270; Sheingorn, 'Flights of Angels', 175–8.

66 Thus when the Laudian dean of Wells Richard Meredith expressed the hope in his will of 1621 'that my soule shalbe carried forthwith by angels into Abraham's bosome', this cannot be considered in itself (*pace* P. E. MacCullough's entry in the *Oxford Dictionary of National Biography*) a 'striking allusion to proscribed Roman rites for the dead'.

67 Dailey, 'Visitation of Sarah Wight', 440.

68 The prevailing interpretative drift of, for example, C. Haigh, *English Reformations: Religion, Politics, and Society under the Tudors* (Oxford, Oxford University Press, 1993).

69 Cf. Tessa Watt's conclusion that the religion of the world of cheap print 'may be described as distinctively "post-Reformation", but not thoroughly "Protestant"'. *Cheap Print*, 327. Christopher Marsh's *Popular Religion in Sixteenth-Century England* (Basingstoke, Macmillan, 1998), which employs as its cover illustration a late medieval image of St Michael re-emerging through an over-painted scriptural text on a Norfolk rood screen, may also be considered a leading examplar of this approach.

70   Cf. Diarmaid MacCulloch's suggestion that angels stepped 'into the shoes of the evicted Catholic saints as ideologically appropriate friends of humanity': *Reformation: Europe's House Divided 1490–1700* (London, Allen Lane, 2003), 581.

71   Sheingorn, 'Flights of Angels', 167; da Lucca, *Dialogue of dying wel*, 46v.

72   Marshall, *Beliefs and the Dead*, 193–4.

73   Becon, *Sick Man's Salve*, 126.

7 The guardian angel in Protestant England

1   D. Keck, *Angels and Angelology in the Middle Ages* (New York and Oxford, Oxford University Press, 1998), 161–5; A. F. Sutton and L. Visser-Fuchs, 'The Cult of Angels in Late Fifteenth-Century England: An Hours of the Guardian Angel Presented to Queen Elizabeth Woodville', in L. Smith and J. H. M. Taylor (eds), *Women and the Book: Assessing the Visual Evidence* (London and Toronto, University of Toronto Press, 1996), 230–65; M. Connolly, 'A Prayer to the Guardian Angel and Wynkyn de Worde's 1506 Edition of *Contemplations of the Dread and Love of God*', *Manuscripta*, 45–6 (2001–2), 1–17; E. Duffy, *The Stripping of the Altars: Traditional Religion in England 1400–1580* (New Haven and London, Yale University Press, 1992), 270; E. Duffy, *Marking the Hours: English People and Their Prayers 1240–1570* (New Haven and London, Yale University Press, 2006), 161; R. N. Swanson, *Religion and Devotion in Europe, c.1215–c.1515* (Cambridge, Cambridge University Press, 1995), 171–2.

2   *Sermons, or Homilies, Appointed to be read in Churches* (London, Prayer-Book and Homily Society, 1833), 223.

3   Keck, *Angels and Angelology*, 162–3; Jacobus de Voragine, *The Golden Legend*, tr. W. Ryan (2 vols, Princeton, Princeton University Press, 1993), II, 207–9.

4   See above, Ch. 6.

5   Richard Baxter, *The Certainty of the Worlds of Spirits* (London, 1691), 233.

6   D. Harkness, *John Dee's Conversations with Angels: Cabala, Alchemy, and the End of Nature* (Cambridge, Cambridge University Press, 1999); K. Harvey, 'The Role of Angels in English Protestant Thought 1580 to 1660', unpublished University of Cambridge PhD thesis (2005); F. Mohamed, *In the Anteroom of Divinity: The Reformation of the Angels from Colet to Milton* (Toronto, University of Toronto Press, 2008); L. Sangha, *Angels and Belief in England, 1480–1700* (London, Pickering & Chatto, 2012); A. Walsham, 'Invisible Helpers: Angelic Intervention in Early Modern England', *Past and Present*, 208 (2010), 77–130; J. Raymond, *Milton's Angels: The Early-Modern Imagination* (Oxford, Oxford University Press, 2010). A useful earlier point of orientation is R. H. West, *Milton and the Angels* (Athens, GA, University of Georgia Press, 1955). See also P. Marshall and A. Walsham, 'Migrations of Angels in the Early Modern World', in Marshall and Walsham (eds), *Angels in the Early Modern World* (Cambridge, Cambridge University Press, 2006), 1–40.

7   C. A. Patrides, 'Renaissance Thought on the Celestial Hierarchy: The Decline of a Tradition', *Journal of the History of Ideas*, 20 (1959), 155–66.

8   See P. Soergel, 'Luther on the Angels', in Marshall and Walsham (eds), *Angels in the Early Modern World*, 64–82.

9   John Calvin, *Institutes of the Christian Religion*, tr. H. Beveridge (2 vols in 1, Grand Rapids, Eerdmans, 1989), I, 146–7. See also Calvin, *Harmony of the Gospels*, ed. T. Torrance (3 vols, Edinburgh, St Andrew Press, 1972), III, 218.

10   William Fulke, *The Text of the New Testament of Iesus Christ, translated out of the vulgar Latine by the Papists of the Traiterous Seminarie at Rhemes* (London, 1589), 36v. See also Fulke, *A Defence of the Sincere and True Translations of the Holy Scriptures into the English Tongue, against the Cavils of Gregory Martin*, ed. C. H. Hartshorne (Cambridge, Cambridge University Press, 1843), 23.

11   Thomas Cartwright, *A Confutation of the Rhemists translation, glosses and annotations on the New Testament* (London, 1618). Though not published in his lifetime, Cartwright's treatise was composed in response to an approach in 1583 from a group of eminent Puritan divines, including Fulke and William Whitaker: Peter Lake, *Moderate Puritans and the Elizabethan Church* (Cambridge, Cambridge University Press, 1982), 69–71.

12   Andrew Willet, *Synopsis Papismi, that is, a generall viewe of papistry* (London, 1592), 294–5.

13   Duffy, *Stripping of the Altars*, 269–70; W. Maskell (ed.), *Monumenta Ritualia Ecclesiae Anglicanae* (3 vols, 2nd edn, Oxford, Oxford University Press, 1882), III, 289–92.

14   Reginald Scot, *The Discovery of Witchcraft* (London, 1584), 505–6.

15   Urbanus Rhegius, *An Homely or Sermon of Good and Euill Angels*, tr. R. Robinson (2nd edn, London, 1590), 30.

16   'An cuique homini creatus angelus, qui eum curet, destinatus sit': Zanchi, *De Operibus Dei*, in *Operum Theologicorum* (3 vols, Geneva, 1617–19), III, cols 142–5.

17   William Perkins, *A golden chaine: or the description of theologie* (Cambridge, 1600), 231–5, quote at 234.

18   Heinrich Bullinger, 'Of Good and Evil Spirits; that is Of the Holy Angels', in *The Decades: The Fourth Decade*, ed. T. Harding (Cambridge, Cambridge University Press, 1851), 327–48. In 1586 Archbishop Whitgift ordered all of his non-preaching clergy to study the *Decades* weekly: D. MacCulloch, *The Later Reformation in England, 1547–1603* (2nd edn, Basingstoke, Macmillan, 2001), 61.

19   John Salkeld, *A Treatise of Angels* (London, 1613), 251–80, quotes at 248, 251, 252.

20   See T. Johnson, 'Guardian Angels and the Society of Jesus', in Marshall and Walsham (eds), *Angels in the Early Modern World*, 191–213; A. Walsham, 'Catholic Reformation and the Cult of Angels in Early Modern England', in J. Raymond (ed.), *Conversations with Angels: Essays towards a History*

of Spiritual Communication, 1100–1700 (Basingstoke, Palgrave Macmillan, 2011), 273–94.

21   J. M. Blom, 'The Adventures of an Angel-Guardian in Seventeenth-Century England', *Recusant History*, 20 (1990–1), 48–57.

22   Godfrey Goodman, *The Fall of Man, or the Corruption of Nature* (London, 1616), 58–9; P. E. McCullough, *Sermons at Court: Politics and Religion in Elizabethan and Jacobean Preaching* (Cambridge, Cambridge University Press, 1998), 72.

23   Richard Montagu, *Immediate Addresse vnto God Alone* (London, 1624), epistle dedicatory, 95–9.

24   Richard Montagu, *A Gagg for the New Gospell?* (London, 1624), 189, 203–5, 199–200.

25   A. Milton, *Catholic and Reformed: The Roman and Protestant Churches in English Protestant Thought, 1600–1640* (Cambridge, Cambridge University Press, 1995), 207. Any notion of offering prayer to angels was condemned by Richard Bernard, *Rhemes Against Rome: Or, The Remooving of the Gagg of the New Gospell* (London, 1626), 187–9.

26   *An Appeal of the Orthodox Ministers of the Church of England against Richard Montague* (Edinburgh [i.e. London], 1629), 10.

27   Thomas Taylor, *Iaphets First Publique Perswasion into Sems tent* (Cambridge, 1612), 98.

28   Thomas Adams, *The Happiness of the Church* (London, 1619), 45–8. Cf. J. Sears McGee, 'Adams, Thomas (1583–1652)', *Oxford Dictionary of National Biography*, online edn.

29   John Prideaux, *The Patronage of Angels. A Sermon Preached at the Court* (Oxford, 1636), 19.

30   For Bayly's altercation with Laud as chancellor of Oxford, see T. F. Tout, 'Bayly, John (1595/6–1633)', rev. Vivienne Larminie, *Oxford Dictionary of National Biography*, online edn.

31   John Bayly, *Two Sermons. The Angell Guardian. The Light Enlightning* (Oxford, 1630), A2r, 7–10, 14–15.

32   Henry Lawrence, *An History of Angells, Being a Theologicall Treatise of Our Communion and Warre with Them* (1646; London, 1649), 19–20, 25.

33   Lawrence, *History of Angells*, 21–2.

34   Lawrence, *History of Angells*, 30–2.

35   Lawrence, *History of Angells*, 35–42.

36   Lawrence, *History of Angells*, 48–9.

37   Robert Dingley, *The Deputation of Angels, or, The Angell-Guardian* (London, 1653), 147.

38   Dingley, *Deputation of Angels*, 59.

39   Dingley, *Deputation of Angels*, 86–9, 117.

40   Dingley, *Deputation of Angels*, 126.

41   Dingley, *Deputation of Angels*, 118, 120–1, 123–4.

42   Dingley, *Deputation of Angels*, 100–8, 127.

43   Dingley, *Deputation of Angels*, 108, 113, 115–16.

44 Dingley, *Deputation of Angels*, 33–4, 58, 98–9, 136–7, 148–9, 158–9, 174–5.

45 Montagu, *New Gagg*, 189–95.

46 Peter Heylyn, *Theologia Veterum, or, The Summe of Christian Theologie* (London, 1654), 70–3.

47 Robert Burton, *The Anatomy of Melancholy*, ed. T. C. Faulkner et al. (6 vols, Oxford, Oxford University Press, 1989–2000), I, 175.

48 Thomas Heywood, *The Hierarchie of the Blessed Angels* (London, 1635), 372–3.

49 Robert Gell, *A Sermon Touching Gods Government of the World by Angels* (London, 1650), 17.

50 John Gumbleden, *Two Sermons: First, an Angel, in a Vision, Appeareth to a Souldier . . . Second, a Saviour, in Mercy, Appeareth to a Sinner* (London, 1657), 8.

51 Thomas Browne, *Religio Medici*, in *The Major Works*, ed. C. A. Patrides (Harmondsworth, Penguin, 1977), 99, 101.

52 Joseph Hall, *The Invisible World, Discovered to Spirituall Eyes* (London, 1651), 113–16, 148.

53 Nicholas Bernard, *The Fare-well Sermons of Comfort and Concord Reached at Drogheda in Ireland* (London, 1651), 197.

54 John Lightfoot, *A Commentary on the Acts of the Apostles* (London, 1645), 324–5.

55 Thomas Fuller, *A Comment on the Eleven First Verses of the Fourth Chapter of S. Matthew's Gospel* (London, 1652), 187–8.

56 Isaac Ambrose, *Ministration of, and Communion with Angels* (London, 1673), 116, 124–5, 128, 129–30.

57 Ambrose, *Communion with Angels*, 168.

58 Benjamin Camfield, *A Theological Discourse of Angels, and their Ministries* (London, 1678), A3r.

59 Camfield, *Theological Discourse of Angels*, 70–5, 117.

60 R. Gillespie, *Devoted People: Belief and Religion in Early Modern Ireland* (Manchester, Manchester University Press, 1997), 46.

61 Thomas Tenison, *Of Idolatry* (London, 1678), 206. Tenison was thus dismissive towards Richard Montagu's suggestion that it was legitimate to pray to the guardian angel: 'he supposeth them to be ever in *propinctu*, nigh at hand to men, and in attendance on them all their days' (207).

62 *Scala Naturae: A Treatise Proving Both from Nature and Scripture the Existence of Good Genii, or Guardian-Angels* (London, 1695), 37–8.

63 Matthew Poole, *Annotations upon the Holy Bible* (London, 1685), Qqq1v.

64 Richard Saunders, *Angelographia sive pneumata leiturgika: Or a Discourse of Angels: their Nature, Office and Ministry* (London, 1701), 121–4.

65 Thomas Shepherd, *Several sermons on angels* (London, 1702), 85–6.

66 Edward Young, *Sermons on Several Occasions* (2nd edn, London, 1706), 219–20. The marginal annotations which the Welsh MP Sir John Salusbury (*c.*1640–84) made to his copy of the translation of Drexler's treatise also seem

to imply a scepticism about guardian angels: Blom, 'Adventures of an Angel-Guardian', 52–5.

67 Robert Nelson, *A Companion for the Festivals and Fasts of the Church of England* (2nd edn, London, 1704), 290–1. See also Nelson, *The Holy-days, or the Holy Feasts and Fasts, as They are Observed in the Church of England* (London, 1706), 54.

68 George Hamond, *A Modest Enquiry into the Opinion Concerning a Guardian Angel* (London, 1702).

69 Isaac Watts, *Hymns and Spiritual Songs* (2nd edn, London, 1709), 154.

70 Hamond, *Modest Enquiry*, 24.

71 Henry More, *An Antidote Against Atheisme* (London, 1653), 148–51.

72 John Pordage, *Innocencie Appearing Through the Dark Mists of Pretended Guilt* (London, 1655), 14–15, 27, 68; Ariel Hessayon, 'Bromley, Thomas (*bap.* 1630, *d.* 1691)', *Oxford Dictionary of National Biography*, online edn. See J. Raymond, 'Radicalism and Mysticism in the Seventeenth Century: John Pordage's Angels', in Raymond (ed.), *Conversations with Angels*, 317–39.

73 Ambrose, *Communion with Angels*, 170.

74 Baxter, *Certainty of the Worlds of Spirits*, 60–1.

75 R. Gillespie, 'Imagining Angels in Early Modern Ireland', in Marshall and Walsham (eds), *Angels in the Early Modern World*, 214–32.

76 *The Autobiography of Mrs. Alice Thornton*, ed. C. Jackson, Surtees Society, 62 (Durham, Andrews & Co., 1875), 3–32, quotes at 4.

77 Izaak Walton, *The Life of Mr Rich. Hooker* (London, 1665), 47.

78 Lawrence, *History of Angells*, 47–8; Henry More, *An Antidote Against Atheism* (London, 1653), 140–4; Camfield, *Theological Discourse of Angels*, 88–90; William Turner, *A Compleat History of the Most Remarkable Providences, Both of Judgement and Mercy, which have Happened in this Present Age* (London, 1697), 7–8; Hamond, *Modest Enquiry*, 17–20. See R. Briggs, 'Dubious Messengers: Bodin's Daemon, the Spirit World and the Sadducees', in Marshall and Walsham (eds), *Angels in the Early Modern World*, 168–90.

79 Ambrose, *Communion with Angels*, 138–9.

80 Hamond, *Modest Enquiry*, 21–2, 12.

81 Keck, *Angels and Angelology*, 161–3.

82 Henry Bourne, *Antiquitates Vulgares: or the Antiquities of the Common People* (Newcastle, 1725), 219–20.

83 *The Athenian Oracle. Being an Entire Collection* (4 vols, London, 1728), I, 4–5.

84 Hamond, *Modest Enquiry*, 1.

85 Hamond, *Modest Enquiry*, 21.

86 Hamond, *Modest Enquiry*, 24; Dingley, *Deputation of Angels*, 191; Adams, *Happiness of the Church*, 52. See also, Lawrence, *History of Angells*, 50; Increase Mather, *Angelographia, or A Discourse concerning the Nature and Power of the Holy Angels* (Boston, 1696), 94.

87 A full-text search for the phrase 'guardian angel' in Early English Books Online (Nov. 2016) produces 328 hits for the period between 1660 and 1700,

many of them passing, and usually metaphorical, references from poetry or drama.

88 Edward Ward, *The World Bewitched: A Dialogue Between Two Astrologers and the Author* (London, 1699), 15.
89 Saunders, *Angelographia*, 124.
90 Bourne, *Antiquitates Vulgares*, 224.
91 Montagu, *New Gagg*, 189.

8 Deceptive appearances: ghosts and reformers in Elizabethan and Jacobean England

1 Robert King, *A funerall sermon that was prepared to have bine preached* (London, 1552), G3v–4r.
2 Thomas Morton, *A Catholike Appeale for Protestants* (London, 1609), 428.
3 Jean Veron, *The Huntyng of Purgatorye to Death* (London, 1561), 201v; James Calfhill, *An Answer to John Martiall's Treatise of the Cross*, ed. R. Gibbings (Cambridge, Cambridge University Press, 1846), 90; Heinrich Bullinger, *The Decades: The Fourth Decade*, ed. T. Harding (Cambridge, Cambridge University Press, 1851), 400; Ludwig Lavater, *Of Ghostes and Spirites Walking by Night 1572*, ed. J. Dover Wilson and M. Yardley (Oxford, Oxford University Press, 1929), 110; William Fulke, *Two Treatises written against the Papistes* (London, 1577), 163–4; George Wither, *A View of the Marginal Notes of the Popish Testament* (London, 1588), 74; Matthew Sutcliffe, *Adversus Roberti Bellarmini de Purgatorio Disputationem* (London, 1599), 101; Edward Hoby, *A Letter to Mr T. H.* (London, 1609), 42; Samuel Purchas, *Purchas his Pilgrimage* (London, 1613),179; Thomas Beard, *A Retractive from the Romish Religion* (London, 1616), 414; Robert Horne, *Certaine Sermons of the Rich Man and Lazarus* (London, 1619), 135; Robert Jenison, *The Height of Israels Heathenish Idolatrie* (London, 1621), 143; John Donne, *Sermons*, ed. E. M. Simpson and G. R. Potter (10 vols, Berkeley and Los Angeles, University of California Press, 1953–62), X, 145–6; Anthony Cooke, *Worke, More Work, and a Little More Worke for a Masse-Priest* (3rd edn, London, 1630), 46.
4 Edmund Grindal, *Remains*, ed. W. Nicholson (Cambridge, Cambridge University Press, 1843), 24.
5 Henry Smith, *Sermons* (London, 1592), 540–1.
6 K. Thomas, *Religion and the Decline of Magic* (new edn, London, Weidenfeld & Nicolson, 1997), 589.
7 See P. Marshall, *Beliefs and the Dead in Reformation England* (Oxford, Oxford University Press, 2002), 53–5.
8 Calfhill, *Answer to Martiall*, 90; Anthony Anderson, *The Shield of our Safetie Set Foorth* (London, 1581), H2r; Reginald Scot, *The Discoverie of Witchcraft* (London, 1584), 139; George Gifford, *A Dialogue concerning Witches and Witchcraftes* (London, 1593), F2r; Horne, *Certaine Sermons*, 134.
9 G. A. [William Alley], *The Poore Mans Librarie* (London, 1571), 53v. See also Bullinger, *Fourth Decade*, 401; Anderson, *Shield of our Safetie*, H2r.

10 Horne, *Certaine Sermons*, 122.

11 Thomas Bilson, *The effect of Certaine Sermons . . . preached at Pauls Crosse* (London, 1599), 204.

12 Robert Bellarmine, *Liber de Purgatorio*, in *De Controversiis Christianae Fidei Adversus Huuis Temporis Haereticos* (5 vols, Ingolstadt, 1601), II, 791–2; *The Holie Bible Faithfully Translated into English . . . by the English College of Doway* (2 vols, Douai, 1609–10), I, 631–2; Noel Taillepied, *A Treatise of Ghosts*, tr. M. Summers (London, Fortune, 1934), 152–7. A more agnostic attitude is evident in William Allen, *A Defence and Declaration of the Catholike Churches Doctrine touching Purgatory* (Antwerp, 1565), 110v.

13 *The Holie Bible* [Bishops' Bible] (London, 1568), 50r; *The Bible* [Geneva version] (London, 1599 edn), 109. The story is treated in detail by Lavater, *Of Ghostes*, 127–45; Anderson, *Shield of our Safetie*, H2v–I1r; Peter Martyr, *The Common Places*, tr. A. Marten (London, 1583), 72–7; Scot, *Discoverie*, 139–52; George Gifford, *A Discourse of the Subtill Practises of Devilles by Witches and Sorcerers* (London, 1587), E1v–E3v; Henry Holland, *A Treatise against Witchcraft* (Cambridge, 1590), C1v–C3r; Andrew Willet, *Synopsis Papismi, that is, a generall viewe of papistry* (London, 1592), 305–6; Randall Hutchins, *Of Specters*, tr. and ed. V. B. Heltzel and C. Murley, *Huntingdon Library Quarterly*, 11 (1947–8), 424–6; John Deacon and John Walker, *Dialogical Discourses of Spirits and Divels* (London, 1601), 120–6; William Perkins, *A Discourse of the Damned Art of Witchcraft* (Cambridge, 1608), 108–20; Thomas Cooper, *The Mystery of Witchcraft* (London, 1617), 151–4.

14 Perkins, *Discourse of the Damned Art*, 113.

15 Smith, *Sermons*, 538.

16 Holland, *Treatise against Witchcraft*, C2r; William Perkins, *A golden chaine: or the description of theologie* (Cambridge, 1600), 515; *Discourse of the Damned Art*, 109–10, 112, 115; Deacon and Walker, *Dialogical Discourses*, 121–2; Cooper, *Mystery of Witchcraft*, 151–2.

17 Willet, *Synopsis Papisimi*, 306; Perkins, *Discourse of the Damned Art*, 111; *Golden chaine*, 50; Gifford, *Discourse of the Subtill Practises of Devilles*, E1v; Holland, *Treatise against Witchcraft*, C2r.

18 Cooper, *Mystery of Witchcraft*, 152.

19 Perkins, *Discourse of the Damned Art*, 118

20 Bellarmine, *De Purgatorio*, 792; *Douai Bible*, II, 441; Taillepied, *Treatise of Ghosts*, 153.

21 Holland, *Treatise against Witchcraft*, C2r; Purchas, *Purchas his Pilgrimage*, 179: 'poore Purgatorie with Jewes and Romists is preached by walking ghosts'.

22 A. Peel (ed.), *The Seconde Parte of a Register* (2 vols, Cambridge, Cambridge University Press, 1915), I, 279. A later conformist response to Puritan objections to this passage admitted that the verse reflected 'the general voice of those times, and the opinion of Saul and the Witch then generalie currant': Thomas Hutton, *Reasons for Refusal of Subscription to the booke of common praier* (Oxford, 1605), 116.

23 Scot, *Discoverie*, 139, 142–50, 152.

24 Scot, *Discoverie*, 462, 139, 152.

25 See S. Anglo, 'Reginald Scot's *Discoverie of Witchcraft*: Scepticism and Sadduceeism', in S. Anglo (ed.), *The Damned Art: Essays in the Literature of Witchcraft* (London, Routledge & Kegan Paul, 1977), 106–39.

26 Samuel Harsnett, *A Declaration of Egregious Popish Impostures*, reprinted in F. W. Brownlow, *Shakespeare, Harnett, and the Devils of Denham* (London and Toronto, Associated University Press, 1993), 309.

27 Gervase Babington, *Workes* (London, 1622), Book II, 189.

28 Erasmus, *The Colloquies*, tr. C. R. Thompson (Chicago, University of Chicago Press, 1965), 230–7; J. Weyer, *De praestigii daemonum*, ed. and tr. G. Mora et al. as *Witches, Devils, and Doctors in the Renaissance* (Binghampton, NY, State University of New York, 1991), 439 ff.; Lavater, *Of Ghostes*, chs 5–9.

29 Taillepied, *Treatise of Ghosts*, ch. 6; Pierre Le Loyer, *A Treatise of Specters or Strange Sights, Visions and Apparitions appearing Sensibly unto Men*, tr. Z. Jones (London, 1605), 75v–79v.

30 Perkins, *Discourse of the Damned Art*, 118; Perkins, *Golden chaine*, 50; Gifford, *Subtill Practises of Devilles*, E3r–v; Holland, *Treatise against Witchcrafjt*, C2r; Cooper, *Mystery of Witchcraft*, 154; Deacon and Walker, *Dialogical Discourses*, 125–6.

31 George Strode, *The Anatomie of Mortalitie* (London, 1632), 205. See also Pierre Du Moulin, *The Waters of Siloe* (Oxford, 1612), 395; Hutchins, *Of Specters*, 426.

32 R. Kieckhefer, *Magic in the Middle Ages* (Cambridge, Cambridge University Press, 1989), 152; Holland, *Treatise of Witchcraft*, D4r; Perkins, *Discourse of the Damned Art*, 107–8; *Golden chaine*, 50; John Cotta, *The Triall of Witchcraft* (London, 1616), 37.

33 Pierre Viret, *The Christian Disputations*, tr. J. Brooke (London, 1579), 104v.

34 Beard, *Retractive from the Romish Religion*, 437.

35 John Preston, *A Sermon Preached at the Funeral of Mr Arthur Upton Esquire in Devon* (London, 1619), 33.

36 Jenison, *Height of Israels Idolatrie*, 141.

37 On inversion and witchcraft, see S. Clark: 'King James's *Daemonologie*: Witchcraft and Kingship', in Anglo (ed.), *Damned Art*, 156–81; Clark, *Thinking with Demons: The Idea of Witchcraft in Early Modern Europe* (Oxford, Clarendon Press, 1997), ch. 6.

38 Richard Bernard, *A Guide to Grand-Iury Men* (London, 1627), 34, 99. See also Cooper, *Mystery of Witchcraft*, 22; John Napeir, *A Plaine Discovery of the Whole Revelation of Saint John* (Edinburgh, 1593), 46; N. Jones, 'Defining Superstitions: Treasonous Catholics and the Act against Witchcraft of 1563', in C. Carlton et al. (eds), *State, Sovereigns and Society in Early Modern England* (Stroud, Sutton, 1998), 187–204.

39 Donne, *Sermons*, VII, 168; VIII, 135.

40 Harsnett's tract was aimed as much at the Puritan exorcist John Darrell as

at the Catholics who were its ostensible targets: see M. Gibson, *Possession,*
Puritanism and Print: Darrell, Harsnett, Shakespeare and the Elizabethan
Exorcism Controversy (London, Pickering & Chatto, 2006).

41   British Library, London, Harleian MS 425, 4–7.
42   Edwin Sandys, *Sermons*, ed. J. Ayre (Cambridge, Cambridge University
     Press, 1841), 60.
43   Lavater, *Of Ghostes*, 89, 183.
44   *Greenes Newes both from Heaven and Hell*, ed. R. B. McKerrow (London,
     Sidgwick and Jackson, 1911), 3.
45   Scot, *Discoverie*, 152–3, 463. He was ill-informed about the situation in
     Germany: see S. Karant-Nunn, *The Reformation of Ritual: An Interpretation*
     of Early Modern Germany (London, Routledge, 1997), 185–6.
46   Harsnett, *Declaration*, 306–7.
47   Donne, *Sermons*, X, 145–6; Bernard, *Guide to Grand-Iury Men*, 99–100;
     Hoby, *Letter to Mr T. H.*, 42.
48   John Northbrooke, *Spiritus est Vicarius Christi in Terra* (London, 1571), 15r.
49   Hutchins, *Of Specters*, 410; Smith, *Sermons*, 536; Perkins, *Golden chaine*, 515;
     Discourse of the Damned Art, 115–16; Strode, *Anatomie of Mortalitie*, 204–5.
50   Veron, *Huntyng of Purgatorye*, 197v–198v.
51   Arthur Dent, *The Plaine Mans Pathway to Heaven* (London, 1605), 265–6.
52   On the rhetoric and function of these texts, see A. Bevan Zlatar, *Reformation*
     Fictions: Polemical Protestant Dialogues in Elizabethan England (Oxford,
     Oxford University Press, 2011).
53   Lavater, *Of Ghostes*, 71.
54   R[obert] H[arrison], 'To the Reader', in Lavater, *Of Ghostes*.
55   Scot, *Discoverie*, 532.
56   Matthew Parker, *Correspondence*, ed. J. Bruce (Cambridge, Cambridge
     University Press, 1853), 222.
57   Anderson, *Shield of our Safetie*, H1v.
58   Preston, *Sermon Preached at the Funeral of Mr Arthur Upton*, 33.
59   Anderson, *Shield of our Safetie*, H2r; Smith, *Sermons*, 537–8.
60   K. L. Parker and E. J. Carlson, *'Practical Divinity': The Works and Life of Revd*
     Richard Greenham (Aldershot, Ashgate, 1998), 217.
61   Smith, *Sermons*, 540.
62   Babington, *Workes*, book II, 188–9; Anderson, *Shield of our Safetie*, H4r.
63   Scot, *Discoverie*, 141; Hutchins, *Of Specters*, 424. On Agrippa and ghosts,
     see R. H. West, *The Invisible World: A Study of Pneumatology in Elizabethan*
     Drama (repr. New York, Octagon Books, 1969), 52–3.
64   N. Z. Davies, 'Some Tasks and Themes in the Study of Popular Religion', in C.
     Trinkaus and H. O. Oberman (eds), *The Pursuit of Holiness in Late Medieval*
     and Renaissance Religion (Leiden, Brill, 1974), 333; R. Muchembled, *Popular*
     and Elite Culture in France 1400–1750, tr. L. Cochrane (Baton Rouge and
     London, Louisiana State University Press, 1985), 64.
65   Barnaby Rich, *The true report of a late practise enterprised by a papist*
     with a yong maiden in Wales (London, 1582). The Orton case is now fully

explored by A. Walsham, 'The Holy Maid of Wales: Visions, Imposture and Catholicism in Elizabethan Britain', *English Historical Review* (forthcoming).

66 John Gee, *New Shreds of the Old Snare* (London, 1624), 1–25.

67 Lavater, *Of Ghostes*, chs 2–4; Scot, *Discoverie*, 152, 462; Taillepied, *Treatise of Ghosts*, chs 3–5, 7; Hutchins, *Of Specters*, 412; Thomas Nashe, *The Terrors of the Night*, in *The Works of Thomas Nashe*, ed. R. B. McKerrow and F. Wilson (Oxford, Clarendon Press, 1958), I, 348, 378; Thomas Lodge, *The Divell Coniured*, in *The Complete Works of Thomas Lodge*, ed. E. Gosse (4 vols, Glasgow, Hunterian Club, 1883), III, 33; Harsnett, *Declaration of Egregious Popish Impostures*, 304–5; Le Loyer, *Treatise of Specters*, 104r–112v; Donne, *Sermons*, VII, 168; Thomas White, *The Middle State of Souls* (London, 1659), 170.

68 Babington, *Workes*, book II, 189.

69 M. MacDonald and T. Murphy, *Sleepless Souls: Suicide in Early Modern England* (Oxford, Oxford University Press, 1990), 34–41; *Hamlet*, II.ii.600–4. On melancholy, see M. MacDonald, *Mystical Bedlam: Madness, Anxiety, and Healing in Seventeenth-Century England* (Cambridge, Cambridge University Press, 1981), 150–60.

70 Cited in MacDonald, *Mystical Bedlam*, 169.

71 MacDonald, *Mystical Bedlam*, 157.

72 Lavater, *Of Ghosts*, B2r, 145, 159–63, 193, 196, 199.

73 Scot, *Discoverie*, 152, 462.

74 William Perkins, *A Reformed Catholike* (Cambridge, 1598), 247.

75 James I, *Daemonologie*, ed. G. B. Harrison (London, The Bodley Head, 1924), 61, 65–6.

76 Bodleian Library, Oxford, MS Rawlinson D 47, 42r–43v. For further examples of alleged angelic appearances, see A. Walsham, 'Invisible Helpers: Angelic Intervention in Early Modern England', *Past and Present*, 208 (2010), 77–130. See also Ch. 6, above.

77 Lavater, *Of Ghosts*, 175, 191; James I, *Daemonologie*, 58.

78 A. Walsham, *Providence in Early Modern England* (Oxford, Oxford University Press, 1999), *passim*.

79 John Foxe, *Actes and Monumentes* (London, 1563), **I*(v); *Actes and Monuments* (London, 1570), 409–10. Foxe was not the first English Protestant to retell the story: Thomas Swinnerton, *A mustre of scismatyke bysshoppes of Rome* (London, 1534), B4r.

80 T. Erbe (ed.), *Mirk's Festial* (London, Oxford University Press, 1905), 270; Jacobus de Voragine, *The Golden Legend*, tr. W. Ryan (2 vols, Princeton, Princeton University Press, 1993), II, 290.

81 Philip Stubbes, *Two Wunderfull and Rare Examples of the Undeferred Judgement of God* (London, 1581).

82 *A Strange and Fearful Warning to all Sonnes and Executors (that fulfill not the will of their dead Fathers)* (London, 1623).

83 David Person, *Varieties: or a Surveigh of rare and excellent matters* (London, 1635), 165.

84 Walsham, *Providence*; P. Lake, 'Deeds against Nature: Cheap Print, Protestantism and Murder in Early Seventeenth-Century England', in K. Sharpe and Lake (eds), *Culture and Politics in Early Stuart England* (Basingstoke, Macmillan, 1994); T. Watt, *Cheap Print and Popular Piety 1550–1640* (Cambridge, Cambridge University Press, 1991).

85 British Library, London, Harleian MS 425, 6v; Northbrooke, *Spiritus est Vicarius Christi in Terra*, 15r; Sandys, *Sermons*, 60; Bullinger, *The Fourth Decade*, 404; Anderson, *Shield of our Safetie*, H1v–2r; Martyr, *Common Places*, 326; Scot, *Discoverie*, 462; Smith, *Sermons*, 525, 541; Hutchins, *Of Specters*, 426; Perkins, *Golden chaine*, 515; *Discourse of the Damned Art*, 33; Robert Pricke, *A Very Godlie and Learned Sermon treating of Mans Mortalitie* (London, 1608), D4v; Harsnett, *Declaration of Egregious Popish Impostures*, 306; Purchas, *Pilgrimage*, 179; Beard, *Retractive from the Romish Religion*, 437; Cooper, *Mystery of Witchcraft*, 152; Babington, *Workes*, book II, 188–9; Strode, *Anatomie of Mortalitie*, 205.

86 Bodleian Library, Oxford, MS Rawlinson D 47, 43r.

87 R. Finucane, *Appearances of the Dead: A Cultural History of Ghosts* (London, Junction Books, 1982), 124.

88 Thomas Browne, *Religio Medici*, in *The Major Works*, ed. C. A. Patrides (Harmondsworth, Penguin, 1977), 108.

89 J. Bossy, *Christianity in the West 1400–1700* (Oxford, Oxford University Press, 1985), 29.

90 J.-C. Schmitt, *Ghosts in the Middle Ages: The Living and the Dead in Medieval Society*, tr. T. L. Fagan (Chicago and London, University of Chicago Press, 1998), 137.

91 Scot, *Discoverie*, 462.

92 D. Oldridge, *The Supernatural in Tudor and Stuart England* (Abingdon, Routledge, 2016), 112.

93 Nashe, *Terrors of the Night*, 348–9.

94 Browne, *Religio Medici*, 108.

95 N. Caciola, 'Wraiths, Revenants and Ritual in Medieval Culture', *Past and Present*, 152 (1996).

96 Lavater, *Of Ghostes*, 171; Veron, *Huntynge of Purgatorye*, 245v; Deacon and Walker, *Dialogical Discourses*, 101–2, 104; Cotta, *Triall of Witchcraft*, 37; John Donne, *No Man Is an Island: A Selection from the Prose of John Donne* (London, Folio Society, 1997), 169.

97 Cooper, *Mystery of Witchcraft*, 151; Preston, *Sermon Preached at the Funeral of Mr Arthur Upton*, 33. See also Whitgift's admission at the 1584 conference at Lambeth that it was 'a question among the learned' whether witches had power to raise the bodies of the dead: Peel, *Seconde Parte of a Register*, I, 279, a comment wrongly attributed to Walter Travers by Thomas, *Religion*, 591.

98 James I, *Daemonologie*, 59, 67, 73; Hutchins, *Of Specters*, 416.

99 G. L. Kittredge, *Witchcraft in Old and New England* (New York, Russell & Russell, 1929), 312.

100 Lodge, *Divell Coniured*, 23, 30. For the very long-standing popular intuition

that the corpses of the dead continued to possess some degree of sentience or life force, see Caciola, 'Wraiths, Revenants and Ritual'; R. Richardson, *Death, Dissection and the Destitute* (London, Routledge & Kegan Paul, 1987), ch. 1.

101 Cited in K. M. Briggs, *The Anatomy of Puck: An Examination of Fairy Beliefs among Shakespeare's Contemporaries* (London, Routledge & Kegan Paul, 1959), 137. For a discussion of the work, see F. Martin, '"Mong'st the furies finde just recompence": Suicide and the Supernatural in William Sampson's The Vow Breaker (1636)', in M. Harmes and V. Bladen (eds), *Supernatural and Secular Power in Early Modern England* (Farnham, Ashgate, 2015), 117–39.

102 E. Prosser, *Hamlet and Revenge* (Stanford, Stanford University Press, 1967), 255. General treatments of ghosts in Elizabethan drama are provided by Briggs, *Anatomy of Puck*, ch. 9; West, *Invisible World*, ch. 9.

103 J. Belfield, 'Tarleton's News out of Purgatory (London, 1590): A Modern-Spelling Edition, with Introduction and Commentary', University of Birmingham PhD thesis (1978), 116–33.

104 Belfield, 'Tarleton's News', 284.

105 Among the works tackling this aspect of the play, and taking very different views on how Shakespeare intended the ghost to be interpreted, are J. Dover Wilson, *What Happens in Hamlet* (Cambridge, Cambridge University Press, 1951), ch. 3; M. Joseph, 'Discerning the Ghost in Hamlet', *Publications of the Modern Language Association of America*, 76 (1961), 493–502; C. Devlin, 'Hamlet's Divinity', in *Hamlet's Divinity and Other Essays* (London, Rupert Hart-Davis, 1963); Prosser, *Hamlet and Revenge*; R. West, *Shakespeare and the Outer Mystery* (Lexington, University of Kentucky Press, 1968), ch. 4; R. M. Frye, *The Renaissance Hamlet: Issues and Responses in 1600* (Princeton, Princeton University Press, 1984), 14–28; A. McGee, *The Elizabethan Hamlet* (New Haven and London, Yale University Press, 1987), chs 1–3; S. Greenblatt, *Hamlet in Purgatory* (Princeton, Princeton University Press, 2001); J. E. Curran, *Hamlet, Protestantism, and the Mourning of Contingency* (Abingdon, Routledge, 2006).

106 John Donne, *Selected Poems*, ed. J. Hayward (Harmondsworth, Penguin, 1950), 52.

107 Henry More, *The Immortality of the Soul* (London, 1659), 286.

108 R. Hutton, 'The English Reformation and the Evidence of Folklore', *Past and Present*, 148 (1995), 114.

109 Smith, *Sermons*, 532.

110 Thomas, *Religion and the Decline of Magic*, ch. 19; O. Davies, *The Haunted: A Social History of Ghosts* (Basingstoke, Palgrave Macmillan, 2007); S. Handley, 'Reclaiming Ghosts in 1690s England', in J. Gregory and K. Cooper (eds), *Signs, Wonders, Miracles: Representations of Divine Power in the Life of the Church* (Woodbridge, Boydell & Brewer, 2005), 345–55; Handley, *Visions of an Unseen World: Ghost Beliefs and Ghost Stories in Eighteenth-Century England* (London, Pickering & Chatto, 2007). See also Ch. 10, below.

9 Piety and poisoning in Restoration Plymouth

1   Lynn Robson, 'No Nine Days Wonder: Embedded Protestant Narratives in Early Modern Prose Murder Pamphlets 1573–1700', University of Warwick PhD thesis (2003).

2   James Sharpe, '"Last Dying Speeches": Religion, Ideology and Public Execution in Seventeenth-Century England', *Past and Present*, 107 (1985), 144–67.

3   Peter Lake, 'Deeds against Nature: Cheap Print, Protestantism and Murder in Early Seventeenth-Century England', in Kevin Sharpe and Peter Lake (eds), *Culture and Politics in Early Stuart England* (Basingstoke, Macmillan, 1994), 257–83; 'Popular Form, Puritan Content? Two Puritan Appropriations of the Murder Pamphlet from Mid-Seventeenth-Century London', in Anthony Fletcher and Peter Roberts (eds), *Religion, Culture and Society in Early Modern Britain* (Cambridge, Cambridge University Press, 1994), 313–34; (with M. Questier), *The Antichrist's Lewd Hat: Protestants, Papists and Players in Post-Reformation England* (New Haven and London, Yale University Press, 2002), 3–183.

4   Robson, 'No Nine Days Wonder', *passim*. Other works making use of the genre include Frances Dolan, *Dangerous Familiars: Representations of Domestic Crime in England 1550–1700* (New York, Cornell University Press, 1994); Malcolm Gaskill, *Crime and Mentalities in Early Modern England* (Cambridge, Cambridge University Press, 2000).

5   C. John Sommerville, *Popular Religion in Restoration England* (Gainesville, University of Florida Press, 1977), 5.

6   John Quick, *Hell Open'd, or, The Infernal Sin of Murther Punished* (London, 1676), 1.

7   Quick, *Hell Open'd*, 3–22, quotes at 7, 11.

8   Quick, *Hell Open'd*, 22–5, 57–67.

9   Sharpe, '"Last Dying Speeches"', 159, 165.

10 A. G. Matthews, *Calamy Revised* (Oxford, Clarendon Press, 1934), 401–2.

11 Peter Linebaugh, 'The Ordinary of Newgate and His Account', in J. S. Cockburn (ed.), *Crime in England 1550–1800* (London, Methuen, 1977), 246–69.

12 Alexander Gordon, 'Quick, John (*bap.* 1636, *d.* 1706)', rev. Stephen Wright, *Oxford Dictionary of National Biography*, online edn; A. C. Clifford, 'Reformed Pastoral Theology under the Cross: John Quick and Claude Brousson', *Western Reformed Seminary Journal*, 5 (1998), 21–35. A collection of lives of eminent nonconformist divines did not make it into print: 'Icones Sacrae Anglicanae' (MS in Dr Williams' Library, London, MS 38.34/5).

13 For example, Quick, *Hell Open'd*, 39, 85, 65–6.

14 Quick, *Hell Open'd*, 26–9.

15 Quick, *Hell Open'd*, 31; John Quick, *The Dead Prophet yet speaking. A Funeral Sermon Preached at Plaisterers-Hall, Feb. 15. 1690* (London, 1691), 20.

16 John Quick, *A Serious Inquiry into that Weighty Case of Conscience Whether a Man may Lawfully Marry his Deceased Wife's Sister* (London, 1703), epistle.

17   Quick, *Hell Open'd*, 41.

18   Quick, *Hell Open'd*, 41–2, 46, 69, 71–3. See Ch. 6, above.

19   Quick, *Hell Open'd*, 45, 50, 64, 77.

20   Quick, *Hell Open'd*, 33–4, 36.

21   Sharpe, '"Last Dying Speeches"', 155–6; Robson, 'No Nine Days Wonder', 264–5.

22   Quick, *Hell Open'd*, 63, 77, 78.

23   N. H. Keeble, *The Literary Culture of Nonconformity* (Leicester, Leicester University Press, 1987).

24   For evidence that murder pamphlets could sometimes fulfil this function, see Peter Lake, 'Puritanism, Arminianism and a Shropshire Axe-Murder', *Midland History*, 15 (1990), 37–64; Robson, 'No Nine Days Wonder', 73.

25   Quick, *Hell Open'd*, 37.

26   John Spurr, *The Restoration Church of England, 1646–1689* (New Haven and London, Yale University Press, 1991), 44–6; Jeremy Gregory, *Restoration, Reformation and Reform, 1660–1828* (Oxford, Clarendon Press, 2000), 187–91.

27   Quick, *Hell Open'd*, 66.

28   Quick, *Hell Open'd*, 74.

29   Cited in N. H. Keeble, *The Restoration* (Oxford, Blackwell, 2002), 145.

30   Quick, *Hell Open'd*, 22–3.

31   Quick, *Hell Open'd*, 28.

32   Quick, *Hell Open'd*, 51.

33   A. Walsham, *Providence in Early Modern England* (Oxford, Oxford University Press, 1999), *passim* and 333–4; K. Thomas, *Religion and the Decline of Magic* (new edn, London, Weidenfeld & Nicolson, 1997), 78–112; Lake, 'Popular Form, Puritan Content?', 331. But for evidence of continued interest in providential occurrences, see W. E. Burns, *An Age of Wonders: Prodigies, Politics and Providence in England 1657–1727* (Manchester, Manchester University Press, 2002).

34   Quick, *Hell Open'd*, 87

35   Quick, *Hell Open'd*, 74–5, 79.

36   Quick, *Hell Open'd*, 20.

37   Quick, *Hell Open'd*, 89. For examples in cheap print of secret murders exposed by ghosts, see M. Gaskill, 'Reporting Murder: Fiction in the Archives in Early Modern England', *Social History*, 23 (1998), 14–16; Robson, 'No Nine Days Wonder', 53–4.

38   British Library, London, Sloane MS 1818, 178r–187v. The accounts were later printed in [Nicholas Bernard], *Some Memorials of the Life and Penitent Death of Dr John Atherton* (London, 1711), 4–14. For a full account of the case, see P. Marshall, *Mother Leakey and the Bishop: A Ghost Story* (Oxford, Oxford University Press, 2007).

39   Quick, *Hell Open'd*, 82–3.

40   Eamon Duffy, 'The Godly and the Multitude in Stuart England', *The Seventeenth Century*, 1 (1985), 31–55.

41 A point made by Robson, 'No Nine Days Wonder', 60.
42 Revealingly, when an abridgement of Quick's text was included in the compendium *The Wonders of Free-Grace: or, A Compleat History of all the Remarkable Penitents that have been Executed at Tyburn and Elsewhere* (London, 1690), the editor decided to 'mostly touch upon the penitent' (161).
43 For instances of this impulse, see Lake, 'Deeds against Nature', 280–2.
44 Quick, *Hell Open'd*, 79.
45 Quick, *Hell Open'd*, 81.
46 Quick, *Hell Open'd*, 65, 79–81.
47 Duffy, 'Godly and the Multitude'; Margaret Spufford, 'The Importance of Religion in the Sixteenth and Seventeenth Centuries', in Spufford (ed.), *The World of Rural Dissenters 1520–1725* (Cambridge, Cambridge University Press, 1995), 1–102.

10 Transformations of the ghost story in post-Reformation England

1 R. C. Finucane, *Appearances of the Dead: A Cultural History of Ghosts* (London, Junction Books, 1982).
2 Noteworthy recent books on the topic include J.-C. Schmitt, *Ghosts in the Middle Ages: The Living and the Dead in Medieval Society*, tr. T. L. Fagan (Chicago and London, University of Chicago Press, 1998); O. Davies, *The Haunted: A Social History of Ghosts* (Basingstoke, Palgrave Macmillan, 2007); S. Handley, *Visions of an Unseen World: Ghost Beliefs and Ghost Stories in Eighteenth-Century England* (London, Pickering & Chatto, 2007); P. Marshall, *Mother Leakey and the Bishop: A Ghost Story* (Oxford, Oxford University Press, 2007); P. G. Maxwell-Stuart, *Ghosts: A History of Phantoms, Ghouls, and Other Spirits of the Dead* (Stroud, Tempus, 2007). See also a major forthcoming survey of ghost beliefs in early modern Europe by Kathryn Edwards.
3 F. W. Moorman, 'The Pre-Shakespearean Ghost', *Modern Language Review*, 1 (1906), 86–95, and 'Shakespeare's Ghosts', *Modern Language Review*, 1 (1906), 192–201. See also pioneering work by R. H. West, *The Invisible World: A Study of Pneumatology in Elizabethan Drama* (Athens, GA, University of Georgia Press, 1939); J. Dover Wilson, *What Happens in Hamlet* (Cambridge, Cambridge University Press, 1951), 51–88; M. Joseph, 'Discerning the Ghost in *Hamlet*', *Publications of the Modern Language Association of America*, 76 (1961), 493–502.
4 Cf. Sasha Handley's contention that 'fictional ghost stories must . . . be positioned within a wider historical framework': *Visions of an Unseen World*, 8.
5 E. J. Clery, *The Rise of Supernatural Fiction, 1762–1800* (Cambridge, Cambridge University Press, 1995), 1–9.
6 C. O. Parsons, 'Ghost-Stories before Defoe', *Notes and Queries* (July 1956), 293–8; J. Bath and J. Newton, '"Sensible Proof of Spirits": Ghost Belief during the Later Seventeenth Century', *Folklore*, 117 (2006), 1–14.

7   M. McKeon, *The Origins of the English Novel, 1600–1740* (Baltimore, Johns Hopkins University Press, 1987), 83–9. See also Clery, *Rise of Supernatural Fiction*, 20: 'The dream of an intrinsically credible, rational ghost story was an impossible one.'

8   Joseph Glanvill, *Saducismus Triumphatus: Or, Full and Plain Evidence Concerning Witches and Apparitions* (London, 1681), 2nd Part, A2 2r.

9   Richard Baxter, *The Certainty of the Worlds of Spirits* (London, 1691), A3v–4r.

10 George Sinclair, *Satans Invisible World Discovered* (Edinburgh, 1685), A1v.

11 Clery, *Rise of Supernatural Fiction*, 25.

12 Parsons, 'Ghost-Stories before Defoe', 293.

13 G. Starr, 'Why Defoe Probably Did Not Write *The Apparition of Mrs. Veal*', *Eighteenth-Century Fiction*, 15 (2003), 421–50; J. Frangos, 'Ghosts in the Machine: The Apparition of Mrs Veal, Rowe's *Friendship in Death* and the Early Eighteenth-Century Invisible World', in C. Göttler and W. Neuber (eds), *Spirits Unseen: The Representation of Subtle Bodies in Early Modern European Culture* (Leiden, Brill, 2008), 313–30.

14 L. J. Davis, *Factual Fictions: The Origins of the English Novel* (New York, Columbia University Press, 1983), 95–101.

15 Michael Cox and R. A. Gilbert (eds), *The Oxford Book of English Ghost Stories* (Oxford, Oxford University Press, 1989), xvi.

16 Maxwell-Stuart, *Ghosts*, 94–116.

17 A point demonstrated brilliantly by Natalie Davis, *Fiction in the Archives: Pardon Tales and Their Tellers in Sixteenth-Century France* (Stanford, Stanford University Press, 1987).

18 Schmitt, *Ghosts in the Middle Ages*, 8. See also C. S. Watkin, *History and the Supernatural in Medieval England* (Cambridge, Cambridge University Press, 2007), ch. 5.

19 M. R. James, 'Twelve Medieval Ghost Stories', *English Historical Review*, 37 (1922), 413–22.

20 Finucane, *Appearances of the Dead*, 79–80.

21 Though for some significant disjunctures between elite and popular understandings, see Nancy Caciola, 'Wraiths, Revenants and Ritual in Medieval Culture', *Past and Present*, 152 (1996), 3–45.

22 W. Welchman (ed.), *The Thirty-Nine Articles of the Church of England* (London, 1834), 52.

23 Stephen Greenblatt, *Hamlet in Purgatory* (Princeton, Princeton University Press, 2001), esp. 10–46.

24 Thomas Cranmer, *Miscellaneous Writings*, ed. J. E. Cox (Cambridge, Cambridge University Press, 1846), 44; D. Oldridge, *The Supernatural in Tudor and Stuart England* (Abingdon, Routledge, 2016), 109.

25 P. Marshall, *Beliefs and the Dead in Reformation England* (Oxford, Oxford University Press, 2002), 55–6.

26 British Library, London, Harleian MS 425, 4–7.

27 Matthew Parker, *Correspondence*, ed. J. Bruce (Cambridge, Cambridge

University Press, 1853), 222; Henry More, *The Immortality of the Soul* (London, 1659), 286. See above, Ch. 8.

28 Scot, *Discoverie*, 152.

29 John Gee, *New Shreds of the Old Snare* (London, 1624), 1–25.

30 See D. P. Walker, 'The Cessation of Miracles', in I. Merkel and A. G. Debus (eds), *Hermeticism and the Renaissance: Intellectual History and the Occult in Early Modern Europe* (Washington, Folger Shakespeare Library, 1988), 111–24; A. Walsham, 'Invisible Helpers: Angelic Intervention in Early Modern England', *Past and Present*, 208 (2010), 77–130. See Ch. 6, above.

31 Bodleian Library, Oxford, MS Rawlinson D 47, 42r–43v; Randall Hutchins, *Of Specters*, tr. and ed. V. B. Heltzel and C. Murley, *Huntingdon Library Quarterly*, 11 (1947–8), 419.

32 Walsham, 'Invisible Helpers', 116.

33 K. L. Parker and E. J. Carlson, *'Practical Divinity': The Works and Life of Revd Richard Greenham* (Aldershot, Ashgate, 1998), 217.

34 Thomas Nashe, *The Terrors of the Night*, in *The Works of Thomas Nashe*, ed. R. B. McKerrow and F. Wilson (5 vols, Oxford, Clarendon Press, 1958), I, 348; Oldridge, *Supernatural in Tudor and Stuart England*, 111.

35 See above, Ch. 8, 134–5.

36 Thomas Cooper, *The Mystery of Witchcraft* (London, 1617), 152.

37 William Perkins, *A Discourse of the Damned Art* (Cambridge, 1608), 118.

38 There is no reference to the topic in the standard work: Ian Green, *The Christian's ABC: Catechisms and Catechizing in England c.1530–1740* (Oxford, Clarendon Press, 1996).

39 John Preston, *A Sermon Preached at the Funeral of Mr Arthur Upton Esquire in Devon* (London, 1619), 33.

40 R[obert] H[arrison], 'To the Reader', in Ludwig Lavater, *Of Ghostes and Spirites Walking by Night 1572*, ed. J. Dover Wilson and M. Yardley (Oxford, Oxford University Press, 1929).

41 Pierre Le Loyer, *A Treatise of Specters or Strange Sights, Visions and Apparitions appearing Sensibly unto Men*, tr. Z. Jones (London, 1605), quote at 145r. Jones's Preface and marginalia offer occasional apologies for Le Loyer's popish opinions: A3v, A4v–5r, 88v.

42 Marshall, *Beliefs and the Dead*, 238.

43 Davies, *The Haunted*, 8.

44 More, *Immortality of the Soul*, 296.

45 Edmund Jones, *The Appearance of Evil: Apparitions of Spirits in Wales*, ed. John Harvey (Cardiff, University of Wales Press, 2003), 126.

46 A. L. Rowse, *Tudor Cornwall* (London, Jonathan Cape, 1941), 334–6.

47 Marshall, *Mother Leakey*, 2–3.

48 Davies, *The Haunted*, 107.

49 Theo Brown, *The Fate of the Dead: A Study in Folk-Eschatology in the West Country after the Reformation* (Ipswich, D. S. Brewer, 1979), 45–54.

50 Thomas, *Religion and the Decline of Magic*, 592.

51 Marshall, *Mother Leakey*, 50.

52 Marshall, *Mother Leakey*, 52.

53 Marshall, *Mother Leakey*, 2; William Shakespeare, *Hamlet*, I.iv.46.

54 Sinclair, *Invisible World Discovered*, A2v.

55 Henry More, *An Antidote Against Atheism*, cited in Handley, *Visions of an Unseen World*, 31.

56 Cited in Jones, *Apparitions in Wales*, 6.

57 P. C. Almond, *Heaven and Hell in Enlightenment England* (Cambridge, Cambridge University Press, 1994), 34.

58 John Roe, *The Certainty of a Future State: or, an Occasional Letter Concerning Apparitions* (London, 1698), 2–3, 14.

59 Davies, *The Haunted*, 109.

60 Baxter, *Certainty of the Worlds of Spirits*, 3, 7.

61 Glanvill, *Saducismus*, 280.

62 Sinclair, *Invisible World Discovered*, 153. See also 19–22, 40–44, 120–2, 128–31.

63 Nathaniel Crouch, *The Kingdom of Darkness* (London, 1688), 167.

64 Baxter, *Certainty of the Worlds of Spirits*, 61–2.

65 See Ch. 2, above.

66 Glanvill, *Saducismus*, 306.

67 Glanvill, *Saducismus*, 60–1; Almond, *Heaven and Hell*.

68 [Edmund Curll], *An account of the most amazing apparition ever heard of*, cited in Marshall, *Mother Leakey*, 204; *A strange but true relation of the discovery of a most horrid and bloudy murder* (London, 1678), 1; *A Narrative of the demon of Spraiton in a letter from a person of quality in the county of Devon* (London, 1683), A1r.

69 Glanvill, *Saducismus*, 276–84.

70 John Aubrey, *Remaines of Gentilisme and Judaisme*, ed. J. Britten (London, W. Satchell, Peyton, and Co., 1881), 24, 159, 164. On Aubrey's relationship to folk culture, see A. Fox, *Oral and Literate Culture in England 1500–1700* (Oxford, Clarendon Press, 2000), 179–81, 186–8.

71 Greenblatt, *Hamlet in Purgatory*, 249.

72 Cox and Gilbert, *Oxford Book of English Ghost Stories*, x.

73 For the diversity in post-Reformation Catholic views, see F. Young, *English Catholics and the Supernatural, 1553–1829* (Farnham, Ashgate, 2013), ch. 3.

11 Ann Jeffries and the fairies: folk belief and the war on scepticism in later Stuart England

1 On Pitt's career, see M. Harris, 'Pitt, Moses (*bap.* 1639, *d.* 1697)', *Oxford Dictionary of National Biography*, online edn. Aspects of the case are discussed by D. Purkiss, *The Witch in History: Early Modern and Twentieth-Century Representations* (London, Routledge, 1996), 161–2; Frederick Valletta, *Witchcraft, Magic and Superstition in England, 1640–1670* (Aldershot, Ashgate, 2001), 78–9; L. McClain, *Lest We Be Damned: Practical Innovation and Lived Experience among Catholics in Protestant England,*

1559–1642 (London, Routledge, 2004), 190–3; R. Buccola, *Fairies, Fractious Women, and the Old Faith: Fairy Lore in Early Modern British Drama and Culture* (Selinsgrove, PA, Susquehanna University Press, 2006), 166–73; J. Shaw, *Miracles in Enlightenment England* (New Haven and London, Yale University Press, 2006), 146–50; P. Elmer, *The Miraculous Conformist: Valentine Greatrakes, the Body Politic, and the Politics of Healing in Restoration Britain* (Oxford, Oxford University Press, 2013), 63–4.

2   Moses Pitt, *An Account of one Ann Jefferies . . . Now Living in the County of Cornwall, who was fed for six Months by a small sort of Airy People call'd fairies*, quotes at 10, 11, 15, 16.

3   Pitt, *Ann Jefferies*, 4–5, 1. Cf. Samuel Barton, *A sermon preach'd before the Honourable House of Commons at St. Margaret's Westminster, upon the 16th of April, 1696 being a day of thanksgiving unto Almighty God for discovering and disappointing an horrid and barbarous conspiracy of papists* (London, 1696), quote at 7.

4   See C. Rose, *England in the 1690s: Revolution, Religion and War* (Oxford, Oxford University Press, 1999), 19–27, 196–201; W. E. Burns, *An Age of Wonders: Prodigies, Politics and Providence in England 1657–1727* (Manchester, Manchester University Press, 2002).

5   Pitt, *Ann Jefferies*, 5–6, 3.

6   J. Spurr, 'Fowler, Edward (1631/2–1714)', *Oxford Dictionary of National Biography*, online edn; S. Handley, *Visions of an Unseen World: Ghost Beliefs and Ghost Stories in Eighteenth-Century England* (London, Pickering & Chatto, 2007), 29, 30. See also M. Goldie and J. Spurr, 'Politics and the Restoration Parish: Edward Fowler and the Struggle for St Giles Cripplegate', *English Historical Review*, 109 (1994), 572–96.

7   Henry More, *An Antidote Against Atheisme* (London, 1653), 164. See above, Ch. 10.

8   See T. H. Jobe, 'The Devil in Restoration Science: The Glanvill–Webster Witchcraft Debate', *Isis*, 72 (1981), 343–56; S. Schaffer, 'Godly Men and Mechanical Philosophers: Souls and Spirits in Restoration Natural Philosophy', *Science in Context*, 1 (1987), 55–85; S. Clark, *Thinking with Demons: The Idea of Witchcraft in Early Modern Europe* (Oxford, Clarendon Press, 1997), ch. 19; M. Hunter (ed.), *The Occult Laboratory: Magic, Science and Second Sight in Late Seventeenth-Century Scotland* (Woodbridge, Boydell Press, 2001), 1–31; M. Hunter, 'Boyle and the Supernatural', in his *Boyle Studies: Aspects of the Life and Thought of Robert Boyle (1627–91)* (Abingdon, Ashgate, 2015), 163–84. On Moses Pitt's connections to Boyle, see A. Johns, *The Nature of the Book: Print and Knowledge in the Making* (Chicago, University of Chicago Press, 1998), 145.

9   A small but growing body of scholarly work has addressed itself to early seventeenth-century fairy belief, largely in order to provide context for the fairy motifs in literary works by Shakespeare, Spenser and others. See J. O. Halliwell (ed.), *Illustrations of the Fairy Mythology of A Midsummer Night's Dream* (London, Shakespeare Society, 1845); M. W. Latham, *The Elizabethan Fairies:*

The Fairies of Folklore and the Fairies of Shakespeare (New York, Columbia University Press, 1930); K. M. Briggs, *The Anatomy of Puck: An Examination of Fairy Beliefs among Shakespeare's Contemporaries and Successors* (London, Routledge & Kegan Paul, 1959); M. E. Lamb, 'Taken by the Fairies: Fairy Practices and the Production of Popular Culture in *A Midsummer Night's Dream*', *Shakespeare Quarterly*, 51 (2000), 277–312; M. Swann, 'The Politics of Fairylore in Early Modern English Literature', *Renaissance Quarterly*, 53 (2000), 449–73; D. Purkiss, 'Old Wives' Tales Retold: The Fairy Queen in Drama and Popular Culture', in D. Clarke and E. Clarke (eds), *'This Double Voice': Gendered Writing in Early Modern England* (Basingstoke, Macmillan, 2003); M. Woodcock, *Fairy in The Faerie Queene: Renaissance Elf-Fashioning and Elizabethan Myth-Making* (Aldershot, Ashgate, 2004); Buccola, *Fairies, Fractious Women, and the Old Faith*. A separate tradition of folklorist study is exemplified by K. M. Briggs, *The Fairies in Tradition and Literature* (repr. London, Routledge, 2002). Among treatments by cultural historians, the short section in K. Thomas, *Religion and the Decline of Magic* (new edn, London, Weidenfeld & Nicolson, 1997), ch. 19, pt IV, maps out the essential ground. See also D. Purkiss, *Troublesome Things: A History of Fairies and Fairy Stories* (London, Penguin, 2000); E. Wilby, *Cunning Folk and Familiar Spirits: Shamanistic Visionary Traditions in Early Modern British Witchcraft and Magic* (Brighton, Sussex Academic Press, 2005); P. Marshall, 'Protestants and Fairies in Early Modern England', in S. Dixon, D. Freist and M. Greengrass (eds), *Living with Religious Diversity in Early-Modern Europe* (Aldershot, Ashgate, 2009), 139–59; R. Hutton, 'The Making of the Early Modern British Fairy Tradition', *Historical Journal*, 57 (2014), 1135–56; D. Oldridge, 'Fairies and the Devil in Early Modern England', *The Seventeenth Century*, 31 (2016), 1–15. There is still no equivalent for England of the excellent early modern survey in L. Henderson and E. Cowan, *Scottish Fairy Belief: A History* (East Linton, Tuckwell Press, 2001).

10   Pitt, *Ann Jefferies*, 7–9, 20–2.

11   Bodleian Library, Oxford, Clarendon MS 29/2443, 102; 2478, 165; 2466. Extracts from these documents are printed in *Devon and Cornwall Notes and Queries*, 13 (1924), 312–14.

12   For other examples of the politicization of prodigies and the supernatural in the Civil War decades, see C. Durston, 'Signs and Wonders and the English Civil War', *History Today* (October 1987), 22–8; J. Friedman, 'The Battle of Frogs and Fairford's Flies: Miracles and Popular Journalism during the English Revolution', *Sixteenth Century Journal*, 23 (1992), 419–42.

13   P. Mack, *Visionary Women: Ecstatic Prophecy in Seventeenth-Century England* (Berkeley, University of California Press, 1992); P. Crawford, *Women and Religion in England 1500–1720* (London, Routledge, 1993), 106–12.

14   B. Capp, *When Gossips Meet: Women, Family and Neighbourhood in Early Modern England* (Oxford, Oxford University Press, 2003), 362.

15   Pitt, *Ann Jefferies*, 16–17. For a broader cultural association between fairies and royalism, see Marshall, 'Protestants and Fairies', 151–2.

16 Latham, *Elizabethan Fairies*, ch. 2; Thomas, *Religion and the Decline of Magic*, 609–10; B. Rosen (ed.), *Witchcraft in England 1558–1618* (Amherst, University of Massachusetts Press, 1991), 64, 68; O. Davies, 'Angels in Elite and Popular Magic, 1650–1790', in P. Marshall and A. Walsham (eds), *Angels in the Early Modern World* (Cambridge, Cambridge University Press, 2006), 301–2. For other Cornish cases, see A. K. Hamilton Jenkins, *Cornwall and the Cornish: The Story, Religion, and Folklore of 'the Western Land'* (London, J. M. Dent, 1933), 248–50; W. Y. Evans-Wentz, *The Fairy Faith in Celtic Countries* (new edn, Gerrards Cross, Colin Smythe, 1977), 163–85.

17 A. Fox, *Oral and Literate Culture in England 1500–1700* (Oxford, Clarendon Press, 2000), 187–8; Buccola, *Fairies, Fractious Women, and the Old Faith*, 45–8.

18 Thomas Nashe, *The Terrors of the Night or, A Discourse of Apparitions* (London, 1594), B2v; Woodcock, *Fairy*, 19.

19 McClain, *Lest We Be Damned*, 191, mistakenly suggests that she was, misinterpreting the 'old form of prayer' Jeffries was advocating (i.e. the abrogated Book of Common Prayer) as a Catholic one.

20 Bodleian Library, Oxford, Clarendon MS 29/2443, 102; Pitt, *Ann Jefferies*, 19. See also Oldridge, 'Fairies and the Devil'. For the demonization of ghost beliefs in this period, see P. Marshall, *Beliefs and the Dead in Reformation England* (Oxford, Oxford University Press, 2002), ch. 6, and Ch. 8, above.

21 Purkiss, *Witch in History*, 135, 138; Wilby, *Cunning Folk*, 63; J. Sharpe, *Witchcraft in Early Modern England* (London, Longman, 2001), 63; A. Gregory, 'Witchcraft, Politics and "God Neighbourhood" in Early Seventeenth-Century Rye', *Past and Present*, 133 (1991), 31–66.

22 *The Bible and Holy Scriptures* (Geneva, 1560), 287v. See also Arthur Dent, *The ruine of Rome: or An exposition vpon the whole Reuelation* (London, 1603), 236–7. See also Thomas Thorowgood, *Digitus dei: new discoveryes with sure arguments to prove that the Jews (a Nation) or people lost in the world for the space of near 200 years, inhabite now in America* (London, 1652), 15; Thomas Heywood, *The Hierarchie of the Blessed Angels* (London, 1635), 567–8.

23 Robert Burton, *The Anatomy of Melancholy* (London, 1621), 64–5. Cf. Heywood, *Hierarchie of the Blessed Angels*, 574.

24 Woodcock, *Fairy*, 24–5.

25 John Gaule, *Select Cases of Conscience Touching Witches and Witchcrafts* (London, 1646), 49–50.

26 Reginald Scot, *The Discoverie of Witchcraft* (London, 1584), 85. See also Scot, *Discoverie*, B2r–3v, 86, 131, 152–3.

27 Samuel Harsnett, *A Declaration of Egregious Popish Impostures* (London, 1603), 134–5; Thomas Ady, *A candle in the dark* (London, 1655), 169.

28 John Webster, *Displaying of supposed witchcraft* (London, 1677), 42, 279–84.

29 Thomas Hobbes, *Leviathan*, ed. K. R. Minogue (London, J. M. Dent, 1973), 381, 7.

30 Ralph Cudworth, *The true intellectual system of the universe, wherein all the*

reason and philosophy of atheism is confuted and its impossibility demonstrated (London, 1679), 834–5.

31   Samuel Pordage, *Mundorum explicatio, or, The explanation of an hieroglyphical figure wherein are couched the mysteries of the external, internal, and eternal worlds* (London, 1661), 37.

32   'A Discourse Concerning Devils and Spirits', in Reginald Scot, *Discovery of Witchcraft* (London, 1665), 50–1.

33   Henry More, *Divine dialogues containing sundry disquisitions & instructions concerning the attributes and providence of God* (London, 1668), 202–3.

34   Richard Bovet, *Pandaemonium, or The Devil's Cloyster, being a Furthe Blow to modern Sadduceism* (London, 1684), 208, recounting an incident from the Blackdown Hills, a place where fairies and spirits 'most ordinarily showed themselves'. See also 173–4, his account of a Scottish case, 'the fairy boy of Leith'. John Beaumont, *An historical, physiological and theological treatise of spirits, apparitions, witchcrafts, and other magical practices* (London, 1705), 104–5, 393–7. Glanvill mentions popular belief in fairies in his account of the famous 'Drummer of Tedworth' case: *Saducismus Triumphatus* (London, 1689), 325.

35   Thomas Browne, *Pseudodoxia epidemica* (London, 1646), 207; Webster, *Displaying of supposed witchcraft*, 40–1. Cf. Davies, 'Angels', 314.

36   Richard Baxter, *The Certainty of the Worlds of Spirits* (London, 1691), 9.

37   John Aubrey, *Miscellanies* (London, 1696), 121, 156, 175–6.

38   Robert Kirk, *The Secret Common-wealth and A Short Treatise of Charms and Spels*, ed. S. Sanderson (Cambridge, D. S. Brewer, 1976), quote at 1. The best scholarly edition is Hunter, *Occult Laboratory*, 77–106. Kirk's holograph manuscript has not survived – the comment about atheism is absent from the earliest surviving copy, but appears on the title page of two eighteenth-century transcriptions. For the textual history, see Hunter, *Occult Laboratory*, 38–41.

39   Hunter, *Occult Laboratory*, 12.

40   Sanderson (ed.), *Secret Commonwealth*, 15.

41   Hunter, *Occult Laboratory*, 96.

42   William Turner, *A Compleat History of the Most Remarkable Providences, Both of Judgement and Mercy, which have Happened in this Present Age* (London, 1697), 'To the Courteous Reader', pt I, 116–20.

43   For expressions of this view, see P. Burke, *Popular Culture in Early Modern Europe* (London, Temple Smith, 1978); K. Wrightson, *English Society 1580–1680* (London, Hutchinson, 1982), 220–8.

44   Thomas, *Religion and the Decline of Magic*, 608, though as Thomas himself concedes, nineteenth-century folklorists found abundant evidence of still current fairy belief.

45   Pitt, *Ann Jefferies*, 5.

46   A. McFarlane, 'Civility and the Decline of Magic', in P. Slack, P. Burke and B. Harrison (eds), *Civil Histories: Essays in Honour of Sir Keith Thomas* (Oxford, Oxford University Press, 2000), 145–60.

47 John Toland, *Christianity not mysterious, or, A treatise shewing that there is nothing in the Gospel contrary to reason, nor above it and that no Christian doctrine can be properly call'd a mystery* (London, 1696), 146–7.

48 John Locke, *An abridgment of Mr. Locke's Essay concerning humane understanding* (London, 1696), 255–6.

49 Anthony Ashley Cooper, earl of Shaftesbury, *A letter concerning enthusiasm, to my Lord ****** (London, 1708), 16–17, 46–7. Cf. Shaw, *Miracles in Enlightenment England*, 149–51; H. C. E. Midelfort, *Exorcism and Enlightenment: Johan Joseph Gassner and the Demons of Eighteenth-Century Germany* (New Haven and London, Yale University Press, 2005), ch. 5. Fowler replied to Shaftesbury's pamphlet, but interestingly ignored the gibe about fairies: Edward Fowler, *Reflections upon a letter concerning enthusiasm, to my Lord *****. In another letter to a lord* (London, 1709).

50 See J. Redwood, *Reason, Ridicule and Religion: The Age of Enlightenment in England 1660–1750* (London, Thames & Hudson, 1976).

51 M. Gaskill, *Crime and Mentalities in Early Modern England* (Cambridge, Cambridge University Press, 2000), 87, 108.

52 Cited in Hunter, *Occult Laboratory*, 29.

53 Fox, *Oral and Literate Culture*, ch. 3.

54 Pitt, *Ann Jefferies*, 16–17, 21, 18.

55 John Aubrey, *Remaines of Gentilisme and Judaisme*, ed. J. Britten (London, W. Satchell, Peyton, and Co., 1881), 29, 102, 122, 125. On Aubrey's cultural and intellectual outlook, see M. Hunter, *John Aubrey and the Realm of Learning* (London, Duckworth, 1975); R. Scurr, *John Aubrey: My Own Life* (London, Chatto & Windus, 2015).

56 Halliwell, *Fairy Mythology*, 235–6. Aubrey's contemporary Robert Plott ascribed fairy rings to the percussive action of lightning: L. Thorndike, *A History of Magic and Experimental Science* (8 vols, New York, Columbia University Press, 1923–58), VIII, 49–50.

57 Pitt, *Ann Jefferies*, 9. For insightful discussion of the relationship between the culture of plebeian women and the world of popular print, see Capp, *When Gossips Meet*, 365–9.

Further reading

General studies of religion, death, the supernatural

Cressy, David, *Birth, Marriage and Death: Ritual, Religion and the Life-Cycle in Tudor and Stuart England* (Oxford, Oxford University Press, 1997).

Duffy, Eamon, *The Stripping of the Altars: Traditional Religion in England 1400–1580* (New Haven and London, Yale University Press, 1992; 2nd edn, 2005).

Gordon, Bruce, and Peter Marshall (eds), *The Place of the Dead: Death and Remembrance in Late Medieval and Early Modern Europe* (Cambridge, Cambridge University Press, 2000).

Houlbrooke, Ralph, *Death, Religion and the Family in England, 1480–1750* (Oxford, Clarendon Press, 1998).

Hutton, Ronald, 'The English Reformation and the Evidence of Folklore', *Past and Present*, 148 (1995).

Marshall, Peter, *Beliefs and the Dead in Reformation England* (Oxford, Oxford University Press, 2002).

Oldridge, Darren, *The Supernatural in Tudor and Stuart England* (Abingdon, Routledge, 2016).

Scribner, Bob, 'The Reformation, Popular Magic, and the "*Disenchantment* of the World"', *Journal of Interdisciplinary History*, 23 (1993).

Thomas, Keith, *Religion and the Decline of Magic* (London, Weidenfeld & Nicolson, 1971; new edn, 1997).

Valletta, Frederick, *Witchcraft, Magic and Superstition in England, 1640–1670* (Aldershot, Ashgate, 2001).

Walsham, Alexandra, 'The Reformation and "the Disenchantment of the World" Reassessed', *Historical Journal*, 51 (2008).

——, *The Reformation of the Landscape: Religion, Identity, and Memory in Early Modern Britain and Ireland* (Oxford, Oxford University Press, 2011).

Young, Francis, *English Catholics and the Supernatural, 1553–1829* (Farnham, Ashgate, 2013).

The afterlife

Almond, Philip C., *Afterlife: A History of Life after Death* (London, I. B. Tauris, 2016).

——, *Heaven and Hell in Enlightenment England* (Cambridge, Cambridge University Press, 1994).

Clarke, Peter, and Tony Claydon (eds), *The Church, the Afterlife and the Fate of the Soul*, Studies in Church History, 45 (Woodbridge: Boydell Press, 2009).

Disley, Emma, 'Degrees of Glory: Protestant Doctrine and the Concept of Rewards Hereafter', *Journal of Theological Studies*, 42 (1991).

Eire, Carlos, *A Very Brief History of Eternity* (Princeton, Princeton University Press, 2010).

Le Goff, Jacques, *The Birth of Purgatory*, tr. A. Goldhammer (Chicago, University of Chicago Press, 1984).

McDannell, Colleen, and Bernhard Lang, *Heaven: A History* (New Haven and London, Yale University Press, 1990).

Moreira, Isabel, and Margaret Toscano (eds), *Hell and Its Afterlife: Historical and Contemporary Perspectives* (Farnham, Ashgate, 2010).

Walker, D. P., *The Decline of Hell: Seventeenth-Century Discussions of Eternal Torment* (London, Routledge & Kegan Paul, 1964).

Angels

Harkness, Deborah, *John Dee's Conversations with Angels: Cabala, Alchemy, and the End of Nature* (Cambridge, Cambridge University Press, 1999).

Keck, David, *Angels and Angelology in the Middle Ages* (New York and Oxford, Oxford University Press, 1998).

Marshall, Peter, and Alexandra Walsham (eds), *Angels in the Early Modern World* (Cambridge, Cambridge University Press, 2006).

Mayr-Harting, Henry, *Perceptions of Angels in History: An Inaugural Lecture Delivered in the University of Oxford on 14 November 1997* (Oxford, Oxford University Press, 1998).

Mohamed, Feisel G., *In the Anteroom of Divinity: The Reformation of the Angels from Colet to Milton* (Toronto, University of Toronto Press, 2008).

Raymond, Joad, *Milton's Angels: The Early-Modern Imagination* (Oxford, Oxford University Press, 2010).

—— (ed.), *Conversations with Angels: Essays towards a History of Spiritual Communication, 1100–1700* (Basingstoke, Palgrave Macmillan, 2011).

Sangha, Laura, *Angels and Belief in England, 1480–1700* (London, Pickering & Chatto, 2012).

Walsham, Alexandra, 'Invisible Helpers: Angelic Intervention in Early Modern England', *Past and Present*, 208 (2010).

Ghosts and revenants

Brown, Theo, *The Fate of the Dead: A Study in Folk-Eschatology in the West Country after the Reformation* (Ipswich, D. S. Brewer, 1979).

Caciola, Nancy, 'Wraiths, Revenants and Ritual in Medieval Culture', *Past and Present*, 152 (1996).

Davidson, H. R. Ellis, and W. M. S. Russell (eds), *The Folklore of Ghosts* (Cambridge, D. S. Brewer, 1981).

Davies, Owen, *The Haunted: A Social History of Ghosts* (Basingstoke, Palgrave Macmillan, 2007).

Finucane, Ronald, *Appearances of the Dead: A Cultural History of Ghosts* (London, Junction Books, 1982).

Greenblatt, Stephen, *Hamlet in Purgatory* (Princeton, Princeton University Press, 2001).

Handley, Sasha, *Visions of an Unseen World: Ghost Beliefs and Ghost Stories in Eighteenth-Century England* (London, Pickering & Chatto, 2007).

Marshall, Peter, *Mother Leakey and the Bishop: A Ghost Story* (Oxford, Oxford University Press, 2007).

Maxwell-Stuart, Peter G., *Ghosts: A History of Phantoms, Ghouls, and Other Spirits of the Dead* (Stroud, Tempus, 2007).

Schmitt, Jean-Claude, *Ghosts in the Middle Ages: The Living and the Dead in Medieval Society*, tr. T. Fagan (Chicago and London, University of Chicago Press, 1998).

Fairies

Briggs, Katharine M., *The Anatomy of Puck: An Examination of Fairy Beliefs among Shakespeare's Contemporaries* (London, Routledge & Kegan Paul, 1959).

Buccola, Regina, *Fairies, Fractious Women, and the Old Faith: Fairy Lore in Early Modern British Drama and Culture* (Selinsgrove, PA, Susquehanna University Press, 2006).

Henderson, Lizanne, and Edward Cowan, *Scottish Fairy Belief: A History* (East Linton, Tuckwell Press, 2001).

Hutton, Ronald, 'The Making of the Early Modern British Fairy Tradition', *Historical Journal*, 57 (2014).

Marshall, Peter, 'Protestants and Fairies in Early Modern England', in Scott Dixon, Dagmar Freist and Mark Greengrass (eds), *Living with Religious Diversity in Early-Modern Europe* (Aldershot, Ashgate, 2009).

Oldridge, Darren, 'Fairies and the Devil in Early Modern England', *The Seventeenth Century*, 31 (2016).

Purkiss, Diane, *Troublesome Things: A History of Fairies and Fairy Stories* (London, Penguin, 2000).

Woodcock, Matthew, *Fairy in The Faerie Queene: Renaissance Elf-Fashioning and Elizabethan Myth-Making* (Aldershot, Ashgate, 2004).

Elite and popular mentalities

Burns, William E., *An Age of Wonders: Prodigies, Politics and Providence in England 1657–1727* (Manchester, Manchester University Press, 2002).

Duffy, Eamon, 'The Godly and the Multitude in Stuart England', *The Seventeenth Century*, 1 (1985).

Fox, Adam, *Oral and Literate Culture in England 1500–1700* (Oxford, Clarendon Press, 2000).

Gaskill, Malcolm, *Crime and Mentalities in Early Modern England* (Cambridge, Cambridge University Press, 2000).

Hunter, Michael (ed.), *The Occult Laboratory: Magic, Science and Second Sight in Late Seventeenth-Century Scotland* (Woodbridge, Boydell Press, 2001).

Lake, Peter, 'Deeds against Nature: Cheap Print, Protestantism and Murder in Early Seventeenth-Century England', in Kevin Sharpe and Peter Lake (eds), *Culture and Politics in Early Stuart England* (Basingstoke, Macmillan, 1994).

Shaw, Jane, *Miracles in Enlightenment England* (New Haven and London, Yale University Press, 2006).

Walsham, Alexandra, *Providence in Early Modern England* (Oxford, Oxford University Press, 1999).

Watt, Tessa, *Cheap Print and Popular Piety 1550–1640* (Cambridge, Cambridge University Press, 1991).

Acknowledgements

Earlier versions of the chapters in this book first appeared in the following locations, and I am indebted to the various publishers and journals for permission to republish them. Chapter 1: T. Rasmussen and J. Øygarden Flaeten (eds), *Preparing for Death, Remembering the Dead* (Vandenhoeck and Ruprecht, 2015), 25–43; Chapter 2: B. Gordon and P. Marshall (eds), *The Place of the Dead: Death and Remembrance in Late Medieval and Early Modern Europe* (Cambridge University Press, 2000), 110–30; Chapter 3: K. Cooper and J. Gregory (eds), *Retribution, Repentance, and Reconciliation*, Studies in Church History, 40 (Boydell Press, 2004), 128–37; Chapter 4: *Journal of Ecclesiastical History* (Cambridge University Press), 61 (2010), 279–98; Chapter 5: *Historical Reflections / Réflexions Historiques* (Berghahn Journals), 26 (2000), 311–33; Chapter 6: P. Marshall and A. Walsham (eds), *Angels in the Early Modern World* (Cambridge University Press, 2006), 83–103; Chapter 7: J. Raymond (ed.), *Conversations with Angels: Essays towards a History of Spiritual Communication, 1100–1700* (Palgrave Macmillan, 2011), 295–316; Chapter 8: H. L. Parish and W. G. Naphy (eds), *Religion and Superstition in Reformation Europe* (Manchester University Press, 2002), 188–208; Chapter 9: K. Cooper and J. Gregory (eds), *Elite and Popular Religion*, Studies in Church History, 42 (Boydell Press, 2006), 261–71; Chapter 10: H. Conrad-O'Briain and J. A. Stevens (eds), *The Ghost Story from the Middle Ages to the Twentieth Century* (Four Courts Press, 2010), 16–33; Chapter 11: A. McShane and G. Walker (eds), *The Extraordinary and the Everyday in Early Modern England* (Palgrave Macmillan, 2010), 127–41.

I am very grateful to Philip Law at SPCK for first suggesting that I put this collection of essays together, and for patiently encouraging me to complete it. That would not have been possible, at the end of an exceptionally busy year, without the forbearance and loving support of my daughters, Bella, Maria and Kit, and of my wife, Ali. Warm thanks are also due, for assistance with the composition of the essays, or for the organization of events at which versions of them were first presented, to Bernard Capp, Helen Conrad-O'Briain, Jon Flaeten, Bruce Gordon, Steve Hindle, Angela McShane, Judith Maltby, Isabel Moreira, Bill Naphy, Helen Parish, Tarald Rasmussen, Joad Raymond, Laura Sangha, Margaret Toscano,

Acknowledgements

Garthine Walker and Alex Walsham. The dedication is to the memory of two outstanding scholars, and very fine men, who set me on the path to becoming a professional historian.

Peter Marshall

Index